Principles, Definitions and Model Rules of European Private Law

Draft Common Frame of Reference (DCFR)

Outline Edition

Principles, Definitions and Model Rules of European Private Law

Draft Common Frame of Reference (DCFR)

Outline Edition

Prepared by the

Study Group on a European Civil Code

and the

Research Group on EC Private Law (Acquis Group)

Based in part on a revised version of the Principles of
European Contract Law

Edited by

Christian von Bar, Eric Clive and Hans Schulte-Nölke

and

Hugh Beale, Johnny Herre, Jérôme Huet, Matthias Storme,
Stephen Swann, Paul Varul, Anna Veneziano and Fryderyk Zoll

sellier.

**european law
publishers**

More texts by the Study Group and the Acquis Group are available at www.law-net.eu.

The print of this edition was supported by the Dieter Fuchs Stiftung in Dissen (Germany).

ISBN 978-3-86653-097-3

The Deutsche Nationalbibliothek lists this publication in the Deutsche Nationalbibliografie; detailed bibliographic data are available on the Internet at http://dnb.d-nb.de.

The Index was prepared by Rechtsanwältin Dr. Martina Schulz, Pohlheim.

Design: Sandra Sellier, Munich. Production: Karina Hack, Munich. Typesetting: fidus Publikations-Service GmbH, Augsburg. Typeface: Goudy Old Style and Goudy Sans from Linotype. Printing and binding: Friedrich Pustet KG, Regensburg. Printed on acid-free, non-ageing paper. Printed in Germany.

Table of contents

Table of contents

Introduction

Revision of the interim outline edition

The coverage of the DCFR

Structure and language of the DCFR model rules

How the DCFR relates to PECL, the SGECC PEL series, the Acquis and the Insurance Contract Group series

General

I. **DCFR and CFR distinguished.** In this volume the Study Group on a European Civil Code (the 'Study Group') and the Research Group on Existing EC Private Law (the 'Acquis Group') present the revised and final academic Draft of a Common Frame of Reference (DCFR). It contains Principles, Definitions and Model Rules of European

Private Law in an outline edition. Among other goals, its completion fulfils an obligation to the European Commission undertaken in 2005. The Commission's Research Directorate-General funded part of the work. One purpose of the text is to serve as a draft for drawing up a 'political' Common Frame of Reference (CFR) which was first called for by the European Commission's 'Action Plan on A More Coherent European Contract Law' of February 2003.[1] As is explained more precisely below, the DCFR and the CFR must be clearly distinguished. The DCFR serves several other important purposes.

2. Revision of the interim outline edition. A year ago, the DCFR was published for the first time in an interim outline edition.[2] This edition is a revision in three main ways. First, the interim edition did not contain model rules in Book IV on loan contracts and contracts for donation, nor in Books VIII to X on acquisition and loss of ownership of goods, on proprietary security rights in movable assets, and on trusts. They have now been included. Secondly, one of the purposes of publishing an interim edition was to provide an opportunity for interested parties to comment on the draft and make suggestions for improvement. The public discussion of the interim outline edition prompted the research groups to revise at various places the text which had already been published. The research groups are grateful to all who have taken part in that critical evaluation, whether in publications, at conferences or in personal correspondence, and who have contributed to the improvement of the text. Naturally, not all the suggestions we received have been acted upon: some, for example, advocated solutions which had already been rejected after full discussion by the Study Group or the Acquis Group. But many suggestions for improvement have been gratefully adopted. Further revisions resulted from our own further reflections and discussions, the results of the research conducted by the evaluative teams in the network and the conclusions which we drew from the process of trans-

---

[1]   COM (2003) final, OJ C 63/1 (referred to below as Action Plan).

[2]   von Bar/Clive/Schulte-Nölke and Beale/Herre/Huet/Schlechtriem/ Storme/Swann/Varul/Veneziano/Zoll, Principles, Definitions and Model Rules of European Private Law. Draft Common Frame of Reference (Munich 2008) (referred to below as IOE).

lating the first three Books into French.[3] That applies in particular to Books I-III, but is not confined to them. (For more details, see paras 26-33). Thirdly, this revised edition contains an additional self-contained section in which we set out four underlying principles underpinning the DCFR. This draws on the *Principes directeurs du droit Européen du contrat*, the subject-matter of an independent research project, which published its output in 2008.[4] The conclusions of the *economic impact group*, which analysed particular rules of the DCFR from an economic perspective, were also made available to us.

3. Paperback and hardcover editions of the final DCFR. Like the 2008 interim edition this revised edition is only an outline edition because it appears without comments and notes. The European Commission received in December 2008 the material published here along with an explanatory and illustrative commentary on each model rule. The Commission has also received the extensive comparative legal material which has been gathered and digested in the past years. The entire work will be published in book form later in the year. At the same time we considered that the publication of a compact and inexpensive second paperback edition would help promote the wider dissemination and discussion of these texts. The complete edition will be voluminous. It will invite study at one's desk at home or in the office, but it will be too bulky to pack into luggage taken to meetings

---

[3] By Professor Jacques Ghestin (Paris); published at http://www.fondation-droitcontinental.org/Documents/Traduc-vBar-livre%20I-II-III-%2008-2008.doc.

[4] Fauvarque-Cosson/Mazeaud and Wicker/Racine/Sautonie-Laguionie/Bujoli (eds.), Principes contractuels commun. Projet de cadre commun de référence (Paris 2008); Fauvarque-Cosson/Mazeaud and Tenenbaum, Terminologie contractuelle commune. Projet de cadre commun de référence (Paris 2008). These studies have also been published in English: European Contract Law. Materials for a Common Frame of Reference: Terminology, Guiding Principles, Model Rules. Produced by Association Henri Capitant des Amis de la Culture Juridique Française and Société de Législation Comparée. Edited by Fauvarque-Cosson and Denis Mazeaud. Prepared by Racine, Sautonie-Laguionie, Tenenbaum and Wicker (Munich 2008).

or conferences. That is another reason for also publishing a second edition in outline form, essentially Articles only.

4. An academic, not a politically authorised text. It must be stressed that what we refer to today as the DCFR originates in an initiative of European legal scholars. It amounts to the compression into rule form of decades of independent research and co-operation by academics with expertise in private law, comparative law and European Community law. The independence of the two Groups and of all the contributors has been maintained and respected unreservedly at every stage of our labours. That in turn has made it possible to take on board many of the suggestions received in the course of a large number of meetings with stakeholders and other experts throughout the continent. The two Groups alone, however, bear responsibility for the content of this volume. In particular, it does not contain a single rule or definition or principle which has been approved or mandated by a politically legitimated body at European or national level (save, of course, where it coincides with existing EU or national legislation). It may be that at a later point in time the DCFR will be carried over at least in part into a CFR, but that is a question for others to decide. This introduction merely sets out some considerations which might usefully be taken into account during the possible process of transformation.

5. About this outline edition. This final outline edition consists of an introduction, the names of the academic contributors and an acknowledgement of our funders and donors, an overview of the guiding principles underlying the model rules, a set of definitions (referred to in I. – 1:108 (Definitions in Annex) and listed later in the Annex to the model rules), tables of derivations and destinations, and the model rules. The introduction explains the purposes pursued in preparing the DCFR and outlines its contents, coverage and structure. It describes the amendments to the 2008 interim edition and elucidates the relationship between the DCFR and the publications which have already appeared or will appear in the course of the preparatory work. Finally, it sketches out how the DCFR might flow into the development of the CFR.

The purposes of the DCFR

6. A possible model for a political CFR. As already indicated, this DCFR is (among other things) a possible model for an actual or 'political' Common Frame of Reference (CFR). The DCFR presents a concrete text, hammered out in all its detail, to those who will be deciding questions relating to a CFR. A 'political' CFR would not necessarily, of course, have the same coverage and contents as this academic DCFR. The question of which functions the DCFR can perform in the development of the CFR is considered under paragraphs 59-74 of this introduction.

7. Legal science, research and education. However, the DCFR ought not to be regarded merely as a building block of a 'political' Common Frame of Reference. The DCFR will stand on its own and retain its significance whatever happens in relation to a CFR. The DCFR is an academic text. It sets out the results of a large European research project and invites evaluation from that perspective. The breadth of that scholarly endeavour will be apparent when the full edition is published. Independently of the fate of the CFR, it is hoped that the DCFR will promote knowledge of private law in the jurisdictions of the European Union. In particular it will help to show how much national private laws resemble one another and have provided mutual stimulus for development – and indeed how much those laws may be regarded as regional manifestations of an overall common European legacy. The function of the DCFR is thus separate from that of the CFR in that the former serves to sharpen awareness of the existence of a European private law and also (via the comparative notes that will appear in the full edition) to demonstrate the relatively small number of cases in which the different legal systems produce substantially different answers to common problems. The DCFR may furnish the notion of a European private law with a new foundation which increases mutual understanding and promotes collective deliberation on private law in Europe.

8. A possible source of inspiration. The drafters of the DCFR nurture the hope that it will be seen also outside the academic world as a text from which inspiration can be gained for suitable solutions for pri-

vate law questions. Shortly after their publication the Principles of
European Contract Law (PECL)[5], which the DCFR (in its second and
third Books) incorporates in a partly revised form (see paragraphs 49-
53), received the attention of many higher courts in Europe and of
numerous official bodies charged with preparing the modernisation
of the relevant national law of contract. This development is set to
continue in the context of the DCFR. It will have repercussions for
reform projects within the European Union, at both national and
Community law levels, and beyond the EU. If the content of the

---

5   Ole Lando and Hugh Beale (eds.), Principles of European Contract Law
     Parts I and II. Prepared by the Commission on European Contract Law
     (The Hague 1999); Ole Lando, Eric Clive, André Prüm and Reinhard
     Zimmermann (eds.), Principles of European Contract Law Part III (The
     Hague, London and Boston 2003). Translations are available in French
     (Principes du droit européen du contract. Version française préparée par
     Georges Rouhette, avec le concours de Isabelle de Lamberterie, Denis
     Tallon et Claude Witz, Droit privé comparé et europeéan, vol. 2, Paris
     2003); German (Grundregeln des Europäisches Vertragsrechts, Teile I
     und II, Kommission für Europäisches Vertragsrecht. Deutsche Ausgabe
     von Christian von Bar und Reinhard Zimmermann, München 2002;
     Grundregeln des Europäisches Vertragsrechts Teil III, Kommission für
     Europäisches Vertragsrecht. Deutsche Ausgabe von Christian von Bar
     und Reinhard Zimmermann, München 2005); Italian (Commissione per
     il Diritto Europeo dei Contratti. Principi di Diritto Europeo dei Contra-
     tti, Parte I & II, Edizione italiana a cura di Carlo Castronovo, Milano
     2001; Commissione per il Diritto Europeo dei Contratti. Principi di Di-
     ritto Europeo dei Contratti, Parte III. Edizione italiana a cura di Carlo
     Castronovo, Milano 2005) and Spanish (Principios de Derecho Contrac-
     tual Europeo, Partes I y II. Edición española a cargo de Pilar Barres Benn-
     loch, José Miguel Embid Irujo, Fernando Martínes Sanz, Madrid 2003).
     Matthias Storme translated the articles of Parts I-III into Dutch (Tijd-
     schrift voor privaatrecht 2005, 1181-1241); M.-A. Zachariasiewicz and
     J. Bełdowski translated the PECL articles of Parts I and II (Kwartalnik
     Prawa Prywatnego 3/2004, 814-881) and J. Bełdowski and A. Kozioł the
     articles of Part III (Kwartalnik Prawa Prywatnego 3/2006, 847-859) into
     the Polish language, Christian Takoff Parts I-III (Targovsko pravo 1/2005,
     15-85) into the Bulgarian language.

DCFR is convincing, it may contribute to a harmonious and informal Europeanisation of private law.

Contents of the DCFR

9. Principles, definitions and model rules. The DCFR contains 'principles, definitions and model rules'. The title of this book thus follows the scheme set out in the European Commission's communications (referred to below in paragraph 59) and in our contract with the Commission. The notion of 'definitions' is reasonably clear. The notions of 'principles' and 'model rules', however, appear to overlap and require some explanation.

10. Meaning of 'principles'. The European Commission's communications concerning the CFR do not elaborate on the concept of 'principles'. The word is susceptible to different interpretations. It is sometimes used, in the present context, as a synonym for rules which do not have the force of law. This is how it appears to be used, for example, in the 'Principles' of European Contract Law (PECL), which referred to themselves in article 1:101(1) as 'Principles ... intended to be applied as general *rules* of contract law in the European Union' (italics added). The word appears to be used in a similar sense in the Unidroit Principles of International Commercial Contracts.[6] In this sense the DCFR can be said to consist of principles and definitions. It is essentially of the same nature as those other instruments in relation to which the word 'principles' has become familiar. Alternatively, the word 'principles' might be reserved for those rules which are of a more general nature, such as those on freedom of contract or good faith. In this sense the DCFR's model rules could be said to include principles. However, in the following paragraphs we explore a third meaning.

---

[6] Unidroit Principles of International Commercial Contracts 2004 (Rome 2004), Preamble (Purpose of the Principles) paragraph (1): "These Principles set forth general rules for international commercial contracts".

11. **Fundamental principles.** The word 'principles' surfaces occasionally in the Commission communications mentioned already, but with the prefix 'fundamental' attached. That suggests that it may have been meant to denote essentially abstract basic values. The model rules of course build on such fundamental principles in any event, whether they are stated or not. There can be no doubt about their importance. Private law is one of those fields of law which are, or at least should be, based on and guided by deep-rooted principles. To some extent such fundamental principles are a matter of interpretation and debate. It is clear that the DCFR does not perceive private law, and in particular contract law, as merely the balancing of private law relations between equally strong natural and legal persons. But different readers may have different interpretations of, and views on, the extent to which the DCFR suggests the correction of market failures or contains elements of 'social justice' and protection for weaker parties.

12. **The approach taken to fundamental principles in the Interim Outline Edition.** In the Introduction to the Interim Outline Edition we asked readers to consider whether it would be useful to include in the DCFR a separate part containing a statement of basic principles and values underlying the model rules. We suggested that this part could possibly be formulated as recitals, i. e. an introductory list of reasons for the essential substance of the following text, or in a discursive preface. To give some idea of what a statement of underlying principles might look like, primarily in relation to contract law, some possible fundamental principles were outlined.[7] The statement of principles in the Interim Outline Edition listed no fewer than fifteen items – justice; freedom; protection of human rights; economic welfare; solidarity and social responsibility; establishing an area of freedom, security and justice; promotion of the internal market; protection of consumers and others in need of protection; preservation of cultural and linguistic plurality; rationality; legal certainty; predictability; efficiency; protection of reasonable reliance; and the proper allocation of responsibility for the creation of risks.[8] These were not

---

[7]   See IOE Introduction at paragraphs 23-36.

[8]   See IOE Introduction at paragraphs 22 and 35.

ranked in any order of priority. It was stressed that the principles would inevitably conflict with each other and that it was the function of the model rules to find an appropriate balance.[9] Feedback was mixed. Some commentators welcomed the express mention of non-mercantile values like human rights and solidarity and social responsibility. Others expressed doubts as to the practical value of such a large, diverse and non-prioritised list. There were powerful calls for full account to be taken of the work done on governing principles by the Association Henri Capitant and the Société de législation comparée[10] as part of the 'CoPECL Network of Excellence' working on the CFR project.[11] To that we now turn.

13. The approach taken by the *Principes directeurs*. The Association Henri Capitant and the Société de législation comparée published their *Principes directeurs du droit européen du contrat* early in 2008.[12] We will refer to these as the *Principes directeurs* to distinguish them from the principles we later discuss. The evaluative group charged with this project approached their task by distilling out the main principles underlying the Principles of European Contract Law, and comparing them with equivalent principles from a number of national systems and international and European instruments.[13] They identified three main principles – *liberté contractuelle, sécurité contrac-*

---

9   IOE Introduction paragraph 23.

10 See note 4 above.

11 Joint Network on European Private Law (CoPECL: Common Principles of European Contract Law), Network of Excellence under the 6th EU Framework Programme for Research and Technological Development, Priority 7 – FP6-2002-CITIZENS-3, Contract N° 513351 (co-ordinator: Professor *Hans Schulte-Nölke*, Osnabrück).

12 The *Principes* form part of the book cited in note 4 above.

13 The national systems used were mainly the Dutch, English, French, German, Italian and Spanish. The international instruments used (in addition to the PECL) were mainly the UN Convention on Contracts for the International Sale of Goods (CISG), the Unidroit Principles on International Commercial Contracts (2004) and the draft European Code of Contract produced by the Academy of European Private Law based in Pavia.

tuelle et loyauté contractuelle – contractual freedom, contractual security and contractual "loyalty" – each with sub-principles. The word "loyalty" is within quotation marks because it does not fully capture the French word *loyauté* in this context. The key elements are good faith, fairness and co-operation in the contractual relationship. *Loyauté* comprises a duty to act in conformity with the requirements of good faith and fair dealing, from the negotiation of the contract until all of its provisions have been given effect, a prohibition on using contractual rights and terms in a way which does not respect the objective that justified their inclusion in the contract and a duty to co-operate so far as necessary for the performance of the contractual obligations; it also requires a party not to act in contradiction of prior declarations or conduct on which the other party might have legitimately relied.[14] The principles and sub-principles were expressed in eleven draft articles drafted in such a way as to be suitable for insertion in one block at the beginning of model rules. The approach adopted by the evaluative group is very attractive. The principles are expressed in an elegant, resonant and focussed way. They are backed up by persuasive analysis and discussion. However, we think that the approach, and to some extent the substance, has to be slightly different for the purposes of the DCFR. There are two reasons for this. First, the *Principes directeurs* relate only to contract law. For the purposes of the DCFR a statement of underlying principles has to be wide enough to cover also non-contractual obligations and aspects of property law. Secondly, it does not seem appropriate to incorporate the governing principles as a block of actual model rules at the beginning of the DCFR. They function at a different level. They are a distillation from the model rules and have a more descriptive function. They sometimes overlap and often conflict with each other. Almost all of the sub-principles, it is true, have direct counterparts in Articles of the DCFR but those Articles appear in, and are adapted to, particular contexts where they may be subject to qualifications and exceptions. It would weaken the DCFR to extract them and put them in one group at the beginning: it would clearly be undesirable to duplicate them. Moreover those Articles are by no means the only ones which reflect and illustrate underlying principles. A discursive

---

14   Op. cit fn 4 above at p. 198.

approach seems more appropriate for an introductory statement of principles of this type. This was the clear preference of the Compilation and Redaction Team and the Co-ordinating Committee of the Study Group when they discussed this matter in April and June 2008.

14. **Lessons learned from the *Principes directeurs*.** Nonetheless lessons can be learned from the *Principes directeurs*. The most important is that the many fundamental principles listed in the introduction to the Interim Outline Edition can be organised and presented in a more effective way. A small group of them (corresponding to some extent to those identified in the *Principes directeurs*) can be extracted and discussed at greater length. These are the principles which are all-pervasive within the DCFR. They can be detected by looking into the model rules. They are underlying principles. They furnished grounds for arguments about the merits of particular rules. The remaining principles mentioned in the introduction to the Interim Outline Edition are generally of a rather high political nature. They could be said to be overriding rather than underlying. Although some of them are strongly reflected in parts of the DCFR, they are primarily relevant to an assessment from the outside of the DCFR as a whole. Before commenting briefly on these two categories of principles we note only that another lesson to be learned from the *Principes directeurs* is that there are different ways of dealing with fundamental principles in an instrument like the DCFR. It will be for others to decide how if at all to deal with fundamental principles in an official CFR. One obvious technique would be to use recitals, but the form and content of these would depend on the form and content of the instrument. It would be premature to adopt that technique here.

15. **Underlying principles.** For the broader purposes of the DCFR we suggest that the underlying principles should be grouped under the headings of freedom, security, justice and efficiency (rather than *liberté contractuelle, sécurité contractuelle et loyauté contractuelle* as in the *Principes directeurs*). This does not mean that the principle of contractual "loyalty" is lost. To a large extent it is covered by the wider principle of justice, without which many of the rules in the DCFR cannot be satisfactorily explained. To some extent it is simply an as-

pect of contractual security viewed from the standpoint of the other party.[15] One party's contractual security is increased by the fact that the other is expected to co-operate and act in accordance with the requirements of good faith and fair dealing. Nothing is more detrimental to contractual security than a contractual partner who does not do so: a cheating and untrustworthy partner, and even an unco-operative partner, may be worse than no partner at all. The heading of efficiency is added because, although this is often an aspect of freedom (freedom from unnecessary impediments and costs), it cannot always be accommodated under one of the other headings. These four principles of freedom, security, justice and efficiency are developed and illustrated at length in the section on underlying principles which precedes the model rules.

16. Overriding principles. Into the category of "overriding principles" of a high political nature we would place the protection of human rights, the promotion of solidarity and social responsibility, the preservation of cultural and linguistic diversity, the protection and promotion of welfare and the promotion of the internal market. Freedom, security, justice and efficiency also have a role to play as overriding principles. They have a double role: the two categories overlap. So they are briefly mentioned here too as well as being discussed at greater length later.

17. Protection of human rights. The DCFR itself recognises the overriding nature of this principle. One of the very first Articles provides that the model rules are to be read in the light of any applicable instruments guaranteeing human rights and fundamental freedoms.[16] However, this is an overriding principle which is also reflected quite strongly in the content of the model rules themselves, most notably in the rules on non-discrimination in Books II and III[17] and in many of the rules in Book VI on non-contractual liability arising out of damage caused to another.[18] These rules could also be seen, of course,

---

[15] This overlap is recognised by the *Principes directeurs* themselves. See article 0:201, alinea 2.

[16] I. – 1:102(2).

[17] See II. – 2:101 to II. – 2:105 and III. – 1:105.

as examples of rules which foster justice and preserve and promote security. Principles overlap as well as conflict.

18. Promotion of solidarity and social responsibility. The promotion of solidarity and social responsibility is generally regarded as primarily the function of public law (using, for example, criminal law, tax law and social welfare law) rather than private law. However, the promotion of solidarity and social responsibility is not absent from the private law rules in the DCFR. In the contractual context the word "solidarity" is often used to mean loyalty or security. It is of great importance to the DCFR. The principle of solidarity and social responsibility is also strongly reflected, for example, in the rules on benevolent intervention in another's affairs, which try to minimise disincentives to acting out of neighbourly solidarity.[19] It is also reflected in the rules on donation, which try to minimise disincentives to charitable giving (an expression of solidarity and social responsibility which was at one time all-important and is still extremely important).[20] Moreover some of the rules in Book VI on non-contractual liability for damage caused to another protect against types of behaviour which are harmful for society in general.[21] Many of these rules could also be regarded as examples of rules which promote security.

19. Preservation of cultural and linguistic diversity. Nothing could illustrate better the point that fundamental principles conflict than the juxtaposition of this item with the preceding one and the two following ones. In a pluralistic society like Europe it is manifest that the preservation of cultural and linguistic diversity is an all-important principle, vital to the very existence of the Union. But where a particular aspect of human life has not only a cultural content but also a strong functional content, this principle may conflict with the

---

[18] See, in particular, VI. – 2:201 (Personal injury and consequential loss); VI. – 2:203 (Infringement of dignity, liberty and privacy) and VI. – 2:206 (Loss upon infringement of property and lawful possession).

[19] Book V.

[20] Book IV, Part H.

[21] VI. – 2:209; see also VI-3:202, VI-3:206 and VI. – 5:103.

principles of solidarity, the protection and promotion of welfare and the promotion of the internal market. Private law is a prime example. Within the rules of the DCFR itself there are some reflections of the principle of respect for cultural and linguistic diversity.[22] However, the impetus for the DCFR in its present form and for its present purposes came from, on the one hand, recognition of cultural and linguistic diversity and, on the other, concerns about the harmful effects for the internal market (and consequently for the welfare of European citizens and businesses) of an excessive diversity of contract law systems. The CFR project is not an attempt to create a single law of the whole of Europe. Rather, the purpose of the CFR as a legislator's guide or toolbox is to enable the meaning of European legislation to be clear to people from diverse legal backgrounds. Moreover, existing cultural diversity was respected by the participation on an equal footing of lawyers from all European legal cultures in the preparation of the DCFR and by the serious attempt to reflect, as far as possible, all legal systems of the EU Member States in the Notes. This resulted in unity out of diversity, at a soft-law level. Linguistic diversity will be respected by ensuring that the DCFR is translated into as many European languages as possible.

20. Protection and promotion of welfare. The Interim Outline Edition referred to "economic welfare" but there is no reason to confine this principle to only one aspect of welfare. This principle embraces all or almost all the others. The whole purpose and raison d'être of the DCFR could be said to derive from this principle. If it does not help to promote the welfare of the citizens and businesses of Europe – however indirectly, however slowly, however slightly – it will have

---

[22] See e.g. II.–1:104(2) (potential applicability of local usages); II.–3:102(2)(c) and (3) (language used for communication when business is marketing to consumers); II.–9:109 (language to be used for communications relating to the contract); IV.A.–6:103(1)(e) (language for consumer guarantee document); IX.–3:310(1)(d) (language to be used for declaration to proposed European register of proprietary security); IX.–3:319(2) (language to be used for request to secured creditor for information about entry in register) and IX.–7:210(3) (language to be used for a type of notice by secured creditor).

failed. Although all-embracing, this principle is too general to be useful on its own.

21. Promotion of the internal market. This principle is really a sub-head of the last. The most obvious way in which the welfare of the citizens and businesses of Europe can be promoted by the DCFR is by the promotion of the smooth functioning of the internal market. Whether this is just by improving the quality, and hence the accessibility and usability, of present and future EU legislation or whether it is by the development of one or more optional instruments are political decisions.

22. Freedom, security, justice and efficiency. As underlying principles within the DCFR, these will be discussed and developed later. They also have a role to play as overriding principles for the purposes of assessment from the outside. The DCFR as a whole falls to be assessed very largely by the criterion of how well it embodies and balances these principles. At the level of overriding political principles, reference may also be made to the EU specific aims of establishing an area of freedom, security and justice and promoting the free movement of goods, persons, services and capital between the Member States. If the political will were there, the DCFR could make a contribution to the achievement of these aims.

23. Definitions. 'Definitions' have the function of suggestions for the development of a uniform European legal terminology. Some particularly important concepts are defined for these purposes at the outset in Book I. For other defined terms DCFR I. – 1:108 provides that 'The definitions in the Annex apply for all the purposes of these rules unless the context otherwise requires.' This expressly incorporates the list of terminology in the Annex as part of the DCFR. This drafting technique, by which the definitions are set out in an appendage to the main text, was chosen in order to keep the first chapter short and to enable the list of terminology to be extended at any time without great editorial labour. The substance is partly distilled from the *acquis*, but predominantly derived from the model rules of the DCFR. If the definitions are essential for the model rules, it is also true that the model rules are essential for the definitions. There would be little value in a set of definitions which was internally incoherent. The definitions can be seen as components which can be used in the making of rules and sets of rules, but there is no point in having components which are incompatible with each other and cannot fit together. In contrast to a dictionary of terms assembled from disparate sources, the definitions in the Annex have been tested in the model rules and revised and refined as the model rules have developed. Ultimately, useful definitions cannot be composed without model rules and useful model rules can hardly be drafted without definitions.

24. Model rules. The greatest part of the DCFR consists of 'model rules'. The adjective 'model' indicates that the rules are not put forward as having any normative force but are soft law rules of the kind contained in the Principles of European Contract Law and similar publications. Whether particular rules might be used as a model for legislation, for example, for the improvement of the internal coherence of the *acquis communautaire* is for others to decide.

25. Comments and notes. In the full edition the model rules will be supplemented by comments and notes. The comments will elucidate each rule, will often illustrate its application by means of examples, and will outline the critical policy considerations at stake. The notes will reflect the legal position in the national legal systems and, where relevant, the current Community law. International instruments such as the UN Convention on Contracts for the International Sale of Goods (CISG) and the Unidroit Principles of International Commercial Contracts 2004 are also mentioned where appropriate. How the notes were assembled is described in the section on the academic contributors and our funders.

Revision of the interim outline edition

26. Overview. This final edition of the DCFR deviates in a number of respects from the Interim Outline Edition of 2008. We referred earlier to the new Books that are included and to the statement of principles which underlie the model rules, now placed in a separate section between this introduction and the model rules. Here we mention some of the more detailed changes to the Articles published in the Interim Outline Edition. One general change has been the elimination of a number of redundant provisions. Another general change has been the expansion of the expression "goods and services" in a number of *acquis*-based provisions to include assets other than "goods" in the narrow sense of corporeal movables in which the word is defined in the DCFR. Finally, the catalogue of definitions has been revised and added to, with material which was misplaced there either expunged or, on occasion, upgraded to the model rules. Here we have frequently taken up points made in public discussion of the text. Although it would be excessive to give details of every drafting or editing change made since the publication of the Interim Outline Edition, a few of the more significant changes will now be mentioned.

27. Book I. The main changes here are the inclusion of some provisions taken from elsewhere in the Interim Outline Edition. Of particular note is I. – 1:103 (Good faith and fair dealing). Paragraph (1) is a more developed version of a definition which formerly appeared only in the Annex of definitions. It is included here because of its importance. Paragraph (2), on inconsistent actings, has been inserted following a recommendation by the evaluative group formed by the Association Henri Capitant and the Société de Législation Comparée. The text of the former Annex 2 (Computation of time) has been integrated into Book I: see I. – 1:110.

28. Book II. The definition of "contract" in II. – 1:101(1) has been shortened. It now refers to "an agreement which is intended to give rise to a binding legal relationship or to have some other legal effect." The definition formerly contained additional words designed to cater for the case where there was no subjective intention but an agreement was carved out of what the parties said or did. However, that point is sufficiently provided for by a later Article (II. – 4:102) and does not need to be repeated here. There is a similar change in the definition of "juridical act" in II. – 1:101(2). The earlier definition had been criticised by commentators on the ground that it did not make the element of intention necessary and was therefore too wide.

Again, the point that intention may have to be objectively ascertained is sufficiently covered by a later Article (II. – 4:302). A reference to the rules on good faith and fair dealing in II. – 1:102 (Party autonomy) gave rise to confusion and has been deleted. The words "promise or undertaking" formerly in II. – 1:103 (Binding effect) were criticised as unnecessary duplication. "Undertaking" alone is now used. A new paragraph (3) has been added to II. – 1:106 (Form). This generalises a rule which originally appeared in the Chapter on donation. There are numerous changes in Chapter 3 in particular with regard to information duties, which reflect further work done by the Acquis Group and also react to many comments received. Of particular note is the provision on specific duties for businesses marketing to consumers (II. – 3:102), where paragraph (1) has been reformulated in order to reflect the underlying acquis more closely. The provisions on sanctions for breach of information duties have been refined and a new Article (II. – 3:501) on liability for damages for breach of a duty imposed by Chapter 3 has been included. The *contra proferentem* rule in II. – 8:103 has been modified and expanded, following a suggestion by the evaluative group formed by the Association Henri Capitant and the Société de Législation Comparée.

29. Book III. A new generalised provision on tacit prolongation (III. – 1:111) has been inserted, again following a suggestion by the evaluative group formed by the Association Henri Capitant and the Société de Législation Comparée. A new paragraph (3) has been inserted in III. – 2:102 (Time of performance) on the recommendation of the Acquis Group, and a new Article has been inserted (III. – 3:205) to make it clear that when a supplier replaces a defective item the supplier has a right and an obligation to take back the replaced item. Some minor adjustments have been made to the rules on the effects of termination for non-performance of contractual obligations (Chapter 3, Section 5, Sub-section 3). New rules on interest in commercial contracts have been inserted on the recommendation of the Acquis Group (III. – 3:710 and III. – 3:711). In Chapter 5 the rule on the requirements for an assignment (III. – 5:104) has been modified to bring it into line with the equivalent rule in the Book on the transfer of ownership of corporeal movables and, for the same reason, a new Article has been added on the effects on an assignment of initial invalidity, subsequent avoidance, withdrawal, termination and revocation (III. – 5:118). The rule on the effect of a contractual prohibition of assignment (III. – 5:108) has been firmed up and part of it removed and generalised in a new rule on competition between an assignee and an assignor receiving the proceeds of performance (III. – 5:122). Chapter 5 has been expanded by the inclusion of Articles on the substitution or addition of a new debtor in such a way that the original debtor is not discharged (Chapter 5, Section 2). A new Article has been added to enable a principal to take over the rights of an agent against a third party if the agent becomes insolvent (III. – 5:401) and to give the third party, in such a case, an option to hold the principal liable for the agent's obligations under the contract ((III. – 5:402). These rules will be particularly relevant in cases of so-called indirect representation where the agent contracts in the agent's own name. As a consequence of some of these changes Chapter 5 has been renamed "Change of parties". The Article on the requirements for set-off (III. – 6:102) has been redrafted after it was drawn to our attention that there was a difference in substance between the English and French texts in the PECL, and it has been expanded to make it clear that the rights being set off against each other must both be available for that purpose, and not for example frozen on the application of an arresting creditor. And, finally, two of the Articles on prescription (III. – 7:302 and III. – 7:303) have been slightly expanded partly to take account of developments in relation to mediation.

30. Book IV. The main change in Book IV has been the elimination of redundant or overlapping provisions, including some provisions which repeated the substance of rules already found in Books II or III. The presence of these redundant provisions had been rightly criticised by commentators on the Interim Outline Edition. Most of these provisions had a proper role to play in the self-standing PEL Books in order to complete the picture but are unnecessary in the DCFR. In a few cases, new or revised rules in earlier Books (e. g. on tacit prolongation and interpretation against the dominant party) enabled provisions in Book IV which were formerly necessary to be now deleted. A slight adjustment has been made in IV. A. – 2:305 (Third party rights or claims in general) in order to bring the text into line with the agreed policy as expressed in the comments. Several changes have been made in the Chapter on mandate. These were made partly to make it more clear that the chapter applies not only to contracts for the conclusion of a contract for the principal but also to contracts, for example with estate agents or brokers of various kinds, for the negotiation or facilitation of a contract to be concluded by the principal and, given that scope, partly in the interests of more precise terminology. For example, an estate agent with authority to negotiate but not conclude a contract for the principal is more accurately described as an "agent" than as a "representative", which was the word used in the Interim Outline Edition.

31. Books V-VII. Only minor drafting changes have been made in these Books.

32. Books VIII-X. Books VIII, IX and X were prepared in the same manner as the other books of the DCFR on the basis of deliberation in working teams, advisory councils and plenary meetings. However, for reasons primarily of time, the Compilation and Redaction Team was not able to give these Books the same complete scrutiny as it was able to bestow on the others.

33. Definitions. Some helpful comments were received on the Annex of definitions. As a result, some definitions which had been inserted primarily as drafting aids rather than to elucidate the meaning of a term or concept have been deleted. This has sometimes meant using a few more words than before in some Articles. A few definitions have been changed in the interests of greater clarity or precision. A few terms which were defined only in the Annex in the Interim Outline Edition have now, because of their importance, been moved to the text of the model rules. The list of definitions still contains definitions taken from, or derived from, the model rules as well as some definitions which, because of their generality, do not have a natural home in any one model rule. This makes for a mixed list but the purpose is simply the convenience of the reader. Where a definition is taken or derived from an Article in the model rules a cross-reference to that Article has been added. Again this responds to a useful suggestion made by commentators.

The coverage of the DCFR

34. Wider coverage than PECL. The coverage of the PECL was already quite wide. They had rules not only on the formation, validity, interpretation and contents of contracts and, by analogy, other juridical acts, but also on the performance of obligations resulting from them and on the remedies for non-performance of such obligations. Indeed the later Chapters had many rules applying to private law rights and obligations in general – for example, rules on a plurality of parties, on the assignment of rights to performance, on set-off and on prescription. To this extent the Principles went well beyond the law on contracts as such. The DCFR continues this coverage but it goes further.

35. Specific contracts. The DCFR also covers (in Book IV) a series of model rules on so-called 'specific contracts' and the rights and obligations arising from them. For their field of application these latter rules expand and make more specific the general provisions (in Books I-III), deviate from them where the context so requires, or address matters not covered by them.

36. Non-contractual obligations. The DCFR also covers other private law rights and obligations within its scope even if they do not arise from a contract. It covers, for example, those arising as the result of an unjustified enrichment, of damage caused to another and of benevolent intervention in another's affairs. It also covers obligations which a person might have, for example, by virtue of being in possession of assets subject to proprietary security or by virtue of being a trustee. It thus embraces non-contractual obligations to a far greater extent than the PECL. It is noted below (paragraphs 44-46) that Book III contains some general rules which are applicable to all obligation within the scope of the DCFR, whether contractual or not. The advantage of this approach is that the rules in Book III can be taken for granted, or slightly modified where appropriate, in the later Books on non-contractual matters. The alternative would be an unacceptable amount of unnecessary repetition.

37. Matters of movable property law. The DCFR also covers some matters of movable property law, namely acquisition and loss of ownership, proprietary security, and trust law. They form the content of Books VIII, IX and X and are published here for the first time.

38. Matters excluded. DCFR I. – 1:101(2) lists all matters which are excluded from its intended field of application. These are in particular: the status or legal capacity of natural persons, wills and succession, family relationships, negotiable instruments, employment relationships, immovable property law, company law, and the law of civil procedure and enforcement of claims.

39. Reasons for the approach adopted. The coverage of the DCFR is thus considerably broader than what the European Commission seems to have in mind for the coverage of the CFR (see paragraph 59 below). The 'academic' frame of reference is not subject to the constraints of the 'political' frame of reference. While the DCFR is linked to the CFR, it is conceived as an independent text. The research teams began in the tradition of the Commission on European Contract Law but with the aim of extending its coverage. When this work started there were no political discussions underway on the creation of a CFR of any kind, neither for contract law nor for any other part of the law. Our contract with the Research Directorate-General to receive funding under the sixth European Framework Programme on Research reflects this; it obliges us to address all the matters listed above. The relatively broad coverage of the DCFR may be seen as advantageous also from a political perspective. Only a comprehensive DCFR creates a concrete basis for the discussion of the coverage of the political CFR and thereby allows for an informed decision of the responsible political institutions.

40. Contract law as part of private law. There are good reasons for including more than rules on general contract law in the DCFR. These general rules need to be tested to see whether or in what respect they have to be adjusted, amended and revised within the framework of the most important of the specific contracts. Nor can the DCFR contain only rules dealing with consumer contracts. The two Groups concur in the view that consumer law is not a self-standing area of private law. It consists of some deviations from the general principles of private law, but it is built on them and cannot be developed without them. And 'private law' for this purpose is not confined to the law on contract and contractual obligations. The correct dividing line between contract law (in this wide sense) and some other areas of law is in any event difficult to determine precisely.[23] The DCFR therefore approaches the whole of the law of obligations as an organic entity or unit. Some areas of property law with regard to movable property are dealt with for more or less identical reasons and because some aspects of property law are of great relevance to the good functioning of the internal market.

Structure and language of the DCFR model rules

41. Structure of the model rules. The structure of the model rules was discussed on many occasions by the Study Group and the joint Compilation and Redaction Team. It was accepted from an early stage that the whole text would be divided into Books and that each Book would be subdivided into Chapters, Sections, Sub-sections (where appropriate) and Articles. In addition the Book on specific contracts and the rights and obligations arising from them was to be divided, because of its size, into Parts, each dealing with a particular type of contract (e. g. Book IV.A: Sale). All of this was relatively uncontroversial.

42. Mode of numbering the model rules. The mode of numbering the model rules corresponds in its basic approach to the technique used in many of the newer European codifications. This too was chosen in order to enable necessary changes to be made later without more than minor editorial labour. Books are numbered by capitalised Roman numerals, i. e., Book I (General provisions), Book II (Contracts and other juridical acts), etc. Only one Book (Book IV (Specific contracts and rights and obligations arising from them)) is di-

---

[23] See, in more detail, von Bar and Drobnig (eds.), The Interaction of Contract Law and Tort and Property Law in Europe (Munich 2004). This study was conducted on behalf of the European Commission.

vided into Parts: Part A (Sale), Part B (Lease of goods), etc. Chapters, sections (and also sub-sections) are numbered using Arabic numerals, e. g. chapter 5, section 2, sub-section 4, etc. Articles are then numbered sequentially within each Book (or Part) using Arabic numerals. The first Arabic digit, preceding the colon, is the number of the relevant chapter. The digit immediately following the colon is the number of the relevant section of that chapter. The remaining digits give the number of the Article within the section; sub-sections do not affect the numbering. For example, III. – 3:509 (Effect on obligations under the contract) is the ninth Article in section 5 (Termination) of the third chapter (Remedies for non-performance) of the third book (Obligations and corresponding rights). It was not possible, however, to devise a numbering system that would indicate every subdivision of the text without the system becoming too complicated to be workable. One cannot see from the numbering that III. – 3:509 is the first Article within sub-section 3 (Effects of termination).

43. Ten books. To a large extent the allocation of the subject matter to the different Books was also uncontroversial. It was readily agreed that Book I should be a short and general guide for the reader on how to use the whole text – dealing, for example, with its intended scope of application, how it should be interpreted and developed and where to find definitions of key terms. The later Books, from Book IV on, also gave rise to little difficulty so far as structure was concerned. There was discussion about the best order, but eventually it was settled that this would be: Specific contracts and rights and obligations arising from them (Book IV); Benevolent intervention in another's affairs (Book V); Non-contractual liability arising out of damage caused to another (Book VI); Unjustified enrichment (Book VII); Acquisition and loss of ownership of goods (Book VIII); Proprietary security rights in movable assets (Book IX) and Trust (Book X). An important argument for putting the rules on specific contracts and their obligational effects in a Book of their own (subdivided into Parts) rather than in separate Books is that it would be easier in the future to add new Parts dealing with other specific contracts without affecting the numbering of later Books and their contents.

44. Books II and III. The difficult decisions concerned Books II and III. There was never much doubt that these Books should cover the material in the existing Principles of European Contract Law (PECL, see paragraph 8 above and paragraphs 49-53 below) – general rules on contracts and other juridical acts, and general rules on contractual and (in most cases) other obligations – but there was considerable difficulty in deciding how this material should be divided up between and within them, and what they should be called. It was only after decisions were taken by the Co-ordinating Group on how the key terms 'contract' and 'obligation' would be used in the model rules, and after a special Structure Group was set up, that the way forward became clear. Book II would deal with contracts and other juridical acts (how they are formed, how they are interpreted, when they are invalid, how their content is determined and so on) while Book III would deal with obligations within the scope of the DCFR – both contractual and non-contractual – and corresponding rights.

45. Contracts and obligations. A feature of this division of material is a clear distinction between a contract seen as a type of agreement – a type of juridical act – and the legal relationship, usually involving reciprocal sets of obligations and rights, which results from it. Book II deals with contracts as juridical acts; Book III deals with the obligations and rights resulting from contracts seen as juridical acts, as well as with non-contractual obligations and rights. To this extent a structural division which in the PECL was only implicit is made explicit in the DCFR. Some commentators on the Interim Outline Edition called for a simpler structure more like that of the PECL, one which, at least in relation to contracts and contractual obligations, would follow a natural "chronological" order. However, it has to be noted that the DCFR does in fact follow such an order. It begins with the pre-contractual stage and then proceeds to formation, right of withdrawal, representation (i. e. how a contract can be concluded for a principal by a representative), grounds of invalidity, interpretation, contents and effects, performance, remedies for non-performance, plurality of debtors and creditors, change of parties, set-off and merger, and prescription. This is essentially the same order as is followed in the PECL. The only difference is that the DCFR inserts a break at the point where the rules cease to talk about contracts as agreements (formation, interpretation, invalidity, contents and effects etc.) and start to talk about the rights and obligations arising from them. At this point a new Book is begun and a new Chapter on obligations and corresponding rights in general is inserted. It is not an enormous change. It hardly affects the order or content of the model rules. And it is justified not only because there *is* a difference between a contract and the rights and obligations arising out of it, and it is an aid to clarity of thought to recognise this, but also because it is useful to have the opening Chapter of Book III as a home for some Articles which are otherwise difficult to place, such as those on conditional and time-limited rights and obligations. To eliminate the break between Books II and III would be a regrettable step backwards for which it is difficult to see any justification.

46. Contractual and non-contractual obligations. A further problem was how best to deal with contractual and non-contractual obligations within Book III. One technique which was tried was to deal first with contractual obligations and then to have a separate part on non-contractual obligations. However, this proved cumbersome and unsatisfactory. It involved either unnecessary repetition or extensive and detailed cross-references to earlier Articles. Either way the text was unattractive and heavy for the reader to use. In the end it was found that the best technique was to frame the Articles in Book III so far as possible in general terms so that they could apply to both contractual and non-contractual obligations. Where a particular Article applied only to contractual obligations this could be clearly stated, see III. – 1:101 ("This Book applies, except as otherwise provided, to all obligations within the scope of these rules, whether they are contractual or not ..."). For example, the rules on termination can only apply to contractual obligations (see III. – 3:501(1) (Scope and definition)); the same is true for III. – 3:601 (Right to reduce price) (the restriction on the scope of application follows from the word "price") and III. – 3:203 (When creditor need not allow debtor an opportunity to cure) paragraph (a), the wording of which limits its application to contractual obligations. It need hardly be added that if a CFR were to be confined to contracts and contractual obligations it would be a very easy matter to use the model rules in Book III for that purpose. Most of them would need no alteration.

47. Language. The DCFR is being published first in English. This has been the working language for all the Groups responsible for formulating the model rules. However, for a substantial portion of the Books (or, in the case of Book IV, its Parts), teams have already composed a large number of translations into other languages. These will be published successively, first in the PEL series (see paragraphs 54-56 below) and later separately for the DCFR. In the course of these translations the English formulation of the model rules has often itself been revised. In autumn 2008 the *Fondation pour le droit continental* (Paris) published a translation of the first three Books of the DCFR (in the version of the interim outline edition).[24] A Czech translation of the interim outline addition appeared shortly afterwards.[25] The research teams are intent on publishing the model rules of the DCFR as quickly and in as many languages as is possible. However, the English version is the only version of the DCFR which has been discussed and adopted by the responsible bodies of the participating groups and by the Compilation and Redaction Team.

48. Accessibility and intelligibility. In the preparation of the DCFR every attempt was made to achieve not only a clear and coherent structure, but also a plain and clear wording. Whether the model rules and definitions are seen as a tool for better lawmaking or as the possible basis for one or more optional instruments it is important that they should be fit for their purpose. The terminology should be precise and should be used consistently. The word "contract" for example should be used in one sense, not three or more. The terminology should be as suitable as possible for use across a large number of translations. It should therefore try to avoid legalese and technicalities drawn from any one legal system. An attempt has been made to find, wherever possible, descriptive language which can be readily translated without carrying unwanted baggage with it. It is for this reason that words like "rescission", "tort" and "delict" have been avoided. The concepts used should be capable of fitting together coherently in model rules, whatever the content of those model

---

[24] By Professor Jacques Ghestin, see fn. 3 above.

[25] By a team led by Professor Přemysl Raban, published in Karlovarská Právní Revuei 2/2008, 1-222.

rules. The text should be well-organised, accessible and readable. Being designed for the Europe of the 21st century, it should be expressed in gender neutral terms. It should be as simple as is consistent with the need to convey accurately the intended meaning. It should not contain irrational, redundant, or conflicting provisions. Whether the DCFR achieves these aims is for others to judge. Certainly, considerable efforts were made to try to achieve them.

How the DCFR relates to PECL, the SGECC PEL series, the Acquis and the Insurance Contract Group series

49. Based in part on the PECL. In Books II and III the DCFR contains many rules derived from the Principles of European Contract Law (PECL). These rules have been adopted with the express agreement of the Commission on European Contract Law, whose successor group is the Study Group. Tables of derivations and destinations will help the reader to trace PECL articles within the DCFR. However, the PECL could not simply be incorporated as they stood. Deviations were unavoidable in part due to the different purpose, structure and coverage of the DCFR and in part because the scope of the PECL needed to be broadened so as to embrace matters of consumer protection.

50. Deviations from the PECL. A primary purpose of the DCFR is to try to develop clear and consistent concepts and terminology. In pursuit of this aim the Study Group gave much consideration to the most appropriate way of using terms like 'contract' and 'obligation', taking into account not only national systems, but also prevailing usage in European and international instruments dealing with private law topics. One reason for many of the drafting changes from the PECL is the clearer distinction now drawn (as noted above) between a contract (seen as a type of agreement or juridical act) and the relationship (usually consisting of reciprocal rights and obligations) to which it gives rise. This has a number of consequences throughout the text.

51. **Examples.** For example, under the DCFR it is not the contract which is performed. A contract is concluded; obligations are performed. Similarly, a contract is not terminated. It is the contractual relationship, or particular rights and obligations arising from it, which will be terminated. The new focus on rights and obligations in Book III also made possible the consistent use of 'creditor' and 'debtor' rather than terms like 'aggrieved party' and 'other party', which were commonly used in the PECL. The decision to use 'obligation' consistently as the counterpart of a right to performance also meant some drafting changes. The PECL sometimes used 'duty' in this sense and sometimes 'obligation'. The need for clear concepts and terminology also meant more frequent references than in the PECL to juridical acts other than contracts. A juridical act is defined in II.–1:101 as a statement or agreement which is intended to have legal effect as such. All legal systems have to deal with various types of juridical act other than contracts, but not all use such a term and not all have generalised rules. Examples of such juridical acts might be offers, acceptances, notices of termination, authorisations, guarantees, acts of assignment, unilateral promises and so on. The PECL dealt with these by an article (1:107) which applied the Principles to them 'with appropriate modifications'. However, this technique is a short-cut which should only be used with great care and only when the appropriate modifications will be slight and fairly obvious. In this instance what modifications would be appropriate was not always apparent. It was therefore decided, as far back as 2004, to deal separately with other juridical acts. Some commentators on the Interim Outline Edition have ascribed a significance to this modest functional decision which it certainly did not have in the eyes of the drafters.

52. **Input from stakeholders.** Other changes in PECL articles resulted from the input from stakeholders to the workshops held by the European Commission on selected topics. For example, the rules on representation were changed in several significant respects for this reason, as were the rules on pre-contractual statements forming part of a contract, the rules on variation by a court of contractual rights and obligations on a change of circumstances and the rules on so-called 'implied terms' of a contract. Sometimes even the process of

preparing for stakeholder meetings which did not, in the end, take place led to proposals for changes in PECL which were eventually adopted. This was the case, for example, with the chapter on plurality of debtors and creditors, where academic criticism on one or two specific points also played a role.

53. Developments since the publication of the PECL. Finally, there were some specific articles or groups of articles from the PECL which, in the light of recent developments or further work and thought, seemed to merit improvement. For example, the PECL rules on stipulations in favour of third parties, although a considerable achievement at the time, seemed in need of some expansion in the light of recent developments in national systems and international instruments. The detailed work which was done on the specific contracts in Book IV, and the rights and obligations resulting from them, sometimes suggested a need for some additions to, and changes in, the general rules in Books II and III. For example, it was found that it would be advantageous to have a general rule on 'mixed contracts' in Book II and a general rule on notifications of non-conformities in Book III. It was also found that the rules on 'cure' by a seller which were developed in the Part of Book IV on sale could usefully be generalised and placed in Book III. The work done on other later Books also sometimes fed back into Books II and III. For example, the work done on unjustified enrichment showed that rather more developed rules were needed on the restitutionary effects of terminated contractual relationships, while the work on the acquisition and loss of ownership of goods (and also on proprietary security rights in movable assets) fed back into the treatment of assignment in Book III. Although the general approach was to follow the PECL as much as possible there were, inevitably, a number of cases where it was found that small drafting changes could increase clarity or consistency. For example, the PECL sometimes used the word "claim" in the sense of a demand based on the assertion of a right and sometimes in the sense of a right to performance. The DCFR uses "claim" only in the first sense and uses a "right to performance" where this is what is meant. Again, the PECL referred sometimes to contract "terms" and sometimes to contract "clauses". The DCFR prefers "terms", which has the advantage of applying with equal facility to written and non-written contracts.

54. The PEL series. The Study Group began its work in 1998. From the outset it was envisaged that at the appropriate time its results would be presented in an integrated complete edition, but it was only gradually that its structure took shape (see paragraphs 41-46 above). As a first step the tasks in the component parts of the project had to be organised and deliberated. The results are being published in a separate series, the 'Principles of European Law' (PEL). To date six volumes have appeared. They cover sales,[26] leases,[27] services,[28] commercial agency, franchise and distribution,[29] personal security contracts,[30] and benevolent interventions in another's affairs.[31] Further books will follow (in 2009 and 2010) on the law regarding non-

---

[26] Principles of European Law. Study Group on a European Civil Code. Sales (PEL S). Prepared by Ewoud Hondius, Viola Heutger, Christoph Jeloschek, Hanna Sivesand, Aneta Wiewiorowska (Sellier, Bruylant, Staempfli, Oxford University Press 2008).

[27] Principles of European Law. Study Group on a European Civil Code. Lease of Goods (PEL LG). Prepared by Kåre Lilleholt, Anders Victorin†, Andreas Fötschl, Berte-Elen R. Konow, Andreas Meidell, Amund Bjøranger Tørum (Sellier, Bruylant, Staempfli, Oxford University Press 2007).

[28] Principles of European Law. Study Group on a European Civil Code. Service Contracts (PEL SC). Prepared by Maurits Barendrecht, Chris Jansen, Marco Loos, Andrea Pinna, Rui Cascão, Stéphanie van Gulijk (Sellier, Bruylant, Staempfli, Oxford University Press 2006).

[29] Principles of European Law. Study Group on a European Civil Code. Commercial Agency, Franchise and Distribution Contracts (PEL CAFDC). Prepared by Martijn W. Hesselink, Jacobien W. Rutgers, Odavia Bueno Díaz, Manola Scotton, Muriel Veldmann (Sellier, Bruylant, Staempfli, Oxford University Press 2006).

[30] Principles of European Law. Study Group on a European Civil Code. Personal Security (PEL Pers.Sec.). Prepared by Ulrich Drobnig (Sellier, Bruylant, Staempfli, Oxford University Press 2007).

[31] Principles of European Law. Study Group on a European Civil Code. Benevolent Intervention in Another's Affairs (PEL Ben.Int.). Prepared

contractual liability arising out of damage caused to another, on unjustified enrichment law, on mandate contracts, and all the subjects related to property law. The volumes published within the PEL series contain additional material which will not be reproduced in the full DCFR, namely the comparative introductions to the various Books, Parts and Chapters and the translations of the model rules published within the PEL series. The continuation of the PEL series will also enable the publication of the full edition of the DCFR independently of whether all gaps in the compilation and editing of the comparative legal material can actually be filled in time.

55. Deviations from the PEL series. In some cases, however, the model rules which the reader encounters in this DCFR deviate from their equivalent published in the PEL series. There are several reasons for such changes. First, in drafting a self-standing set of model rules for a given subject (such as e. g. service contracts) it proved necessary to have much more repetition of rules which were already part of the PECL. Such repetitions became superfluous in an integrated DCFR text which states these rules at a more general level (i. e. in Books II and III). The DCFR is therefore considerably shorter than it would have been had all PEL model rules been included as they stood.

56. Improvements. The second reason for changing some already published PEL model rules is that, at the stage of revising and editing for DCFR purposes, the Compilation and Redaction Team saw room for some improvements. After consulting the authors of the relevant PEL book, the CRT submitted the redrafted rules to the Study Group's Co-ordinating Committee for approval, amendment or rejection. Resulting changes are in part limited to mere drafting, but occasionally go to substance. They are a consequence of the systematic revision of the model rules which commenced in 2006, the integration of ideas from others (including stakeholders) and the compilation of the list of terminology, which revealed some incon-

---

by Christian von Bar (Sellier, Bruylant, Staempfli, Oxford University Press 2006).

sistencies in the earlier texts. The DCFR in turn, in its full edition, reflects yet further refinements as compared with the interim outline edition.

57. The Acquis Principles (ACQP). The Research Group on the Existing EC Private Law, commonly called the Acquis Group, is also publishing its findings in a separate series.[32] The Acquis Principles are an attempt to present and structure the bulky and rather incoherent patchwork of EC private law in a way that should allow the current state of its development to be made clear and relevant legislation and case law to be found easily. This also permits identification of shared features, contradictions and gaps in the *acquis*. Thus, the ACQP may have a function for themselves, namely as a source for the drafting, transposition and interpretation of EC law. Within the process of elaborating the DCFR, the Acquis Group and its output contribute to the task of ensuring that the existing EC law is appropriately reflected. The ACQP are consequently one of the sources from which the Compilation and Redaction Team has drawn.

58. Principles of European Insurance Contract Law. The CoPECL network of researchers established under the sixth framework programme for research (see below: academic contributors and funders) also includes the 'Project Group Restatement of European Insurance Contract Law (Insurance Group)'. That body is expected to deliver its 'Principles of European Insurance Contract Law' to the European Commission contemporaneously with our submission of the DCFR.

---

[32] Principles of the Existing EC Contract Law (Acquis Principles). Contract I – Pre-Contractual Obligations, Conclusion of Contract, Unfair Terms. Prepared by the Research Group on the Existing EC Private Law (Acquis Group) (Munich 2007); in print: Contract II (Munich 2009), which includes general provisions, delivery of goods, package travel and payment services. Further volumes on specific contracts and extra-contractual matters in preparation.

How the DCFR may be used as preparatory work for the CFR

59. Announcements by the Commission. The European Commission's 'Action Plan on A More Coherent European Contract Law' of January 2003[33] called for comments on three proposed measures: increasing the coherence of the *acquis communautaire*, the promotion of the elaboration of EU-wide standard contract terms,[34] and further examination of whether there is a need for a measure that is not limited to particular sectors, such as an 'optional instrument.' Its principal proposal for improvement was to develop a Common Frame of Reference (CFR) which could then be used by the Commission in reviewing the existing *acquis* and drafting new legislation.[35] In October 2004 the Commission published a further paper, 'European Contract Law and the revision of the acquis: the way forward'.[36] This proposed that the CFR should provide 'fundamental principles, definitions and model rules' which could assist in the improvement of the existing *acquis communautaire*, and which might form the basis of an optional instrument if it were decided to create one. Model rules would form the bulk of the CFR,[37] its main purpose being to serve as a kind of legislators' guide or 'tool box'. This DCFR responds to these announcements by the Commission and contains proposals for the principles, definitions and model rules mentioned in them.

60. Purposes of the CFR. It remains to be seen what purposes the CFR may be called upon to serve. Some indication may be obtained from the expression 'principles, definitions and model rules' itself. Other indications can be obtained from the Commission's papers on

---

[33] See fn. 1 above.

[34] This aspect of the plan is not being taken forward. See Commission of the European Communities. First Progress Report on The Common Frame of Reference, COM (2005), 456 final, p. 10.

[35] Action Plan para. 72.

[36] Communication from the Commission to the European Parliament and the Council, COM (2004) 651 final, 11 October 2004 (referred to as Way Forward).

[37] Way Forward para. 3.1.3, p. 11.

this subject. These, and their implications for the coverage of the DCFR, will now be explored.

61. Green Paper on the Review of the Consumer Acquis. The 'Way Forward' communication had announced that parallel to the preparation of the DCFR a review of eight consumer Directives[38] would be carried out. Members of the Acquis Group were involved in this review.[39] In 2007 the European Commission published a Green Paper on the review of the consumer acquis.[40] It asked questions at a number of different levels: for example, whether full harmonisation is desirable,[41] whether there should be a horizontal instrument,[42] (as to which see paragraph 62 below) and whether various additional matters should be dealt with by the Consumer Sales Directive.[43] It is possible that other Directives will also be revised, for example those relating to the provision of information to recipients of financial services. In the longer term, there may be proposals for further harmonisation measures in sectors where there still appears to be a need for consumer protection (e. g. contracts for services and for personal security) or where the differences between the laws of the Member States appear to cause difficulties for the internal market (e. g. insurance and security over movable property).

62. Draft proposal for a Directive on consumer contractual rights. The Green Paper on the review of the consumer *acquis* has now been followed by the publication of a draft proposal for a 'horizontal'

---

[38] Directives 85/577, 90/314, 93/13, 94/47, 97/7, 98/6; 98/27, 99/44. See Way Forward para. 2.1.1.

[39] See Schulte-Nölke/Twigg-Flesner/Ebers (eds), EC Consumer Law Compendium. The Consumer Acquis and its transposition in the Member States (Munich 2008).

[40] Green Paper on the Review of the Consumer Acquis, COM(2006) 744 final of 8 February 2007 (http://ec.europa.eu/consumers/cons_int/safe_sh op/acquis/green-paper_cons_acquis_en.pdf).

[41] Question A3, p. 15.

[42] Question A2, p. 14.

[43] Directive 1999/44/EC. See questions H1-M3, pp. 24-32.

directive.[44] In its present form, however, and perhaps for reasons of timing, the latter does not make any explicit use of the DCFR. Whereas terminology and drafting style are rather different, there are nevertheless some characteristic similarities with regard to substance. For instance, both the DCFR and the draft horizontal directive propose general rules on pre-contractual information duties or withdrawal rights, which are different in detail but follow the same basic ideas. One such idea is that, in general, a right of withdrawal and the corresponding information duties should apply to all types of contracts negotiated away from business premises (the draft horizontal directive calls them "distance and off-premises contracts"), except under clearly defined circumstances, which can be easily proved. It will have to be seen what use will be made of the DCFR or a possible political CFR in later stages of the elaboration of the directive.

63. Improving the existing and future acquis: model rules. The DCFR is intended to help in this process of improving the existing *acquis* and in drafting any future EU legislation in the field of private law. By teasing out and stating clearly the principles that underlie the *acquis*, the DCFR can show how the existing Directives can be made more consistent and how various sectoral provisions might be given a wider application, so as to eliminate current gaps and overlaps – the 'horizontal approach' referred to in the draft proposal. (For instance the DCFR provides for general model rules on pre-contractual information duties and withdrawal rights, which are also the subject of the draft horizontal directive, though this, unlike the DCFR, mainly leaves it to the national laws to determine the consequences of any breach of information duties. The DCFR offers both the EC legislator and the national legislators a model set of sanctions for breach of information duties.) The DCFR also seeks to identify improvements in substance that might be considered. The research preparing the DCFR 'will aim to identify best solutions, taking into account national contract laws (both case law and established practice), the EC *acquis* and relevant international instruments, particularly the UN

---

[44] Proposal for a Directive of the European Parliament and of the Council on consumer rights, COM(2008) 614.

Convention on Contracts for the International Sale of Goods of 1980'.[45] The DCFR therefore provides recommendations, based on extensive comparative research and careful analysis, of what should be considered if legislators are minded to alter or add to EU legislation within the broad framework of existing basic assumptions. The DCFR does not challenge these basic assumptions of the *acquis* (such as the efficacy of information duties or the value of the notion of the consumer as a basis for providing necessary protection) any more than shared propositions of national law. It would not have been appropriate for a group of academic lawyers in an exercise of this nature to do so: these are fundamental and politically sensitive questions which are not primarily of a legal nature. The DCFR simply makes proposals as to how, given the present policy assumptions, the relevant rules might with advantage be modified and made more coherent. In a very few cases it is proposed that, as has been done in some Member States, particular *acquis* rules applying to consumers should be applied more generally. We do not of course suggest that even those proposals should simply be adopted without further debate. They are no more than model rules from which the legislator and other interested parties may draw inspiration.

64. Improving the acquis: developing a coherent terminology. Directives frequently employ legal terminology and concepts which they do not define.[46] The classic example, seemingly referred to in the Commission's papers, is the *Simone Leitner* case,[47] but there are many

---

[45] Way Forward para. 3.1.3.

[46] In the CFR workshops on the consumer *acquis*, texts providing definitions of concepts used or pre-supposed in the EU acquis were referred to as 'directly relevant' material. See Second Progress Report on the Common Frame of Reference, COM (2007) 447 final, p. 2.

[47] Case C-168/00 Simone Leitner v TUI Deutschland [2002] ECR I-2631. The ECJ had to decide whether the damages to which a consumer was entitled under the provisions of the Package Travel Directive must include compensation for non-economic loss suffered when the holiday was not as promised. This head of damages is recognised by many national laws, but was not recognised by Austrian law. The ECJ held that 'damage' in the Directive must be given an autonomous, 'European' legal mean-

others. A CFR which provides definitions of these legal terms and concepts would be useful for questions of interpretation of this kind, particularly if it were adopted by the European institutions – for example, as a guide for legislative drafting.[48] It would be presumed that the word or concept contained in a Directive was used in the sense in which it is used in the CFR unless the Directive stated otherwise.[49] National legislators seeking to implement the Directive, and national courts faced with interpreting the implementing legislation, would be able to consult the CFR to see what was meant. Moreover, if comparative notes on the Articles are included, as they will be in the full version of the DCFR, the notes will often provide useful background information on how national laws currently deal with the relevant questions.

65. No functional terminology list without rules. As said before, it is impossible to draft a functional list of terminology without a set of model rules behind it, and vice versa. That in turn makes it desirable to consider a rather wide coverage of the CFR. For example, it would be very difficult to develop a list of key notions of the law on contract and contractual obligations (such as "conduct", "creditor", "damage", "indemnify", "loss", "negligence", "property" etc.), without a sufficient awareness of the fact that many of these notions also play a role in the area of non-contractual obligations.

66. Coverage of the CFR. The purposes to be served by the DCFR have a direct bearing on its coverage. As explained in paragraphs 34-39 above, the coverage of the DCFR goes well beyond the coverage

---

ing – and in this context 'damage' is to be interpreted as including non-economic loss.

[48] In the absence of any formal arrangement, legislators could achieve much the same result for individual legislative measures by stating in the recitals that the measure should be interpreted in accordance with the CFR.

[49] We note that the draft Directive on consumer rights (fn. 44 above) at present often adopts the words of the existing Directives, even where these are known not to be very clear. We hope that before the Directive is adopted, its drafting will be checked against the DCFR and brought into line with it, save where a different outcome is intended.

of the CFR as contemplated by the Commission in its communications (whereas the European Parliament in several resolutions envisages for the CFR more or less the same coverage as this DCFR).[50] Today, the coverage of the CFR still seems to be an open question. How far should it reach if it is to be effective as a legislators' guide or 'tool box'? How may this DCFR be used if it is decided that the coverage of the CFR will be narrower (or even much narrower) than the coverage of the DCFR? The following aspects would seem to be worthy of being taken into consideration when making the relevant political decisions.

67. Consumer law and e-commerce. It seems clear that the CFR must at any rate cover the fields of application of the existing Directives that are under review, and any others likely to be reviewed in the foreseeable future. Thus all consumer law and questions of e-commerce should be included, and probably all contracts and contractual relationships that are the subject of existing Directives affecting questions of private law, since these may also be reviewed at some stage.

68. Revision of the acquis and further harmonisation measures. Secondly, the CFR should cover any field in which revision of the *acquis* or further harmonisation measures is being considered. This includes both areas currently under review (e. g. sales, and also leasing which is discussed in the Green Paper on revision of the consumer *acquis*[51]) and also areas where harmonisation is being considered, even if there are no immediate proposals for new legislation. Thus contracts for services should be covered, and also security over movable property, where divergences of laws cause serious problems.

---

[50] European Parliament, Resolution of 15 November 2001, OJ C 140E of 13 June 2002, p. 538; Resolution of 23 March 2006, OJ C 292E of 1 December 2006, p. 109; Resolution of 7 September 2007, OJ C 305E of 14 December 2006, p. 247; Resolution of 12 December 2007, OJ C 323E of 18 December 2008, p. 364; Resolution of 3 September 2008, Texts adopted, P6_TA(2008)0397.

[51] See fn. 40 above.

69. Terms and concepts referred to in Directives. Thirdly, in order to provide the definitions that are wanted, the CFR must cover many terms and concepts that are referred to in Directives without being defined. In practice this includes almost all of the general law on contract and contractual obligations. There are so few topics that are not at some point referred to in the *acquis*, or at least presupposed by it, that it is simpler to include all of this general law than to work out what few topics can be omitted. It is not only contract law terminology in the strict sense which is referred to, however, and certainly not just contract law which is presupposed in EU instruments. For example, consumer Directives frequently presuppose rules on unjustified enrichment law; and Directives on pre-contractual information refer to or presuppose rules that in many systems are classified as rules of non-contractual liability for damage, i. e. delict or tort. It is thus useful to provide definitions of terms and model rules in these fields – not because they are likely to be subjected to regulation or harmonisation by European legislation in the foreseeable future, but because existing European legislation already builds on assumptions that the laws of the Member States have relevant rules and provide appropriate remedies. Whether they do so in ways that fit well with the European legislation, actual or proposed, is another matter. It is for the European institutions to decide what might be needed or might be useful. What seems clear is that it is not easy to identify in advance topics which will never be wanted.

70. When in doubt, topics should be included. There are good arguments for the view that in case of doubt, topics should be included. Excluding too many topics will result in the CFR being a fragmented patchwork, thus replicating a major fault in existing EU legislation on a larger scale. Nor can there be any harm in a broad CFR. It is not legislation, nor even a proposal for legislation. It merely provides language and definitions for use, when needed, in the closely targeted legislation that is, and will probably remain, characteristic of European Union private law.

71. Essential background information. There is a further way in which the CFR would be valuable as a legislators' guide, and it has been prepared with a view to that possible purpose. If EU legislation is to fit harmoniously with the laws of the Member States, and in particular if it is neither to leave unintended gaps nor to be more invasive than is necessary, the legislator needs to have accurate information about the different laws in the various Member States. The national notes to be included in the full version of the DCFR will be very useful in this respect. They would, of course, have to be frequently updated if this purpose is to be served on a continuing basis.

72. Good faith as an example. The principle of good faith can serve as an example. In many laws the principle is accepted as fundamental, but it is not accorded the same recognition in the laws of all the Member States. In some systems it is not recognised as a general rule of direct application. It is true that such systems contain many particular rules which perform the same function as a requirement of good faith, in the sense that they are aimed at preventing the parties from acting in ways that are incompatible with good faith, but there is no *general* rule. So the European legislator cannot assume that whatever requirements it chooses to impose on consumer contracts in order to protect consumers will always be supplemented by a general requirement that the parties act in good faith. If it wants a general requirement to apply in the particular context, in all jurisdictions, the legislator will have to incorporate the requirement into the Directive in express words – as of course it did with the Directive on Unfair Terms in Consumer Contracts.[52] Alternatively, it will need to insert into the Directive specific provisions to achieve the results that in some jurisdictions would be reached by the application of the principle of good faith. To take another example, in drafting or revising a Directive dealing with pre-contractual information, legislators will want to know what they need to deal with and what is already covered adequately, and in a reasonably harmonious way, by the law of all Member States. Thus general principles on mistake, fraud and provision of incorrect information form essential background to the consumer *acquis* on pre-contractual information. In this sense, even a 'legislators' guide' needs statements of the common principles found in the different laws, and a note of the variations. It needs information about what is in the existing laws and what can be

---

[52] Council Directive 93/13/EEC, art. 3(1).

omitted from the *acquis* because, in one form or another, all Member States already have it.

73. Presupposed rules of national law. Further, a Directive normally presupposes the existence of certain rules in national law. For example, when a consumer exercises a right to withdraw from a contract, questions of liability in restitution are mainly left to national law. It may be argued that information about the law that is presupposed is more than 'essential background'. The Commission's Second Progress Report describes it as 'directly relevant'.[53] Whatever the correct classification, this information is clearly important. Put simply, European legislators need to know what is a problem in terms of national laws and what is not. This is a further reason why the DCFR has a wide coverage and why the full DCFR will contain extensive notes, comparing the model rules to the various national laws.

74. DCFR not structured on an 'everything or nothing' basis. The DCFR is, so far as possible, structured in such a way that the political institutions, if they wish to proceed with an official Common Frame of Reference on the basis of some of its proposals, can sever certain parts of it and leave them to a later stage of deliberation or just to general discussion amongst academics. In other words, the DCFR is carefully not structured on an 'everything or nothing' basis. Perhaps not every detail can be cherry-picked intact, but in any event larger areas could be taken up without any need to accept the entirety. For example, the reader will soon see that the provisions of Book III are directly applicable to contractual rights and obligations; it is simply that they also apply to non-contractual rights and obligations. Were the Commission to decide that the CFR should deal only with the former, it would be a quick and simple task to adjust the draft to apply only to contractual rights and obligations. We would not advise this, for reasons explained earlier. It would create the appearance of a gulf between contractual and other obligations that does not in fact exist in the laws of Member States, and it would put the coherence of the structure at risk. But it could be done if required.[54]

---

[53] See fn. 46 above, p. 2.

Developments after this edition

75. Full version of the DCFR. The full version of the DCFR was submitted to the European Commission at the end of December 2008. It will soon be reproduced in book form as a larger publication. The outline and full editions will differ in that the latter will contain the comments and the comparative notes supplemented by an index and bibliographic tables.

76. Consumer credit contracts not covered. The DCFR does not contain any model rules on consumer credit law. This is the subject-matter of a Directive which was only adopted during the concluding phase of the work on the DCFR.[55] The DCFR could not be revised in time to take account of it.

77. Evaluating the DCFR. The research teams which combined their endeavours under the 6th Framework Programme for Research will have concluded their work with the publication of the DCFR. The network will continue to exist only until the end of April 2009. The discussion about the DCFR and about the CFR which will possibly develop from it will, however, go on. The researchers offer to be a part of that development and the implementation of new forms of cooperation between the various legal professional groups, but must point out that fresh funding would have to be found to make that possible.

78. CFR. The creation of a CFR is a question for the European Institutions. We suggest that they make decisions about the questions of legal policy which arise in this context only after consultation with the various groups involved. If desired, the researchers remain willing to participate.

---

[54] We would strongly urge that if anything like this were done, the Comments should be re-written to explain that in most systems the rules apply also to non-contractual obligations.

[55] Directive 2008/48/EC of the European Parliament and of the Council of 23 April 2008 on Consumer Credit Contracts and abrogating Directive 87/102/EEC, OJ L 133/66 of 22 May 2008

79. Square brackets. The square brackets in Interim Outline Edition II. – 9:404 (Meaning of "unfair" in contracts between a business and a consumer) (now II. – 9:403) remain. The question here is whether the control on unfair terms in a contract between a business and a consumer should apply (a) only to terms which have not been individually negotiated or (b) to any terms which have been supplied by the business. The practical consequences of keeping or removing the words "which has not been individually negotiated" would probably not be great in this context (given that most terms supplied by the business would in any event not be individually negotiated) but the question is a delicate one and better left to a political decision. The square brackets in Interim Outline Edition III. – 5:108 (Assignability: effect of contractual prohibition) have been deleted as it proved possible to reach a decision in favour of a less complicated solution than that formerly presented in paragraph (5).

80. The CFR as the basis for an optional instrument. What has been said about the purposes of the CFR relates to its function as a legislators' guide or toolbox. It is still unclear whether or not the CFR, or parts of it, might at a later stage be used as the basis for one or more optional instruments, i. e. as the basis for an additional set of legal rules which parties might choose to govern their mutual rights and obligations. In the view of the two Groups such an optional instrument would open attractive perspectives, not least for consumer transactions. A more detailed discussion of this issue, however, seems premature at this stage. It suffices to say that this DCFR is consciously drafted in a way that, given the political will, would allow progress to be made towards the creation of such an optional instrument.

January 2009   *Christian von Bar,*
                                                        Hugh Beale,
                                                        Eric Clive,
                                                        Hans Schulte-Nölke

Academic contributors and funders

The pan-European teams

As indicated already, the DCFR is the result of more than 25 years' collaboration of jurists from all jurisdictions of the present Member States within the European Union. It began in 1982 with the constitution of the Commission on European Contract Law (CECL) and was furthered by the establishment of the Study Group in 1998 and the Acquis Group in 2002. From 2005 the Study Group, Acquis Group and Insurance Contract Group formed the so-called 'drafting teams' of the CoPECL network. The following DCFR is the result of the work of the Study Group, Acquis Group and CECL.

The Study Group on a European Civil Code

The Study Group has had the benefit of Working (or Research) Teams – groups of younger legal scholars under the supervision of a senior member of the Group (a Team Leader). The Teams undertook the basic comparative legal research, developed the drafts for discussion and assembled the extensive material required for the notes. To each Working Team was allocated a consultative body –

an Advisory Council. These bodies – deliberately kept small in the interests of efficiency – were formed from leading experts in the relevant field of law, who represented the major European legal systems. The proposals drafted by the Working Teams and critically scrutinised and improved in a series of meetings by the respective Advisory Council were submitted for discussion on a revolving basis to the actual decision-making body of the Study Group on a European Civil Code, the Co-ordinating Group. Until June 2004 the Co-ordinating Group consisted of representatives from all the jurisdictions belonging to the EU immediately prior to its enlargement in Spring 2004 and in addition legal scholars from Estonia, Hungary, Norway, Poland, Slovenia and Switzerland. Representatives from the Czech Republic, Malta, Latvia, Lithuania and Slovakia joined us after the June 2004 meeting in Warsaw and representatives from Bulgaria and Romania after the December 2006 meeting in Lucerne. Besides its permanent members, other participants in the Co-ordinating Group with voting rights included all the Team Leaders and – when the relevant material was up for discussion – the members of the Advisory Council concerned. The results of the deliberations during the week-long sittings of the Co-ordinating Group were incorporated into the text of the Articles and the commentaries which returned to the agenda for the next meeting of the Co-ordinating Group (or the next but one depending on the work load of the Group and the Team affected). Each part of the project was the subject of debate on manifold occasions, some stretching over many years. Where a unanimous opinion could not be achieved, majority votes were taken.

Its Co-ordinating Group

The Study Group's Co-ordinating Group has (or had) the following members: Professor *Guido Alpa* (Genoa/Rome, until May 2005), Professor *Christian von Bar* (Osnabrück, chairman), Professor *Maurits Barendrecht* (Tilburg, until May 2005), Professor *Hugh Beale* (Warwick), Dr. *Mircea-Dan Bob* (Cluj, since June 2007), Professor *Michael Joachim Bonell* (Rome), Professor *Mifsud G. Bonnici* (Valetta, since December 2004), Professor *Carlo Castronovo* (Milan), Professor *Eric*

Clive (Edinburgh), Professor *Eugenia Dacoronia* (Athens), Professor *Ulrich Drobnig* (Hamburg), Professor *Bénédicte Fauvarque-Cosson* (Paris), Professor *Marcel Fontaine* (Louvain, until December 2003), Professor *Andreas Furrer* (Lucerne, since December 2003), Professor *Júlio Manuel Vieira Gomes* (Oporto), Professor *Viggo Hagstrøm* (Oslo, since June 2002), Supreme Court Judge *Torgny Håstad* (Stockholm), Professor *Johnny Herre* (Stockholm), Professor *Martijn Hesselink* (Amsterdam), Professor *Ewoud Hondius* (Utrecht, until May 2005), Professor *Jérôme Huet* (Paris), Professor *Giovanni Iudica* (Milan, since June 2004), Dr. *Monika Jurčova* (Trnava, since June 2006), Professor *Konstantinos Kerameus* (Athens), Professor *Ole Lando* (Copenhagen), Professor *Kåre Lilleholt* (Bergen/Oslo, since June 2003), Professor *Marco Loos* (Amsterdam); Professor *Brigitta Lurger* (Graz), Professor *Hector MacQueen* (Edinburgh), Professor *Ewan McKendrick* (Oxford), Professor *Valentinas Mikelenas* (Vilnius, since December 2004), Professor *Eoin O'Dell* (Dublin, until June 2006), Professor *Edgar du Perron* (Amsterdam), Professor *Denis Philippe* (Louvain, since June 2004), Professor *Jerzy Rajski* (Warsaw), Professor *Christina Ramberg* (Gothenburg), Supreme Court Judge Professor *Encarna Roca y Trias* (Madrid/Barcelona), Professor *Peter Schlechtriem†* (Freiburg i. Br.), Professor *Martin Schmidt-Kessel* (Osnabrück, since December 2004), Professor *Jorge Sinde Monteiro* (Coimbra, until December 2004), Professor *Lena Sisula-Tulokas* (Helsinki), Professor *Sophie Stijns* (Leuven), Professor *Matthias Storme* (Leuven), Dr. *Stephen Swann* (Osnabrück), Professor *Christian Takoff* (Sofia, since June 2007), Professor *Luboš Tichý* (Prague, since June 2005), Professor *Verica Trstenjak* (Maribor, until December 2006), Professor *Vibe Ulfbeck* (Copenhagen, since June 2006), Professor *Paul Varul* (Tartu, since June 2003), Professor *Lajos Vékás* (Budapest), Professor *Anna Veneziano* (Teramo).

The Study Group's Working Teams

Permanent working teams were based in various European universities and research institutions. The teams' former and present 'junior members' conducted research into basically three main areas of private law: the law of specific contracts, the law of extra-contractual obligations, and property law. They sometimes stayed for one or two years only, but often considerably longer in order additionally to pursue their own research projects. The meetings of the Co-ordinating Group and of numerous Advisory Councils were organised from Osnabrück, in conjunction with the relevant host, by *Ina El Kobbia*.

The members of the Working Teams were: *Begoña Alfonso de la Riva, Georgios Arnokouros,* Dr. *Erwin Beysen, Christopher Bisping, Ole Böger, Michael Bosse, Manuel Braga,* Dr. *Odavia Bueno Díaz, Sandie Calme,* Dr. *Rui Cascão, Cristiana Cicoria, Martine Costa, Inês Couto Guedes,* Dr. *John Dickie, Tobias Dierks,* Dr. *Evlalia Eleftheriadou,* Dr. *Wolfgang Faber, Silvia Fedrizzi,* Dr. *Francesca Fiorentini,* Dr. *Andreas Fötschl, Laetitia Franck,* Dr. *Caterina Gozzi, Alessio Greco, Lodewijk Gualthérie van Weezel, Stéphanie van Gulijk, Judith Hauck,* Dr. *Lars Haverkamp,* Dr. *Annamaria Herpai,* Dr. *Viola Heutger,* Dr. *Matthias Hünert,* Professor *Chris Jansen,* Dr. *Christoph Jeloschek, Menelaos Karpathakis,* Dr. *Stefan Kettler, Ina El Kobbia,* Dr. *Berte-Elen R. Konow, Rosalie Koolhoven, Caroline Lebon, Jacek Lehmann, Martin Lilja, Roland Lohnert, Birte Lorenzen,* Dr. *María Ángeles Martín Vida, Almudena de la Mata Muñoz, Pádraic McCannon,* Dr. *Mary-Rose McGuire, Paul McKane, José Carlos de Medeiros Nóbrega,* Dr. *Andreas Meidell, Philip Mielnicki, Anastasios Moraitis, Sandra Müller, Franz Nieper, Teresa Pereira,* Dr. *Andrea Pinna, Sandra Rohlfing,* Dr. *Jacobien W. Rutgers, Johan Sandstedt, Marta Lívia dos Santos Silva,* Dr. *Mårten Schultz, Manola Scotton†, Frank Seidel, Anna von Seht, Susan Singleton,* Dr. *Hanna Sivesand, Daniel Smith,* Dr. *Malene Stein Poulsen, Dimitar Stoimenov,* Dr. *Stephen Swann, Ferenc Szilágyi,* Dr. *Amund Bjøranger Tørum, Pia Ulrich, Muriel Veldman, Carles Vendrell Cervantes, Ernest Weiker, Aneta Wiewiorowska, Bastian Willers.*

The Study Group's Advisory Councils

The members of the Advisory Councils to the permanent working teams (who not infrequently served more than one team or performed other functions besides) were: Professor *Hugh Beale* (Warwick), Professor *John W. Blackie* (Strathclyde), Professor *Michael G. Bridge* (London), Professor *Angel Carrasco* (Toledo), Professor

Carlo Castronovo (Milan), Professor *Eric Clive* (Edinburgh), Professor *Pierre Crocq* (Paris); Professor *Eugenia Dacoronia* (Athens), Professor *Bénédicte Fauvarque-Cosson* (Paris), Professor *Jacques Ghestin* (Paris), Professor *Júlio Manuel Vieira Gomes* (Oporto), Professor *Helmut Grothe* (Berlin), Supreme Court Judge *Torgny Håstad* (Stockholm), Professor *Johnny Herre* (Stockholm), Professor *Jérôme Huet* (Paris), Professor *Giovanni Iudica* (Milan), Dr. *Monika Jurčova* (Trnava), Professor *Jan Kleineman* (Stockholm), Professor *Irene Kull* (Tartu), Professor *Marco Loos* (Amsterdam), Professor *Denis Mazeaud* (Paris), Professor *Hector MacQueen* (Edinburgh), Professor *Ewan McKendrick* (Oxford), Professor *Graham Moffat* (Warwick), Professor *Andrea Nicolussi* (Milan), Professor *Eoin O'Dell* (Dublin), Professor *Guillermo Palao Moreno* (Valencia), Professor *Edgar du Perron* (Amsterdam), Professor *Maria A. L. Puelinckx-van Coene* (Antwerp), Professor *Philippe Rémy* (Poitiers), Professor *Peter Schlechtriem*† (Freiburg i. Br.), Professor *Martin Schmidt-Kessel* (Osnabrück), Dr. *Kristina Siig* (Arhus), Professor *Reinhard Steennot* (Ghent), Professor *Matthias Storme* (Leuven), Dr. *Stephen Swann* (Osnabrück), Professor *Luboš Tichý* (Prague), Professor *Stefano Troiano* (Verona), Professor *Antoni Vaquer Aloy* (Lleida), Professor *Anna Veneziano* (Teramo), Professor *Alain Verbeke* (Leuven and Tilburg), Professor *Anders Victorin*† (Stockholm), Professor *Sarah Worthington* (London).

The Acquis Group

The Acquis Group texts result from a drafting process which involved individual Drafting Teams, the Redaction Committee, the Terminology Group, and the Plenary Meeting. The Drafting Teams produced a first draft of rules with comments for their topic or area on the basis of a survey of existing EC law. The drafts were then passed on to the Redaction Committee and to the Terminology Group which formulated proposals for making the various drafts by different teams dovetail with each other, also with a view towards harmonising the use of terminology and improving the language and consistency of drafts. All draft rules were debated several times at, and finally adopted by, Plenary Meetings of the Acquis Group, which convened twice a year. Several drafts which were adopted by Plenary

Meetings (in particular those on pre-contractual information duties, unfair terms and withdrawal) were subsequently presented and discussed at CFR-net stakeholder meetings. Their comments were considered within a second cycle of drafting and consolidation of the Acquis Principles.

The following members of the Acquis Group took part in the *Plenary Meetings:* Professor *Gianmaria Ajani* (Torino, speaker), Professor *Esther Arroyo i Amayuelas* (Barcelona), Professor *Carole Aubert de Vincelles* (Lyon), Dr. *Guillaume Busseuil* (Paris), Dr. *Simon Chardenoux* (Paris), Professor *Giuditta Cordero Moss* (Oslo), Professor *Gerhard Dannemann* (Berlin), Professor *Silvia Ferreri* (Torino), Professor *Lars Gorton* (Lund), Professor *Michele Graziadei* (Torino), Professor *Hans Christoph Grigoleit* (Regensburg), Professor *Luc Grynbaum* (Paris), Professor *Geraint Howells* (Manchester), Professor *Jan Hurdik* (Brno), Professor *Tsvetana Kamenova* (Sofia), Professor *Konstantinos Kerameus* (Athens), Professor *Stefan Leible* (Bayreuth), Professor *Eva Lindell-Frantz* (Lund), Dr. hab. *Piotr Machnikowski* (Wrocław), Professor *Ulrich Magnus* (Hamburg), Professor *Peter Møgelvang-Hansen* (Copenhagen), Professor *Susana Navas Navarro* (Barcelona), Dr. *Paolisa Nebbia* (Leicester), Professor *Anders Ørgaard* (Aalborg), Dr. *Barbara Pasa* (Torino), Professor *Thomas Pfeiffer* (Heidelberg), Professor *António Pinto Monteiro* (Coimbra), Professor *Jerzy Pisulinski* (Kraków), Professor *Elise Poillot* (Lyon), Professor *Judith Rochfeld* (Paris), Professor *Ewa Rott-Pietrzyk* (Katowice), Professor *Søren Sandfeld Jakobsen* (Copenhagen), Dr. *Markéta Selucká* (Brno), Professor *Hans Schulte-Nölke* (Osnabrück, co-ordinator), Professor *Reiner Schulze* (Münster), Professor *Carla Sieburgh* (Nijmegen), Dr. *Sophie Stalla-Bourdillon* (Florence), Professor *Matthias Storme* (Antwerp and Leuven), Professor *Gert Straetmans* (Antwerp), Dr. hab. *Maciej Szpunar* (Katowice), Professor *Evelyne Terryn* (Leuven), Dr. *Christian Twigg-Flesner* (Hull), Professor *Antoni Vaquer Aloy* (Lleida), Professor *Thomas Wilhelmsson* (Helsinki), Professor *Fryderyk Zoll* (Kraków).

The members of the *Redaction Committee* were, besides the speaker (*Gianmaria Ajani*) and the co-ordinator (*Hans Schulte-Nölke*) of the Acquis Group, *Gerhard Dannemann* (chair), *Luc Grynbaum, Reiner Schulze, Matthias Storme, Christian Twigg-Flesner* and *Fryderyk Zoll*.

The *Terminology Group* consisted of *Gerhard Dannemann* (Chair), *Silvia Ferreri* and *Michele Graziadei*.

Members of the individual Acquis Group Drafting Teams are: 'Contract I' (originally organised in the subteams Definition of Consumer and Business, Form, Good Faith, Pre-contractual Information Duties, Formation, Withdrawal, Non-negotiated Terms): *Esther Arroyo i Amayuelas*, *Christoph Grigoleit*, *Peter Møgelvang-Hansen*, *Barbara Pasa*, *Thomas Pfeiffer*, *Hans Schulte-Nölke*, *Reiner Schulze*, *Evelyne Terryn*, *Christian Twigg-Flesner*, *Antoni Vaquer Aloy*; 'Contract II' (responsible for Performance, Non-Performance, Remedies): *Carole Aubert de Vincelles*, *Piotr Machnikowski*, *Ulrich Magnus*, *Jerzy Pisuliłski*, *Judith Rochfeld*, *Ewa Rott-Pietrzyk*, *Reiner Schulze*, *Matthias Storme*, *Maciej Szpunar*, *Fryderyk Zoll*; 'E-Commerce': *Stefan Leible*, *Jerzy Pisulinski*, *Fryderyk Zoll*; 'Non-discrimination': *Stefan Leible*, *Susana Navas Navarro*, *Jerzy Pisulinski*, *Fryderyk Zoll*; 'Specific Performance': *Lars Gorton*, *Geraint Howells*. Numerous further colleagues supported the Plenary and the Drafting Teams or contributed to the Comments, among them Dr. *Christoph Busch*, Dr. *Martin Ebers*, Dr. *Krzysztof Korus*, Professor *Matthias Lehmann* and Dr. *Filip Wejman*.

The former Commission on European Contract Law

The members of the three consecutive commissions of the Commission on European Contract Law which met under the chairmanship of Professor *Ole Lando* (Copenhagen) from 1982 to 1999 were: Professor *Christian von Bar* (Osnabrück), Professor *Hugh Beale* (Warwick); Professor *Alberto Berchovitz* (Madrid), Professor *Brigitte Berlioz-Houin* (Paris), Professor *Massimo Bianca* (Rome), Professor *Michael Joachim Bonell* (Rome), Professor *Michael Bridge* (London), Professor *Carlo Castronovo* (Milan), Professor *Eric Clive* (Edinburgh), Professor *Isabel de Magalhães Collaço*† (Lisbon), Professor *Ulrich Drobnig* (Hamburg), Bâtonnier Dr. *André Elvinger* (Luxembourg), Maître *Marc Elvinger* (Luxembourg), Professor *Dimitri Evrigenis*† (Thessaloniki), Professor *Carlos Ferreira de Almeida* (Lisbon), Professor Sir *Roy M. Goode* (Oxford), Professor *Arthur Hartkamp* (The Hague), Professor *Ewoud Hondius* (Utrecht), Professor *Guy Hors-*

mans (Louvain la Neuve), Professor *Roger Houin†* (Paris), Professor *Konstantinos Kerameus* (Athens), Professor *Bryan MacMahon* (Cork), Professor *Hector MacQueen* (Edinburgh), Professor *Willibald Posch* (Graz), Professor *André Prum* (Nancy), Professor *Jan Ramberg* (Stockholm), Professor *Georges Rouhette* (Clermont-Ferrand), Professor *Pablo Salvador Coderch* (Barcelona), Professor *Fernando Marti-nez Sanz* (Castellon), Professor *Matthias E. Storme* (Leuven), Professor *Denis Tallon* (Paris), Dr. *Frans J. A. van der Velden* (Utrecht), Dr. *J. A. Wade* (The Hague), Professor *William A. Wilson†* (Edinburgh), Professor *Thomas Wilhelmsson* (Helsinki), Professor *Claude Witz* (Saarbrücken), Professor *Reinhard Zimmermann* (Regensburg).

The Compilation and Redaction Team

To co-ordinate between the Study and Acquis Groups, to integrate the PECL material revised for the purposes of the DCFR, and for revision and assimilation of the drafts from the sub-projects we established a "Compilation and Redaction Team" (CRT) at the beginning of 2006. The CRT members were Professors *Christian von Bar* (Osnabrück), *Hugh Beale* (Warwick), *Eric Clive* (Edinburgh), *Johnny Herre* (Stockholm), *Jérôme Huet* (Paris), *Peter Schlechtriem†* (Freiburg i. Br.), *Hans Schulte-Nölke* (Osnabrück), *Matthias Storme* (Leuven), *Stephen Swann* (Osnabrück), *Paul Varul* (Tartu), *Anna Veneziano* (Teramo) and *Fryderyk Zoll* (Cracow); it was chaired by *Eric Clive* and *Christian von Bar*. Professor *Clive* carried the main drafting and editorial burden at the later (CRT) stages; he is also the main drafter of the list of terminology in the Annex of the DCFR. Professor *Gerhard Danne-mann* (Berlin), Chair of the Acquis Group's redaction committee, attended several of the later meetings of the CRT by invitation and made important drafting contributions.

Professor Clive was assisted by *Ashley Theunissen* (Edinburgh), Professor von Bar by *Daniel Smith* (Osnabrück). Over the course of several years *Johan Sandstedt* (Bergen) and *Daniel Smith* (Osnabrück) took care of the Master copy of the DCFR.

Funding

The DCFR is the result of years of work by many pan-European teams of jurists. They have been financed from diverse sources which cannot all be named here.[1] Before we came together with other teams in May 2005 to form the 'CoPECL Network of Excellence'[2] under the European Commission's sixth framework programme for research, from which funds our research has since been supported, the members of the Study Group on a European Civil Code had the benefit of funding from national research councils. Among others the *Deutsche Forschungsgemeinschaft (DFG)* provided over several years the lion's share of the financing including the salaries of the Working Teams based in Germany and the direct travel costs for the meetings of the Co-ordinating Group and the numerous Advisory Councils. The work of the Dutch Working Teams was financed by the *Nederlandse Organisatie voor Wetenschappelijk Onderzoek (NWO)*. Further personnel costs were met by the Flemish *Fonds voor Wetenschappelijk Onderzoek-Vlaanderen (FWO)*, the Greek *Onassis-Foundation*, the Austrian *Fonds zur Förderung der wissenschaftlichen Forschung*, the Portuguese *Fundação Calouste Gulbenkian* and the *Norges forskningsråd* (the Research Council of Norway). The Acquis Group received substantial support from its preceding Training and Mobility Networks on 'Common Principles of European Private Law' (1997-2002) under the fourth EU Research Framework Programme[3] and

---

1   A complete survey of the donors of the Study Group on a European Civil Code will be found in the opening pages of the most recent volume of the Study Group's "Principles of European Law (PEL)" series (as to which see para. 54 of the introduction). The donors of the Commission on European Contract Law are mentioned in the preface of both volumes of the Principles of European Contract Law.

2   Joint Network on European Private Law (CoPECL: Common Principles of European Contract Law), Network of Excellence under the 6th EU Framework Programme for Research and Technological Development, Priority 7 – FP6-2002-CITIZENS-3, Contract N° 513351 (co-ordinator: Professor *Hans Schulte-Nölke*, Osnabrück).

3   TMR (Training and Mobility) Network 'Common Principles of European Private Law' of the Universities of Barcelona, Berlin (Humboldt), Lyon

on 'Uniform Terminology for European Private Law' (2002-2006) under the fifth Research Framework Programme.[4] We are extremely indebted to all who in this way have made our work possible.

III, Münster (co-ordinator of the Network: Professor *Reiner Schulze*), Nijmegen, Oxford and Turin, funded under the 4th EU Research Framework Programme 1997-2002.

[4] TMR (Training and Mobility) Network 'Uniform Terminology for European Private Law' of the Universities of Barcelona, Lyon III, Münster, Nijmegen, Oxford, Turin (co-ordinator of the Network: Professor *Gianmaria Ajani*), Warsaw, funded under the 5th EU Research Framework Programme 2002-2006.

Principles

The underlying principles of freedom, security, justice and efficiency

1. **The four principles.** The four principles of freedom, security, justice and efficiency underlie the whole of the DCFR. Each has several aspects. Freedom is, for obvious reasons, comparatively more important in relation to contracts and unilateral undertakings and the obligations arising from them, but is not absent elsewhere. Security, justice and efficiency are equally important in all areas. The fact that four principles are identified does not mean that all have equal value. Efficiency is more mundane and less fundamental than the others. It is not at the same level but it is nonetheless important and has to be included. Law is a practical science. The idea of efficiency underlies a number of the model rules and they cannot be fully explained without reference to it.

At one level, freedom, security, and justice are ends in themselves. People have fought and died for them. Efficiency is less dramatic. In the context of private law, however, these values are best regarded not as ends in themselves but as means to other ends – the promotion of welfare, the empowering of people to pursue their legitimate aims and fulfil their potential.

In preparing the first part of this account of the role played by these underlying principles in the DCFR, we have drawn heavily on the *Principes directeurs du droit européen du contrat*[1] and we refer the reader to the analytical and comparative work done in their elaboration. However, we have had to take a slightly different approach for the purposes of the DCFR, which is not confined to traditional contract law.

It is characteristic of principles such as those discussed here that they conflict with each other. For example, on occasion, justice in a particular case may have to make way for legal security or efficiency, as happens under the rules of prescription. Sometimes, on the other hand, rules designed to promote security have to be balanced by considerations of justice, as happens under the rules in Books V and

---

[1]   See Introduction p. 5, note 4.

VI which allow for a reduction of liability on equitable grounds. Freedom, in particular freedom of contract, may be limited for the sake of an aspect of justice – for instance, to prevent some forms of discrimination or to prevent the abuse of a dominant position. Principles can even conflict with themselves, depending on the standpoint from which a situation is viewed: freedom from discrimination restricts another's freedom to discriminate. One aspect of justice (e. g. equality of treatment) may conflict with another (e. g. protection of the weak). Therefore the principles can never be applied in a pure and rigid way.

The principles also overlap. As will be seen below, there are many examples of rules which can be explained on the basis of more than one principle. In particular, many of the rules which are designed to ensure genuine freedom of contract can also be explained in terms of contractual justice.

Freedom

2. General remarks. There are several aspects to freedom as an underlying principle in private law. Freedom can be protected by not laying down mandatory rules or other controls and by not imposing unnecessary restrictions of a formal or procedural nature on peoples' legal transactions. It can be promoted by enhancing the capabilities of people to do things. Both aspects are present throughout the DCFR. The first is illustrated by the general approach to party autonomy, particularly but not exclusively in the rules on contracts and contractual obligations. The assumption is that party autonomy should be respected unless there is a good reason to intervene. Often, of course, there is a good reason to intervene – for example, in order to ensure that a party can escape from a contract concluded in the absence of genuine freedom to contract. The assumption is also that formal and procedural hurdles should be kept to a minimum. The second aspect – enhancing capabilities – is also present throughout the DCFR. People are provided with default rules (including default rules for a wide variety of specific contracts) which make it easier and less costly for them to enter into well-regulated legal relationships.

They are provided with efficient and flexible ways of transferring rights and goods, of securing rights to the performance of obligations and of managing their property. The promotion of freedom overlaps with the promotion of efficiency and some of these examples are discussed more fully below under that heading.

Contractual freedom

3. Freedom of contract the starting point. As a rule, natural and legal persons should be free to decide whether or not to contract and with whom to contract. They should also be free to agree on the terms of their contract. This basic idea is recognised in the DCFR.[2] It is also expressed in the first article of the *Principes directeurs*.[3] In both cases the freedom is subject to any applicable mandatory rules. Parties should also be free to agree at any time to modify the terms of their contract or to put an end to their relationship. These ideas are also expressed in the DCFR[4] and in the *Principes directeurs*.[5] In normal situations there is no incompatibility between contractual freedom

---

[2]   II.–1:102(1). "Parties are free to make a contract or other juridical act and to determine its contents, subject to any applicable mandatory rules." It follows from the general rules on the formation of contracts that the parties can agree not to be contractually bound unless the contract is in a particular form. See II.–4:101. Also in the Book on Proprietary Security the principle of party autonomy is fully recognised in the freedom of the parties to regulate their mutual relationship at the predefault stage, IX.–5:101.

[3]   Art. 0:101 of the *Principes directeurs*: "Each party is free to contract and to choose who will be the other party. The parties are free to determine the content of the contract and the rules of form which apply to it. Freedom of contract operates subject to compliance with mandatory rules".

[4]   II.–1:103 (3). See also III.–1:108(1) "A right, obligation or contractual relationship may be varied or terminated by agreement at any time."

[5]   Art. 0:103. The second paragraph of this Article adds that unilateral revocation is effective only in the case of contracts of indeterminate duration. The same idea is expressed in the DCFR in II.–1:103(1) read with III.–1:109(2) but there are some special rules for contracts for services (including mandate contracts).

and justice. Indeed it has been claimed that, in some situations, freedom of contract, without more, leads to justice. If, for instance, the parties to a contract are fully informed and in an equal bargaining position when concluding it, the content of their agreement can be presumed to be in their interest and to be just as between themselves. "*Qui dit contractuel, dit juste.*"[6] In normal situations there is also no incompatibility between contractual freedom and efficiency. In general terms it can be assumed that agreements made by parties who are both fully informed and of equal bargaining power will be profit-maximising in the sense of bringing gains to each party (the exact division of the gain is a distributive question of little concern to economic analysis.) The only caveat is that the agreement should not impose costs on third parties (externalities). This is why in most systems certain contracts which are likely to have detrimental effects on third persons are rendered void as a matter of public policy.

4. Limitations with regard to third parties. There is one principle in the section on contractual freedom in the *Principes directeurs* which is not expressly stated in the DCFR. It provides that "Parties can contract only for themselves, unless otherwise provided. A contract can produce an effect only in so far as it does not result in an infringement or unlawful modification of third party rights".[7] The DCFR does not contain explicit provisions at such a general level on the relation of contracts to third parties. It takes it as self-evident that parties can contract only for themselves, unless otherwise provided, and that contracts, as a rule, regulate only the rights and obligations between the parties who conclude them. The DCFR merely spells out the exceptions, principally the rules on representation[8] and the rules on stipulations in favour of a third party.[9] So far as the attempted inva-

---

[6] Alfred Fouillée, La science sociale contemporaine. Paris (Hachette) 1880, p. 410.

[7] Art. 0-102 (Respect for the freedom and rights of third parties).

[8] Book II, Chapter 6. Under these rules one party (the representative) can contract for another (the principal).

[9] See II. – 9:301 to II. – 9:303. The rules in Book III, Chapter 5 on change of parties (assignment and substitution of new debtor) and the rule in III. – 5:401 on indirect representation (under which, when the representative

sion of third party rights is concerned the DCFR takes the view that this will often be simply impossible to achieve by a contract, because of the content of other rules. The parties to a contract could not, for example, effectively deprive another person of his or her property by simply contracting to this effect. There is no need for a special rule to achieve that result. In so far as such invasions or infringements are possible they are dealt with partly by the rules on illegal contracts[10] and partly by the rules in Book VI on non-contractual liability for damage caused to another. An example of the latter is the inducement of a contract party to breach the contract. The DCFR qualifies such conduct as a ground for non-contractual liability under Book VI.[11] A rather different case is when the purpose of a contract is to disadvantage creditors, usually by putting property beyond their reach. Classical systems based on Roman law tried to respond to such contracts by the so called *actio pauliana*, which gave the affected creditor an action against the contract party holding the property in question. The DCFR does not contain explicit provisions on this issue. The reason is that – although an *actio pauliana* can be brought before the opening of insolvency proceedings – the issue is closely linked to insolvency law, with which the DCFR does not deal. But it would be possible to deal with fraudulent conveyances which aim at the disadvantage of creditors under the rules of Book VI.[12]

5. Contracts harmful to third persons and society in general. A ground on which a contract may be invalidated, even though it was freely agreed between two equal parties, is that it (or more often the performance of the obligation under it) would have a seriously harmful effect on third persons or society. Thus contracts which are illegal or contrary to public policy in this sense are invalid. (Within the

---

has become insolvent, the principal and the third party may acquire rights against each other) can also be seen as exceptions to the rule that a contract can produce effects only for the contracting parties.

[10] II. – 7:301 to II. – 7:304. A contract to injure, or steal from, another person would, for example, be void. This topic is further explored in the following paragraph.

[11] VI. – 2:211.

[12] Cf. in particular VI. – 2:101 paragraph (3).

framework of the EU a common example is contracts which infringe the competition articles of the Treaty.) The DCFR does not spell out when a contract is contrary to public policy in this sense, because that is a matter for law outside the scope of the DCFR – the law of competition or the criminal law of the Member State where the relevant performance takes place. However the fact that a contract might harm particular third persons or society at large is clearly a ground on which the legislator should consider invalidating it.

6. Interventions when consent defective. Even classical contract law recognises that it may not be just to enforce a contract if one party to it was in a weaker position, typically because when giving consent the party was not free or was misinformed. For example, a contract concluded as the result of mistake or fraud, or which was the result of duress or unfair exploitation, can be set aside by the aggrieved party. These grounds for invalidity are often explained in terms of justice but equally it can be said that they are designed to ensure that contractual freedom was genuine freedom; and in the DCFR, as in the laws of the Member States, they are grounds for the invalidity of a contract. Moreover, at least where the contract has been made only as the result of deliberate conduct by one party that infringed the other party's freedom or misled the other party, the right to set it aside should be inalienable, i.e. mandatory. The remedies given by the DCFR in cases of fraud and duress cannot be excluded or restricted.[13] In contrast, remedies provided in cases of mistake and similar cases which do not involve deliberate wrongdoing may be excluded or restricted.[14]

7. Restrictions on freedom to choose contracting party. While in general persons should remain free to contract or to refuse to contract with anyone else, this freedom may need to be qualified where it might result in unacceptable discrimination, for example discrimination on the grounds of gender, race or ethnic origin. Discrimination

---

[13] II. – 7:215 paragraph (1).

[14] II. – 7:215 paragraph (2). However, any attempt to exclude or restrict remedies for mistake will itself be subject to the controls over unfair terms that have not been negotiated. See II. – 9:401 et seq.

on those grounds is a particularly anti-social form of denying the contractual freedom, and indeed the human dignity, of the other party. EU law and the DCFR therefore prohibit these forms of discrimination and provide appropriate remedies.[15] The DCFR is drafted in such a way that it easily allows the addition of further grounds for discrimination, as they exist – for general contract law – in some Member States and as they may be enacted in EC law in the future.

8. Restrictions on freedom to withhold information at pre-contractual stage. Similarly, restrictions on the parties' freedom to contract as they choose may be justified even outside the classic cases of procedural unfairness such as mistake, fraud, duress and the exploitation of a party's circumstances to obtain an excessive advantage. A particular concern is to ensure that parties were fully informed. The classical grounds for invalidity because of mistake, which are reflected in the provisions of the DCFR mentioned above, were quite limited: for example, in many laws the mistake had to be as to the substance of the thing sold. This notion was developed when the goods or services which were to be supplied were usually very much simpler than they are today. In today's conditions parties often need much more information before it can be said that they were fully informed. Thus the law needs to deal not only with cases of inequality of information about the basic characteristics of the goods or services to be supplied but also as to other relevant circumstances. It may also need to go beyond the general contract law of some Member States and impose positive duties to give information to the uninformed party. In the DCFR, the classical defence of mistake has been supplemented by duties to give the other party the information which is essential to enable that party to make a properly informed decision. These rules apply particularly to consumer contracts, but the problem may arise also in contracts between businesses. Normally a business can be expected to make full enquiries before concluding a contract, but if good commercial practice dictates that certain information be provided by one of the parties, the other party is likely to assume that it has been provided. If in fact full information has not been provided,

---

[15]   See, for the DCFR, II. – 2:101 to II. – 2:105 and III. – 1:105.

and as a result the party concludes a contract which would not have been concluded, or would have been concluded only on fundamentally different terms, the party has a remedy.

9. Information as to the terms of the contract. Modern law must also deal with lack of information as to the terms of the contract. The classical defences were developed at a time when most contracts were of a simple kind that the parties could understand readily. This too has changed, particularly with the development of longer-term (and therefore more complex) contracts and the use of standard terms. Standard terms are very useful but there is the risk that the parties may not be aware of their contents or may not fully understand them. Existing EC law addresses this problem and gives protection to consumers when the term in question is in a consumer contract and was not individually negotiated.[16] However, as the laws of many Member States recognise, the problem may occur also in contracts between businesses. Particularly when one party is a small business that lacks expertise or where the relevant term is contained in a standard form contract document prepared by the party seeking to rely on the term, the other party may not be aware of the existence or extent of the term. The DCFR contains controls which deal with similar problems in contracts between businesses, though the controls are of a more restricted kind than for consumer contracts.

10. Correcting inequality of bargaining power. The classical grounds for avoidance deal with some simple cases of lack of bargaining power, for example when one party takes advantage of the other party's urgent needs and lack of choice to extort an unfairly high price for goods or services.[17] But modern conditions, and particularly the use of standard contract terms, lead to new forms of inequality that need to be addressed. A party who is offered a standard form contract and who knows what it contains and understands its meaning, and is unhappy with the terms offered, may find that it is impossible to get the other party, or any other possible contracting

---

[16] Directive on Unfair Terms in Consumer Contracts, 1993/13/EEC.

[17] See the illustrations to II. – 7:207.

party, to offer better terms: the party may be told to "take it or leave it." Such problems are most common when a consumer is dealing with a business, but can also occur in contracts between businesses, particularly when one party is a small business that lacks bargaining power. The provisions on unfair terms are thus also based on notions of preserving freedom of contract, but – just as in the existing EC law – in a more extended sense than in classical law. The laws of some Member States apply these provisions to contracts of all types, not just to contracts between businesses and consumers. Again the DCFR takes a balanced view, suggesting a cautious extension beyond the existing *acquis*.

11. **Minimum intervention.** Even when some intervention can be justified on one of the grounds just mentioned, thought must be given to the form of intervention. Is the problem one that can be solved adequately by requiring one party to provide the other with information before the contract is made, with perhaps a right in the other party to withdraw from the contract if the information was not given? In general terms we are concerned, as explained above, to ensure that when parties conclude contracts they should be adequately informed. This suggests that if they were provided with the relevant information, they should be bound by the contract to which they agreed. But in some cases problems will persist even if consumers (for example) are 'informed', possibly because they will not be able to make effective use of the information. In such a case a mandatory rule giving the consumer certain minimum rights (for example, to withdraw from a timeshare contract, as such contracts are typically concluded without sufficient reflection) may be justified. In general terms, the interference with freedom of contract should be the minimum that will solve the problem while providing the other party (e. g. the business seller) with sufficient guidance to be able to arrange its affairs efficiently. Similarly with contract terms: it must be asked whether it is necessary to make a particular term mandatory or whether a flexible test such as 'fairness' would suffice to protect the weaker party. A fairness test may allow certain terms to be used providing these are clearly brought home to the consumer or other party before the contract is made. The fairness test thus interferes less with the parties' freedom of contract than making a particular

term mandatory would do. Usually it will be sufficient that a term is
not binding on the aggrieved party if in the particular circumstances
it is unfair. This leaves parties who are fully informed and dealing at
arms' length free (when the term will normally be fair: see above) to
arrange their affairs as they wish. However, sometimes it may be
easier to have a simple rule rather than a standard that varies according to the circumstances of each case.

Non-contractual obligations

12. Emphasis on obligations rather than freedom. The purpose of the
law on benevolent intervention in another's affairs, on non-contractual liability for damage caused to another and on unjustified enrichment is not to promote freedom but rather to limit it by imposing
obligations. Here we see the principle of freedom being counteracted
by the competing principles of security and justice.

13. Freedom respected so far as consistent with policy objectives.
Nonetheless the underlying principle of freedom is recognised in
that the model rules impose these non-contractual obligations only
where that is clearly justified. So, a benevolent intervener has rights
as such only if there was a reasonable ground for acting; and there
will be no such ground if the intervener had a reasonable opportunity
to discover the principal's wishes but failed to do so or if the intervener knew or could be expected to know that the intervention was
against the principal's wishes.[18] To the maximum extent possible the
principal's freedom of action and control is respected. In the rules on
non-contractual liability for damage caused to another, the imposition of an obligation of reparation is carefully limited to cases where
it is justified. It is this concern which explains why this Book does
not simply adopt some sweeping statement to the effect that people
are liable for damage they cause. Respect for freedom (not to mention security and justice viewed from the point of view of the person
causing the damage) requires careful and detailed formulation of
rules imposing liability. Again, in the law on unjustified enrichment

---

[18] V. – 1:101(2).

the underlying principle is that people are free to hold what they have. An obligation to redress an enrichment is imposed only in carefully regulated circumstances. In particular, rules ensure that one person cannot force another to pay for an enrichment resulting from a disadvantage to which the first person has consented freely and without error.[19] That would be an unwarranted infringement of freedom. Rules also ensure that those who are enriched by receiving a non-transferable benefit without their consent (such as receiving an unwanted service) are not compelled to reverse that enrichment by paying for its value, since this would in substance require the recipient of an enrichment to perform a bargain not voluntarily concluded. If they are liable at all, their liability is therefore not allowed to exceed any sum which they would have spent in any case in order to enjoy the benefit which they have unwittingly or unwillingly received.[20]

Property

14. **Limited scope for party autonomy.** The principle of party autonomy has to be considerably modified in property law. Because proprietary rights affect third parties generally, the parties to a transaction are not free to create their own basic rules as they wish. They cannot, for example, define for themselves basic concepts like "possession". Nor are they free to modify the basic rules on how ownership can be acquired, transferred or lost. Under the DCFR they cannot even agree to an effective contractual prohibition on alienation.[21] The free alienability of goods is important not only to the persons concerned but also to society at large. One type of freedom is restricted in order to promote another – and efficiency.

15. **Recognition and enhancement of freedom in some respects.** Within the essential limits just noted, the principle of party autonomy is reflected in Book VIII. It can be seen in the rule that the parties to a

---

[19] VII. – 2:101(1)(b).

[20] VII. – 5:102(2).

[21] VIII. – 1:301.

transfer of goods can generally determine by agreement the point in time when ownership passes,[22] and in the rule that the consequences of the production of new goods out of another's goods or of the combination or commingling of goods belonging to different persons can be regulated by party agreement.[23] The rules on proprietary security in Book IX can be seen as enhancing freedom (and efficiency) by opening up wide possibilities for the provision of non-possessory security, something which has not traditionally been possible in many legal systems. Similarly, the rules on trusts in Book X could enhance freedom by opening up possibilities for setting property aside for particular purposes (commercial, familial or charitable) in a flexible way which has been much used and much valued in some systems for a very long time and is gradually spreading to others.

Security

16. General remarks. The importance of the principle of security in private law can be understood by considering some of the ways in which the security of natural and legal persons in the normal conducting of their lives and affairs can be threatened. The most obvious way is by unlawful invasions of their rights and interests or indeed by any unwanted disturbance of the status quo. Security, particularly in forward planning, is also threatened by uncertainty of outcomes. This can be caused by inaccessible or confusing or badly drafted laws. It can also be caused by the unpredictability of others. Will they perform their obligations? Will they do so properly? Will they give good value or attempt to cut corners and get away with the minimum possible? Will they be uncooperative and difficult to work with? Will they be able to pay? Are there effective remedies if things go wrong?

---

[22] VIII. – 2:103.
[23] VIII. – 5:101(1).

Contractual security

17. **The main ingredients.** The *Principes directeurs* identify as the main ingredients in contractual security:

(1) the obligatory force of contracts (but subject to the possibility of challenge where an unforeseeable change of circumstances gravely prejudices the utility of the contract for one of the parties);

(2) the fact that each party has duties flowing from contractual loyalty (i. e. to behave in accordance with the requirements of good faith; to co-operate when that is necessary for performance of the obligations; not to act inconsistently with prior declarations or conduct on which the other party has relied);

(3) the right to enforce performance of the contractual obligations in accordance with the terms of the contract;

(4) the fact that third parties must respect the situation created by the contract and may rely on that situation; and

(5) the approach of "favouring the contract" (*faveur pour le contrat*) (whereby, in questions relating to interpretation, invalidity or performance, an approach which gives effect to the contract is preferred to one which does not, if the latter is harmful to the legitimate interests of one of the parties).[24]

Almost all of these ingredients of contractual security are clearly recognised and expressed in the DCFR. A most important further ingredient of contractual security is the availability of adequate remedies (in addition to enforcement of performance) for non-performance of the contractual obligations. This too is addressed by the DCFR and will be considered below immediately after the topic of enforcement of performance at no. 27. Another ingredient of contractual security is the protection of reasonable reliance and expectations in situations not covered by the doctrine of contractual loyalty.

---

[24] See arts. 0:201 to 0:204.

18. Third party respect and reliance. The only aspect of contractual security which is mentioned in the *Principes directeurs* but which does not appear explicitly in the DCFR is the fourth one – that third parties must respect the situation created by the contract and may rely on that situation. It was not thought necessary to provide for this as it is not precluded by any rule in the DCFR and, if understood in a reasonable way, seems to follow sufficiently from other rules and essential assumptions. One case of practical importance is where a person not being a party to a contract or an intended beneficiary of it nonetheless relies on the proper performance of a contractual obligation (e.g. a tenant's visitor claims damages from the landlord as the tenant could do under the contract, because the visitor falls down the stairs as a result of a broken handrail the landlord was obliged to repair under the contract). In the DCFR such cases fall under the rules on non-contractual liability of Book VI.

19. Protection of reasonable reliance and expectations. This is an aspect of security which appears in different parts of the DCFR. It first appears in relation to contract formation. It may happen that one party does not intend to undertake an obligation when that party's actions suggest to the other party that an obligation is being undertaken. A typical case is where an apparent offer is made by mistake. If the other party reasonably believed that the first party was undertaking the obligation as apparently stated, the other party's reliance will be protected in most legal systems. This may be achieved either by using the law on non-contractual liability for damage caused to another or, more simply, by holding the mistaken party to the outward appearance of what was said. The protection of reasonable reliance and expectations is a core aim of the DCFR, just as it was in PECL. Usually this protection is achieved by holding the mistaken party to the obligation which the other party reasonably assumed was being undertaken. Examples are the objective rules on interpretation[25], the restriction of avoidance for mistake to cases in which the non-mistaken party contributed to the mistake, should have known of it or shared it[26] and the rule that imposes on a busi-

---

[25] See II. – 8:101.

[26] See II. – 7:201.

ness which has failed to comply with a pre-contractual information duty such obligations under a contract as the other party has reasonably expected as the consequence of the absence or incorrectness of the information.[27]

20. The principle of binding force. If the parties have concluded a contract freely and with adequate information, then the contract should normally be treated as binding on them unless they (again freely) agree to modification or termination or, where the contract is for an indefinite period, one has given the other notice of a wish to end the relationship.[28] These rules are set out clearly in the DCFR.[29] It also sets out rules on the termination of a contractual relationship in more detail. Examples are – besides the rules on termination for non-performance – the right to terminate by notice where that is provided for by the contract terms and the right to terminate where the contract is for an indefinite duration. In the latter case the party wishing to terminate must give a reasonable period of notice.[30] The principle of binding force (often expressed still by the Latin tag, *pacta sunt servanda*) was qualified classically only when without the fault of either party performance of the contractual obligations became impossible for reasons that could not have been foreseen. A more modern development is the right of withdrawal granted to consumers in certain situations. The reasons for this exception vary, but can be seen in the specific situations where such withdrawal rights exist. One example is the right to withdraw from contracts negotiated away from business premises (e. g. at the doorstep or at a distance).[31]

---

[27] See II. – 3:107(3).

[28] The *Principes directeurs* state in art. 0-201 (Principle of binding force) paragraph (1): "A contract which is lawfully concluded has binding force between the parties". Art. 0-103 (Freedom of the parties to modify or terminate the contract) provides that: "By their mutual agreement, the parties are free, at any moment, to terminate the contract or to modify it. Unilateral revocation is only effective in respect of contracts for an indefinite period."

[29] II. – 1:103 read with III. – 1:108 and III. – 1:109.

[30] See III. – 1:109.

[31] See II. – 5:201.

In such situations the consumer may have been taken by surprise or have been less attentive than he or she would have been in a shop. A further example is provided by some complex contracts (e. g. time-share contracts)[32], where consumers may need an additional period for reflection. The right to withdraw gives the consumer who concluded a contract in such situations a 'cooling off period' for acquiring additional information and for further consideration whether he or she wants to continue with the contract. For reasons of simplicity and legal certainty, withdrawal rights are granted to consumers, irrespective of whether they individually need protection, as a considerable number of consumers are considered to be typically in need of protection in such situations.

21. Exceptional change of circumstances. Many modern laws have recognised that in extreme circumstances it may be unjust to enforce the performance of contractual obligations that can literally still be performed according to the original contract terms if the circumstances in which the obligations were assumed were completely different to those in which they fall to be enforced. As noted above, this qualification is stated in general terms in the *Principes directeurs*.[33] It is also recognised in the DCFR but the parties remain free, if they wish, to exclude any possibility of adjustment without the consent of all the parties.[34]

22. Certainty or flexibility. A more general question is whether contractual security is better promoted by rigid rules or by rules which, by using open terms like "reasonable" or by other means, leave room for flexibility. The answer probably turns on the nature of the contract. In contracts for the purchase of certain commodities or types of incorporeal assets where prices fluctuate rapidly and where one deal is likely to be followed rapidly by another which relies on the first

---

[32] See II. – 5:202.

[33] Art. 0-201(3): "In the course of performance, the binding force of the contract can be called into question if an unforeseeable change in circumstances seriously compromises the usefulness of the contract for one of the parties."

[34] II. – 1:102. See also III. – 1:110(3)(c).

and so on within a short space of time, certainty is all important. Nobody wants a link in a chain of transactions to be broken by an appeal to some vague criterion. Certainty means security. However, in long term contracts for the provision of services of various kinds (including construction services), where the contractual relationship may last for years and where the background situation may change dramatically in the course of it, the reverse is true. Here true security comes from the knowledge that there are fair mechanisms in place to deal with changes in circumstances. It is for this reason that the default rules in the part of the DCFR on service contracts have special provisions on the giving of warnings of impending changes known to one party, on co-operation, on directions by the client and on variation of the contract.[35] The general rules on contractual and other obligations in Book III have to cater for all types of contract. So their provisions on changes of circumstances are much more restricted. However, even in the general rules it is arguable that it does more good than harm to build in a considerable measure of flexibility because open criteria will either be disapplied by highly specific standard terms devised for fields of commercial activity where certainty is particularly important or will disapply themselves automatically in cases where they are inappropriate. The effects of terms such as "reasonable" and "fair dealing" depend entirely on the circumstances. Rigid rules (e. g. "within 5 days" instead of "within a reasonable time") would be liable to increase insecurity by applying in circumstances where they were totally unexpected and unsuitable.

23. Good faith and fair dealing. As the *Principes directeurs* recognise, one party's contractual security is enhanced by the other's duty to act in accordance with the requirements of good faith. However, the converse of that is that there may be some uncertainty and insecurity for the person who is required to act in accordance with good faith and fair dealing, which are rather open-ended concepts. Moreover, the role of good faith and fair dealing in the DCFR goes beyond the provision of contractual security. These concepts are therefore discussed later under the heading of justice.

---

[35] See e. g. IV. C. – 2:102, IV. C. – 2:103, IV. C. – 2:107, IV. C. – 2:108, IV. C. – 2:109, IV. C. – 2:110.

24. Co-operation. Contractual security is also enhanced by the imposition of an obligation to co-operate. The *Principes directeurs* put it this way: "The parties are bound to cooperate with each other when this is necessary for the performance of their contract".[36] The DCFR provision goes a little further than the case where co-operation is *necessary*: the debtor and the creditor are obliged to co-operate with each other when and to the extent that this *can reasonably be expected* for the performance of the debtor's obligation.[37]

25. Inconsistent behaviour. A particular aspect of the protection of reasonable reliance and expectations is to prevent a party, on whose conduct another party has reasonably acted in reliance, from adopting an inconsistent position and thereby frustrating the reliance of the other party. This principle is often expressed in the Latin formula *venire contra factum proprium*. The *Principes directeurs* express it as follows: "No party shall act inconsistently with any prior statements made by the party or behaviour on the part of the party, upon which the other party may legitimately have relied."[38] The Interim Outline Edition of the DCFR did not contain an express rule of this nature; it was thought that it could be arrived at by applying the general principles of good faith and fair dealing. Inspired by the *Principes directeurs*, the DCFR now incorporates an express provision which qualifies inconsistent behaviour as being contrary to good faith and fair dealing.[39]

26. Enforcement of performance. If one party fails to perform contractual obligations, the other should have an effective remedy. One of the main remedies under the DCFR is the right to enforce actual performance, whether the obligation which has not been performed is to pay money or is non-monetary, e. g. to do or to transfer something else. This basic idea is also expressed in the *Principes directeurs*.[40] The DCFR slightly modifies and supplements this principle

---

[36] Art. 0-303 (Duty to cooperate)

[37] III. – 1:104.

[38] Art. 0-304 (Duty of consistency).

[39] See I. – 1:103 paragraph (2).

[40] Art. 0-202: "Each party can demand from the other party the performance of the other party's obligation as provided in the contract".

by some exceptions as the right to enforce performance should not apply in various cases in which literal performance is impossible or would be inappropriate.[41] However, in a change from the PECL,[42] under the DCFR the right to enforce performance is less of a "secondary" remedy, reflecting the underlying principle that obligations should be performed unless there are good reasons to the contrary.

27. Other remedies. In addition to the right to enforcement, the DCFR contains a full set of other remedies to protect the creditor in a contractual obligation: withholding of performance, termination, reduction of price and damages. The creditor faced with a non-performance which is not excused may normally exercise any of these remedies, and may use more than one remedy provided that the remedies sought are not incompatible.[43] If the non-performance is excused because of impossibility, the creditor may not enforce the obligation or claim damages, but the other remedies are available.[44] The remedy of termination provided in the DCFR is a powerful remedy which adds to the contractual security of the creditor faced with a fundamental non-performance by the debtor. The creditor knows that if the expected counter-performance is not forthcoming it is possible to escape from the relationship and obtain what is wanted elsewhere. However the powerful nature of the remedy is also a threat to the debtor's contractual security and, potentially at least, contrary to the idea of maintaining contractual relationships whenever possible. Termination will often leave the debtor with a loss (for example, wasted costs incurred in preparing to perform; or loss caused by a change in the market). The creditor should not be entitled to use some minor non-performance, or a non-performance that can readily be put right, by the debtor as a justification for termination. The rules governing termination therefore restrict termination to cases in which the creditor's interests will be seriously affected by the non-performance, while leaving the parties free to agree on termination in other circumstances.

---

[41] See III. – 3:301 and 3:302

[42] Compare PECL art 9:102, esp. (2)(d).

[43] III. – 3:102.

[44] III. – 3:101.

28. Maintaining the contractual relationship. This aim, recognised in the *Principes directeurs* under the heading of *faveur pour le contrat*,[45] is also recognised in various provisions in the DCFR – for example those on interpretation,[46] and on the power of the court to adapt a contract which is affected by invalidity.[47] Also, the debtor's right to cure a non-conforming performance[48] can be seen as being aimed at the preservation of the contractual relationship, as this right may avoid the execution of remedies, including termination. The same aim underlies the provisions which supplement the parties' agreement when there are points which the parties appear to have overlooked. In a sense, many rules of contract law – for example, the remedies available for non-performance – are "default rules" that fill gaps in what the parties had agreed, thus helping to maintain an effective working relationship. But there are a number of rules dealing specifically with points which in some systems of law have led the courts to hold that there can be no obligation, even though it seems clear that the parties, despite the incompleteness of their agreement, wished to be bound. These include provisions on determination of the price and other terms.[49] Further, the DCFR provides a more general mechanism to supplement the agreement in order to make it workable when it is necessary to provide for a matter which the parties have not foreseen or provided for, thus "favouring the contract" and increasing contractual security.[50]

29. Other rules promoting security. The rules on personal security in Book IV.G obviously promote contractual security by giving the

---

[45] Art. 0:204. "When the contract is subject to interpretation, or when its validity or performance is threatened, the effectiveness of the contract should be preferred if its destruction would harm the legitimate interests of one of the parties".

[46] See II. – 8:106. "An interpretation which renders the terms of the contract lawful, or effective, is to be preferred to one which would not."

[47] See II. – 7:203.

[48] III. – 3:202 to III. – 3:204.

[49] See II. – 9:104 ff.

[50] II. – 9:101. The relevant provisions of PECL were slightly less restrictive. They were changed in the light of representations by stakeholders.

creditor an extra person from whom to seek performance if the debtor defaults. In a different way, the rules on prescription can be seen as promoting security by preventing disturbance of the status quo by the making of stale claims. This example shows that even in the area covered by the PECL the underlying principle of security is not confined to contractual security for the creditor. Security is also important for the debtor.

Non-contractual obligations

30. Security a core aim and value in the law on non-contractual obligations. The protection and promotion of security is a core aim and value in the law on non-contractual obligations. These branches of the law can be regarded as supplementing contract law. Under contract law parties typically acquire assets. The protection of assets once acquired and the protection from infringement of innate rights of personality is not something which contract law is able to provide. That is the task of the law on non-contractual liability for damage (Book VI). A person who has parted with something without a legal basis, e. g. because the contract which prompted the performance is void, must be able to recover it. That is provided for in the law on unjustified enrichment (Book VII). In cases in which one party would have wanted action to be taken, in particular where help is rendered, but due to the pressure of circumstances or in a case of emergency it is not possible to obtain that party's consent, the situation has a resemblance to contract. But the security which would normally be provided for both parties by the conclusion of a contract for necessary services has to be provided by the rules on benevolent intervention in another's affairs (Book V).

31. Protection of the status quo: non-contractual liability arising out of damage caused to another. The notion of contract would be meaningless if it were not flanked by a notion of compensation for loss involuntarily sustained. Contracts are aimed at a voluntary change in relationships. That presupposes, however, a regime for the protection of the *status quo* against involuntary changes. The law on non-contractual liability for damage caused to another is thus directed at reinstating the person suffering such damage in the position that person would have been in had the damage not occurred.[51] It does not seek to punish anybody, neither does it aspire to enrich the injured party. Nor does it aim at a social redistribution of wealth or at integrating an individual in a community founded on the principle of social solidarity. Rather it is aimed at protection.

32. Protection of the person. A particular concern of non-contractual liability law is the protection of the person. The individual stands at the focus of the legal system. A person's rights to physical wellbeing (health, physical integrity, freedom) are of fundamental importance, as are other personality rights, in particular that of dignity and with it protection against discrimination and exposure. Injuries to the person give rise to non-economic loss besides economic loss; the former also deserves compensation.

33. Protection of human rights. The non-contractual liability law of the DCFR has the function primarily (albeit not exclusively) of providing "horizontal" protection of human rights – that is to say, a protection not vis-à-vis the state, but in relation to fellow citizens and others subject to private law. This protection is provided in the first instance by the claim to reparation for loss suffered, but is not confined to that. Prevention of damage is better than making good the damage; hence Book VI confers on a person who would suffer it a right to prevent an impending damage.[52]

34. Protection of other rights and interests. Book VI contains specific provisions on various kinds of legally relevant damage (including loss upon infringement of property or lawful possession) which may give rise to liability. However, it is not confined to providing security in such listed cases. Loss or injury can, subject to certain controlling provisions, also be legally relevant damage for the purposes of Book VI if it results from a violation of a right otherwise conferred by the law or of an interest worthy of legal protection.[53]

---

[51]   VI. – 6:101(1).

[52]   VI. – 1:102.

[53]   VI. – 2:101.

35. Protection of security by the law on unjustified enrichment. The rules on unjustified enrichment respect the binding force of contracts in that a valid contract between the parties will provide a justifying basis for an enrichment conferred by one party on the other within the terms of that contract.[54] The rules on unjustified enrichment buttress the protection of rights within private law by the principle that a wrongdoer is not permitted to profit from the exploitation of another's rights. A non-innocent use of another's assets as a rule creates an obligation to pay for the value of that use,[55] so helping to remove any incentive to make improper use of another's property. Protection of reasonable reliance and expectations as a value and aim is relevant to both the elements of the claim and the grounds of defence within the rules on unjustified enrichment. A person who confers an enrichment on another in circumstances where it is reasonable to expect a counter-benefit, or the return of the benefit if events do not turn out as expected, is protected by being entitled to a reversal of the enrichment if the agreement on which reliance was placed turns out not to be valid or if the mutually anticipated outcome does not occur.[56] Equally, the interests of the recipient of a benefit are protected if the recipient relies on the apparent entitlement to the benefit received. Such protection is conferred by the defence of disenrichment, where the recipient disposes of the benefit in a bona fide assumption that there is a right to do so,[57] or by a defence, protecting faith in the market, where an acquirer has given value to a third party in good faith for the benefit received.[58]

Property

36. Security a core aim. Security is a paramount value in relation to property law and pervades the whole of Book VIII. The rules in Chapter 6 on the protection of ownership and possession provide a

---

[54] VII. – 2:101(1)(a).

[55] See in particular VII. – 4:101(c) and VII. – 5:102(1).

[56] Cf. VII. – 2:101(4).

[57] VII. – 6:101.

[58] VII. – 6:102.

particularly clear example. Indeed, in relation to the acquisition and loss of ownership in movables, certainty and predictability of outcome may sometimes be more important that the actual content of the rules. Different approaches, even fundamentally different approaches, can all lead to acceptable results. Again, however, different values have to be balanced against each other. Some methods of increasing security might, for example, inhibit easy transferability. And certainty has to be balanced against fairness, as can be seen very clearly in the rules in Book VIII on production, combination and commingling.[59] It almost goes without saying that security is also a core aim of the Book on proprietary security. The whole objective is to enable parties to provide and obtain security for the proper performance of obligations. The rules are comprehensive and cover all types of proprietary security over moveable assets, including retention of ownership devices. They aim at maximum certainty by recommending a registration system for the effectiveness of a proprietary security against third parties.[60] A large part of Book IX is concerned with the detailed regulation of this system. Its rules provide effective remedies for creditors wishing to enforce their security.[61]

37. Protection of reasonable reliance and expectations. This value is strongly reflected in Book VIII. It can be seen most obviously in the rules on good faith acquisition from a person who has no right or authority to transfer ownership[62] and in the rules on the acquisition of ownership by continuous possession.[63] In the Book on proprietary security this value is most obviously reflected in rules protecting the good faith acquisition of assets, or of security rights in assets, free from a prior security right.[64]

---

[59] VIII.–5:101 to VIII.–5:105.

[60] Chapter 3.

[61] Chapter 7.

[62] VIII. – 3:101 and VIII. – 3:102.

[63] VIII. – 4:101 to 4:302.

[64] IX. – 2:108, IX. – 2:109 and IX. – 6:102.

38. The provision of effective remedies. This is just as important as in contract law but the remedies are different. They are designed to enable ownership and possession to be protected.[65] So the owner is given a right to obtain or recover possession of the goods from any person exercising physical control over them.[66] The possessor of goods is also given protective remedies against those who interfere unlawfully with the possession.[67]

39. Protection of the status quo. This value lies behind some of the rules in Book VIII designed to protect possession, particularly those for the protection of "better possession".[68]

Justice

40. General remarks. Justice is an all-pervading principle within the DCFR. It can conflict with other principles, such as efficiency, but is not lightly to be displaced. Justice is hard to define, impossible to measure and subjective at the edges, but clear cases of injustice are universally recognised and universally abhorred.

As with the other principles discussed above, there are several aspects to justice in the present context. Within the DCFR, promoting justice can refer to: ensuring that like are treated alike; not allowing people to rely on their own unlawful, dishonest or unreasonable conduct; not allowing people to take undue advantage of the weakness, misfortune or kindness of others; not making grossly excessive demands; and holding people responsible for the consequences of their own actions or their own creation of risks. Justice can also refer to protective justice – where protection is afforded, sometimes in a generalised preventative way, to those in a weak or vulnerable position.

---

[65] See Book VIII, Chapter 6.

[66] VIII. – 6:101.

[67] VIII. – 6:201 to VIII. – 6:204.

[68] VIII. – 6:301 and VIII. – 6:302.

Contract

41. Treating like alike. The most obvious manifestation of this aspect of justice in the DCFR is in the rules against discrimination[69] but it is an implicit assumption behind most of the rules on contracts and contractual obligations that parties should be treated equally by the law unless there is a good reason to the contrary. The big exception to the rule of equal treatment is that there are situations where businesses and consumers are not treated alike. This has been mentioned already and is discussed further below. The "equality" aspect of justice also surfaces in a rather different way in the notion that if both parties have obligations under a contract what goes for one party also goes for the other. This idea – sometimes called the principle of mutuality in contractual relations. – appears, for example, in the rule on the order of performance of reciprocal obligations: in the absence of any provision or indication to the contrary one party need not perform before the other.[70] It also appears in the rules on withholding performance until the other party performs[71] and in the rules allowing one party to terminate the relationship if there is a fundamental non-performance by the other,[72] although the primary explanation for these rules is the need to provide effective remedies to enhance contractual security. A further example of the "equality" aspect of justice can be seen in the rules on a plurality of debtors or creditors: the default rule is that as between themselves solidary debtors and creditors are liable or entitled in equal shares.[73]

42. Not allowing people to rely on their own unlawful, dishonest or unreasonable conduct. There are several examples of this aspect of justice in the DCFR provisions on contract law. A recurring and important idea is that parties are expected to act in accordance with good faith and fair dealing. For example, a party engaged in negotiations has a duty to negotiate in accordance with good faith and fair

---

[69]   II. – 2:101 to II. – 2:105 and III. – 1:105.

[70]   III. – 2:104.

[71]   III. – 3:401.

[72]   III. – 3:502.

[73]   III. – 4:106 and III. – 4:204.

dealing and is liable for loss caused by a breach of the duty.[74] For later stages in the relationship it is provided that:

> *A person has a duty to act in accordance with good faith and fair dealing in performing an obligation, in exercising a right to perform-ance, in pursuing or defending a remedy for non-performance, or in exercising a right to terminate an obligation or contractual relation-ship.*[75]

A breach of this duty does not in itself give rise to a liability to pay damages but may prevent a party from exercising or relying on a right, remedy or defence. The *Principes directeurs* say that "Each party is bound to act in conformity with the requirements of good faith and fair dealing, from the negotiation of the contract until all of its provisions have been given effect".[76] They also have an additional provision on performance: "Every contract must be performed in good faith. The parties may avail themselves of the contractual rights and terms only in accordance with the objective that justified their inclusion in the contract."[77] Taken together, these provisions are slightly wider than those of the DCFR but whether there would be much difference in practical effect may be doubted.

There are many specific provisions in the DCFR which can be re-garded as concretisations of the idea that people should not be al-lowed to rely on their own unlawful, dishonest or unreasonable con-duct. An example is the rule that the debtor is not liable for loss suffered by the creditor to the extent that the creditor could have reduced the loss by taking reasonable steps.[78] Another recurring ex-ample is in the requirements to give reasonable notice before certain steps are taken which would be harmful to the other party's interest. And there are several rules which allow a person to rely on an ap-parent situation only if that person is in good faith.[79] The rules on

---

[74] II. – 3:301 (2) and (3).

[75] III. – 1:103.

[76] Art. 0-301 (General duty of good faith and fair dealing).

[77] Art. 0-302 (Performance in good faith).

[78] III. – 3:705.

voidable contracts, even if their primary purpose is to ensure that a party can escape from a contract concluded in the absence of genuine freedom to contract, often have the incidental effect of preventing the other party from gaining an advantage from conduct such as fraud,[80] coercion or threats.[81]

43. No taking of undue advantage. This aspect overlaps with the last one. The most explicit recognition of this aspect of justice in contract law is the rule which allows a party, in carefully specified circumstances, to avoid a contract on the ground of unfair exploitation if the party was dependent on or had a relationship of trust with the other party, was in economic distress or had urgent needs, or was improvident, ignorant, inexperienced or lacking in bargaining skill. It is necessary that the other party knew or could reasonably be expected to have known of the vulnerability and exploited the first party's situation by taking an excessive benefit or grossly unfair advantage.[82] Again, it is clear that the rule also has the function of ensuring that the victim of the exploitation can escape from a contract concluded in the absence of genuine freedom to contract.

44. No grossly excessive demands. This aspect of justice is reflected in a number of rules which qualify the binding effect of contracts. It is recognised in the rule which regards non-performance of an obligation as excused (so that performance cannot be enforced and damages cannot be recovered) if the non-performance is due to an impediment beyond the debtor's control and if the debtor could not reasonably be expected to have avoided or overcome the impediment or its consequences.[83] It lies behind the rule allowing contractual obligations to be varied or terminated by a court if they have become so onerous as a result of an exceptional change of circumstances that it would be "manifestly unjust to hold the debtor to the

---

[79] See e.g. II.–6:103(3) (Apparent authority of representative); II.–9:201(Effect of simulation) paragraph (2).

[80] II.–7:205.

[81] II.–7:206.

[82] II.–7:207.

[83] III.–3:104.

obligation".[84] It is the basis of the rule that performance of an obligation cannot be specifically enforced if it would be unreasonably burdensome or expensive.[85] And it appears in the rule that a stipulated payment for non-performance can be reduced to a reasonable amount where it is "grossly excessive" in the circumstances.[86] It is clear, however, that this aspect of justice has to be kept within strict limits. The emphasis is on "grossly", and the oft-repeated warning that principles conflict and have to be balanced against each other is particularly apposite here. There is nothing against people profiting from a good bargain or losing from a bad one. The DCFR does not have any general notion that contracts can be challenged on the ground of lesion. This is explicitly illustrated in the rule excluding the adequacy of the price from the unfairness test in the part of the DCFR dealing with unfair contract terms.[87]

45. Responsibility for consequences. This aspect is most prominent in Book VI on non-contractual liability arising out of damage caused to another but it also surfaces in Book III. For example, a person cannot resort to a remedy for non-performance of an obligation to the extent that that person has caused the non-performance.[88]

46. Protecting the vulnerable. Many of the qualifications on freedom of contract mentioned above can also be explained as rules designed to protect the vulnerable. Here we consider some other examples. Within the DCFR the main example of this aspect of justice is the special protection afforded to consumers. This appears prominently in the rules on marketing and pre-contractual duties in Book II, Chapter 3; on the right of withdrawal in Book II, Chapter 5; and on unfair contract terms in Book II, Chapter 9, Section 4. It also appears prominently in the parts of Book IV dealing with sale, the lease of goods and personal security.[89] Often the protection takes the form of

---

[84] III. – 1:110.

[85] III. – 3:302.

[86] III. – 3:710.

[87] II. – 9:407(2). The exclusion applies only if the terms are drafted in plain and intelligible language.

[88] III. – 3:101(3).

recommending that, in a contract between a business and a consumer, it should not be possible for the parties to derogate from particular rules to the detriment of the consumer. Most of the consumer protection rules in the DCFR come from the *acquis*. They are, in substance if not in actual wording, part of EU law and of the laws of Member States and seem likely to remain so. The "consumer" is defined as "any natural person who is acting primarily for purposes which are not related to his or her trade, business or profession".[90] Whether the notion of the consumer is necessarily the best way of identifying those in need of special protection is a question which has been raised and will no doubt be raised again. Some argue that small businesses or "non-repeat players" of any kind may be equally in need of protection. However this question may be answered in the future, the point remains that the protection of those in a weak or vulnerable position can be considered an aspect of the underlying principle of justice within the DCFR. Another example in the DCFR is that some of the rules on contracts for the provision of treatment services (medical and other) afford special protection to patients.[91] And yet other examples are the protections afforded to the debtor when a right to performance is assigned[92] and the protections afforded to non-professional providers of personal security.[93] Both are in an inherently exposed position. People presented with standard terms prepared by the other party are also in a vulnerable position in practice, whether or not they are consumers, and there are rules in the DCFR to protect them.[94] Of a rather similar nature is the rule that in cases of doubt an ambiguous term which has not been individually negotiated will be interpreted against the person who supplied it.[95]

---

[89] See e.g. (for sale) IV. A. – 2:304, IV. A. – 2:309, IV. A. – 4:102, IV. A. – 5:103, IV. A. – 6:101 to IV. A. – 6:106; (for the lease of goods) IV. B. – 1:102 to IV. B. – 1:104, IV. B. – 3:105; IV. B. – 6:102; and (for personal security) IV. G. – 4:101 to IV. G. – 4:107.

[90] I. – 1:105(1).

[91] IV. C. – 8:103; IV. C. – 8:104; IV. C. – 8:106; IV. C. – 8:108; IV. C. – 8:109(5); IV. C. – 8:111.

[92] III. – 5:118 and III. – 5:119.

[93] See in particular IV. G. – 4:101 to IV. G. – 4:107.

[94] II. – 9:103, II. – 9:405 and II. – 9:406.

Non-contractual obligations

47. General. Most of the rules on obligations and corresponding rights in Book III apply to non-contractual as well as contractual obligations. Many of the points made above for contractual obligations therefore apply equally to non-contractual obligations. Moreover, most of the aspects of justice mentioned above feature strongly in the rules in Books V to VII.

48. Not allowing people to gain an advantage from their own unlawful, dishonest or unreasonable conduct. An example of this aspect of justice in Book VI is the rule denying reparation (where to allow it would be contrary to public policy) for damage caused unintentionally by one criminal collaborator to another in the course of committing an offence.[96] It has already been noted that the law on unjustified enrichment recognises the principle that a wrongdoer is not permitted to profit from the exploitation of another's rights. A non-innocent use of another's assets as a rule creates an obligation to pay for the value of that use.[97] There are also several rules in the Book in unjustified enrichment from which a person can benefit only if in good faith.[98]

49. No taking of undue advantage. The rules on benevolent intervention reflect the idea that it would be unfair to allow a person who has been assisted in an emergency by the kindness of a stranger to take advantage of that kindness. The assisted person is therefore obliged to pay at least the necessary expenses incurred. This idea is also at the root of the law on unjustified enrichment. The rules on unjustified enrichment primarily give effect to a deep-rooted principle of justice that one person should not be permitted unfairly to profit at another's expense. Where one person, due to mistake, fraud or some equivalent reason, has conferred a benefit on another which

---

95   II. – 8:103.

96   VI. – 5:103.

97   See in particular VII. – 4:101(c) and VII. – 5:102(1).

98   See e.g. VII. – 4:103, VII. – 5:101(4), VII. – 5:102(2), VII. – 5:104(2), VII. – 6:101(2) and VII. – 6:102.

would not have been conferred if the true circumstances had been known and the recipient has no countervailing reason to retain that benefit, other than that they have fortuitously received it, the recipient should not be permitted to retain the benefit to the prejudice of the person who was disadvantaged by conferring it.[99]

50. No grossly excessive demands. This aspect of justice is also found in Books V to VII. For example, it is at the root of rules which enable the normal entitlements of a benevolent intervener to be reduced in certain cases on grounds of fairness.[100] There are similar rules allowing for an equitable reduction in Book VI.[101] These reflect the fact that there may be a gross disproportion between the amount of blameworthiness and the amount of the damage caused: a very slight degree of negligence may cause enormous damage. This aspect of justice is also represented, as a countervailing consideration to the normal rules on liability, in the rules on unjustified enrichment. It is most relevant to the defence of disenrichment, where a person who has disposed of a benefit in good faith is protected.[102] It would be unfair in such circumstances to burden an innocent recipient, who no longer has the benefit received, with the expense of the claimant's mistake.

51. Responsibility for consequences. This aspect of justice features prominently in the rules of Book VI on non-contractual liability arising out of damage caused to another. It is the very basis of this branch of the law. Responsibility for damage caused does not rest on a contractual undertaking; it rests instead on intention, negligence or a special responsibility for the source of the damage. Everyone is entitled to rely on neighbours observing the law and behaving as can be expected from a reasonably careful person in the circumstances of the case. It is a requirement of fairness that an employer should be responsible for damage which an employee has caused in the course

---

[99] VII.–1:101.

[100] V.–3:104. Paragraph (2) allows regard to be had to "whether the liability of the principal would be excessive".

[101] VI.–6:202.

[102] VII.–6:101.

of the employment. For the same reason the keeper of a motor vehicle, the owner of premises and the producer of goods must all
answer for the personal injuries and damage to property which are
caused by their things. In the other direction, a person may be unable
to recover reparation, if that person consented to the damage suffered or knowingly accepted the risk.[103] Similarly, reparation may be
reduced if there was contributory fault on the part of the person
suffering the damage.[104]

52. **Protecting the vulnerable.** Although the law on non-contractual
liability aims at protection, it is framed by reference to types of damage and not by reference to the need for protection of particular
groups. There are, however, some recognitions of this aspect of the
principle of justice. One is indirect: in the definition of negligence
reference is made to failure to come up to the standard of care provided by a statutory provision whose purpose is the protection of the
injured person (the assumption being that the statute protects a
vulnerable group of which the injured person is a member).[105] The
others are more direct but operate in the other direction, by protecting the people in the categories concerned from full liability for
damage caused where it would be unfair to expose them to such
liability. Children under 7, young persons under 18 and mentally
incompetent persons are all given some protection in this way.[106]

Property

53. **Importance of certainty.** Certainty is so important in property
law that there are fewer rules which rely overtly on justice than in
the other branches of the law already discussed. However, the idea of
treating like alike (specifically, treating all the creditors of the transferor alike) played an important part in the debates on the question
of whether ownership should as a rule pass on the conclusion of the

---

[103] VI. – 5:101.

[104] VI. – 5:102.

[105] VI. – 3:102.

[106] VI. – 3:103 and VI.–5:301.

relevant contract (e. g. a contract for the sale of goods) or only on delivery of the goods or in accordance with another system.[107] Moreover the notion of good faith plays a crucial role in the rules of Book VIII which deal with the acquisition of goods. Chapter 3 deals with good faith acquisition from a person who is not the owner. The main objective of those rules is the promotion of security by favouring the status quo but they are heavily qualified by notions of justice. The acquirer will get ownership only if the acquisition was in good faith.[108] The position is the same in the rules on the acquisition of ownership by continuous possession.[109] Justice is also an important element in the rules on the consequences of production, combination or commingling. It is not enough to produce an answer to the question of who owns the resulting goods. The result must also be fair. Where, for example, one person acquires ownership by producing something out of material owned by another, a fair result is achieved by giving the person who loses ownership a right to payment of an amount equal to the value of the material at the moment of production, secured by a proprietary security right in the new goods.[110] This prevents the taking of an undue advantage at the expense of another. The only example of consumer protection in Book VIII is the rule on the ownership of unsolicited goods sent by a business to a consumer.[111] Justice lies behind many of the rules in Book IX on proprietary security and particularly the rules on priority[112] and enforcement.[113] In this context it means not only fairness as between the security provider and the secured creditor but also fairness between different secured creditors and indeed others having a proprietary right in the encumbered assets. The emphasis is on the protective aspect of justice and it is the security provider who often requires protection. There are provisions designed to afford particu-

---

[107] For the outcome, see VIII. – 2:101.

[108] VIII. – 3:101. See also VIII. – 3:101 on acquisition free of limited proprietary rights.

[109] VIII. – 4:101.

[110] VIII. – 5:201.

[111] VIII. – 2:304.

[112] Chapter 4.

[113] Chapter 7.

lar protection to consumer security providers.[114] Another aspect of justice is reflected in the rules on good faith acquisition of assets, or of security rights in assets, free from a prior security right.[115]

Efficiency

54. General remarks. The principle of efficiency lay behind many of the debates and decisions made in the course of preparing the DCFR. There are two overlapping aspects – efficiency for the purposes of the parties who might use the rules; and efficiency for wider public purposes.

Efficiency for the purposes of the parties

55. Minimal formal and procedural restrictions. The DCFR tries to keep formalities to a minimum. For example, neither writing nor any other formality is generally required for a contract or other juridical act.[116] There are exceptions for a few cases where protection seems to be specially required,[117] and it is recognised that in areas beyond the scope of the DCFR (such as conveyances of land or testaments) national laws may require writing or other formalities, but the general approach is informality. Where the parties to a transaction want writing or some formality for their own purposes they can stipulate for that. Another recurring example of this aspect of the principle of efficiency is that unnecessary procedural steps are kept to a minimum. Voidable contracts can be avoided by simple notice, without any need for court procedures.[118] Contractual relationships can be terminated in the same way if there has been a fundamental non-

---

[114] IX. – 2:107, IX. – 7:103(2), IX. – 7:105(3), IX. – 7:107, IX. – 7:201(2), IX. – 7:204, IX. – 7:207(2).

[115] IX. – 2:108, IX. – 2:109 and IX. – 6:102.

[116] II. – 1:106.

[117] E. g. personal security provided by a consumer (IV. G. – 4:104) and donations (IV. H. – 2:101).

[118] II. – 7:209.

performance of the other party's obligations.[119] A right to performance can be assigned without the need for notification to the debt-
or.[120] The ownership of goods can be transferred without delivery.[121]
Non-possessory proprietary security can be readily created. To be
effective against third parties registration will often be necessary but,
again, the formalities are kept to a minimum in the interests of efficiency.[122] The rules on set-off can be seen as based on the principle
of efficiency. There is no reason for X to pay Y and then for Y to pay
X, if the cross-payments can simply be set off against each other.[123]
Again, in the DCFR set-off is not limited to court proceedings and
can be effected by simple notice.[124]

56. Minimal substantive restrictions. The absence of any need for
consideration or *causa* for the conclusion of an effective contract,[125]
the recognition that there can be binding unilateral undertakings[126]
and the recognition that contracts can confer rights on third parties[127] all promote efficiency (and freedom!) by making it easier for
parties to achieve the legal results they want in the way they want
without the need to resort to legal devices or distortions.

57. Provision of efficient default rules. It is an aid to efficiency to provide extensive default rules for common types of contract and common
types of contractual problem. This is particularly useful for individuals
and small businesses who do not have the same legal resources as big
businesses. If matters which experience shows are likely to cause difficulty can be regulated in advance, in a fair and reasonable manner, that
is much more efficient than having to litigate about them later. It is
hoped that the content of the default rules will also promote efficiency.

---

[119] III. – 3:507.
[120] III. – 5:104(2).
[121] VIII. – 2:101
[122] See Book IX generally.
[123] II. – 6:102.
[124] III. – 6:105.
[125] II. – 4:101.
[126] II. – 1:103(2).
[127] II. – 9:301 to II. – 9:303.

The DCFR does not take the view (occasionally heard but rarely supported and never adopted) that default rules should be so unreasonable that the parties are pushed to negotiate and think things out for themselves. In cases involving only the parties to a transaction, it tries to base the default rules on what the parties would probably have agreed but for the costs of trying to do so. Such rules should produce efficient outcomes since that is presumably what the parties would have wanted.

Efficiency for wider public purposes

58. General. The rules in the DCFR are in general intended to be such as will promote economic welfare; and this is a criterion against which any legislative intervention should be checked. The promotion of market efficiency could be a useful outcome of the CFR project as a whole but that is not the aspect with which we are here concerned. The question here is the extent to which market efficiency is reflected in and promoted by the model rules *within* the DCFR. It is a matter of regret that the condensed timescale for the preparation and evaluation of the DCFR did not allow the evaluative work of the Economic Impact Group within the CoPECL project to be taken into account in the formulation of the model rules from the earliest stages. However, that evaluative work will form a valuable part of the *corona* of evaluation which will surround the DCFR and will be available to those taking the project further. What follows is a very brief note of a few areas in which it could be said that this aspect of efficiency is exemplified in the DCFR.

59. Information duties. Rules which might be said to promote market efficiency (at least when compared to some more traditional approaches) are those on information duties in Book II.[128] There is

---

[128] II. – 3:101 to II. – 3:107. In De Geest and Kovac, "The Formation of Contracts in the DCFR – A Law and Economics Perspective" (publication forthcoming in Chirico/Larouche (eds.), Economic analysis of the DCFR – The work of the Economic Impact Group within the CoPECL network of excellence (Munich 2009)) the authors cast doubt on the continued value of rights to avoid contracts on the basis of defects of consent and on

a public value in better-informed decision making across the board. Interferences with freedom of contract may be justified on the ground that they can serve to promote economic welfare if there is reason to think that because of some market failure (such as that caused by inequality of information) the agreement is less than fully efficient. Consumer protection rules, for example, can be seen not only as protective for the benefit of typically weaker parties but also as favourable to general welfare because they may lead to more competition and thus to a better functioning of markets. This holds true in particular for information duties, where consumers' lack of information about either the characteristics of the goods sold or the terms being offered leads to forms of market failure. Rules that, in relation to the making of a contract of a particular type or in a particular situation, require one party (typically a business) to provide the other (typically a consumer) with specified information about its nature, terms and effect, where such information is needed for a well-informed decision and is not otherwise readily available to that other party, can be justified as promoting efficiency in the relevant market. Indeed a legislator should consider whether this is the justification for the proposed intervention, or whether it is based on a protective notion that consumers simply should have the right in question. The answer to that question may influence the choice of the extent and form of intervention.

60. Remedies for non-performance. The Article on stipulated payments for non-performance[129] could be said to be more favourable to market efficiency than rules which regard penalty clauses as completely unenforceable.[130] Questions might be asked about the second

---

the way in which the rules on invalidity for mistake etc are formulated in the DCFR.

[129] III. – 3:712.

[130] See Schweizer, "Obligations and Remedies for non-Performance: Book III of the DCFR from an Economist's Perspective" http://www.wipol.uni-bonn.de/fileadmin/Fachbereich_Wirtschaft/Einrichtungen/Wirtschaftspolitik/Mitarbeiter/Prof._Dr._Urs_Schweizer/DCFRSchweizerRev.pdf; Ogus, "Measure of Damages, Expectation, Reliance and Opportunity Cost" (publication forthcoming in the work cited in fn. 128).

paragraph of the Article which allows a stipulated payment to be reduced to a reasonable amount when it is grossly excessive in relation to the loss resulting from the non-performance,[131] but here there are considerations of justice to weigh in the balance. The allowance of damages for pure economic loss seems to be preferable from the point of view of efficiency to the denial of such recovery, as happens under some systems.[132] It is difficult to see any justification for distinguishing between pure economic loss and loss caused by damage to property or injury to the person. The question of whether the other rules on damages are optimal from the point of view of general efficiency seems to be a matter of debate.[133]

61. Other rules. The rules on prescription in Book III, Chapter 7 are designed to promote efficiency by encouraging the prompt making of claims before evidence becomes stale and expensive to provide and by freeing assets which might otherwise be held against the possibility of old claims being made. The rules on withholding performance and terminating the contractual relationship in cases of anticipated non-performance[134] are designed to promote efficiency by not requiring the creditor to wait until non-performance actually happens. There are also rules which promote efficiency by discouraging the providing of unwanted performance.[135] The rules denying effect to contractual prohibitions on the alienation of assets are also designed to promote general efficiency by favouring the free circulation of goods and other assets.[136] The same applies to the rules on acquisition in good faith or by continuous possession.[137] A core aim of the rules in Book IX on proprietary security in movable assets is the facilitation of economic activity and economic welfare by enabling credit to be obtained on favourable terms against the provision of proprietary security.

---

[131] Ibid.

[132] Schweizer, cited above, at p.9.

[133] See e.g. the differing views of Schweizer and Ogus cited above.

[134] III. – 3:401 and III. – 3:504.

[135] See III. – 3:301(2), IV. C. – 2:111 and IV. D. – 6:101.

[136] See III. – 5:108 and VIII. – 1:301.

[137] See VIII. – 3:101 and VIII. – 4:101.

Conclusion

62. Stability. There is one aspect of efficiency and security which deserves separate mention because it lay, consciously or subconsciously, behind many of the debates on the model rules and because it accounts for an overwhelming part of the actual shape and content of the DCFR. It is stability. People feel more secure with solutions which are familiar, tried, tested and traditional. Other things being more or less equal, such solutions also promote efficiency because there is no need to understand new rules and work out all their possible implications. A valuable store of knowledge and experience is not wasted. This aspect of security and efficiency seems to be particularly valued in the legal sphere. There is a story of a famous judge of a former era who addressed a large and distinguished audience for a full hour and then said at the end, with perfect sincerity, "I hope I have said nothing new." We would not go quite so far. But we hope and believe that there is much in the DCFR which will indeed be perfectly familiar to private lawyers from every part of Europe. We hope that no lawyer from any part of Europe will see it as an alien product but that all will see it as growing out of a shared tradition and a shared legal culture. It is our great good fortune that that legal culture, thanks to the work of many legal thinkers from many countries over many centuries, is strongly imbued with the principles of freedom, security, justice and efficiency.

> *Christian von Bar,*
> *Hugh Beale,*
> *Eric Clive,*
> *Hans Schulte-Nölke*

Table of Destinations[*]

An entry in this table indicates a model rule which addresses the same legal issue as that dealt with in the relevant article of the PECL. It does not imply that the corresponding model rule is in the same terms or to the same effect. Relocations of Model Rules since the publication of the Interim Outline Edition (IOE) are indicated in italics in square brackets. Reference should be made to the IOE to ascertain changes in wording.

	PECL	DCFR Model Rules
Chapter 1	1:101	
	(1)	I. – 1:101(1)
	(2)	–
	(3)	–
	(4)	–
	1:102	
	(1)	II. – 1:102(1)
	(2)	II. – 1:102(2)
	1:103	–
	1:104	–
	1:105	II. – 1:104(1), (2)
	1:106	I. – 1:102(1), (3), (4)
	1:107	–
	1:201	
	(1)	II. – 3:301(2); III. – 1:103(1)
	(2)	III. – 1:103(2)
	1:202	III. – 1:104

---

* This and the following table were compiled by *Daniel Smith* (Osnabrück) with assistance from Dr. *Stephen Swann* (Osnabrück).

	PECL	DCFR Model Rules
	1:301	
	(1)	I. – 1:108(1) (with the Annex) *[ex IOE I. – 1:103(1) (with Annex 1: "Conduct")]*
	(2)	I. – 1:108(1) (with the Annex) *[ex IOE I. – 1:103(1) (with Annex 1: "Court")]*
	(3)	–
	(4)	I. – 1:108(1) (with the Annex) *[ex IOE I. – 1:103(1) (with Annex 1: "Non-performance")]*; III. – 1:102(3) *[ex IOE III.–1:101]*
	(5)	–
	(6)	I. – 1:106 *[ex IOE I. – 1:105]*
	1:302	I. – 1:104 *[ex IOE I. – 1:103(1) (with Annex 1: "Reasonable")]*
	1:303	
	(1)	I. – 1:109(2) *[ex IOE II.–1:106(2)]*
	(2)	I. – 1:109(3) *[ex IOE II.–1:106(3)]*
	(3)	I. – 1:109(4) *[ex IOE II.–1:106(4)]*
	(4)	III. – 3:106
	(5)	I. – 1:109(5) *[ex IOE II.–1:106(5)]*
	(6)	I. – 1:109(1) *[ex IOE II.–1:106(1)]*
	1:304	I. – 1:110 *[ex IOE I. – 1:104 (with Annex 2)]*
	1:305	II. – 1:105
Chapter 2	2:101	
	(1)	II. – 4:101
	(2)	II. – 1:106(1) *[ex IOE II.–1:107]*

	PECL	DCFR Model Rules
	2:102	II. – 4:102
	2:103	II. – 4:103
	2:104	
	(1)	II. – 9:103(1)
	(2)	II. – 9:103(3)(b)
	2:105	II. – 4:104
	2:106	II. – 4:105
	2:107	II. – 1:103(2)
	2:201	II. – 4:201
	2:202	II. – 4:202(1)-(3)
	2:203	II. – 4:203
	2:204	II. – 4:204
	2:205	II. – 4:205
	2:206	II. – 4:206
	2:207	II. – 4:207
	2:208	II. – 4:208
	2:209	
	(1)	II. – 4:209(1)
	(2)	II. – 4:209(2)
	(3)	I. – 1:108(1) (with the Annex) *[ex IOE I. – 1:103(1) (with Annex 1: "Standard terms")]*
	2:210	II. – 4:210
	2:211	II. – 4:211
	2:301	
	(1)	II. – 3:301(1)
	(2)	II. – 3:301(3)
	(3)	II. – 3:301(4)
	2:302	II. – 3:302(1), (4)
Chapter 3	3:101	
	(1)	II. – 6:101(1)
	(2)	–
	(3)	II. – 6:101(3)
	3:102	–

	PECL	DCFR Model Rules
	3:201	
	(1)	II. – 6:103(2)
	(2)	II. – 6:104(2)
	(3)	II. – 6:103(3)
	3:202	II. – 6:105
	3:203	II. – 6:108
	3:204	
	(1)	II. – 6:107(1)
	(2)	II. – 6:107(2), (3)
	3:205	II. – 6:109
	3:206	II. – 6:104(3)
	3:207	II. – 6:111(1), (2)
	3:208	–
	3:209	
	(1)	II. – 6:112(1)
	(2)	II. – 6:112(3)
	(3)	II. – 6:112(4)
	3:301	II. – 6:106
	3:302	–
	3:303	–
	3:304	–
Chapter 4	4:101	II. – 7:101(2)
	4:102	II. – 7:102
	4:103	II. – 7:201
	4:104	II. – 7:202
	4:105	II. – 7:203
	4:106	II. – 7:204
	4:107	II. – 7:205
	4:108	II. – 7:206
	4:109	II. – 7:207
	4:110	
	(1)	II. – 9:403-9:405 *[ex IOE II.–9:404-9:406]*; II. – 9:407(1) *[ex IOE II.–9:408(1)]*;

	PECL	DCFR Model Rules
	(2)	II. – 9:408 *[ex IOE II.–9:409]* II. – 9:406(2) *[ex IOE II.–9:407(2)]*
	4:111	II. – 7:208
	4:112	II. – 7:209
	4:113 (1) (2)	 II. – 7:210 –
	4:114	II. – 7:211
	4:115	II. – 7:212(2)
	4:116	II. – 7:213
	4:117	II. – 7:214
	4:118	II. – 7:215
	4:119	II. – 7:216
Chapter 5	5:101	II. – 8:101
	5:102	II. – 8:102(1)
	5:103	II. – 8:103(1)
	5:104	II. – 8:104
	5:105	II. – 8:105
	5:106	II. – 8:106
	5:107	II. – 8:107
Chapter 6	6:101 (1) (2) (3)	 II. – 9:102(1) II. – 9:102(2) II. – 9:102(3), (4)
	6:102	II. – 9:101(2)
	6:103	II. – 9:201(1)
	6:104	II. – 9:104
	6:105	II. – 9:105
	6:106	II. – 9:106
	6:107	II. – 9:107
	6:108	II. – 9:108
	6:109	III. – 1:109(2)

	PECL	DCFR Model Rules
	8:107	III. – 2:106
	8:108	III. – 3:104(1), (3), (5)
	8:109	III. – 3:105(2)
Chapter 9	9:101	III. – 3:301
	9:102	
	(1)	III. – 3:302(1), (2)
	(2)	III. – 3:302(3), (5)
	(3)	III. – 3:302(4)
	9:103	III. – 3:303
	9:201	
	(1)	III. – 3:401(1), (4)
	(2)	III. – 3:401(2)
	9:301	
	(1)	III. – 3:502(1)
	(2)	–
	9:302	III. – 3:506(2)
	9:303	
	(1)	III. – 3:507(1)
	(2)	III. – 3:508
	(3)	III. – 3:508
	(4)	III. – 3:104(4)
	9:304	III. – 3:504
	9:305	III. – 3:509(1), (2)
	9:306	III. – 3:511(2) *[ex IOE III.–3:510 and III. – 3:512(2)]*
	9:307	III. – 3:510 *[ex IOE III.–3:511]*
	9:308	III. – 3:510 *[ex IOE III.–3:511]*
	9:309	III. – 3:510 *[ex IOE III.–3:511]*
		III. – 3:512 *[ex IOE III.–3:513]*
	9:401	III. – 3:601
	9:501	III. – 3:701

	PECL	DCFR Model Rules
Chapter 11	(4)	III. – 5:103(1)
	(5)	–
	11:102	
	(1)	III. – 5:105(1)
	(2)	III. – 5:106(1)
	11:103	III. – 5:107
	11:104	III. – 5:110
	11:201	III. – 5:115
	11:202	III. – 5:114(1), (2)
	11:203	III. – 5:108(1);
		III. – 5:122 *[ex IOE III. – 5:108(3)]*
	11:204	III. – 5:112(2), (4), (6)
	11:301	
	(1)	III. – 5:108(2),
		III. – 5:108(3) *[ex IOE III. – 5:108(4), (5)]*
	(2)	III. – 5:108(4) *[ex IOE III. – 5:108(6)*
	11:302	III. – 5:109
	11:303	
	(1)	III. – 5:119(1) *[ex IOE III. – 5:118(1)]*;
		III. – 5:120(2) *[ex IOE III. – 5:119(2)]*
	(2)	III. – 5:120(3), (4) *[ex IOE III. – 5:119(3), (4)]*
	(3)	III. – 5:120(1) *[ex IOE III. – 5:119(1)]*
	(4)	III. – 5:119(1) *[ex IOE III. – 5:118(1)]*
	11:304	III. – 5:119(2) *[ex IOE III. – 5:118(2)]*
	11:305	–
	11:306	III. – 5:117
	11:307	III. – 5:116(1), (3)
	11:308	–

	PECL	DCFR Model Rules
	11:401	
	(1)	III. – 5:121(1) *[ex IOE III. – 5:120(1)]*
	(2)	III. – 5:114(3)
	(3)	III. – 5:122 *[ex IOE III. – 5:108(3)]*
	(4)	III. – 5:122 *[ex IOE III. – 5:108(3)]*
Chapter 12	12:101	
	(1)	III. – 5:202(1)(a) *[ex IOE III. – 5:201(1)]* III. – 5:203(1) *[ex IOE III. – 5:201(1)]*
	(2)	III. – 5:203(2) *[ex IOE III. – 5:201(2)]*
	12:102	
	(1)	III. – 5:205(3) *[ex IOE III. – 5:202(1)]*
	(2)	III. – 5:205(4) *[ex IOE III. – 5:202(2)]*
	(3)	III. – 5:205(5) *[ex IOE III. – 5:202(3)]*
	(4)	III. – 5:205(1) *[ex IOE III. – 5:202(4)]*
	12:201	
	(1)	III. – 5:302(1) *[ex IOE III. – 5:301(1)]*
	(2)	III. – 5:302(2) *[ex IOE III. – 5:301(2)]*
Chapter 13	13:101	III. – 6:102(a), (b)
	13:102	III. – 6:103
	13:103	III. – 6:104
	13:104	III. – 6:105
	13:105	III. – 6:106
	13:106	III. – 6:107
	13:107	III. – 6:108
Chapter 14	14:101	III. – 7:101
	14:201	III. – 7:201

Table of Destinations

Table of Derivations

An entry in this table indicates an article of the PECL which addresses the same legal issue as that dealt with in the relevant model rule. It does not imply that the article of the PECL is in the same terms or to the same effect.

Relocations of Model Rules since the publication of the Interim Outline Edition (IOE) are indicated in italics in square brackets; newly inserted Articles or Paragraphs are pointed out by an asterisk. Reference should be made to the IOE to ascertain changes in wording.

	DCFR Model Rules	PECL
Book I	I. – 1:101	
	(1)	1:101(1)
	(2)	–
	(3)	–
	I. – 1:102	
	(1)	1:106(1), 1st sent.
	(2)	–
	(3)	1:106(1), 2nd sent.
	(4)	1:106(2), 1st sent.
	(5)	–
	I. – 1:103* [ex IOE Annex 1: "Good faith and fair dealing"]	–
	I. – 1:104* [ex IOE Annex 1: "Reasonable"]	1:302
	I. – 1:105* [ex IOE Annex 1: "Consumer" and "Business"]	–
	I. – 1:106 [ex IOE I. – 1:105]	1:301(6)

	DCFR Model Rules	PECL
Book I	I. – 1:107 *[ex IOE I. – 1:106]*	–
	I. – 1:108	
	(1) (with Annex: "Conduct"; "Court"; "Non-performance"; "Standard terms") *[ex IOE I. – 1:103(1) (with Annex 1: "Conduct"; "Court"; "Non-perform- ance"; "Standard terms")]*	1:301(1), (2), (4); 2:209(3)
	(2) *[ex IOE I. – 1:103(2)]*	–
	I. – 1:109 *[ex IOE II.–1:106]*	
	(1)	1:303(6)
	(2)	1:303(1)
	(3)	1:303(2)
	(4)	1:303(3)
	(5)	1:303(5)
	(6)	–
	(7)	–
	I. – 1:110* *[ex IOE I. – 1:104 (with Annex 2)]*	1:304
Book II	II. – 1:101	–
	II. – 1:102	
	(1)	1:102(1)
	(2)	1:102(2)
	(3)	–
	II. – 1:103	
	(1)	–
	(2)	2:107
	(3)	–
	II. – 1:104	
	(1)	1:105(1)
	(2)	1:105(2)
	(3)	–

Table of Derivations

	DCFR Model Rules	PECL
Book II	II. – 1:105	1:305
	II. – 1:106 [ex IOE II.–1:107] (1) (2)*	 2:101(2) –
	II. – 1:107 [ex IOE II.–1:108]	–
	II. – 1:108 [ex IOE II.–1:109]	–
	II. – 1:109* [ex IOE Annex 1: "Standard terms"]	–
	II. – 1:110 [ex IOE II.–9:403]	–
	II. – 2:101	–
	II. – 2:102	–
	II. – 2:103	–
	II. – 2:104	–
	II. – 2:105	–
	II. – 3:101	–
	II. – 3:102 (1) (2) (3)*	 – – –
	II. – 3:103	–
	II. – 3:104 (1) (2) (3) (4)* (5)*	– – – – – –
	II. – 3:105 (1) (2) (3)* (4)*	– – – – –

	DCFR Model Rules	PECL
Book II	II. – 3:106	–
	(1)	–
	(2)*	–
	(3)	–
	II. – 3:107*	–
	II. – 3:108*	–
	II. – 3:109 [ex IOE II.–3:107]	–
	II. – 3:201	–
	II. – 3:202*	–
	II. – 3:301	
	(1)	2:301(1)
	(2)	1:201(1)
	(3)	2:301(2)
	(4)	2:301(3)
	II. – 3:302	
	(1)	2:302, 1st sent.
	(2)	–
	(3)	–
	(4)	2:302, 2nd sent.
	II. – 3:401	–
	II. – 3:501*	–
	II. – 4:101	2:101(1)
	II. – 4:102	2:102
	II. – 4:103	2:103
	II. – 4:104	2:105
	II. – 4:105	2:106
	II. – 4:201	2:201
	II. – 4:202	
	(1)	2:202(1)
	(2)	2:202(2)
	(3)	2:202(3)
	(4)*	–

	DCFR Model Rules	PECL
Book II	II. – 4:203	2:203
	II. – 4:204	2:204
	II. – 4:205	2:205
	II. – 4:206	2:206
	II. – 4:207	2:207
	II. – 4:208	2:208
	II. – 4:209	2:209(1), (2)
	II. – 4:210	2:210
	II. – 4:211	2:211
	II. – 4:301	–
	II. – 4:302	–
	II. – 4:303	–
	II. – 5:101	–
	II. – 5:102	–
	II. – 5:103	–
	II. – 5:104	–
	II. – 5:105	–
	(1)	–
	(2)	–
	(3)*	–
	(4)	–
	(5)	–
	(6)	–
	(7)*	–
	II. – 5:106	–
	II. – 5:201	–
	II. – 5:202	–
	II. – 6:101	
	(1)	3:101(1)
	(2)	–
	(3)	3:101(3)
	II. – 6:102	–

	DCFR Model Rules	PECL
Book II	II. – 6:103	
	(1)	–
	(2)	3:201(1)
	(3)	3:201(3)
	II. – 6:104	
	(1)	–
	(2)	3:201(2)
	(3)	3:206
	II. – 6:105	3:202
	II. – 6:106	3:301
	II. – 6:107	
	(1)	3:204(1)
	(2)	3:204(2), 1st sent.
	(3)	3:204(2), 2nd sent.
	II. – 6:108	3:203
	II. – 6:109	3:205
	II. – 6:110	–
	II. – 6:111	
	(1)	3:207(1)
	(2)	3:207(2)
	(3)	–
	II. – 6:112	
	(1)	3:209(1)
	(2)	–
	(3)	3:209(2)
	(4)	3:209(3)
	II. – 7:101	
	(1)	–
	(2)	4:101
	(3)	–
	II. – 7:102	4:102
	II. – 7:201	4:103
	II. – 7:202	4:104

	DCFR Model Rules	PECL
Book II	II. – 7:203	4:105
	II. – 7:204	4:106
	II. – 7:205	4:107
	II. – 7:206	4:108
	II. – 7:207	4:109
	II. – 7:208	4:111
	II. – 7:209	4:112
	II. – 7:210	4:113(1)
	II. – 7:211	4:114
	II. – 7:212	
	(1)	–
	(2)	4:115
	(3)	–
	II. – 7:213	4:116
	II. – 7:214	4:117
	II. – 7:215	4:118
	II. – 7:216	4:119
	II. – 7:301	15:101
	II. – 7:302	15:102
	II. – 7:303	15:104
	II. – 7:304	15:105
	II. – 8:101	5:101
	II. – 8:102	
	(1)	5:102
	(2)	–
	II. – 8:103	
	(1)	5:103
	(2)*	–
	II. – 8:104	5:104
	II. – 8:105	5:105
	II. – 8:106	5:106
	II. – 8:107	5:107
	II. – 8:201	–
	II. – 8:202	–

	DCFR Model Rules	PECL
Book II	II. – 9:101	
	(1)	–
	(2)	6:102
	(3)	–
	(4)	–
	II. – 9:102	
	(1)	6:101(1)
	(2)	6:101(2)
	(3)	6:101(3)
	(4)	6:101(3)
	(5)	–
	(6)*	–
	II. – 9:103	
	(1)	2:104(1)
	(2)	–
	(3)(a)	–
	(3)(b)	2:104(2)
	II. – 9:104	6:104
	II. – 9:105	6:105
	II. – 9:106	6:106
	II. – 9:107	6:107
	II. – 9:108	6:108
	II. – 9:109*	–
	II. – 9:201	
	(1)	6:103
	(2)	–
	II. – 9:301	
	(1)	6:110(1)
	(2)	–
	(3)	–
	II. – 9:302	–
	II. – 9:303	6:110(2), (3)
	II. – 9:401	–
	II. – 9:402	–

	DCFR Model Rules	PECL
Book II	II. – 9:403 *[ex IOE II.–9:404]*	4:110(1)
	II. – 9:404 *[ex IOE II.–9:405]*	4:110(1)
	II. – 9:405 *[ex IOE II.–9:406]*	4:110(1)
	II. – 9:406 *[ex IOE II.–9:407]* (1) (2)	 – 4:110(2)
	II. – 9:407 *[ex IOE II.–9:408]* (1) (2)	 4:110(1) –
	II. – 9:408 *[ex IOE II.–9:409]*	4:110(1)
	II. – 9:409 *[ex IOE II.–9:410]*	–
	II. – 9:410 *[ex IOE II.–9:411]*	–
Book III	III. – 1:101 *[ex IOE III.–1:102]*	–
	III. – 1:102 *[ex IOE III.–1:101]* (1) (2) (3) (4) (5)	 – – 1:301(4) – –
	III. – 1:103 (1) (2) (3)	 1:201(1) 1:201(2) –
	III. – 1:104	1:202
	III. – 1:105	–

	DCFR Model Rules	PECL
Book III	III. – 1:106	
	(1)	16:101
	(2)	16:103(1)
	(3)	16:103(2)
	(4)	16:102
	(5)	–
	III. – 1:107	–
	III. – 1:108	–
	III. – 1:109	
	(1)	–
	(2)	6:109
	(3)	–
	III. – 1:110	6:111
	III. – 1:111*	–
	III. – 2:101	
	(1)	7:101(1)
	(2)	7:101(2), (3)
	(3)	–
	III. – 2:102	
	(1)	7:102(1), (3)
	(2)	7:102(2)
	(3)*	–
	(4)*	–
	III. – 2:103	7:103
	III. – 2:104	7:104
	III. – 2:105	7:105
	III. – 2:106	8:107
	III. – 2:107	
	(1)	7:106(1)
	(2)	7:106(2)
	(3)	–
	III. – 2:108	7:107

Table of Derivations

	DCFR Model Rules	PECL
Book III	III. – 2:109	
	(1)	7:108(1)
	(2)	7:108(2)
	(3)	7:108(3)
	(4)	–
	III. – 2:110	
	(1)	7:109(1)
	(2)	7:109(2)
	(3)	7:109(2)
	(4)	7:109(3)
	(5)	7:109(4)
	III. – 2:111	7:110
	III. – 2:112	
	(1)	7:111
	(2)	–
	III. – 2:113	
	(1)	7:112
	(2)	–
	III. – 2:114	–
	III. – 3:101	8:101
	III. – 3:102	8:102
	III. – 3:103	
	(1)	8:106(1)
	(2)	8:106(2), 1st sent.
	(3)	8:106(2), 2nd sent.
	III. – 3:104	
	(1)	8:108(1)
	(2)	–
	(3)	8:108(2)
	(4)	9:303(4)
	(5)	8:108(3)
	III. – 3:105	
	(1)	–
	(2)	8:109

	DCFR Model Rules	PECL
Book III	III. – 3:106	
	(1)	1:303(4), 1st sent.
	(2)	1:303(4), 2nd sent.
	III. – 3:107	–
	III. – 3:108*	–
	III. – 3:201	–
	III. – 3:202	8:104
	III. – 3:203	
	(a)	8:104
	(b)	–
	(c)	–
	(d)	–
	III. – 3:204	–
	III. – 3:205*	–
	III. – 3:301	9:101
	III. – 3:302	
	(1)	9:102(1)
	(2)	9:102(1)
	(3)	9:102(2)(a)-(c)
	(4)	9:102(3)
	(5)	9:102(2)(d)
	III. – 3:303	9:103
	III. – 3:401	
	(1)	9:201(1), 1st sent.
	(2)	8:105(1); 9:201(2)
	(3)	–
	(4)	9:201(1), 2nd sent.
	III. – 3:501	–
	III. – 3:502	
	(1)	9:301(1)
	(2)	8:103
	III. – 3:503	8:106(3)
	III. – 3:504	9:304
	III. – 3:505	8:105(2)

	DCFR Model Rules	PECL
Book III	III. – 3:506	
	(1)*	–
	(2)	9:302
	III. – 3:507	
	(1)	9:303(1)
	(2)	8:106(3)
	III. – 3:508	9:303(2), (3)
	III. – 3:509	
	(1)	9:305(1)
	(2)	9:305(2)
	(3)	–
	III. – 3:510 *[ex IOE III.–3:511]*	9:307; 9:308; 9:309
	III. – 3:511 *[ex IOE III.–3:512]*	
	(1)	–
	(2) *[ex IOE III.–3:510]*	9:306
	(3)*	–
	III. – 3:512 *[ex IOE III.–3:513]*	9:309
	III. – 3:513 *[ex IOE III.–3:514]*	–
	III. – 3:514 *[ex IOE III.–3:515]*	–
	III. – 3:601	9:401
	III. – 3:701	9:501
	III. – 3:702	9:502
	III. – 3:703	9:503
	III. – 3:704	9:504
	III. – 3:705	9:505
	III. – 3:706	9:506
	III. – 3:707	9:507
	III. – 3:708	9:508
	III. – 3:709	17:101
	III. – 3:710*	–

	DCFR Model Rules	PECL
Book III	III. – 3:711*	–
	III. – 3:712 *[ex IOE III.–3:710]*	9:509
	III. – 3:713 *[ex IOE III.–3:711]*	9:510
	III. – 4:101	–
	III. – 4:102	10:101
	III. – 4:103	10:102
	III. – 4:104	10:103
	III. – 4:105	10:104
	III. – 4:106	10:105
	III. – 4:107	10:106
	III. – 4:108	10:107
	III. – 4:109	
	(1)	10:108(1)
	(2)	10:108(3)
	(3)	–
	III. – 4:110	10:109
	III. – 4:111	10:110
	III. – 4:112	10:111
	III. – 4:201	–
	III. – 4:202	10:201
	III. – 4:203	–
	III. – 4:204	10:202
	III. – 4:205	10:203
	III. – 4:206	10:204
	III. – 4:207	10:205
	III. – 5:101	
	(1)	11:101(1), (2)
	(2)	11:101(3)
	III. – 5:102	–
	III. – 5:103	
	(1)	11:101(4)
	(2)	–

	DCFR Model Rules	PECL
Book III	III. – 5:104	
	(1)	–
	(2)*	–
	(3)*	–
	(4)	–
	III. – 5:105	
	(1)	11:102(1)
	(2)	–
	III. – 5:106	
	(1)	11:102(2)
	(2)	–
	III. – 5:107	11:103
	III. – 5:108	
	(1)	11:203
	(2)	11:301(1)
	(3) *[ex IOE III.–5:108(4), (5)]*	11:301(1)
	(4) *[ex IOE III.–5:108(6)]*	11:301(2)
	III. – 5:109	11:302
	III. – 5:110	11:104
	III. – 5:111	–
	III. – 5:112	
	(1)	–
	(2)	11:204(a)
	(3)	–
	(4)	11:204(b)
	(5)	–
	(6)	11:204(c)
	(7)	–
	III. – 5:113	–
	III. – 5:114	
	(1)	11:202(1)
	(2)	11:202(2)
	(3)	11:401(2)

	DCFR Model Rules	PECL
Book III	III. – 5:115	11:201
	III. – 5:116	
	(1)	11:307(1)
	(2)	–
	(3)	11:307(2)
	III. – 5:117	11:306
	III. – 5:118*	–
	III. – 5:119 *[ex IOE III.–5:118]*	
	(1)	11:303(1), (4)
	(2)	11:304
	(3)*	–
	III. – 5:120 *[ex IOE III.–5:119]*	
	(1)	11:303(3)
	(2)	11:303(1)
	(3)	11:303(2)
	(4)	11:303(2)
	III. – 5:121 *[ex IOE III.–5:120]*	
	(1)	11:401(1)
	(2)	–
	III. – 5:122* *[ex IOE III.–5:108(3)]*	11:203; 11:401(3), (4)
	III. – 5:201*	–
	III. – 5:202	
	(1)	
	(a) *[ex IOE III.–5:201(1)]*	12:101(1)
	(b)*	–
	(c)*	–
	(2)*	–

	DCFR Model Rules	PECL
Book III	III. – 5:203	
	(1) *[ex IOE III.–5:201(1)]*	12:101(1)
	(2) *[ex IOE III.–5:201(2)]*	12:101(2)
	(3)*	–
	III. – 5:204*	–
	III. – 5:205	
	(1) *[ex IOE III.–5:202(4)]*	12:102(4)
	(2)*	–
	(3) *[ex IOE III.–5:202(1)]*	12:102(1)
	(4) *[ex IOE III.–5:202(2)]*	12:102(2)
	(5) *[ex IOE III.–5:202(3)]*	12:102(3)
	III. – 5:206*	
	III. – 5:207*	
	III. – 5:208*	
	III. – 5:209*	
	III. – 5:301*	
	III. – 5:302	
	(1) *[ex IOE III.–5:301(1)]*	12:201(1), 1st sent.
	(2) *[ex IOE III.–5:301(1)]*	12:201(1), 2nd sent.
	(3) *[ex IOE III.–5:301(2)]*	12:201(2)
	III. – 5:401*	–
	III. – 5:402*	–
	III. – 6:101	
	(1)	–
	(2)*	–
	III. – 6:102	
	(a), (b)	13:101
	(c)*	–

	DCFR Model Rules	PECL
Book III	III. – 6:103	13:102
	III. – 6:104	13:103
	III. – 6:105	13:104
	III. – 6:106	13:105
	III. – 6:107	13:106
	III. – 6:108	13:107
	III. – 6:201	–
	III. – 7:101	14:101
	III. – 7:201	14:201
	III. – 7:202	14:202
	III. – 7:203	14:203
	III. – 7:301	14:301
	III. – 7:302	
	(1)	14:302(1)
	(2)	14:302(2)
	(3)	14:302(3)
	(4)*	–
	III. – 7:303	
	(1)	14:303(1)
	(2)	14:303(2)
	(3)*	–
	(4)	–
	III. – 7:304	14:304
	III. – 7:305	14:305
	III. – 7:306	14:306
	III. – 7:307	14:307
	III. – 7:401	14:401
	III. – 7:402	14:402
	III. – 7:501	14:501
	III. – 7:502	14:502
	III. – 7:503	14:503
	III. – 7:601	14:601

Model Rules

Book I
General provisions

Book II
Contracts and other juridical acts

Chapter 1: General provisions

Book III
Obligations and corresponding rights

Chapter 1: General

Chapter 4: Plurality of debtors and creditors

Chapter 5: Change of parties

Book IV
Specific contracts and the rights and obligations arising from them

Part A. Sales

Part B. Lease of goods

Chapter 3: Construction

Chapter 4: Processing

Chapter 5: Storage

Part F. Loan contracts

Part G. Personal security

Chapter 1: Common rules

Book V
Benevolent intervention in another's affairs

Book VI
Non-contractual liability arising out of damage caused to another

Book VIII
Acquisition and loss of ownership of goods

Book IX
Proprietary security in movable assets

Chapter 7: Default and enforcement

Book X
Trusts

Chapter 1: Fundamental provisions

Chapter 2: Constitution of trusts

Chapter 8: Change of trustees or trust auxiliary

Chapter 9: Termination and variation of trusts and transfer of rights to benefit

Book I
General provisions

I. – I:101: Intended field of application
(1) These rules are intended to be used primarily in relation to contracts and other juridical acts, contractual and non-contractual rights and obligations and related property matters.
(2) They are not intended to be used, or used without modification or supplementation, in relation to rights and obligations of a public law nature or, except where otherwise provided, in relation to:
    (a) the status or legal capacity of natural persons;
    (b) wills and succession;
    (c) family relationships, including matrimonial and similar relationships;
    (d) bills of exchange, cheques and promissory notes and other negotiable instruments;
    (e) employment relationships;
    (f) the ownership of, or rights in security over, immovable property;
    (g) the creation, capacity, internal organisation, regulation or dissolution of companies and other bodies corporate or unincorporated;
    (h) matters relating primarily to procedure or enforcement.
(3) Further restrictions on intended fields of application are contained in later Books.

I. – I:102: Interpretation and development
(1) These rules are to be interpreted and developed autonomously and in accordance with their objectives and the principles underlying them.
(2) They are to be read in the light of any applicable instruments guaranteeing human rights and fundamental freedoms and any applicable constitutional laws.
(3) In their interpretation and development regard should be had to the need to promote:
    (a) uniformity of application;
    (b) good faith and fair dealing; and
    (c) legal certainty.

(4) Issues within the scope of the rules but not expressly settled by them are so far as possible to be settled in accordance with the principles underlying them.

(5) Where there is a general rule and a special rule applying to a particular situation within the scope of the general rule, the special rule prevails in any case of conflict.

I. – 1:103: Good faith and fair dealing

(1) The expression "good faith and fair dealing" refers to a standard of conduct characterised by honesty, openness and consideration for the interests of the other party to the transaction or relationship in question.

(2) It is, in particular, contrary to good faith and fair dealing for a party to act inconsistently with that party's prior statements or conduct when the other party has reasonably relied on them to that other party's detriment.

I. – 1:104: Reasonableness

Reasonableness is to be objectively ascertained, having regard to the nature and purpose of what is being done, to the circumstances of the case and to any relevant usages and practices.

I. – 1:105: "Consumer" and "business"

(1) A "consumer" means any natural person who is acting primarily for purposes which are not related to his or her trade, business or profession.

(2) A "business" means any natural or legal person, irrespective of whether publicly or privately owned, who is acting for purposes relating to the person's self-employed trade, work or profession, even if the person does not intend to make a profit in the course of the activity.

(3) A person who is within both of the preceding paragraphs is regarded as falling exclusively within paragraph (1) in relation to a rule which would provide protection for that person if that person were a consumer, and otherwise as falling exclusively within paragraph (2).

I. – 1:106: "In writing" and similar expressions

(1) For the purposes of these rules, a statement is "in writing" if it is in textual form and in characters which are directly legible from paper or another tangible durable medium.

(2) "Textual form" means a text which is expressed in alphabetical or other intelligible characters by means of any support which permits reading, recording of the information contained in the text and its reproduction in tangible form.

(3) "Durable medium" means any material on which information is stored so that it is accessible for future reference for a period of time adequate to the purposes of the information, and which allows the unchanged reproduction of this information.

I. – 1:107: "Signature" and similar expressions

(1) A reference to a person's signature includes a reference to that person's handwritten signature, electronic signature or advanced electronic signature, and references to anything being signed by a person are to be construed accordingly.

(2) A "handwritten signature" means the name of, or sign representing, a person written by that person's own hand for the purpose of authentication.

(3) An "electronic signature" means data in electronic form which are attached to or logically associated with other electronic data, and which serve as a method of authentication.

(4) An "advanced electronic signature" means an electronic signature which is:
   (a) uniquely linked to the signatory;
   (b) capable of identifying the signatory;
   (c) created using means which can be maintained under the signatory's sole control; and
   (d) linked to the data to which it relates in such a manner that any subsequent change of the data is detectable.

(5) In this Article, "electronic" means relating to technology with electrical, digital, magnetic, wireless, optical, electromagnetic, or similar capabilities.

I. – I:108: Definitions in Annex

(1) The definitions in the Annex apply for all the purposes of these rules unless the context otherwise requires.

(2) Where a word is defined, other grammatical forms of the word have a corresponding meaning.

I. – I:109: Notice

(1) This Article applies in relation to the giving of notice for any purpose under these rules. "Notice" includes the communication of information or of a juridical act.

(2) The notice may be given by any means appropriate to the circumstances.

(3) The notice becomes effective when it reaches the addressee, unless it provides for a delayed effect.

(4) The notice reaches the addressee:

    (a) when it is delivered to the addressee;

    (b) when it is delivered to the addressee's place of business or, where there is no such place of business or the notice does not relate to a business matter, to the addressee's habitual residence;

    (c) in the case of a notice transmitted by electronic means, when it can be accessed by the addressee; or

    (d) when it is otherwise made available to the addressee at such a place and in such a way that the addressee could reasonably be expected to obtain access to it without undue delay.

(5) The notice has no effect if a revocation of it reaches the addressee before or at the same time as the notice.

(6) Any reference in these rules to a notice given by or to a person includes a notice given by or to an agent of that person who has authority to give or receive it.

(7) In relations between a business and a consumer the parties may not, to the detriment of the consumer, exclude the rule in paragraph (4)(c) or derogate from or vary its effects.

I. – I:110: Computation of time

(1) The provisions of this Article apply in relation to the computation of time for any purpose under these rules.

(2) Subject to the following provisions of this Article:

  (a) a period expressed in hours starts at the beginning of the first hour and ends with the expiry of the last hour of the period;

  (b) a period expressed in days starts at the beginning of the first hour of the first day and ends with the expiry of the last hour of the last day of the period;

  (c) a period expressed in weeks, months or years starts at the beginning of the first hour of the first day of the period, and ends with the expiry of the last hour of whichever day in the last week, month or year is the same day of the week, or falls on the same date, as the day from which the period runs; with the qualification that if, in a period expressed in months or in years, the day on which the period should expire does not occur in the last month, it ends with the expiry of the last hour of the last day of that month;

  (d) if a period includes part of a month, the month is considered to have thirty days for the purpose of calculating the length of the part.

(3) Where a period is to be calculated from a specified event or action, then:

  (a) if the period is expressed in hours, the hour during which the event occurs or the action takes place is not considered to fall within the period in question; and

  (b) if the period is expressed in days, weeks, months or years, the day during which the event occurs or the action takes place is not considered to fall within the period in question.

(4) Where a period is to be calculated from a specified time, then:

  (a) if the period is expressed in hours, the first hour of the period is considered to begin at the specified time; and

  (b) if the period is expressed in days, weeks, months or years, the day during which the specified time arrives is not considered to fall within the period in question.

(5) The periods concerned include Saturdays, Sundays and public holidays, save where these are expressly excepted or where the periods are expressed in working days.

(6) Where the last day of a period expressed otherwise than in hours is a Saturday, Sunday or public holiday at the place where a prescribed act is to be done, the period ends with the expiry of the last hour of the following working day. This provision does not apply to periods calculated retroactively from a given date or event.

(7) Any period of two days or more is regarded as including at least two working days.

(8) Where a person sends another person a document which sets a period of time within which the addressee has to reply or take other action but does not state when the period is to begin, then, in the absence of indications to the contrary, the period is calculated from the date stated as the date of the document or, if no date is stated, from the moment the document reaches the addressee.

(9) In this Article:

   (a) "public holiday" with reference to a member state, or part of a member state, of the European Union means any day designated as such for that state or part in a list published in the official journal; and

   (b) "working days" means all days other than Saturdays, Sundays and public holidays.

Book II
Contracts and other juridical acts

Chapter 1:
General provisions

II. – 1:101: Meaning of "contract" and "juridical act"
(1) A contract is an agreement which is intended to give rise to a binding legal relationship or to have some other legal effect. It is a bilateral or multilateral juridical act.
(2) A juridical act is any statement or agreement, whether express or implied from conduct, which is intended to have legal effect as such. It may be unilateral, bilateral or multilateral.

II. – 1:102: Party autonomy
(1) Parties are free to make a contract or other juridical act and to determine its contents, subject to any applicable mandatory rules.
(2) Parties may exclude the application of any of the following rules relating to contracts or other juridical acts, or the rights and obligations arising from them, or derogate from or vary their effects, except as otherwise provided.
(3) A provision to the effect that parties may not exclude the application of a rule or derogate from or vary its effects does not prevent a party from waiving a right which has already arisen and of which that party is aware.

II. – 1:103: Binding effect
(1) A valid contract is binding on the parties.
(2) A valid unilateral undertaking is binding on the person giving it if it is intended to be legally binding without acceptance.
(3) This Article does not prevent modification or termination of any resulting right or obligation by agreement between the debtor and creditor or as provided by law.

II. – 1:104: Usages and practices
(1) The parties to a contract are bound by any usage to which they have agreed and by any practice they have established between themselves.
(2) The parties are bound by a usage which would be considered generally applicable by persons in the same situation as the parties, except where the application of such usage would be unreasonable.
(3) This Article applies to other juridical acts with any necessary adaptations.

II. – 1:105: Imputed knowledge etc.
If a person who with a party's assent was involved in making a contract or other juridical act or in exercising a right or performing an obligation under it:
(a) knew or foresaw a fact, or is treated as having knowledge or foresight of a fact; or
(b) acted intentionally or with any other relevant state of mind
this knowledge, foresight or state of mind is imputed to the party.

II. – 1:106: Form
(1) A contract or other juridical act need not be concluded, made or evidenced in writing nor is it subject to any other requirement as to form.
(2) Where a contract or other juridical act is invalid only by reason of non-compliance with a particular requirement as to form, one party (the first party) is liable for any loss suffered by the other (the second party) by acting in the mistaken, but reasonable, belief that it was valid if the first party:
    (a) knew it was invalid;
    (b) knew or could reasonably be expected to know that the second party was acting to that party's potential prejudice in the mistaken belief that it was valid; and
    (c) contrary to good faith and fair dealing, allowed the second party to continue so acting.

II. – 1:107: Mixed contracts
(1) For the purposes of this Article a mixed contract is a contract which contains:
    (a) parts falling within two or more of the categories of contracts regulated specifically in these rules; or

(b) a part falling within one such category and another part falling within the category of contracts governed only by the rules applicable to contracts generally.

(2) Where a contract is a mixed contract then, unless this is contrary to the nature and purpose of the contract, the rules applicable to each relevant category apply, with any appropriate adaptations, to the corresponding part of the contract and the rights and obligations arising from it.

(3) Paragraph (2) does not apply where:
    (a) a rule provides that a mixed contract is to be regarded as falling primarily within one category; or
    (b) in a case not covered by the preceding sub-paragraph, one part of a mixed contract is in fact so predominant that it would be unreasonable not to regard the contract as falling primarily within one category.

(4) In cases covered by paragraph (3) the rules applicable to the category into which the contract primarily falls (the primary category) apply to the contract and the rights and obligations arising from it. However, rules applicable to any elements of the contract falling within another category apply with any appropriate adaptations so far as is necessary to regulate those elements and provided that they do not conflict with the rules applicable to the primary category.

(5) Nothing in this Article prevents the application of any mandatory rules.

II. – 1:108: Partial invalidity or ineffectiveness

Where only part of a contract or other juridical act is invalid or ineffective, the remaining part continues in effect if it can reasonably be maintained without the invalid or ineffective part.

II. – 1:109: Standard terms

A "standard term" is a term which has been formulated in advance for several transactions involving different parties and which has not been individually negotiated by the parties.

II. – 1:110: Terms "not individually negotiated"

(1) A term supplied by one party is not individually negotiated if the other party has not been able to influence its content, in particular because it has been drafted in advance, whether or not as part of standard terms.

(2) If one party supplies a selection of terms to the other party, a term will not be regarded as individually negotiated merely because the other party chooses that term from that selection.

(3) If it is disputed whether a term supplied by one party as part of standard terms has since been individually negotiated, that party bears the burden of proving that it has been.

(4) In a contract between a business and a consumer, the business bears the burden of proving that a term supplied by the business has been individually negotiated.

(5) In contracts between a business and a consumer, terms drafted by a third person are considered to have been supplied by the business, unless the consumer introduced them to the contract.

Chapter 2:
Non-discrimination

II. – 2:101: Right not to be discriminated against
A person has a right not to be discriminated against on the grounds of sex or ethnic or racial origin in relation to a contract or other juridical act the object of which is to provide access to, or supply, goods, other assets or services which are available to the public.

II. – 2:102: Meaning of discrimination
(1) "Discrimination" means any conduct whereby, or situation where, on grounds such as those mentioned in the preceding Article:
  (a) one person is treated less favourably than another person is, has been or would be treated in a comparable situation; or
  (b) an apparently neutral provision, criterion or practice would place one group of persons at a particular disadvantage when compared to a different group of persons.

(2) Discrimination also includes harassment on grounds such as those mentioned in the preceding Article. "Harassment" means unwanted conduct (including conduct of a sexual nature) which violates a person's dignity, particularly when such conduct creates an intimidating, hostile, degrading, humiliating or offensive environment, or which aims to do so.

(3) Any instruction to discriminate also amounts to discrimination.

II. – 2:103: Exception

Unequal treatment which is justified by a legitimate aim does not amount to discrimination if the means used to achieve that aim are appropriate and necessary.

II. – 2:104: Remedies

(1) If a person is discriminated against contrary to II. – 2:101 (Right not to be discriminated against) then, without prejudice to any remedy which may be available under Book VI (Non-contractual liability for damage caused to another), the remedies for non-performance of an obligation under Book III, Chapter 3 (including damages for economic and non-economic loss) are available.

(2) Any remedy granted should be proportionate to the injury or anticipated injury; the dissuasive effect of remedies may be taken into account.

II. – 2:105: Burden of proof

(1) If a person who considers himself or herself discriminated against on one of the grounds mentioned in II. – 2:101 (Right not to be discriminated against) establishes, before a court or another competent authority, facts from which it may be presumed that there has been such discrimination, it falls on the other party to prove that there has been no such discrimination.

(2) Paragraph (1) does not apply to proceedings in which it is for the court or another competent authority to investigate the facts of the case.

Chapter 3:
Marketing and pre-contractual duties
Section 1:
Information duties

II. – 3:101: Duty to disclose information about goods, other assets and services

(1) Before the conclusion of a contract for the supply of goods, other assets or services by a business to another person, the business has a duty to disclose to the other person such information concerning the goods, other assets or services to be supplied as the other person can

reasonably expect, taking into account the standards of quality and performance which would be normal under the circumstances.

(2) In assessing what information the other person can reasonably expect to be disclosed, the test to be applied, if the other person is also a business, is whether the failure to provide the information would deviate from good commercial practice.

II. – 3:102: Specific duties for businesses marketing to consumers

(1) Where a business is marketing goods, other assets or services to a consumer, the business has a duty not to give misleading information. Information is misleading if it misrepresents or omits material facts which the average consumer could expect to be given for an informed decision on whether to take steps towards the conclusion of a contract. In assessing what an average consumer could expect to be given, account is to be taken of all the circumstances and of the limitations of the communication medium employed.

(2) Where a business uses a commercial communication which gives the impression to consumers that it contains all the relevant information necessary to make a decision about concluding a contract, the business has a duty to ensure that the communication in fact contains all the relevant information. Where it is not already apparent from the context of the commercial communication, the information to be provided comprises:

(a) the main characteristics of the goods, other assets or services, the identity and address, if relevant, of the business, the price, and any available right of withdrawal;

(b) peculiarities related to payment, delivery, performance and complaint handling, if they depart from the requirements of professional diligence; and

(c) the language to be used for communications between the parties after the conclusion of the contract, if this differs from the language of the commercial communication.

(3) A duty to provide information under this Article is not fulfilled unless all the information to be provided is provided in the same language.

II. – 3:103: Duty to provide information when concluding contract with a consumer who is at a particular disadvantage

(1) In the case of transactions that place the consumer at a significant informational disadvantage because of the technical medium used for contracting, the physical distance between business and consumer, or the nature of the transaction, the business has a duty, as appropriate in the circumstances, to provide clear information about the main characteristics of any goods, other assets or services to be supplied, the price, the address and identity of the business with which the consumer is transacting, the terms of the contract, the rights and obligations of both contracting parties, and any available right of withdrawal or redress procedures. This information must be provided a reasonable time before the conclusion of the contract. The information on the right of withdrawal must, as appropriate in the circumstances, also be adequate in the sense of II. – 5:104 (Adequate information on the right to withdraw).

(2) Where more specific information duties are provided for specific situations, these take precedence over the general information duty under paragraph (1).

(3) The business bears the burden of proof that it has provided the information required by this Article.

II. – 3:104: Information duties in real time distance communication

(1) When initiating real time distance communication with a consumer, a business has a duty to provide at the outset explicit information on its name and the commercial purpose of the contact.

(2) Real time distance communication means direct and immediate distance communication of such a type that one party can interrupt the other in the course of the communication. It includes telephone and electronic means such as voice over internet protocol and internet related chat, but does not include communication by electronic mail.

(3) The business bears the burden of proof that the consumer has received the information required under paragraph (1).

(4) If a business has failed to comply with the duty under paragraph (1) and a contract has been concluded as a result of the communication,

the other party has a right to withdraw from the contract by giving
notice to the business within the period specified in II. – 5:103 (Withdrawal period).

(5) A business is liable to the consumer for any loss caused by a breach of
the duty under paragraph (1).

II. – 3:105: Formation by electronic means

(1) If a contract is to be concluded by electronic means and without individual communication, a business has a duty to provide information
about the following matters before the other party makes or accepts an
offer:

   (a) the technical steps to be taken in order to conclude the contract;
   (b) whether or not a contract document will be filed by the business
       and whether it will be accessible;
   (c) the technical means for identifying and correcting input errors be-
       fore the other party makes or accepts an offer;
   (d) the languages offered for the conclusion of the contract;
   (e) any contract terms used.

(2) The business has a duty to ensure that the contract terms referred to in
paragraph (1)(e) are available in textual form.

(3) If a business has failed to comply with the duty under paragraph (1)
and a contract has been concluded in the circumstances there stated,
the other party has a right to withdraw from the contract by giving
notice to the business within the period specified in II. – 5:103 (Withdrawal period).

(4) A business is liable to the consumer for any loss caused by a breach of
the duty under paragraph (1).

II. – 3:106: Clarity and form of information

(1) A duty to provide information imposed on a business under this Chapter is not fulfilled unless the requirements of this Article are satisfied.

(2) The information must be clear and precise, and expressed in plain and
intelligible language.

(3) Where rules for specific contracts require information to be provided
on a durable medium or in another particular form it must be provided
in that way.

(4) In the case of contracts between a business and a consumer concluded
at a distance, information about the main characteristics of any goods,

other assets or services to be supplied, the price, the address and identity of the business with which the consumer is transacting, the terms
of the contract, the rights and obligations of both contracting parties,
and any available redress procedures, as may be appropriate in the particular case, must be confirmed in textual form on a durable medium at
the time of conclusion of the contract. The information on the right of
withdrawal must also be adequate in the sense of II. – 5:104 (Adequate
information on the right to withdraw).

II. – 3:107: Information about price and additional charges
Where under this Chapter a business has a duty to provide information
about price, the duty is not fulfilled unless what is provided:
(a) includes information about any deposits payable, delivery charges and
    any additional taxes and duties where these may be indicated separate-
    ly;
(b) if an exact price cannot be indicated, gives such information on the
    basis for the calculation as will enable the consumer to verify the price;
    and
(c) if the price is not payable in one sum, includes information about the
    payment schedule.

II. – 3:108: Information about address and identity of business
(1) Where under this Chapter a business has a duty to provide information
    about its address and identity, the duty is not fulfilled unless the in-
    formation includes:
    (a) the name of the business;
    (b) any trading names relevant to the contract in question;
    (c) the registration number in any official register, and the name of
        that register;
    (d) the geographical address of the business;
    (e) contact details;
    (f) where the business has a representative in the consumer's state of
        residence, the address and identity of that representative;
    (g) where the activity of the business is subject to an authorisation
        scheme, the particulars of the relevant supervisory authority; and
    (h) where the business exercises an activity which is subject to VAT,
        the relevant VAT identification number.

(2) For the purpose of II. – 3:103 (Duty to provide information when concluding contract with a consumer who is at a particular disadvantage),
the address and identity of the business include only the information
indicated in paragraph (1)(a), (c), (d) and (e).

II. – 3:109: Remedies for breach of information duties

(1) If a business has a duty under II. – 3:103 (Duty to provide information
when concluding contract with a consumer who is at a particular disadvantage) to provide information to a consumer before the conclusion
of a contract from which the consumer has the right to withdraw, the
withdrawal period does not commence until all this information has
been provided. Regardless of this, the right of withdrawal lapses after
one year from the time of the conclusion of the contract.

(2) If a business has failed to comply with any duty imposed by the preceding Articles of this Section and a contract has been concluded, the
business has such obligations under the contract as the other party has
reasonably expected as a consequence of the absence or incorrectness
of the information. Remedies provided under Book III, Chapter 3 apply
to non-performance of these obligations.

(3) Whether or not a contract is concluded, a business which has failed to
comply with any duty imposed by the preceding Articles of this Section
is liable for any loss caused to the other party to the transaction by such
failure. This paragraph does not apply to the extent that a remedy is
available for non-performance of a contractual obligation under the
preceding paragraph.

(4) The remedies provided under this Article are without prejudice to any
remedy which may be available under II. – 7:201 (Mistake).

(5) In relations between a business and a consumer the parties may not, to
the detriment of the consumer, exclude the application of this Article
or derogate from or vary its effects.

Section 2:
Duty to prevent input errors and acknowledge receipt

II. – 3:201: Correction of input errors

(1) A business which intends to conclude a contract by making available
electronic means without individual communication for concluding it

has a duty to make available to the other party appropriate, effective and accessible technical means for identifying and correcting input errors before the other party makes or accepts an offer.

(2) Where a person concludes a contract in error because of a failure by a business to comply with the duty under paragraph (1) the business is liable for any loss caused to that person by such failure. This is without prejudice to any remedy which may be available under II. – 7:201 (Mistake).

(3) In relations between a business and a consumer the parties may not, to the detriment of the consumer, exclude the application of this Article or derogate from or vary its effects.

II. – 3:202: Acknowledgement of receipt

(1) A business which offers the facility to conclude a contract by electronic means and without individual communication has a duty to acknowledge by electronic means the receipt of an offer or an acceptance by the other party.

(2) If the other party does not receive the acknowledgement without undue delay, that other party may revoke the offer or withdraw from the contract.

(3) The business is liable for any loss caused to the other party by a breach of the duty under paragraph (1).

(4) In relations between a business and a consumer the parties may not, to the detriment of the consumer, exclude the application of this Article or derogate from or vary its effects.

Section 3:
Negotiation and confidentiality duties

II. – 3:301: Negotiations contrary to good faith and fair dealing

(1) A person is free to negotiate and is not liable for failure to reach an agreement.

(2) A person who is engaged in negotiations has a duty to negotiate in accordance with good faith and fair dealing and not to break off negotiations contrary to good faith and fair dealing. This duty may not be excluded or limited by contract.

(3) A person who is in breach of the duty is liable for any loss caused to the other party by the breach.

(4) It is contrary to good faith and fair dealing, in particular, for a person to enter into or continue negotiations with no real intention of reaching an agreement with the other party.

II. – 3:302: Breach of confidentiality

(1) If confidential information is given by one party in the course of negotiations, the other party is under a duty not to disclose that information or use it for that party's own purposes whether or not a contract is subsequently concluded.

(2) In this Article, "confidential information" means information which, either from its nature or the circumstances in which it was obtained, the party receiving the information knows or could reasonably be expected to know is confidential to the other party.

(3) A party who reasonably anticipates a breach of the duty may obtain a court order prohibiting it.

(4) A party who is in breach of the duty is liable for any loss caused to the other party by the breach and may be ordered to pay over to the other party any benefit obtained by the breach.

Section 4:
Unsolicited goods or services

II. – 3:401: No obligation arising from failure to respond

(1) If a business delivers unsolicited goods to, or performs unsolicited services for, a consumer:

    (a) no contract arises from the consumer's failure to respond or from any other action or inaction by the consumer in relation to the goods and services; and

    (b) no non-contractual obligation arises from the consumer's acquisition, retention, rejection or use of the goods or receipt of benefit from the services.

(2) Sub-paragraph (b) of the preceding paragraph does not apply if the goods or services were supplied:

(a) by way of benevolent intervention in another's affairs; or

(b) in error or in such other circumstances that there is a right to re-versal of an unjustified enrichment.

(3) This Article is subject to the rules on delivery of excess quantity under a contract for the sale of goods.

(4) For the purposes of paragraph (1) delivery occurs when the consumer obtains physical control over the goods.

Section 5:
Damages for breach of duty under this Chapter

II. – 3:501: Liability for damages

(1) Where any rule in this Chapter makes a person liable for loss caused to another person by a breach of a duty, the other person has a right to damages for that loss.

(2) The rules on III. – 3:704 (Loss attributable to creditor) and III. – 3:705 (Reduction of loss) apply with the adaptation that the reference to non-performance of the obligation is to be taken as a reference to breach of the duty.

Chapter 4:
Formation
Section 1:
General provisions

II. – 4:101: Requirements for the conclusion of a contract

A contract is concluded, without any further requirement, if the parties:

(a) intend to enter into a binding legal relationship or bring about some other legal effect; and

(b) reach a sufficient agreement.

II. – 4:102: How intention is determined

The intention of a party to enter into a binding legal relationship or bring about some other legal effect is to be determined from the party's state-ments or conduct as they were reasonably understood by the other party.

II. – 4:103: Sufficient agreement

(1) Agreement is sufficient if:
- (a) the terms of the contract have been sufficiently defined by the parties for the contract to be given effect; or
- (b) the terms of the contract, or the rights and obligations of the parties under it, can be otherwise sufficiently determined for the contract to be given effect.

(2) If one of the parties refuses to conclude a contract unless the parties have agreed on some specific matter, there is no contract unless agreement on that matter has been reached.

II. – 4:104: Merger clause

(1) If a contract document contains an individually negotiated term stating that the document embodies all the terms of the contract (a merger clause), any prior statements, undertakings or agreements which are not embodied in the document do not form part of the contract.

(2) If the merger clause is not individually negotiated it establishes only a presumption that the parties intended that their prior statements, undertakings or agreements were not to form part of the contract. This rule may not be excluded or restricted.

(3) The parties' prior statements may be used to interpret the contract. This rule may not be excluded or restricted except by an individually negotiated term.

(4) A party may by statements or conduct be precluded from asserting a merger clause to the extent that the other party has reasonably relied on such statements or conduct.

II. – 4:105: Modification in certain form only

(1) A term in a contract requiring any agreement to modify its terms, or to terminate the relationship resulting from it, to be in a certain form establishes only a presumption that any such agreement is not intended to be legally binding unless it is in that form.

(2) A party may by statements or conduct be precluded from asserting such a term to the extent that the other party has reasonably relied on such statements or conduct.

Section 2:
Offer and acceptance

II. – 4:201: Offer
(1) A proposal amounts to an offer if:
  (a) it is intended to result in a contract if the other party accepts it; and
  (b) it contains sufficiently definite terms to form a contract.
(2) An offer may be made to one or more specific persons or to the public.
(3) A proposal to supply goods from stock, or a service, at a stated price made by a business in a public advertisement or a catalogue, or by a display of goods, is treated, unless the circumstances indicate otherwise, as an offer to supply at that price until the stock of goods, or the business's capacity to supply the service, is exhausted.

II. – 4:202: Revocation of offer
(1) An offer may be revoked if the revocation reaches the offeree before the offeree has dispatched an acceptance or, in cases of acceptance by conduct, before the contract has been concluded.
(2) An offer made to the public can be revoked by the same means as were used to make the offer.
(3) However, a revocation of an offer is ineffective if:
  (a) the offer indicates that it is irrevocable;
  (b) the offer states a fixed time for its acceptance; or
  (c) it was reasonable for the offeree to rely on the offer as being irrevocable and the offeree has acted in reliance on the offer.
(4) Paragraph (3) does not apply to an offer if the offeror would have a right under any rule in Books II to IV to withdraw from a contract resulting from its acceptance. The parties may not, to the detriment of the offeror, exclude the application of this rule or derogate from or vary its effects.

II. – 4:203: Rejection of offer
When a rejection of an offer reaches the offeror, the offer lapses.

II. – 4:204: Acceptance
(1) Any form of statement or conduct by the offeree is an acceptance if it indicates assent to the offer.
(2) Silence or inactivity does not in itself amount to acceptance.

II. – 4:205: Time of conclusion of the contract
(1) If an acceptance has been dispatched by the offeree the contract is concluded when the acceptance reaches the offeror.
(2) In the case of acceptance by conduct, the contract is concluded when notice of the conduct reaches the offeror.
(3) If by virtue of the offer, of practices which the parties have established between themselves, or of a usage, the offeree may accept the offer by doing an act without notice to the offeror, the contract is concluded when the offeree begins to do the act.

II. – 4:206: Time limit for acceptance
(1) An acceptance of an offer is effective only if it reaches the offeror within the time fixed by the offeror.
(2) If no time has been fixed by the offeror the acceptance is effective only if it reaches the offeror within a reasonable time.
(3) Where an offer may be accepted by performing an act without notice to the offeror, the acceptance is effective only if the act is performed within the time for acceptance fixed by the offeror or, if no such time is fixed, within a reasonable time.

II. – 4:207: Late acceptance
(1) A late acceptance is nonetheless effective as an acceptance if without undue delay the offeror informs the offeree that it is treated as an effective acceptance.
(2) If a letter or other communication containing a late acceptance shows that it has been dispatched in such circumstances that if its transmission had been normal it would have reached the offeror in due time, the late acceptance is effective as an acceptance unless, without undue delay, the offeror informs the offeree that the offer is considered to have lapsed.

II. – 4:208: Modified acceptance

(1) A reply by the offeree which states or implies additional or different terms which materially alter the terms of the offer is a rejection and a new offer.

(2) A reply which gives a definite assent to an offer operates as an acceptance even if it states or implies additional or different terms, provided these do not materially alter the terms of the offer. The additional or different terms then become part of the contract.

(3) However, such a reply is treated as a rejection of the offer if:
    (a) the offer expressly limits acceptance to the terms of the offer;
    (b) the offeror objects to the additional or different terms without undue delay; or
    (c) the offeree makes the acceptance conditional upon the offeror's assent to the additional or different terms, and the assent does not reach the offeree within a reasonable time.

II. – 4:209: Conflicting standard terms

(1) If the parties have reached agreement except that the offer and acceptance refer to conflicting standard terms, a contract is nonetheless formed. The standard terms form part of the contract to the extent that they are common in substance.

(2) However, no contract is formed if one party:
    (a) has indicated in advance, explicitly, and not by way of standard terms, an intention not to be bound by a contract on the basis of paragraph (1); or
    (b) without undue delay, informs the other party of such an intention.

II. – 4:210: Formal confirmation of contract between businesses

If businesses have concluded a contract but have not embodied it in a final document, and one without undue delay sends the other a notice in textual form on a durable medium which purports to be a confirmation of the contract but which contains additional or different terms, such terms become part of the contract unless:

(a) the terms materially alter the terms of the contract; or

(b) the addressee objects to them without undue delay.

II. – 4:211: Contracts not concluded through offer and acceptance
The rules in this Section apply with appropriate adaptations even though
the process of conclusion of a contract cannot be analysed into offer and
acceptance.

Section 3:
Other juridical acts

II. – 4:301: Requirements for a unilateral juridical act
The requirements for a unilateral juridical act are:
(a) that the party doing the act intends to be legally bound or to achieve
the relevant legal effect;
(b) that the act is sufficiently certain; and
(c) that notice of the act reaches the person to whom it is addressed or, if
the act is addressed to the public, the act is made public by advertisement, public notice or otherwise.

II. – 4:302: How intention is determined
The intention of a party to be legally bound or to achieve the relevant legal
effect is to be determined from the party's statements or conduct as they
were reasonably understood by the person to whom the act is addressed.

II. – 4:303: Right or benefit may be rejected
Where a unilateral juridical act confers a right or benefit on the person to
whom it is addressed, that person may reject it by notice to the maker of the
act, provided that is done without undue delay and before the right or
benefit has been expressly or impliedly accepted. On such rejection, the
right or benefit is treated as never having accrued.

Chapter 5:
Right of withdrawal
Section I:
Exercise and effect

II. – 5:101: Scope and mandatory nature
(1) The provisions in this Section apply where under any rule in Books II to IV a party has a right to withdraw from a contract within a certain period.
(2) The parties may not, to the detriment of the entitled party, exclude the application of the rules in this Chapter or derogate from or vary their effects.

II. – 5:102: Exercise of right to withdraw
(1) A right to withdraw is exercised by notice to the other party. No reasons need to be given.
(2) Returning the subject matter of the contract is considered a notice of withdrawal unless the circumstances indicate otherwise.

II. – 5:103: Withdrawal period
(1) A right to withdraw may be exercised at any time after the conclusion of the contract and before the end of the withdrawal period.
(2) The withdrawal period ends fourteen days after the latest of the following times;
    (a) the time of conclusion of the contract;
    (b) the time when the entitled party receives from the other party adequate information on the right to withdraw; or
    (c) if the subject matter of the contract is the delivery of goods, the time when the goods are received.
(3) The withdrawal period ends no later than one year after the time of conclusion of the contract.
(4) A notice of withdrawal is timely if dispatched before the end of the withdrawal period.

II. – 5:104: Adequate information on the right to withdraw

Adequate information on the right to withdraw requires that the right is appropriately brought to the entitled party's attention, and that the information provides, in textual form on a durable medium and in clear and comprehensible language, information about how the right may be exercised, the withdrawal period, and the name and address of the person to whom the withdrawal is to be communicated.

II. – 5:105: Effects of withdrawal

(1) Withdrawal terminates the contractual relationship and the obligations of both parties under the contract.
(2) The restitutionary effects of such termination are governed by the rules in Book III, Chapter 3, Section 5, Sub-section 4 (Restitution) as modified by this Article, unless the contract provides otherwise in favour of the withdrawing party.
(3) Where the withdrawing party has made a payment under the contract, the business has an obligation to return the payment without undue delay, and in any case not later than thirty days after the withdrawal becomes effective.
(4) The withdrawing party is not liable to pay:
    (a) for any diminution in the value of anything received under the contract caused by inspection and testing;
    (b) for any destruction or loss of, or damage to, anything received under the contract, provided the withdrawing party used reasonable care to prevent such destruction, loss or damage.
(5) The withdrawing party is liable for any diminution in value caused by normal use, unless that party had not received adequate notice of the right of withdrawal.
(6) Except as provided in this Article, the withdrawing party does not incur any liability through the exercise of the right of withdrawal.
(7) If a consumer exercises a right to withdraw from a contract after a business has made use of a contractual right to supply something of equivalent quality and price in case what was ordered is unavailable, the business must bear the cost of returning what the consumer has received under the contract.

II. – 5:106: Linked contracts

(1) If a consumer exercises a right of withdrawal from a contract for the supply of goods, other assets or services by a business, the effects of withdrawal extend to any linked contract.

(2) Where a contract is partially or exclusively financed by a credit contract, they form linked contracts, in particular:

    (a) if the business supplying goods, other assets or services finances the consumer's performance;

    (b) if a third party which finances the consumer's performance uses the services of the business for preparing or concluding the credit contract;

    (c) if the credit contract refers to specific goods, assets or services to be financed with this credit, and if this link between both contracts was suggested by the supplier of the goods, other assets or services, or by the supplier of credit; or

    (d) if there is a similar economic link.

(3) The provisions of II. – 5:105 (Effects of withdrawal) apply accordingly to the linked contract.

(4) Paragraph (1) does not apply to credit contracts financing the contracts mentioned in paragraph (2)(f) of the following Article.

Section 2:
Particular rights of withdrawal

II. – 5:201: Contracts negotiated away from business premises

(1) A consumer is entitled to withdraw from a contract under which a business supplies goods, other assets or services, including financial services, to the consumer, or is granted a personal security by the consumer, if the consumer's offer or acceptance was expressed away from the business premises.

(2) Paragraph (1) does not apply to:

    (a) a contract concluded by means of an automatic vending machine or automated commercial premises;

    (b) a contract concluded with telecommunications operators through the use of public payphones;

    (c) a contract for the construction and sale of immovable property or relating to other immovable property rights, except for rental;

(d) a contract for the supply of foodstuffs, beverages or other goods intended for everyday consumption supplied to the home, residence or workplace of the consumer by regular roundsmen;

(e) a contract concluded by means of distance communication, but outside of an organised distance sales or service-provision scheme run by the supplier;

(f) a contract for the supply of goods, other assets or services whose price depends on fluctuations in the financial market outside the supplier's control, which may occur during the withdrawal period;

(g) a contract concluded at an auction;

(h) travel and baggage insurance policies or similar short-term insurance policies of less than one month's duration.

(3) If the business has exclusively used means of distance communication for concluding the contract, paragraph (1) also does not apply if the contract is for:

(a) the supply of accommodation, transport, catering or leisure services, where the business undertakes, when the contract is concluded, to supply these services on a specific date or within a specific period;

(b) the supply of services other than financial services if performance has begun, at the consumer's express and informed request, before the end of the withdrawal period referred to in II. – 5:103 (Withdrawal period) paragraph (1);

(c) the supply of goods made to the consumer's specifications or clearly personalised or which, by reason of their nature, cannot be returned or are liable to deteriorate or expire rapidly;

(d) the supply of audio or video recordings or computer software
   (i) which were unsealed by the consumer, or
   (ii) which can be downloaded or reproduced for permanent use, in case of supply by electronic means;

(e) the supply of newspapers, periodicals and magazines;

(f) gaming and lottery services.

(4) With regard to financial services, paragraph (1) also does not apply to contracts that have been fully performed by both parties, at the consumer's express request, before the consumer exercises his or her right of withdrawal.

II. – 5:202: Timeshare contracts

(1) A consumer who acquires a right to use immovable property under a timeshare contract with a business is entitled to withdraw from the contract.

(2) Where a consumer exercises the right of withdrawal under paragraph (1), the contract may require the consumer to reimburse those expenses which:

(a) have been incurred as a result of the conclusion of and withdrawal from the contract;

(b) correspond to legal formalities which must be completed before the end of the period referred to in II. – 5:103 (Withdrawal period) paragraph (1);

(c) are reasonable and appropriate;

(d) are expressly mentioned in the contract; and

(e) are in conformity with any applicable rules on such expenses.

The consumer is not obliged to reimburse any expenses when exercising the right of withdrawal in the situation covered by paragraph (1) of II. – 3:109 (Remedies for breach of information duties).

(3) The business must not demand or accept any advance payment by the consumer during the period in which the latter may exercise the right of withdrawal. The business is obliged to return any such payment received.

Chapter 6:
Representation

II. – 6:101: Scope

(1) This Chapter applies to the external relationships created by acts of representation – that is to say, the relationships between:

(a) the principal and the third party; and

(b) the representative and the third party.

(2) It applies also to situations where a person purports to be a representative without actually being a representative.

(3) It does not apply to the internal relationship between the representative and the principal.

II. – 6:102: Definitions

(1) A "representative" is a person who has authority to affect directly the legal position of another person, the principal, in relation to a third party by acting on behalf of the principal.

(2) The "authority" of a representative is the power to affect the principal's legal position.

(3) The "authorisation" of the representative is the granting or maintaining of the authority.

(4) "Acting without authority" includes acting beyond the scope of the authority granted.

(5) A "third party", in this Chapter, includes the representative who, when acting for the principal, also acts in a personal capacity as the other party to the transaction.

II. – 6:103: Authorisation

(1) The authority of a representative may be granted by the principal or by the law.

(2) The principal's authorisation may be express or implied.

(3) If a person causes a third party reasonably and in good faith to believe that the person has authorised a representative to perform certain acts, the person is treated as a principal who has so authorised the apparent representative.

II. – 6:104: Scope of authority

(1) The scope of the representative's authority is determined by the grant.

(2) The representative has authority to perform all incidental acts necessary to achieve the purposes for which the authority was granted.

(3) A representative has authority to delegate authority to another person (the delegate) to do acts on behalf of the principal which it is not reasonable to expect the representative to do personally. The rules of this Chapter apply to acts done by the delegate.

II. – 6:105: When representative's act affects principal's legal position

When the representative acts:

(a) in the name of a principal or otherwise in such a way as to indicate to the third party an intention to affect the legal position of a principal; and

(b) within the scope of the representative's authority,

the act affects the legal position of the principal in relation to the third party as if it had been done by the principal. It does not as such give rise to any legal relation between the representative and the third party.

II. – 6:106: Representative acting in own name
When the representative, despite having authority, does an act in the representative's own name or otherwise in such a way as not to indicate to the third party an intention to affect the legal position of a principal, the act affects the legal position of the representative in relation to the third party as if done by the representative in a personal capacity. It does not as such affect the legal position of the principal in relation to the third party unless this is specifically provided for by any rule of law.

II. – 6:107: Person purporting to act as representative but not having authority
(1) When a person acts in the name of a principal or otherwise in such a way as to indicate to the third party an intention to affect the legal position of a principal but acts without authority, the act does not affect the legal position of the purported principal or, save as provided in paragraph (2), give rise to legal relations between the unauthorised person and the third party.
(2) Failing ratification by the purported principal, the person is liable to pay the third party such damages as will place the third party in the same position as if the person had acted with authority.
(3) Paragraph (2) does not apply if the third party knew or could reasonably be expected to have known of the lack of authority.

II. – 6:108: Unidentified principal
If a representative acts for a principal whose identity is to be revealed later, but fails to reveal that identity within a reasonable time after a request by the third party, the representative is treated as having acted in a personal capacity.

II. – 6:109: Conflict of interest
(1) If an act done by a representative involves the representative in a conflict of interest of which the third party knew or could reasonably be expected to have known, the principal may avoid the act according to the provisions of II. – 7:209 (Notice of avoidance) to II. – 7:213 (Partial avoidance).

(2) There is presumed to be a conflict of interest where:
  (a) the representative also acted as representative for the third party; or
  (b) the transaction was with the representative in a personal capacity.
(3) However, the principal may not avoid the act:
  (a) if the representative acted with the principal's prior consent; or
  (b) if the representative had disclosed the conflict of interest to the principal and the principal did not object within a reasonable time;
  (c) if the principal otherwise knew, or could reasonably be expected to have known, of the representative's involvement in the conflict of interest and did not object within a reasonable time; or
  (d) if, for any other reason, the representative was entitled as against the principal to do the act by virtue of IV. D. – 5:101 (Self-contracting) or IV. D. – 5:102 (Double mandate).

II. – 6:110: Several representatives
Where several representatives have authority to act for the same principal, each of them may act separately.

II. – 6:111: Ratification
(1) Where a person purports to act as a representative but acts without authority, the purported principal may ratify the act.
(2) Upon ratification, the act is considered as having been done with authority, without prejudice to the rights of other persons.
(3) The third party who knows that an act was done without authority may by notice to the purported principal specify a reasonable period of time for ratification. If the act is not ratified within that period ratification is no longer possible.

II. – 6:112: Effect of ending or restriction of authorisation
(1) The authority of a representative continues in relation to a third party who knew of the authority notwithstanding the ending or restriction of the representative's authorisation until the third party knows or can reasonably be expected to know of the ending or restriction.
(2) Where the principal is under an obligation to the third party not to end or restrict the representative's authorisation, the authority of a representative continues notwithstanding an ending or restriction of the authorisation even if the third party knows of the ending or restriction.

(3) The third party can reasonably be expected to know of the ending or restriction if, in particular, it has been communicated or publicised in the same way as the granting of the authority was originally communicated or publicised.

(4) Notwithstanding the ending of authorisation, the representative continues to have authority for a reasonable time to perform those acts which are necessary to protect the interests of the principal or the principal's successors.

Chapter 7:
Grounds of invalidity
Section 1:
General provisions

II. – 7:101: Scope
(1) This Chapter deals with the effects of:
　　(a) mistake, fraud, threats, or unfair exploitation; and
　　(b) infringement of fundamental principles or mandatory rules.
(2) It does not deal with lack of capacity.
(3) It applies in relation to contracts and, with any necessary adaptations, other juridical acts.

II. – 7:102: Initial impossibility or lack of right or authority to dispose
A contract is not invalid, in whole or in part, merely because at the time it is concluded performance of any obligation assumed is impossible, or because a party has no right or authority to dispose of any assets to which the contract relates.

Section 2:
Vitiated consent or intention

II. – 7:201: Mistake
(1) A party may avoid a contract for mistake of fact or law existing when the contract was concluded if:

(a) the party, but for the mistake, would not have concluded the contract or would have done so only on fundamentally different terms and the other party knew or could reasonably be expected to have known this; and

(b) the other party:

    (i) caused the mistake;

    (ii) caused the contract to be concluded in mistake by leaving the mistaken party in error, contrary to good faith and fair dealing, when the other party knew or could reasonably be expected to have known of the mistake;

    (iii) caused the contract to be concluded in mistake by failing to comply with a pre-contractual information duty or a duty to make available a means of correcting input errors; or

    (iv) made the same mistake.

(2) However a party may not avoid the contract for mistake if:

    (a) the mistake was inexcusable in the circumstances; or

    (b) the risk of the mistake was assumed, or in the circumstances should be borne, by that party.

II. – 7:202: Inaccuracy in communication may be treated as mistake

An inaccuracy in the expression or transmission of a statement is treated as a mistake of the person who made or sent the statement.

II. – 7:203: Adaptation of contract in case of mistake

(1) If a party is entitled to avoid the contract for mistake but the other party performs, or indicates a willingness to perform, the obligations under the contract as it was understood by the party entitled to avoid it, the contract is treated as having been concluded as that party understood it. This applies only if the other party performs, or indicates a willingness to perform, without undue delay after being informed of the manner in which the party entitled to avoid it understood the contract and before that party acts in reliance on any notice of avoidance.

(2) After such performance or indication the right to avoid is lost and any earlier notice of avoidance is ineffective.

(3) Where both parties have made the same mistake, the court may at the request of either party bring the contract into accordance with what might reasonably have been agreed had the mistake not occurred.

II. – 7:204: Liability for loss caused by reliance on incorrect information

(1) A party who has concluded a contract in reasonable reliance on incorrect information given by the other party in the course of negotiations has a right to damages for loss suffered as a result if the provider of the information:

    (a) believed the information to be incorrect or had no reasonable grounds for believing it to be correct; and

    (b) knew or could reasonably be expected to have known that the recipient would rely on the information in deciding whether or not to conclude the contract on the agreed terms.

(2) This Article applies even if there is no right to avoid the contract.

II. – 7:205: Fraud

(1) A party may avoid a contract when the other party has induced the conclusion of the contract by fraudulent misrepresentation, whether by words or conduct, or fraudulent non-disclosure of any information which good faith and fair dealing, or any pre-contractual information duty, required that party to disclose.

(2) A misrepresentation is fraudulent if it is made with knowledge or belief that the representation is false and is intended to induce the recipient to make a mistake. A non-disclosure is fraudulent if it is intended to induce the person from whom the information is withheld to make a mistake.

(3) In determining whether good faith and fair dealing required a party to disclose particular information, regard should be had to all the circumstances, including:

    (a) whether the party had special expertise;

    (b) the cost to the party of acquiring the relevant information;

    (c) whether the other party could reasonably acquire the information by other means; and

    (d) the apparent importance of the information to the other party.

II. – 7:206: Coercion or threats

(1) A party may avoid a contract when the other party has induced the conclusion of the contract by coercion or by the threat of an imminent and serious harm which it is wrongful to inflict, or wrongful to use as a means to obtain the conclusion of the contract.

(2) A threat is not regarded as inducing the contract if in the circumstances the threatened party had a reasonable alternative.

II. – 7:207: Unfair exploitation

(1) A party may avoid a contract if, at the time of the conclusion of the contract:

    (a) the party was dependent on or had a relationship of trust with the other party, was in economic distress or had urgent needs, was improvident, ignorant, inexperienced or lacking in bargaining skill; and

    (b) the other party knew or could reasonably be expected to have known this and, given the circumstances and purpose of the contract, exploited the first party's situation by taking an excessive benefit or grossly unfair advantage.

(2) Upon the request of the party entitled to avoidance, a court may if it is appropriate adapt the contract in order to bring it into accordance with what might have been agreed had the requirements of good faith and fair dealing been observed.

(3) A court may similarly adapt the contract upon the request of a party receiving notice of avoidance for unfair exploitation, provided that this party informs the party who gave the notice without undue delay after receiving it and before that party has acted in reliance on it.

II. – 7:208: Third persons

(1) Where a third person for whose acts a party is responsible or who with a party's assent is involved in the making of a contract:

    (a) causes a mistake, or knows of or could reasonably be expected to know of a mistake; or

    (b) is guilty of fraud, coercion, threats or unfair exploitation,

remedies under this Section are available as if the behaviour or knowledge had been that of the party.

(2) Where a third person for whose acts a party is not responsible and who does not have the party's assent to be involved in the making of a contract is guilty of fraud, coercion, threats or unfair exploitation, remedies under this Section are available if the party knew or could reasonably be expected to have known of the relevant facts, or at the time of avoidance has not acted in reliance on the contract.

II. – 7:209: Notice of avoidance
Avoidance under this Section is effected by notice to the other party.

II. – 7:210: Time
A notice of avoidance under this Section is ineffective unless given within a reasonable time, with due regard to the circumstances, after the avoiding party knew or could reasonably be expected to have known of the relevant facts or became capable of acting freely.

II. – 7:211: Confirmation
If a party who is entitled to avoid a contract under this Section confirms it, expressly or impliedly, after the period of time for giving notice of avoidance has begun to run, avoidance is excluded.

II. – 7:212: Effects of avoidance
(1) A contract which may be avoided under this Section is valid until avoided but, once avoided, is retrospectively invalid from the beginning.
(2) The question whether either party has a right to the return of whatever has been transferred or supplied under a contract which has been avoided under this Section, or a monetary equivalent, is regulated by the rules on unjustified enrichment.
(3) The effect of avoidance under this Section on the ownership of property which has been transferred under the avoided contract is governed by the rules on the transfer of property.

II. – 7:213: Partial avoidance
If a ground of avoidance under this Section affects only particular terms of a contract, the effect of an avoidance is limited to those terms unless, giving due consideration to all the circumstances of the case, it is unreasonable to uphold the remaining contract.

II. – 7:214: Damages for loss
(1) A party who has the right to avoid a contract under this Section (or who had such a right before it was lost by the effect of time limits or confirmation) is entitled, whether or not the contract is avoided, to damages from the other party for any loss suffered as a result of the mistake, fraud, coercion, threats or unfair exploitation, provided that

the other party knew or could reasonably be expected to have known of the ground for avoidance.

(2) The damages recoverable are such as to place the aggrieved party as nearly as possible in the position in which that party would have been if the contract had not been concluded, with the further limitation that, if the party does not avoid the contract, the damages are not to exceed the loss caused by the mistake, fraud, coercion, threats or unfair exploitation.

(3) In other respects the rules on damages for non-performance of a contractual obligation apply with any appropriate adaptation.

II. – 7:215: Exclusion or restriction of remedies

(1) Remedies for fraud, coercion, threats and unfair exploitation cannot be excluded or restricted.

(2) Remedies for mistake may be excluded or restricted unless the exclusion or restriction is contrary to good faith and fair dealing.

II. – 7:216: Overlapping remedies

A party who is entitled to a remedy under this Section in circumstances which afford that party a remedy for non-performance may pursue either remedy.

Section 3:
Infringement of fundamental principles or mandatory rules

II. – 7:301: Contracts infringing fundamental principles

A contract is void to the extent that:

(a) it infringes a principle recognised as fundamental in the laws of the Member States of the European Union; and

(b) nullity is required to give effect to that principle.

II. – 7:302: Contracts infringing mandatory rules

(1) Where a contract is not void under the preceding Article but infringes a mandatory rule of law, the effects of that infringement on the validity of the contract are the effects, if any, expressly prescribed by that mandatory rule.

(2) Where the mandatory rule does not expressly prescribe the effects of an infringement on the validity of a contract, a court may:
  (a) declare the contract to be valid;
  (b) avoid the contract, with retrospective effect, in whole or in part; or
  (c) modify the contract or its effects.
(3) A decision reached under paragraph (2) should be an appropriate and proportional response to the infringement, having regard to all relevant circumstances, including:
  (a) the purpose of the rule which has been infringed;
  (b) the category of persons for whose protection the rule exists;
  (c) any sanction that may be imposed under the rule infringed;
  (d) the seriousness of the infringement;
  (e) whether the infringement was intentional; and
  (f) the closeness of the relationship between the infringement and the contract.

II. – 7:303: Effects of nullity or avoidance
(1) The question whether either party has a right to the return of whatever has been transferred or supplied under a contract, or part of a contract, which is void or has been avoided under this Section, or a monetary equivalent, is regulated by the rules on unjustified enrichment.
(2) The effect of nullity or avoidance under this Section on the ownership of property which has been transferred under the void or avoided contract, or part of a contract, is governed by the rules on the transfer of property.
(3) This Article is subject to the powers of the court to modify the contract or its effects.

II. – 7:304: Damages for loss
(1) A party to a contract which is void or avoided, in whole or in part, under this Section is entitled to damages from the other party for any loss suffered as a result of the invalidity, provided that the first party did not know and could not reasonably be expected to have known, and the other party knew or could reasonably be expected to have known, of the infringement.

(2) The damages recoverable are such as to place the aggrieved party as nearly as possible in the position in which that party would have been if the contract had not been concluded or the infringing term had not been included.

Chapter 8:
Interpretation
Section 1:
Interpretation of contracts

II. – 8:101: General rules
(1) A contract is to be interpreted according to the common intention of the parties even if this differs from the literal meaning of the words.
(2) If one party intended the contract, or a term or expression used in it, to have a particular meaning, and at the time of the conclusion of the contract the other party was aware, or could reasonably be expected to have been aware, of the first party's intention, the contract is to be interpreted in the way intended by the first party.
(3) The contract is, however, to be interpreted according to the meaning which a reasonable person would give to it:
  (a) if an intention cannot be established under the preceding paragraphs; or
  (b) if the question arises with a person, not being a party to the contract or a person who by law has no better rights than such a party, who has reasonably and in good faith relied on the contract's apparent meaning.

II. – 8:102: Relevant matters
(1) In interpreting the contract, regard may be had, in particular, to:
  (a) the circumstances in which it was concluded, including the preliminary negotiations;
  (b) the conduct of the parties, even subsequent to the conclusion of the contract;
  (c) the interpretation which has already been given by the parties to terms or expressions which are the same as, or similar to, those used in the contract and the practices they have established between themselves;

   (d) the meaning commonly given to such terms or expressions in the
       branch of activity concerned and the interpretation such terms or
       expressions may already have received;
   (e) the nature and purpose of the contract;
   (f) usages; and
   (g) good faith and fair dealing.
(2) In a question with a person, not being a party to the contract or a
    person such as an assignee who by law has no better rights than such
    a party, who has reasonably and in good faith relied on the contract's
    apparent meaning, regard may be had to the circumstances mentioned
    in sub-paragraphs (a) to (c) above only to the extent that those cir-
    cumstances were known to, or could reasonably be expected to have
    been known to, that person.

II. – 8:103: Interpretation against supplier of term or dominant party

(1) Where there is doubt about the meaning of a term not individually
    negotiated, an interpretation of the term against the party who sup-
    plied it is to be preferred.
(2) Where there is doubt about the meaning of any other term, and that
    term has been established under the dominant influence of one party,
    an interpretation of the term against that party is to be preferred.

II. – 8:104: Preference for negotiated terms

Terms which have been individually negotiated take preference over those
which have not.

II. – 8:105: Reference to contract as a whole

Terms and expressions are to be interpreted in the light of the whole contract in which they appear.

II. – 8:106: Preference for interpretation which gives terms effect

An interpretation which renders the terms of the contract lawful, or effective, is to be preferred to one which would not.

II. – 8:107: Linguistic discrepancies

Where a contract document is in two or more language versions none of
which is stated to be authoritative, there is, in case of discrepancy between
the versions, a preference for the interpretation according to the version in
which the contract was originally drawn up.

Section 2:
Interpretation of other juridical acts

II. – 8:201: General rules

(1) A unilateral juridical act is to be interpreted in the way in which it could
    reasonably be expected to be understood by the person to whom it is
    addressed.
(2) If the person making the juridical act intended the act, or a term or
    expression used in it, to have a particular meaning, and at the time of
    the act the person to whom it was addressed was aware, or could rea-
    sonably be expected to have been aware, of the first person's intention,
    the act is to be interpreted in the way intended by the first person.
(3) The act is, however, to be interpreted according to the meaning which
    a reasonable person would give to it:
    (a) if neither paragraph (1) nor paragraph (2) applies; or
    (b) if the question arises with a person, not being the addressee or a
        person who by law has no better rights than the addressee, who
        has reasonably and in good faith relied on the contract's apparent
        meaning.

II. – 8:202: Application of other rules by analogy

The provisions of Section 1, apart from its first Article, apply with appropriate adaptations to the interpretation of a juridical act other than a contract.

Chapter 9:
Contents and effects of contracts
Section 1:
Contents

II. – 9:101: Terms of a contract
(1) The terms of a contract may be derived from the express or tacit agreement of the parties, from rules of law or from practices established between the parties or usages.
(2) Where it is necessary to provide for a matter which the parties have not foreseen or provided for, a court may imply an additional term, having regard in particular to:
    (a) the nature and purpose of the contract;
    (b) the circumstances in which the contract was concluded; and
    (c) the requirements of good faith and fair dealing.
(3) Any term implied under paragraph (2) should, where possible, be such as to give effect to what the parties, had they provided for the matter, would probably have agreed.
(4) Paragraph (2) does not apply if the parties have deliberately left a matter unprovided for, accepting the consequences of so doing.

II. – 9:102: Certain pre-contractual statements regarded as contract terms
(1) A statement made by one party before a contract is concluded is regarded as a term of the contract if the other party reasonably understood it as being made on the basis that it would form part of the contract terms if a contract were concluded. In assessing whether the other party was reasonable in understanding the statement in that way account may be taken of:
    (a) the apparent importance of the statement to the other party;
    (b) whether the party was making the statement in the course of business; and
    (c) the relative expertise of the parties.
(2) If one of the parties to a contract is a business and before the contract is concluded makes a statement, either to the other party or publicly,

about the specific characteristics of what is to be supplied by that business under the contract, the statement is regarded as a term of the contract unless:

(a) the other party was aware when the contract was concluded, or could reasonably be expected to have been so aware, that the statement was incorrect or could not otherwise be relied on as such a term; or

(b) the other party's decision to conclude the contract was not influenced by the statement.

(3) For the purposes of paragraph (2), a statement made by a person engaged in advertising or marketing on behalf of the business is treated as being made by the business.

(4) Where the other party is a consumer then, for the purposes of paragraph (2), a public statement made by or on behalf of a producer or other person in earlier links of the business chain between the producer and the consumer is treated as being made by the business unless the business, at the time of conclusion of the contract, did not know and could not reasonably be expected to have known of it.

(5) In the circumstances covered by paragraph (4) a business which at the time of conclusion of the contract did not know and could not reasonably be expected to have known that the statement was incorrect has a right to be indemnified by the person making the statement for any liability incurred as a result of that paragraph.

(6) In relations between a business and a consumer the parties may not, to the detriment of the consumer, exclude the application of this Article or derogate from or vary its effects.

II. – 9:103: Terms not individually negotiated

(1) Terms supplied by one party and not individually negotiated may be invoked against the other party only if the other party was aware of them, or if the party supplying the terms took reasonable steps to draw the other party's attention to them, before or when the contract was concluded.

(2) If a contract is to be concluded by electronic means, the party supplying any terms which have not been individually negotiated may invoke them against the other party only if they are made available to the other party in textual form.

(3) For the purposes of this Article
   (a) "not individually negotiated" has the meaning given by II. – 1:110 (Terms "not individually negotiated"); and
   (b) terms are not sufficiently brought to the other party's attention by a mere reference to them in a contract document, even if that party signs the document.

II. – 9:104: Determination of price

Where the amount of the price payable under a contract cannot be determined from the terms agreed by the parties, from any other applicable rule of law or from usages or practices, the price payable is the price normally charged in comparable circumstances at the time of the conclusion of the contract or, if no such price is available, a reasonable price.

II. – 9:105: Unilateral determination by a party

Where the price or any other contractual term is to be determined by one party and that party's determination is grossly unreasonable then, notwithstanding any provision in the contract to the contrary, a reasonable price or other term is substituted.

II. – 9:106: Determination by a third person

(1) Where a third person is to determine the price or any other contractual term and cannot or will not do so, a court may, unless this is inconsistent with the terms of the contract, appoint another person to determine it.
(2) If a price or other term determined by a third person is grossly unreasonable, a reasonable price or term is substituted.

II. – 9:107: Reference to a non-existent factor

Where the price or any other contractual term is to be determined by reference to a factor which does not exist or has ceased to exist or to be accessible, the nearest equivalent factor is substituted unless this would be unreasonable in the circumstances, in which case a reasonable price or other term is substituted.

II. – 9:108: Quality

Where the quality of anything to be supplied or provided under the contract cannot be determined from the terms agreed by the parties, from any other applicable rule of law or from usages or practices, the quality required is the quality which the recipient could reasonably expect in the circumstances.

II. – 9:109: Language

Where the language to be used for communications relating to the contract or the rights or obligations arising from it cannot be determined from the terms agreed by the parties, from any other applicable rule of law or from usages or practices, the language to be used is that used for the conclusion of the contract.

Section 2:
Simulation

II. – 9:201: Effect of simulation

(1) When the parties have concluded a contract or an apparent contract and have deliberately done so in such a way that it has an apparent effect different from the effect which the parties intend it to have, the parties' true intention prevails.

(2) However, the apparent effect prevails in relation to a person, not being a party to the contract or apparent contract or a person who by law has no better rights than such a party, who has reasonably and in good faith relied on the apparent effect.

Section 3:
Effect of stipulation in favour of a third party

II. – 9:301: Basic rules

(1) The parties to a contract may, by the contract, confer a right or other benefit on a third party. The third party need not be in existence or identified at the time the contract is concluded.

(2) The nature and content of the third party's right or benefit are determined by the contract and are subject to any conditions or other limitations under the contract.

(3) The benefit conferred may take the form of an exclusion or limitation of the third party's liability to one of the contracting parties.

II. – 9:302: Rights, remedies and defences

Where one of the contracting parties is bound to render a performance to the third party under the contract, then, in the absence of provision to the contrary in the contract:

(a) the third party has the same rights to performance and remedies for non-performance as if the contracting party was bound to render the performance under a binding unilateral undertaking in favour of the third party; and

(b) the contracting party may assert against the third party all defences which the contracting party could assert against the other party to the contract.

II. – 9:303: Rejection or revocation of benefit

(1) The third party may reject the right or benefit by notice to either of the contracting parties, if that is done without undue delay after being notified of the right or benefit and before it has been expressly or impliedly accepted. On such rejection, the right or benefit is treated as never having accrued to the third party.

(2) The contracting parties may remove or modify the contractual term conferring the right or benefit if this is done before either of them has given the third party notice that the right or benefit has been conferred. The contract determines whether and by whom and in what circumstances the right or benefit can be revoked or modified after that time.

(3) Even if the right or benefit conferred is by virtue of the contract revocable or subject to modification, the right to revoke or modify is lost if the parties have, or the party having the right to revoke or modify has, led the third party to believe that it is not revocable or subject to modification and if the third party has reasonably acted in reliance on it.

Section 4:
Unfair terms

II. – 9:401: Mandatory nature of following provisions
The parties may not exclude the application of the provisions in this Section or derogate from or vary their effects.

II. – 9:402: Duty of transparency in terms not individually negotiated
(1) A person who supplies terms which have not been individually negotiated has a duty to ensure that they are drafted and communicated in plain, intelligible language.
(2) In a contract between a business and a consumer a term which has been supplied by the business in breach of the duty of transparency imposed by paragraph (1) may on that ground alone be considered unfair.

II. – 9:403: Meaning of "unfair" in contracts between a business and a consumer
In a contract between a business and a consumer, a term [which has not been individually negotiated] is unfair for the purposes of this Section if it is supplied by the business and if it significantly disadvantages the consumer, contrary to good faith and fair dealing.

II. – 9:404: Meaning of "unfair" in contracts between non-business parties
In a contract between parties neither of whom is a business, a term is unfair for the purposes of this Section only if it is a term forming part of standard terms supplied by one party and significantly disadvantages the other party, contrary to good faith and fair dealing.

II. – 9:405: Meaning of "unfair" in contracts between businesses
A term in a contract between businesses is unfair for the purposes of this Section only if it is a term forming part of standard terms supplied by one party and of such a nature that its use grossly deviates from good commercial practice, contrary to good faith and fair dealing.

II. – 9:406: Exclusions from unfairness test

(1) Contract terms are not subjected to an unfairness test under this Section if they are based on:
  (a) provisions of the applicable law;
  (b) international conventions to which the Member States are parties, or to which the European Union is a party; or
  (c) these rules.

(2) For contract terms which are drafted in plain and intelligible language, the unfairness test extends neither to the definition of the main subject matter of the contract, nor to the adequacy of the price to be paid.

II. – 9:407: Factors to be taken into account in assessing unfairness

(1) When assessing the unfairness of a contractual term for the purposes of this Section, regard is to be had to the duty of transparency under II. – 9:402 (Duty of transparency in terms not individually negotiated), to the nature of what is to be provided under the contract, to the circumstances prevailing during the conclusion of the contract, to the other terms of the contract and to the terms of any other contract on which the contract depends.

(2) For the purposes of II. – 9:403 (Meaning of "unfair" in contracts between a business and a consumer) the circumstances prevailing during the conclusion of the contract include the extent to which the consumer was given a real opportunity to become acquainted with the term before the conclusion of the contract.

II. – 9:408: Effects of unfair terms

(1) A term which is unfair under this Section is not binding on the party who did not supply it.

(2) If the contract can reasonably be maintained without the unfair term, the other terms remain binding on the parties.

II. – 9:409: Exclusive jurisdiction clauses

(1) A term in a contract between a business and a consumer is unfair for the purposes of this Section if it is supplied by the business and if it confers exclusive jurisdiction for all disputes arising under the contract on the court for the place where the business is domiciled.

(2) Paragraph (1) does not apply if the chosen court is also the court for the place where the consumer is domiciled.

II. – 9:410: Terms which are presumed to be unfair in contracts between a business and a consumer

(1) A term in a contract between a business and a consumer is presumed to be unfair for the purposes of this Section if it is supplied by the business and if it:

(a) excludes or limits the liability of a business for death or personal injury caused to a consumer through an act or omission of that business;

(b) inappropriately excludes or limits the remedies, including any right to set-off, available to the consumer against the business or a third party for non-performance by the business of obligations under the contract;

(c) makes binding on a consumer an obligation which is subject to a condition the fulfilment of which depends solely on the intention of the business;

(d) permits a business to keep money paid by a consumer if the latter decides not to conclude the contract, or perform obligations under it, without providing for the consumer to receive compensation of an equivalent amount from the business in the reverse situation;

(e) requires a consumer who fails to perform his or her obligations to pay a disproportionately high amount of damages;

(f) entitles a business to withdraw from or terminate the contractual relationship on a discretionary basis without giving the same right to the consumer, or entitles a business to keep money paid for services not yet supplied in the case where the business withdraws from or terminates the contractual relationship;

(g) enables a business to terminate a contractual relationship of indeterminate duration without reasonable notice, except where there are serious grounds for doing so; this does not affect terms in financial services contracts where there is a valid reason, provided that the supplier is required to inform the other contracting party thereof immediately;

(h) automatically extends a contract of fixed duration unless the consumer indicates otherwise, in cases where such terms provide for an unreasonably early deadline;

(i) enables a business to alter the terms of the contract unilaterally
without a valid reason which is specified in the contract; this does
not affect terms under which a supplier of financial services reserves the right to change the rate of interest to be paid by, or to,
the consumer, or the amount of other charges for financial services
without notice where there is a valid reason, provided that the
supplier is required to inform the consumer at the earliest opportunity and that the consumer is free to terminate the contractual
relationship with immediate effect; neither does it affect terms under which a business reserves the right to alter unilaterally the conditions of a contract of indeterminate duration, provided that the
business is required to inform the consumer with reasonable notice, and that the consumer is free to terminate the contractual
relationship;

(j) enables a business to alter unilaterally without a valid reason any
characteristics of the goods, other assets or services to be provided;

(k) provides that the price of goods or other assets is to be determined
at the time of delivery or supply, or allows a business to increase
the price without giving the consumer the right to withdraw if the
increased price is too high in relation to the price agreed at the
conclusion of the contract; this does not affect price-indexation
clauses, where lawful, provided that the method by which prices
vary is explicitly described;

(l) gives a business the right to determine whether the goods, other
assets or services supplied are in conformity with the contract, or
gives the business the exclusive right to interpret any term of the
contract;

(m) limits the obligation of a business to respect commitments undertaken by its agents, or makes its commitments subject to compliance with a particular formality;

(n) obliges a consumer to fulfil all his or her obligations where the
business fails to fulfil its own;

(o) allows a business to transfer its rights and obligations under the
contract without the consumer's consent, if this could reduce the
guarantees available to the consumer;

(p) excludes or restricts a consumer's right to take legal action or to
exercise any other remedy, in particular by referring the consumer

to arbitration proceedings which are not covered by legal provisions, by unduly restricting the evidence available to the consumer, or by shifting a burden of proof on to the consumer;

(q) allows a business, where what has been ordered is unavailable, to supply an equivalent without having expressly informed the consumer of this possibility and of the fact that the business must bear the cost of returning what the consumer has received under the contract if the consumer exercises a right to withdraw.

(2) Subparagraphs (g), (i) and (k) do not apply to:

(a) transactions in transferable securities, financial instruments and other products or services where the price is linked to fluctuations in a stock exchange quotation or index or a financial market rate beyond the control of the business;

(b) contracts for the purchase or sale of foreign currency, traveller's cheques or international money orders denominated in foreign currency.

Book III
Obligations and corresponding rights

Chapter 1:
General

III. – 1:101: Scope of Book
This Book applies, except as otherwise provided, to all obligations within the scope of these rules, whether they are contractual or not, and to corresponding rights to performance.

III. – 1:102: Definitions
(1) An obligation is a duty to perform which one party to a legal relationship, the debtor, owes to another party, the creditor.
(2) Performance of an obligation is the doing by the debtor of what is to be done under the obligation or the not doing by the debtor of what is not to be done.
(3) Non-performance of an obligation is any failure to perform the obligation, whether or not excused, and includes delayed performance and any other performance which is not in accordance with the terms regulating the obligation.
(4) An obligation is reciprocal in relation to another obligation if:
    (a) performance of the obligation is due in exchange for performance of the other obligation;
    (b) it is an obligation to facilitate or accept performance of the other obligation; or
    (c) it is so clearly connected to the other obligation or its subject matter that performance of the one can reasonably be regarded as dependent on performance of the other.
(5) The terms regulating an obligation may be derived from a contract or other juridical act, the law or a legally binding usage or practice, or a court order; and similarly for the terms regulating a right.

III. – 1:103: Good faith and fair dealing

(1) A person has a duty to act in accordance with good faith and fair dealing in performing an obligation, in exercising a right to performance, in pursuing or defending a remedy for non-performance, or in exercising a right to terminate an obligation or contractual relationship.

(2) The duty may not be excluded or limited by contract or other juridical act.

(3) Breach of the duty does not give rise directly to the remedies for non-performance of an obligation but may preclude the person in breach from exercising or relying on a right, remedy or defence which that person would otherwise have.

III. – 1:104: Co-operation

The debtor and creditor are obliged to co-operate with each other when and to the extent that this can reasonably be expected for the performance of the debtor's obligation.

III. – 1:105: Non-discrimination

Chapter 2 (Non-discrimination) of Book II applies with appropriate adaptations to:

(a) the performance of any obligation to provide access to, or supply, goods, other assets or services which are available to members of the public;

(b) the exercise of a right to performance of any such obligation or the pursuing or defending of any remedy for non-performance of any such obligation; and

(c) the exercise of a right to terminate any such obligation.

III. – 1:106: Conditional rights and obligations

(1) The terms regulating a right, obligation or contractual relationship may provide that it is conditional upon the occurrence of an uncertain future event, so that it takes effect only if the event occurs (suspensive condition) or comes to an end if the event occurs (resolutive condition).

(2) Upon fulfilment of a suspensive condition, the relevant right, obligation or relationship takes effect.

(3) Upon fulfilment of a resolutive condition, the relevant right, obligation or relationship comes to an end.

(4) When a party, contrary to the duty of good faith and fair dealing or the obligation to co-operate, interferes with events so as to bring about the fulfilment or non-fulfilment of a condition to that party's advantage, the other party may treat the condition as not having been fulfilled or as having been fulfilled as the case may be.

(5) When a contractual obligation or relationship comes to an end on the fulfilment of a resolutive condition any restitutionary effects are regulated by the rules in Chapter 3, Section 5, Sub-section 4 (Restitution) with appropriate adaptations.

III. – 1:107: Time-limited rights and obligations

(1) The terms regulating a right, obligation or contractual relationship may provide that it is to take effect from or end at a specified time, after a specified period of time or on the occurrence of an event which is certain to occur.

(2) It will take effect or come to an end at the time or on the event without further steps having to be taken.

(3) When a contractual obligation or relationship comes to an end under this Article any restitutionary effects are regulated by the rules in Chapter 3, Section 5, Sub-section 4 (Restitution) with appropriate adaptations.

III. – 1:108: Variation or termination by agreement

(1) A right, obligation or contractual relationship may be varied or terminated by agreement at any time.

(2) Where the parties do not regulate the effects of termination, then:

    (a) it has prospective effect only and does not affect any right to damages, or a stipulated payment, for non-performance of any obligation performance of which was due before termination;

    (b) it does not affect any provision for the settlement of disputes or any other provision which is to operate even after termination; and

    (c) in the case of a contractual obligation or relationship any restitutionary effects are regulated by the rules in Chapter 3, Section 5, Sub-section 4 (Restitution) with appropriate adaptations.

III. – 1:109: Variation or termination by notice

(1) A right, obligation or contractual relationship may be varied or terminated by notice by either party where this is provided for by the terms regulating it.

(2) Where, in a case involving continuous or periodic performance of a contractual obligation, the terms of the contract do not say when the contractual relationship is to end or say that it will never end, it may be terminated by either party by giving a reasonable period of notice. In assessing whether a period of notice is reasonable, regard may be had to the interval between performances or counter-performances.

(3) Where the parties do not regulate the effects of termination, then:
  (a) it has prospective effect only and does not affect any right to damages, or a stipulated payment, for non-performance of any obligation performance of which was due before termination;
  (b) it does not affect any provision for the settlement of disputes or any other provision which is to operate even after termination; and
  (c) in the case of a contractual obligation or relationship any restitutionary effects are regulated by the rules in Chapter 3, Section 5, Sub-section 4 (Restitution) with appropriate adaptations.

III. – 1:110: Variation or termination by court on a change of circumstances

(1) An obligation must be performed even if performance has become more onerous, whether because the cost of performance has increased or because the value of what is to be received in return has diminished.

(2) If, however, performance of a contractual obligation or of an obligation arising from a unilateral juridical act becomes so onerous because of an exceptional change of circumstances that it would be manifestly unjust to hold the debtor to the obligation a court may:
  (a) vary the obligation in order to make it reasonable and equitable in the new circumstances; or
  (b) terminate the obligation at a date and on terms to be determined by the court.

(3) Paragraph (2) applies only if:
  (a) the change of circumstances occurred after the time when the obligation was incurred;

(b) the debtor did not at that time take into account, and could not reasonably be expected to have taken into account, the possibility or scale of that change of circumstances;

(c) the debtor did not assume, and cannot reasonably be regarded as having assumed, the risk of that change of circumstances; and

(d) the debtor has attempted, reasonably and in good faith, to achieve by negotiation a reasonable and equitable adjustment of the terms regulating the obligation.

III. – 1:111: Tacit prolongation

Where a contract provides for continuous or repeated performance of obligations for a definite period and the obligations continue to be performed by both parties after that period has expired, the contract becomes a contract for an indefinite period, unless the circumstances are inconsistent with the tacit consent of the parties to such prolongation.

Chapter 2:
Performance

III. – 2:101: Place of performance

(1) If the place of performance of an obligation cannot be otherwise determined from the terms regulating the obligation it is:

    (a) in the case of a monetary obligation, the creditor's place of business;

    (b) in the case of any other obligation, the debtor's place of business.

(2) For the purposes of the preceding paragraph:

    (a) if a party has more than one place of business, the place of business is that which has the closest relationship to the obligation; and

    (b) if a party does not have a place of business, or the obligation does not relate to a business matter, the habitual residence is substituted.

(3) If, in a case to which paragraph (1) applies, a party causes any increase in the expenses incidental to performance by a change in place of business or habitual residence subsequent to the time when the obligation was incurred, that party is obliged to bear the increase.

III. – 2:102: Time of performance

(1) If the time at which, or a period of time within which, an obligation is to be performed cannot otherwise be determined from the terms regulating the obligation it must be performed within a reasonable time after it arises.

(2) If a period of time within which the obligation is to be performed can be determined from the terms regulating the obligation, the obligation may be performed at any time within that period chosen by the debtor unless the circumstances of the case indicate that the creditor is to choose the time.

(3) Unless the parties have agreed otherwise, a business must perform the obligations incurred under a contract concluded at a distance for the supply of goods, other assets or services to a consumer no later than 30 days after the contract was concluded.

(4) If a business has an obligation to reimburse money received from a consumer for goods, other assets or services supplied, the reimbursement must be made as soon as possible and in any case no later than 30 days after the obligation arose.

III. – 2:103: Early performance

(1) A creditor may reject an offer to perform before performance is due unless the early performance would not cause the creditor unreasonable prejudice.

(2) A creditor's acceptance of early performance does not affect the time fixed for the performance by the creditor of any reciprocal obligation.

III. – 2:104: Order of performance

If the order of performance of reciprocal obligations cannot be otherwise determined from the terms regulating the obligations then, to the extent that the obligations can be performed simultaneously, the parties are bound to perform simultaneously unless the circumstances indicate otherwise.

III. – 2:105: Alternative obligations or methods of performance

(1) Where a debtor is bound to perform one of two or more obligations, or to perform an obligation in one of two or more ways, the choice belongs to the debtor, unless the terms regulating the obligations or obligation provide otherwise.

(2) If the party who is to make the choice fails to choose by the time when performance is due, then:
   (a) if the delay amounts to a fundamental non-performance, the right to choose passes to the other party;
   (b) if the delay does not amount to a fundamental non-performance, the other party may give a notice fixing an additional period of reasonable length within which the party to choose is required to do so. If the latter still fails to do so, the right to choose passes to the other party.

III. – 2:106: Performance entrusted to another
A debtor who entrusts performance of an obligation to another person remains responsible for performance.

III. – 2:107: Performance by a third person
(1) Where personal performance by the debtor is not required by the terms regulating the obligation, the creditor cannot refuse performance by a third person if:
   (a) the third person acts with the assent of the debtor; or
   (b) the third person has a legitimate interest in performing and the debtor has failed to perform or it is clear that the debtor will not perform at the time performance is due.
(2) Performance by a third person in accordance with paragraph (1) discharges the debtor except to the extent that the third person takes over the creditor's right by assignment or subrogation.
(3) Where personal performance by the debtor is not required and the creditor accepts performance of the debtor's obligation by a third party in circumstances not covered by paragraph (1) the debtor is discharged but the creditor is liable to the debtor for any loss caused by that acceptance.

III. – 2:108: Method of payment
(1) Payment of money due may be made by any method used in the ordinary course of business.
(2) A creditor who accepts a cheque or other order to pay or a promise to pay is presumed to do so only on condition that it will be honoured. The creditor may not enforce the original obligation to pay unless the order or promise is not honoured.

III. – 2:109: Currency of payment

(1) The debtor and the creditor may agree that payment is to be made only in a specified currency.

(2) In the absence of such agreement, a sum of money expressed in a currency other than that of the place where payment is due may be paid in the currency of that place according to the rate of exchange prevailing there at the time when payment is due.

(3) If, in a case falling within the preceding paragraph, the debtor has not paid at the time when payment is due, the creditor may require payment in the currency of the place where payment is due according to the rate of exchange prevailing there either at the time when payment is due or at the time of actual payment.

(4) Where a monetary obligation is not expressed in a particular currency, payment must be made in the currency of the place where payment is to be made.

III. – 2:110: Imputation of performance

(1) Where a debtor has to perform several obligations of the same nature and makes a performance which does not suffice to extinguish all of the obligations, then subject to paragraph (5), the debtor may at the time of performance notify the creditor of the obligation to which the performance is to be imputed.

(2) If the debtor does not make such a notification the creditor may, within a reasonable time and by notifying the debtor, impute the performance to one of the obligations.

(3) An imputation under paragraph (2) is not effective if it is to an obligation which is not yet due, or is illegal, or is disputed.

(4) In the absence of an effective imputation by either party, and subject to the following paragraph, the performance is imputed to that obligation which satisfies one of the following criteria in the sequence indicated:
   (a) the obligation which is due or is the first to fall due;
   (b) the obligation for which the creditor has the least security;
   (c) the obligation which is the most burdensome for the debtor;
   (d) the obligation which has arisen first.
   If none of the preceding criteria applies, the performance is imputed proportionately to all the obligations.

(5) In the case of a monetary obligation, a payment by the debtor is to be imputed, first, to expenses, secondly, to interest, and thirdly, to principal, unless the creditor makes a different imputation.

III. – 2:111: Property not accepted
(1) A person who has an obligation to deliver or return corporeal property other than money and who is left in possession of the property because of the creditor's failure to accept or retake the property, has an ancillary obligation to take reasonable steps to protect and preserve it.
(2) The debtor may obtain discharge from the obligation to deliver or return and from the ancillary obligation mentioned in the preceding paragraph:
    (a) by depositing the property on reasonable terms with a third person to be held to the order of the creditor, and notifying the creditor of this; or
    (b) by selling the property on reasonable terms after notice to the creditor, and paying the net proceeds to the creditor.
(3) Where, however, the property is liable to rapid deterioration or its preservation is unreasonably expensive, the debtor has an obligation to take reasonable steps to dispose of it. The debtor may obtain discharge from the obligation to deliver or return by paying the net proceeds to the creditor.
(4) The debtor left in possession is entitled to be reimbursed or to retain out of the proceeds of sale any costs reasonably incurred.

III. – 2:112: Money not accepted
(1) Where a creditor fails to accept money properly tendered by the debtor, the debtor may after notice to the creditor obtain discharge from the obligation to pay by depositing the money to the order of the creditor in accordance with the law of the place where payment is due.
(2) Paragraph (1) applies, with appropriate adaptations, to money properly tendered by a third party in circumstances where the creditor is not entitled to refuse such performance.

III. – 2:113: Costs and formalities of performance
(1) The costs of performing an obligation are borne by the debtor.
(2) In the case of a monetary obligation the debtor's obligation to pay includes taking such steps and complying with such formalities as may be necessary to enable payment to be made.

III. – 2:114: Extinctive effect of performance
Full performance extinguishes the obligation if it is:
(a) in accordance with the terms regulating the obligation; or
(b) of such a type as by law to afford the debtor a good discharge.

Chapter 3:
Remedies for non-performance
Section 1:
General

III. – 3:101: Remedies available
(1) If an obligation is not performed by the debtor and the non-performance is not excused, the creditor may resort to any of the remedies set out in this Chapter.
(2) If the debtor's non-performance is excused, the creditor may resort to any of those remedies except enforcing specific performance and damages.
(3) The creditor may not resort to any of those remedies to the extent that the creditor caused the debtor's non-performance

III. – 3:102: Cumulation of remedies
Remedies which are not incompatible may be cumulated. In particular, a creditor is not deprived of the right to damages by resorting to any other remedy.

III. – 3:103: Notice fixing additional period for performance
(1) In any case of non-performance of an obligation the creditor may by notice to the debtor allow an additional period of time for performance.
(2) During the additional period the creditor may withhold performance of the creditor's reciprocal obligations and may claim damages, but may not resort to any other remedy.

(3) If the creditor receives notice from the debtor that the debtor will not perform within that period, or if upon expiry of that period due performance has not been made, the creditor may resort to any available remedy.

III. – 3:104: Excuse due to an impediment

(1) A debtor's non-performance of an obligation is excused if it is due to an impediment beyond the debtor's control and if the debtor could not reasonably be expected to have avoided or overcome the impediment or its consequences.

(2) Where the obligation arose out of a contract or other juridical act, non-performance is not excused if the debtor could reasonably be expected to have taken the impediment into account at the time when the obligation was incurred.

(3) Where the excusing impediment is only temporary the excuse has effect for the period during which the impediment exists. However, if the delay amounts to a fundamental non-performance, the creditor may treat it as such.

(4) Where the excusing impediment is permanent the obligation is extinguished. Any reciprocal obligation is also extinguished. In the case of contractual obligations any restitutionary effects of extinction are regulated by the rules in Chapter 3, Section 5, Sub-section 4 (Restitution) with appropriate adaptations.

(5) The debtor has a duty to ensure that notice of the impediment and of its effect on the ability to perform reaches the creditor within a reasonable time after the debtor knew or could reasonably be expected to have known of these circumstances. The creditor is entitled to damages for any loss resulting from the non-receipt of such notice.

III. – 3:105: Term excluding or restricting remedies

(1) A term of a contract or other juridical act which purports to exclude or restrict liability to pay damages for personal injury (including fatal injury) caused intentionally or by gross negligence is void.

(2) A term excluding or restricting a remedy for non-performance of an obligation, even if valid and otherwise effective, having regard in particular to the rules on unfair contract terms in Book II, Chapter 9, Section 4, may nevertheless not be invoked if it would be contrary to good faith and fair dealing to do so.

III. – 3:106: Notices relating to non-performance

(1) If the creditor gives notice to the debtor because of the debtor's non-performance of an obligation or because such non-performance is anticipated, and the notice is properly dispatched or given, a delay or inaccuracy in the transmission of the notice or its failure to arrive does not prevent it from having effect.

(2) The notice has effect from the time at which it would have arrived in normal circumstances.

III. – 3:107: Failure to notify non-conformity

(1) If, in the case of an obligation to supply goods, other assets or services, the debtor supplies goods, other assets or services which are not in conformity with the terms regulating the obligation, the creditor may not rely on the lack of conformity unless the creditor gives notice to the debtor within a reasonable time specifying the nature of the lack of conformity.

(2) The reasonable time runs from the time when the goods or other assets are supplied or the service is completed or from the time, if it is later, when the creditor discovered or could reasonably be expected to have discovered the non-conformity.

(3) The debtor is not entitled to rely on paragraph (1) if the failure relates to facts which the debtor knew or could reasonably be expected to have known and which the debtor did not disclose to the creditor.

(4) This Article does not apply where the creditor is a consumer.

III. – 3:108: Business unable to fulfil consumer's order by distance communication

(1) Where a business is unable to perform its obligations under a contract concluded with a consumer by means of distance communication, it is obliged to inform the consumer immediately and refund any sums paid by the consumer without undue delay and in any case within 30 days. The consumer's remedies for non-performance remain unaffected.

(2) The parties may not, to the detriment of the consumer, exclude the application of this Article or derogate from or vary its effects.

Section 2:
Cure by debtor of non-conforming performance

III. – 3:201: Scope
This Section applies where a debtor's performance does not conform to the terms regulating the obligation.

III. – 3:202: Cure by debtor: general rules
(1) The debtor may make a new and conforming tender if that can be done within the time allowed for performance.
(2) If the debtor cannot make a new and conforming tender within the time allowed for performance but, promptly after being notified of the lack of conformity, offers to cure it within a reasonable time and at the debtor's own expense, the creditor may not pursue any remedy for non-performance, other than withholding performance, before allowing the debtor a reasonable period in which to attempt to cure the non-conformity.
(3) Paragraph (2) is subject to the provisions of the following Article.

III. – 3:203: When creditor need not allow debtor an opportunity to cure
The creditor need not, under paragraph (2) of the preceding Article, allow the debtor a period in which to attempt cure if:
(a) failure to perform a contractual obligation within the time allowed for performance amounts to a fundamental non-performance;
(b) the creditor has reason to believe that the debtor's performance was made with knowledge of the non-conformity and was not in accordance with good faith and fair dealing;
(c) the creditor has reason to believe that the debtor will be unable to effect the cure within a reasonable time and without significant inconvenience to the creditor or other prejudice to the creditor's legitimate interests; or
(d) cure would be inappropriate in the circumstances.

III. – 3:204: Consequences of allowing debtor opportunity to cure

(1) During the period allowed for cure the creditor may withhold performance of the creditor's reciprocal obligations, but may not resort to any
other remedy.

(2) If the debtor fails to effect cure within the time allowed, the creditor
may resort to any available remedy.

(3) Notwithstanding cure, the creditor retains the right to damages for any
loss caused by the debtor's initial or subsequent non-performance or
by the process of effecting cure.

III. – 3:205: Return of replaced item

(1) Where the debtor has, whether voluntarily or in compliance with an
order under III. – 3:302 (Enforcement of non-monetary obligations),
remedied a non-conforming performance by replacement, the debtor
has a right and an obligation to take back the replaced item at the
debtor's expense.

(2) The creditor is not liable to pay for any use made of the replaced item in
the period prior to the replacement.

Section 3:
Right to enforce performance

III. – 3:301: Enforcement of monetary obligations

(1) The creditor is entitled to recover money payment of which is due.

(2) Where the creditor has not yet performed the reciprocal obligation for
which payment will be due and it is clear that the debtor in the monetary obligation will be unwilling to receive performance, the creditor
may nonetheless proceed with performance and may recover payment
unless:

(a) the creditor could have made a reasonable substitute transaction
without significant effort or expense; or

(b) performance would be unreasonable in the circumstances.

III. – 3:302: Enforcement of non-monetary obligations

(1) The creditor is entitled to enforce specific performance of an obligation
other than one to pay money.

(2) Specific performance includes the remedying free of charge of a performance which is not in conformity with the terms regulating the obligation.

(3) Specific performance cannot, however, be enforced where:

    (a) performance would be unlawful or impossible;

    (b) performance would be unreasonably burdensome or expensive; or

    (c) performance would be of such a personal character that it would be unreasonable to enforce it.

(4) The creditor loses the right to enforce specific performance if performance is not requested within a reasonable time after the creditor has become, or could reasonably be expected to have become, aware of the non-performance.

(5) The creditor cannot recover damages for loss or a stipulated payment for non-performance to the extent that the creditor has increased the loss or the amount of the payment by insisting unreasonably on specific performance in circumstances where the creditor could have made a reasonable substitute transaction without significant effort or expense.

III. – 3:303: Damages not precluded

The fact that a right to enforce specific performance is excluded under the preceding Article does not preclude a claim for damages.

Section 4:
Withholding performance

III. – 3:401: Right to withhold performance of reciprocal obligation

(1) A creditor who is to perform a reciprocal obligation at the same time as, or after, the debtor performs has a right to withhold performance of the reciprocal obligation until the debtor has tendered performance or has performed.

(2) A creditor who is to perform a reciprocal obligation before the debtor performs and who reasonably believes that there will be non-performance by the debtor when the debtor's performance becomes due may withhold performance of the reciprocal obligation for as long as the

reasonable belief continues. However, the right to withhold performance is lost if the debtor gives an adequate assurance of due performance.

(3) A creditor who withholds performance in the situation mentioned in
paragraph (2) has a duty to give notice of that fact to the debtor as
soon as is reasonably practicable and is liable for any loss caused to the
debtor by a breach of that duty.

(4) The performance which may be withheld under this Article is the
whole or part of the performance as may be reasonable in the circumstances.

Section 5:
Termination

III. – 3:50I: Scope and definition

(I) This Section applies only to contractual obligations and contractual
relationships.

(2) In this Section "termination" means the termination of the contractual
relationship in whole or in part and "terminate" has a corresponding
meaning.

Sub-section I:
Grounds for termination

III. – 3:502: Termination for fundamental non-performance

(I) A creditor may terminate if the debtor's non-performance of a contractual obligation is fundamental.

(2) A non-performance of a contractual obligation is fundamental if:

  (a) it substantially deprives the creditor of what the creditor was entitled to expect under the contract, as applied to the whole or relevant part of the performance, unless at the time of conclusion of
the contract the debtor did not foresee and could not reasonably be
expected to have foreseen that result; or

  (b) it is intentional or reckless and gives the creditor reason to believe
that the debtor's future performance cannot be relied on.

III. – 3:503: Termination after notice fixing additional time for performance

(1) A creditor may terminate in a case of delay in performance of a contractual obligation which is not in itself fundamental if the creditor gives a notice fixing an additional period of time of reasonable length for performance and the debtor does not perform within that period.

(2) If the period fixed is unreasonably short, the creditor may terminate only after a reasonable period from the time of the notice.

III. – 3:504: Termination for anticipated non-performance

A creditor may terminate before performance of a contractual obligation is due if the debtor has declared that there will be a non-performance of the obligation, or it is otherwise clear that there will be such a non-performance, and if the non-performance would have been fundamental.

III. – 3:505: Termination for inadequate assurance of performance

A creditor who reasonably believes that there will be a fundamental non-performance of a contractual obligation by the debtor may terminate if the creditor demands an adequate assurance of due performance and no such assurance is provided within a reasonable time.

Sub-section 2:
Scope, exercise and loss of right to terminate

III. – 3:506: Scope of right to terminate

(1) Where the debtor's obligations under the contract are not divisible the creditor may only terminate the contractual relationship as a whole.

(2) Where the debtor's obligations under the contract are to be performed in separate parts or are otherwise divisible, then:
   (a) if there is a ground for termination under this Section of a part to which a counter-performance can be apportioned, the creditor may terminate the contractual relationship so far as it relates to that part;
   (b) the creditor may terminate the contractual relationship as a whole only if the creditor cannot reasonably be expected to accept performance of the other parts or there is a ground for termination in relation to the contractual relationship as a whole.

III. – 3:507: Notice of termination

(1) A right to terminate under this Section is exercised by notice to the debtor.

(2) Where a notice under III. – 3:503 (Termination after notice fixing additional time for performance) provides for automatic termination if the debtor does not perform within the period fixed by the notice, termination takes effect after that period or a reasonable length of time from the giving of notice (whichever is longer) without further notice.

III. – 3:508: Loss of right to terminate

(1) If performance has been tendered late or a tendered performance otherwise does not conform to the contract the creditor loses the right to terminate under this Section unless notice of termination is given within a reasonable time.

(2) Where the creditor has given the debtor a period of time to cure the non-performance under III. – 3:202 (Cure by debtor: general rules) the time mentioned in paragraph (1) begins to run from the expiry of that period. In other cases that time begins to run from the time when the creditor has become, or could reasonably be expected to have become, aware of the tender or the non-conformity.

(3) A creditor loses a right to terminate by notice under III. – 3:503 (Termination after notice fixing additional time for performance), III. – 3:504 (Termination for anticipated non-performance) or III. – 3:505 (Termination for inadequate assurance of performance) unless the creditor gives notice of termination within a reasonable time after the right has arisen.

Sub-section 3:
Effects of termination

III. – 3:509: Effect on obligations under the contract

(1) On termination under this Section, the outstanding obligations or relevant part of the outstanding obligations of the parties under the contract come to an end.

(2) Termination does not, however, affect any provision of the contract for the settlement of disputes or other provision which is to operate even after termination.

(3) A creditor who terminates under this Section retains existing rights to damages or a stipulated payment for non-performance and in addition has the same right to damages or a stipulated payment for non-performance as the creditor would have had if there had been non-performance of the now extinguished obligations of the debtor. In relation to such extinguished obligations the creditor is not regarded as having caused or contributed to the loss merely by exercising the right to terminate.

Sub-section 4:
Restitution

III. – 3:510: Restitution of benefits received by performance
(1) On termination under this Section a party (the recipient) who has received any benefit by the other's performance of obligations under the terminated contractual relationship or terminated part of the contractual relationship is obliged to return it. Where both parties have obligations to return, the obligations are reciprocal.
(2) If the performance was a payment of money, the amount received is to be repaid.
(3) To the extent that the benefit (not being money) is transferable, it is to be returned by transferring it. However, if a transfer would cause unreasonable effort or expense, the benefit may be returned by paying its value.
(4) To the extent that the benefit is not transferable it is to be returned by paying its value in accordance with III. – 3:512 (Payment of value of benefit).
(5) The obligation to return a benefit extends to any natural or legal fruits received from the benefit.

III. – 3:511: When restitution not required
(1) There is no obligation to make restitution under this Sub-section to the extent that conforming performance by one party has been met by conforming performance by the other.

(2) The terminating party may elect to treat performance as non-conforming if what was received by that party is of no, or fundamentally reduced, value to that party because of the other party's non-performance.

(3) Restitution under this Sub-section is not required where the contract was gratuitous.

III. – 3:512: Payment of value of benefit

(1) The recipient is obliged to:
   - (a) pay the value (at the time of performance) of a benefit which is not transferable or which ceases to be transferable before the time when it is to be returned; and
   - (b) pay recompense for any reduction in the value of a returnable benefit as a result of a change in the condition of the benefit between the time of receipt and the time when it is to be returned.

(2) Where there was an agreed price the value of the benefit is that proportion of the price which the value of the actual performance bears to the value of the promised performance. Where no price was agreed the value of the benefit is the sum of money which a willing and capable provider and a willing and capable recipient, knowing of any non-conformity, would lawfully have agreed.

(3) The recipient's liability to pay the value of a benefit is reduced to the extent that as a result of a non-performance of an obligation owed by the other party to the recipient:
   - (a) the benefit cannot be returned in essentially the same condition as when it was received; or
   - (b) the recipient is compelled without compensation either to dispose of it or to sustain a disadvantage in order to preserve it.

(4) The recipient's liability to pay the value of a benefit is likewise reduced to the extent that it cannot be returned in the same condition as when it was received as a result of conduct of the recipient in the reasonable, but mistaken, belief that there was no non-conformity.

III. – 3:513: Use and improvements

(1) The recipient is obliged to pay a reasonable amount for any use which the recipient makes of the benefit except in so far as the recipient is liable under III. – 3:512 (Payment of value of benefit) paragraph (1) in respect of that use.

(2) A recipient who has improved a benefit which the recipient is obliged under this Section to return has a right to payment of the value of improvements if the other party can readily obtain that value by dealing with the benefit unless:

(a) the improvement was a non-performance of an obligation owed by the recipient to the other party; or

(b) the recipient made the improvement when the recipient knew or could reasonably be expected to know that the benefit would have to be returned.

III. – 3:514: Liabilities arising after time when return due

(1) The recipient is obliged to:

(a) pay the value (at the time of performance) of a benefit which ceases to be transferable after the time when its return was due; and

(b) pay recompense for any reduction in the value of a returnable benefit as a result of a change in the condition of the benefit after the time when its return was due.

(2) If the benefit is disposed of after the time when return was due, the value to be paid is the value of any proceeds, if this is greater.

(3) Other liabilities arising from non-performance of an obligation to return a benefit are unaffected.

Section 6:
Price reduction

III. – 3:601: Right to reduce price

(1) A creditor who accepts a performance not conforming to the terms regulating the obligation may reduce the price. The reduction is to be proportionate to the decrease in the value of what was received by virtue of the performance at the time it was made compared to the value of what would have been received by virtue of a conforming performance.

(2) A creditor who is entitled to reduce the price under the preceding paragraph and who has already paid a sum exceeding the reduced price may recover the excess from the debtor.

(3) A creditor who reduces the price cannot also recover damages for the loss thereby compensated but remains entitled to damages for any further loss suffered.

(4) This Article applies with appropriate adaptations to a reciprocal obligation of the creditor other than an obligation to pay a price.

Section 7:
Damages and interest

III. – 3:701: Right to damages
(1) The creditor is entitled to damages for loss caused by the debtor's non-performance of an obligation, unless the non-performance is excused.
(2) The loss for which damages are recoverable includes future loss which is reasonably likely to occur.
(3) "Loss" includes economic and non-economic loss. "Economic loss" includes loss of income or profit, burdens incurred and a reduction in the value of property. "Non-economic loss" includes pain and suffering and impairment of the quality of life.

III. – 3:702: General measure of damages
The general measure of damages for loss caused by non-performance of an obligation is such sum as will put the creditor as nearly as possible into the position in which the creditor would have been if the obligation had been duly performed. Such damages cover loss which the creditor has suffered and gain of which the creditor has been deprived.

III. – 3:703: Foreseeability
The debtor in an obligation which arises from a contract or other juridical act is liable only for loss which the debtor foresaw or could reasonably be expected to have foreseen at the time when the obligation was incurred as a likely result of the non-performance, unless the non-performance was intentional, reckless or grossly negligent.

III. – 3:704: Loss attributable to creditor
The debtor is not liable for loss suffered by the creditor to the extent that the creditor contributed to the non-performance or its effects.

III. – 3:705: Reduction of loss
(1) The debtor is not liable for loss suffered by the creditor to the extent that the creditor could have reduced the loss by taking reasonable steps.
(2) The creditor is entitled to recover any expenses reasonably incurred in attempting to reduce the loss.

III. – 3:706: Substitute transaction
A creditor who has terminated a contractual relationship in whole or in part under Section 5 and has made a substitute transaction within a reasonable time and in a reasonable manner may, in so far as entitled to damages, recover the difference between the value of what would have been payable under the terminated relationship and the value of what is payable under the substitute transaction, as well as damages for any further loss.

III. – 3:707: Current price
Where the creditor has terminated a contractual relationship in whole or in part under Section 5 and has not made a substitute transaction but there is a current price for the performance, the creditor may, in so far as entitled to damages, recover the difference between the contract price and the price current at the time of termination as well as damages for any further loss.

III. – 3:708: Interest on late payments
(1) If payment of a sum of money is delayed, whether or not the non-performance is excused, the creditor is entitled to interest on that sum from the time when payment is due to the time of payment at the average commercial bank short-term lending rate to prime borrowers prevailing for the currency of payment at the place where payment is due.
(2) The creditor may in addition recover damages for any further loss.

III. – 3:709: When interest to be added to capital
(1) Interest payable according to the preceding Article is added to the out-standing capital every 12 months.
(2) Paragraph (1) of this Article does not apply if the parties have provided for interest upon delay in payment.

III. – 3:710: Interest in commercial contracts

(1) If a business delays the payment of a price due under a contract for the supply of goods, other assets or services without being excused under III. – 3:104 (Excuse due to an impediment), interest is due at the rate specified in paragraph (4), unless a higher interest rate is applicable.

(2) Interest at the rate specified in paragraph (4) starts to run on the day which follows the date or the end of the period for payment provided in the contract. If there is no such date or period, interest at that rate starts to run:

    (a) 30 days after the date when the debtor receives the invoice or an equivalent request for payment; or

    (b) 30 days after the date of receipt of the goods or services, if the date under (a) is earlier or uncertain, or if it is uncertain whether the debtor has received an invoice or equivalent request for payment.

(3) If conformity of goods or services to the contract is to be ascertained by way of acceptance or verification, the 30 day period under paragraph (2)(b) starts to run on the date of acceptance or verification.

(4) The interest rate for delayed payment is the interest rate applied by the European Central Bank to its most recent main refinancing operation carried out before the first calendar day of the half-year in question ("the reference rate"), plus seven percentage points. For the currency of a Member State which is not participating in the third stage of economic and monetary union, the reference rate is the equivalent rate set by its national central bank.

(5) The creditor may in addition recover damages for any further loss.

III. – 3:711: Unfair terms relating to interest

(1) A term whereby a business pays interest from a date later than that specified in the preceding Article paragraph (2) (a) and (b) and paragraph (3), or at a rate lower than that specified in paragraph (4), is not binding to the extent that this would be unfair.

(2) A term whereby a debtor is allowed to pay the price for goods, other assets or services later than the time when interest starts to run under the preceding Article paragraph (2)(a) and (b) and paragraph (3) does not deprive the creditor of interest to the extent that this would be unfair.

(3) Something is unfair for the purposes of this Article if it grossly deviates from good commercial practice, contrary to good faith and fair dealing.

III. – 3:712: Stipulated payment for non-performance

(1) Where the terms regulating an obligation provide that a debtor who fails to perform the obligation is to pay a specified sum to the creditor for such non-performance, the creditor is entitled to that sum irrespective of the actual loss.

(2) However, despite any provision to the contrary, the sum so specified in a contract or other juridical act may be reduced to a reasonable amount where it is grossly excessive in relation to the loss resulting from the non-performance and the other circumstances.

III. – 3:713: Currency by which damages to be measured

Damages are to be measured by the currency which most appropriately reflects the creditor's loss.

Chapter 4:
Plurality of debtors and creditors
Section 1:
Plurality of debtors

III. – 4:101: Scope of Section

This Section applies where two or more debtors are bound to perform one obligation.

III. – 4:102: Solidary, divided and joint obligations

(1) An obligation is solidary when each debtor is bound to perform the obligation in full and the creditor may require performance from any of them until full performance has been received.

(2) An obligation is divided when each debtor is bound to perform only part of the obligation and the creditor may claim from each debtor only performance of that debtor's part.

(3) An obligation is joint when the debtors are bound to perform the obligation together and the creditor may require performance only from all of them together.

III. – 4:103: When different types of obligation arise

(1) Whether an obligation is solidary, divided or joint depends on the terms regulating the obligation.

(2) If the terms do not determine the question, the liability of two or more debtors to perform the same obligation is solidary. Liability is solidary in particular where two or more persons are liable for the same damage.

(3) The fact that the debtors are not liable on the same terms or grounds does not prevent solidarity.

III. – 4:104: Liability under divided obligations

Debtors bound by a divided obligation are liable in equal shares.

III. – 4:105: Joint obligations: special rule when money claimed for non-performance

Notwithstanding III. – 4:102 (Solidary, divided and joint obligations) paragraph (3), when money is claimed for non-performance of a joint obligation, the debtors have solidary liability for payment to the creditor.

III. – 4:106: Apportionment between solidary debtors

(1) As between themselves, solidary debtors are liable in equal shares.

(2) If two or more debtors have solidary liability for the same damage, their share of liability as between themselves is equal unless different shares of liability are more appropriate having regard to all the circumstances of the case and in particular to fault or to the extent to which a source of danger for which one of them was responsible contributed to the occurrence or extent of the damage.

III. – 4:107: Recourse between solidary debtors

(1) A solidary debtor who has performed more than that debtor's share has a right to recover the excess from any of the other debtors to the extent of each debtor's unperformed share, together with a share of any costs reasonably incurred.

(2) A solidary debtor to whom paragraph (1) applies may also, subject to any prior right and interest of the creditor, exercise the rights and actions of the creditor, including any supporting security rights, to recover the excess from any of the other debtors to the extent of each debtor's unperformed share.

(3) If a solidary debtor who has performed more than that debtor's share is unable, despite all reasonable efforts, to recover contribution from another solidary debtor, the share of the others, including the one who has performed, is increased proportionally.

III. – 4:108: Performance, set-off and merger in solidary obligations

(1) Performance or set-off by a solidary debtor or set-off by the creditor against one solidary debtor discharges the other debtors in relation to the creditor to the extent of the performance or set-off.

(2) Merger of debts between a solidary debtor and the creditor discharges the other debtors only for the share of the debtor concerned.

III. – 4:109: Release or settlement in solidary obligations

(1) When the creditor releases, or reaches a settlement with, one solidary debtor, the other debtors are discharged of liability for the share of that debtor.

(2) As between solidary debtors, the debtor who is discharged from that debtor's share is discharged only to the extent of the share at the time of the discharge and not from any supplementary share for which that debtor may subsequently become liable under III. – 4:107 (Recourse between solidary debtors) paragraph (3).

(3) When the debtors have solidary liability for the same damage the discharge under paragraph (1) extends only so far as is necessary to prevent the creditor from recovering more than full reparation and the other debtors retain their rights of recourse against the released or settling debtor to the extent of that debtor's unperformed share.

III. – 4:110: Effect of judgment in solidary obligations

A decision by a court as to the liability to the creditor of one solidary debtor does not affect:

(a) the liability to the creditor of the other solidary debtors; or

(b) the rights of recourse between the solidary debtors under III. – 4:107 (Recourse between solidary debtors).

III. – 4:111: Prescription in solidary obligations

Prescription of the creditor's right to performance against one solidary debtor does not affect:

(a) the liability to the creditor of the other solidary debtors; or

(b) the rights of recourse between the solidary debtors under III. – 4:107 (Recourse between solidary debtors).

III. – 4:112: Opposability of other defences in solidary obligations

(1) A solidary debtor may invoke against the creditor any defence which another solidary debtor can invoke, other than a defence personal to that other debtor. Invoking the defence has no effect with regard to the other solidary debtors.

(2) A debtor from whom contribution is claimed may invoke against the claimant any personal defence that that debtor could have invoked against the creditor.

Section 2:
Plurality of creditors

III. – 4:201: Scope of section

This Section applies where two or more creditors have a right to performance under one obligation.

III. – 4:202: Solidary, divided and joint rights

(1) A right to performance is solidary when any of the creditors may require full performance from the debtor and the debtor may perform to any of the creditors.

(2) A right to performance is divided when each creditor may require performance only of that creditor's share and the debtor owes each creditor only that creditor's share.

(3) A right to performance is joint when any creditor may require performance only for the benefit of all the creditors and the debtor must perform to all the creditors.

III. – 4:203: When different types of right arise

(1) Whether a right to performance is solidary, divided or communal depends on the terms regulating the right.

(2) If the terms do not determine the question, the right of co-creditors is divided.

III. – 4:204: Apportionment in cases of divided rights

In the case of divided rights the creditors have equal shares.

III. – 4:205: Difficulties of performing in cases of joint rights

If one of the creditors who have joint rights to performance refuses to accept, or is unable to receive, the performance, the debtor may obtain discharge from the obligation by depositing the property or money with a third party according to III. – 2:111 (Property not accepted) or III. – 2:112 (Money not accepted).

III. – 4:206: Apportionment in cases of solidary rights

(1) In the case of solidary rights the creditors have equal shares.
(2) A creditor who has received more than that creditor's share has an obligation to transfer the excess to the other creditors to the extent of their respective shares.

III. – 4:207: Regime of solidary rights

(1) A release granted to the debtor by one of the solidary creditors has no effect on the other solidary creditors.
(2) The rules of III. – 4:108 (Performance, set-off and merger in solidary obligations), III. – 4:110 (Effect of judgment in solidary obligations), III. – 4:111 (Prescription in solidary obligations) and III. – 4:112 (Opposability of other defences in solidary obligations) paragraph (1) apply, with appropriate adaptations, to solidary rights to performance.

Chapter 5:
Change of parties
Section 1:
Assignment of rights
Sub-section 1:
General

III. – 5:101: Scope of Section

(1) This Section applies to the assignment, by a contract or other juridical act, of a right to performance of an obligation.
(2) It does not apply to the transfer of a financial instrument or investment security where such transfer is required to be by entry in a register maintained by or for the issuer or where there are other requirements for transfer or restrictions on transfer.

III. – 5:102: Definitions

(1) An "assignment" of a right is the transfer of the right from one person (the "assignor") to another person (the "assignee").

(2) An "act of assignment" is a contract or other juridical act which is intended to effect a transfer of the right.

(3) Where part of a right is assigned, any reference in this Section to a right includes a reference to the assigned part of the right.

III. – 5:103: Priority of provisions on proprietary securities and trusts

(1) In relation to assignments for purposes of security, the provisions of Book IX apply and have priority over the provisions in this Chapter.

(2) In relation to assignments for purposes of a trust, or to or from a trust, the provisions of Book X apply and have priority over the provisions in this Chapter.

Sub-section 2:
Requirements for assignment

III. – 5:104: Basic requirements

(1) The requirements for an assignment of a right to performance are that:
    (a) the right exists;
    (b) the right is assignable;
    (c) the person purporting to assign the right has the right or authority to transfer it;
    (d) the assignee is entitled as against the assignor to the transfer by virtue of a contract or other juridical act, a court order or a rule of law; and
    (e) there is a valid act of assignment of the right.

(2) The entitlement referred to in paragraph (1)(d) need not precede the act of assignment.

(3) The same contract or other juridical act may operate as the conferment of an entitlement and as the act of assignment.

(4) Neither notice to the debtor nor the consent of the debtor to the assignment is required.

III. – 5:105: Assignability: general rule

(1) All rights to performance are assignable except where otherwise provided by law.
(2) A right to performance which is by law accessory to another right is not assignable separately from that right.

III. – 5:106: Future and unspecified rights

(1) A future right to performance may be the subject of an act of assignment but the transfer of the right depends on its coming into existence and being identifiable as the right to which the act of assignment relates.
(2) A number of rights to performance may be assigned without individual specification if, at the time when the assignment is to take place in relation to them, they are identifiable as rights to which the act of assignment relates.

III. – 5:107: Assignability in part

(1) A right to performance of a monetary obligation may be assigned in part.
(2) A right to performance of a non-monetary obligation may be assigned in part only if:
   (a) the debtor consents to the assignment; or
   (b) the right is divisible and the assignment does not render the obligation significantly more burdensome.
(3) Where a right is assigned in part the assignor is liable to the debtor for any increased costs which the debtor thereby incurs.

III. – 5:108: Assignability: effect of contractual prohibition

(1) A contractual prohibition of, or restriction on, the assignment of a right does not affect the assignability of the right.
(2) However, where a right is assigned in breach of such a prohibition or restriction:
   (a) the debtor may perform in favour of the assignor and is discharged by so doing; and
   (b) the debtor retains all rights of set-off against the assignor as if the right had not been assigned.
(3) Paragraph (2) does not apply if:
   (a) the debtor has consented to the assignment;

(b) the debtor has caused the assignee to believe on reasonable grounds that there was no such prohibition or restriction; or

(c) the assigned right is a right to payment for the provision of goods or services.

(4) The fact that a right is assignable notwithstanding a contractual prohibition or restriction does not affect the assignor's liability to the debtor for any breach of the prohibition or restriction.

III. – 5:109: Assignability: rights personal to the creditor

(1) A right is not assignable if it is a right to a performance which the debtor, by reason of the nature of the performance or the relationship between the debtor and the creditor, could not reasonably be required to render to anyone except that creditor.

(2) Paragraph (1) does not apply if the debtor has consented to the assignment.

III. – 5:110: Act of assignment: formation and validity

(1) Subject to paragraphs (2) and (3), the rules of Book II on the formation and validity of contracts and other juridical acts apply to acts of assignment.

(2) The rules of Book IV.H on the formation and validity of contracts of donation apply to gratuitous acts of assignment.

(3) The rules of Book IX on the formation and validity of security agreements apply to acts of assignment for purposes of security.

III. – 5:111: Right or authority to assign

The requirement of right or authority in III. – 5:104 (Basic requirements) paragraph (1)(c) need not be satisfied at the time of the act of assignment but has to be satisfied at the time the assignment is to take place.

Sub-section 3:
Undertakings by assignor

III. – 5:112: Undertakings by assignor

(1) The undertakings in paragraphs (2) to (6) are included in the act of assignment unless the act of assignment or the circumstances indicate otherwise.

(2) The assignor undertakes that:

    (a) the assigned right exists or will exist at the time when the assignment is to take effect;

    (b) the assignor is entitled to assign the right or will be so entitled at the time when the assignment is to take effect.

    (c) the debtor has no defences against an assertion of the right;

    (d) the right will not be affected by any right of set-off available as between the assignor and the debtor; and

    (e) the right has not been the subject of a prior assignment to another assignee and is not subject to any right in security in favour of any other person or to any other incumbrance.

(3) The assignor undertakes that any terms of a contract or other juridical act which have been disclosed to the assignee as terms regulating the right have not been modified and are not affected by any undisclosed agreement as to their meaning or effect which would be prejudicial to the assignee.

(4) The assignor undertakes that the terms of any contract or other juridical act from which the right arises will not be modified without the consent of the assignee unless the modification is provided for in the act of assignment or is one which is made in good faith and is of a nature to which the assignee could not reasonably object.

(5) The assignor undertakes not to conclude or grant any subsequent act of assignment of the same right which could lead to another person obtaining priority over the assignee.

(6) The assignor undertakes to transfer to the assignee, or to take such steps as are necessary to complete the transfer of, all transferable rights intended to secure the performance which are not already transferred by the assignment, and to transfer the proceeds of any non-transferable rights intended to secure the performance.

(7) The assignor does not represent that the debtor has, or will have, the ability to pay.

Sub-section 4:
Effects of assignment

III. – 5:113: New creditor
As soon as the assignment takes place the assignor ceases to be the creditor and the assignee becomes the creditor in relation to the right assigned.

III. – 5:114: When assignment takes place
(1) An assignment takes place when the requirements of III. – 5:104 (Basic requirements) are satisfied, or at such later time as the act of assignment may provide.
(2) However, an assignment of a right which was a future right at the time of the act of assignment is regarded as having taken place when all requirements other than those dependent on the existence of the right were satisfied.
(3) Where the requirements of III. – 5:104 (Basic requirements) are satisfied in relation to successive acts of assignment at the same time, the earliest act of assignment takes effect unless it provides otherwise.

III. – 5:115: Rights transferred to assignee
(1) The assignment of a right to performance transfers to the assignee not only the primary right but also all accessory rights and transferable supporting security rights.
(2) Where the assignment of a right to performance of a contractual obligation is associated with the substitution of the assignee as debtor in respect of any obligation owed by the assignor under the same contract, this Article takes effect subject to III. – 5:302 (Transfer of contractual position).

III. – 5:116: Effect on defences and rights of set-off
(1) The debtor may invoke against the assignee all substantive and procedural defences to a claim based on the assigned right which the debtor could have invoked against the assignor.
(2) The debtor may not, however, invoke a defence against the assignee:
    (a) if the debtor has caused the assignee to believe that there was no such defence; or
    (b) if the defence is based on breach by the assignor of a prohibition or restriction on assignment.

(3) The debtor may invoke against the assignee all rights of set-off which would have been available against the assignor in respect of rights against the assignor:
  (a) existing at the time when the debtor could no longer obtain a discharge by performing to the assignor; or
  (b) closely connected with the assigned right.

III. – 5:117: Effect on place of performance

(1) Where the assigned right relates to an obligation to pay money at a particular place, the assignee may require payment at any place within the same country or, if that country is a Member State of the European Union, at any place within the European Union, but the assignor is liable to the debtor for any increased costs which the debtor incurs by reason of any change in the place of performance.
(2) Where the assigned right relates to a non-monetary obligation to be performed at a particular place, the assignee may not require performance at any other place.

III. – 5:118: Effect of initial invalidity, subsequent avoidance, withdrawal, termination and revocation

(1) This Article applies where the assignee's entitlement for the purposes of III. – 5:104 (Basic requirements) paragraph (1)(d) arises from a contract or other juridical act (the underlying contract or other juridical act) whether or not it is followed by a separate act of assignment for the purposes of paragraph (1)(e) of that Article.
(2) Where the underlying contract or other juridical act is void from the beginning, no assignment takes place.
(3) Where, after an assignment has taken place, the underlying contract or other juridical act is avoided under Book II, Chapter 7, the right is treated as never having passed to the assignee (retroactive effect on assignment).
(4) Where, after an assignment has taken place, the underlying contract or other juridical act is withdrawn in the sense of Book II, Chapter 5, or the contractual relationship is terminated under any rule of Book III, or a donation is revoked in the sense of Book IV. H Chapter 4, there is no retroactive effect on the assignment.
(5) This Article does not affect any right to recover based on other provisions of these model rules.

Sub-section 5:
Protection of debtor

III. – 5:119: Performance to person who is not the creditor

(1) The debtor is discharged by performing to the assignor so long as the debtor has not received a notice of assignment from either the assignor or the assignee and does not know that the assignor is no longer entitled to receive performance.

(2) Notwithstanding that the person identified as the assignee in a notice of assignment received from the assignor is not the creditor, the debtor is discharged by performing in good faith to that person.

(3) Notwithstanding that the person identified as the assignee in a notice of assignment received from a person claiming to be the assignee is not the creditor, the debtor is discharged by performing to that person if the creditor has caused the debtor reasonably and in good faith to believe that the right has been assigned to that person.

III. – 5:120: Adequate proof of assignment

(1) A debtor who believes on reasonable grounds that the right has been assigned but who has not received a notice of assignment, may request the person who is believed to have assigned the right to provide a notice of assignment or a confirmation that the right has not been assigned or that the assignor is still entitled to receive payment.

(2) A debtor who has received a notice of assignment which is not in textual form on a durable medium or which does not give adequate information about the assigned right or the name and address of the assignee may request the person giving the notice to provide a new notice which satisfies these requirements.

(3) A debtor who has received a notice of assignment from the assignee but not from the assignor may request the assignee to provide reliable evidence of the assignment. Reliable evidence includes, but is not limited to, any statement in textual form on a durable medium emanating from the assignor indicating that the right has been assigned.

(4) A debtor who has made a request under this Article may withhold performance until the request is met.

Sub-section 6:
Priority rules

III. – 5:121: Competition between successive assignees
(1) Where there are successive purported assignments by the same person of the same right to performance the purported assignee whose assignment is first notified to the debtor has priority over any earlier assignee if at the time of the later assignment the assignee under that assignment neither knew nor could reasonably be expected to have known of the earlier assignment.
(2) The debtor is discharged by paying the first to notify even if aware of competing demands.

III. – 5:122: Competition between assignee and assignor receiving proceeds
Where the debtor is discharged under III. – 5:108 (Assignability: effect of contractual prohibition) paragraph (2)(a) or III. – 5:119 (Performance to person who is not the creditor) paragraph (1), the assignee's right against the assignor to the proceeds has priority over the right of a competing claimant so long as the proceeds are held by the assignor and are reasonably identifiable from the other assets of the assignor.

Section 2:
Substitution and addition of debtors

III. – 5:201: Scope
This Section applies only to the substitution or addition of a new debtor by agreement.

III. – 5:202: Types of substitution or addition
(1) A new debtor may be substituted or added:
  (a) in such a way that the original debtor is discharged (complete substitution of new debtor);
  (b) in such a way that the original debtor is retained as a debtor in case the new debtor does not perform properly (incomplete substitution of new debtor); or

  (c) in such a way that the original debtor and the new debtor have
    solidary liability (addition of new debtor).
(2) If it is clear that there is a new debtor but not clear what type of substitution or addition was intended, the original debtor and the new
  debtor have solidary liability.

III. – 5:203: Consent of creditor

(1) The consent of the creditor is required for the substitution of a new
  debtor, whether complete or incomplete.
(2) The consent of the creditor to the substitution of a new debtor may be
  given in advance. In such a case the substitution takes effect only when
  the creditor is given notice by the new debtor of the agreement between the new and the original debtor.
(3) The consent of the creditor is not required for the addition of a new
  debtor but the creditor, by notice to the new debtor, can reject the right
  conferred against the new debtor if that is done without undue delay
  after being informed of the right and before it has been expressly or
  impliedly accepted. On such rejection the right is treated as never having been conferred.

III. – 5:204: Complete substitution

A third person may undertake with the agreement of the creditor and the
original debtor to be completely substituted as debtor, with the effect that
the original debtor is discharged.

III. – 5:205: Effects of complete substitution on defences, set-off and security rights

(1) The new debtor may invoke against the creditor all defences which the
  original debtor could have invoked against the creditor.
(2) The new debtor may not exercise against the creditor any right of set-
  off available to the original debtor against the creditor.
(3) The new debtor cannot invoke against the creditor any rights or defences arising from the relationship between the new debtor and the
  original debtor.
(4) The discharge of the original debtor also extends to any personal or
  proprietary security provided by the original debtor to the creditor for
  the performance of the obligation, unless the security is over an asset

which is transferred to the new debtor as part of a transaction between the original and the new debtor.

(5) Upon discharge of the original debtor, a security granted by any person other than the new debtor for the performance of the obligation is released, unless that other person agrees that it should continue to be available to the creditor.

III. – 5:206: Incomplete substitution
A third person may agree with the creditor and with the original debtor to be incompletely substituted as debtor, with the effect that the original debtor is retained as a debtor in case the original debtor does not perform properly.

III. – 5:207: Effects of incomplete substitution
(1) The effects of an incomplete substitution on defences and set-off are the same as the effects of a complete substitution.
(2) To the extent that the original debtor is not discharged, any personal or proprietary security provided for the performance of that debtor's obligations is unaffected by the substitution.
(3) So far as not inconsistent with paragraphs (1) and (2) the liability of the original debtor is governed by the rules on the liability of a provider of dependent personal security with subsidiary liability.

III. – 5:208: Addition of new debtor
A third person may agree with the debtor to be added as a debtor, with the effect that the original debtor and the new debtor have solidary liability.

III. – 5:209: Effects of addition of new debtor
(1) Where there is a contract between the new debtor and the creditor, or a separate unilateral juridical act by the new debtor in favour of the creditor, whereby the new debtor is added as a debtor, the new debtor cannot invoke against the creditor any rights or defences arising from the relationship between the new debtor and the original debtor. Where there is no such contract or unilateral juridical act the new debtor can invoke against the creditor any ground of invalidity affecting the agreement with the original debtor.
(2) So far as not inconsistent with paragraph (1), the rules of Book III, Chapter 4, Section 1 (Plurality of debtors) apply.

Section 3:
Transfer of contractual position

III. – 5:301: Scope
This Section applies only to transfers by agreement.

III. – 5:302: Transfer of contractual position
(1) A party to a contractual relationship may agree with a third person, with the consent of the other party to the contractual relationship, that that person is to be substituted as a party to the relationship.
(2) The consent of the other party may be given in advance. In such a case the transfer takes effect only when that party is given notice of it.
(3) To the extent that the substitution of the third person involves a transfer of rights, the provisions of Section 1 of this Chapter on the assignment of rights apply; to the extent that obligations are transferred, the provisions of Section 2 of this Chapter on the substitution of a new debtor apply.

Section 4:
Transfer of rights and obligations on agent's insolvency

III. – 5:401: Principal's option to take over rights
in case of agent's insolvency
(1) This Article applies where an agent has concluded a contract with a third party on the instructions of and on behalf of a principal but has done so in such a way that the agent, and not the principal, is a party to the contract.
(2) If the agent becomes insolvent the principal may by notice to the third party and to the agent take over the rights of the agent under the contract in relation to the third party.
(3) The third party may invoke against the principal any defence which the third party could have invoked against the agent and has all the other protections which would be available if the rights had been voluntarily assigned by the agent to the principal.

III. – 5:402: Third party's counter-option

Where the principal has taken over the rights of the agent under the preceding Article, the third party may by notice to the principal and the agent opt to exercise against the principal the rights which the third party has against the agent, subject to any defences which the agent has against the third party.

Chapter 6:
Set-off and merger
Section 1:
Set-off

III. – 6:101: Definition and scope

(1) "Set-off" is the process by which a person may use a right to performance held against another person to extinguish in whole or in part an obligation owed to that person.
(2) This Chapter does not apply to set-off in insolvency.

III. – 6:102: Requirements for set-off

If two parties owe each other obligations of the same kind, either party may set off that party's right against the other party's right, if and to the extent that, at the time of set-off:
(a) the performance of the first party is due or, even if it is not due, the first party can oblige the other party to accept performance;
(b) the performance of the other party is due; and
(c) each party has authority to dispose of that party's right for the purpose of the set-off.

III. – 6:103: Unascertained rights

(1) A debtor may not set off a right which is unascertained as to its existence or value unless the set-off will not prejudice the interests of the creditor.
(2) Where the rights of both parties arise from the same legal relationship it is presumed that the creditor's interests will not be prejudiced.

III. – 6:104: Foreign currency set-off
Where parties owe each other money in different currencies, each party may set off that party's right against the other party's right, unless the parties have agreed that the party declaring set-off is to pay exclusively in a specified currency.

III. – 6:105: Set-off by notice
Set-off is effected by notice to the other party.

III. – 6:106: Two or more rights and obligations
(1) Where the party giving notice of set-off has two or more rights against the other party, the notice is effective only if it identifies the right to which it relates.
(2) Where the party giving notice of set-off has to perform two or more obligations towards the other party, the rules on imputation of performance apply with appropriate adaptations.

III. – 6:107: Effect of set-off
Set-off extinguishes the obligations, as far as they are coextensive, as from the time of notice.

III. – 6:108: Exclusion of right of set-off
Set-off cannot be effected:
(a) where it is excluded by agreement;
(b) against a right to the extent that that right is not capable of attachment; and
(c) against a right arising from an intentional wrongful act.

Section 2:
Merger of debts

III. – 6:201: Extinction of obligations by merger
(1) An obligation is extinguished if the same person becomes debtor and creditor in the same capacity.
(2) Paragraph (1) does not, however, apply if the effect would be to deprive a third person of a right.

Chapter 7:
Prescription
Section 1:
General provision

III. – 7:101: Rights subject to prescription
A right to performance of an obligation is subject to prescription by the expiry of a period of time in accordance with the rules in this Chapter.

Section 2:
Periods of prescription and their commencement

III. – 7:201: General period
The general period of prescription is three years.

III. – 7:202: Period for a right established by legal proceedings
(1) The period of prescription for a right established by judgment is ten years.
(2) The same applies to a right established by an arbitral award or other instrument which is enforceable as if it were a judgment.

III. – 7:203: Commencement
(1) The general period of prescription begins to run from the time when the debtor has to effect performance or, in the case of a right to damages, from the time of the act which gives rise to the right.
(2) Where the debtor is under a continuing obligation to do or refrain from doing something, the general period of prescription begins to run with each breach of the obligation.
(3) The period of prescription set out in III. – 7:202 (Period for a right established by legal proceedings) begins to run from the time when the judgment or arbitral award obtains the effect of res judicata, or the other instrument becomes enforceable, though not before the debtor has to effect performance.

Section 3:
Extension of period

III. – 7:301: Suspension in case of ignorance

The running of the period of prescription is suspended as long as the creditor does not know of, and could not reasonably be expected to know of:

(a) the identity of the debtor; or

(b) the facts giving rise to the right including, in the case of a right to damages, the type of damage.

III. – 7:302: Suspension in case of judicial and other proceedings

(1) The running of the period of prescription is suspended from the time when judicial proceedings to assert the right are begun.

(2) Suspension lasts until a decision has been made which has the effect of res judicata, or until the case has been otherwise disposed of. Where the proceedings end within the last six months of the prescription period without a decision on the merits, the period of prescription does not expire before six months have passed after the time when the proceedings ended.

(3) These provisions apply, with appropriate adaptations, to arbitration proceedings, to mediation proceedings, to proceedings whereby an issue between two parties is referred to a third party for a binding decision and to all other proceedings initiated with the aim of obtaining a decision relating to the right.

(4) Mediation proceedings mean structured proceedings whereby two or more parties to a dispute attempt to reach an agreement on the settlement of their dispute with the assistance of a mediator.

III. – 7:303: Suspension in case of impediment beyond creditor's control

(1) The running of the period of prescription is suspended as long as the creditor is prevented from pursuing proceedings to assert the right by an impediment which is beyond the creditor's control and which the creditor could not reasonably have been expected to avoid or overcome.

(2) Paragraph (1) applies only if the impediment arises, or subsists, within the last six months of the prescription period.

(3) Where the duration or nature of the impediment is such that it would be unreasonable to expect the creditor to take proceedings to assert the right within the part of the period of prescription which has still to run after the suspension comes to an end, the period of prescription does not expire before six months have passed after the time when the impediment was removed.

(4) In this Article an impediment includes a psychological impediment.

III. – 7:304: Postponement of expiry in case of negotiations

If the parties negotiate about the right, or about circumstances from which a claim relating to the right might arise, the period of prescription does not expire before one year has passed since the last communication made in the negotiations.

III. – 7:305: Postponement of expiry in case of incapacity

(1) If a person subject to an incapacity is without a representative, the period of prescription of a right held by or against that person does not expire before one year has passed after either the incapacity has ended or a representative has been appointed.

(2) The period of prescription of rights between a person subject to an incapacity and that person's representative does not expire before one year has passed after either the incapacity has ended or a new representative has been appointed.

III. – 7:306: Postponement of expiry: deceased's estate

Where the creditor or debtor has died, the period of prescription of a right held by or against the deceased's estate does not expire before one year has passed after the right can be enforced by or against an heir, or by or against a representative of the estate.

III. – 7:307: Maximum length of period

The period of prescription cannot be extended, by suspension of its running or postponement of its expiry under this Chapter, to more than ten years or, in case of rights to damages for personal injuries, to more than thirty years. This does not apply to suspension under III. – 7:302 (Suspension in case of judicial and other proceedings).

Section 4:
Renewal of period

III. – 7:401: Renewal by acknowledgement
(1) If the debtor acknowledges the right, vis-à-vis the creditor, by part pay-
    ment, payment of interest, giving of security, or in any other manner, a
    new period of prescription begins to run.
(2) The new period is the general period of prescription, regardless of
    whether the right was originally subject to the general period of pre-
    scription or the ten year period under III. – 7:202 (Period for a right
    established by legal proceedings). In the latter case, however, this Ar-
    ticle does not operate so as to shorten the ten year period.

III. – 7:402: Renewal by attempted execution
The ten year period of prescription laid down in III. – 7:202 (Period for a
right established by legal proceedings) begins to run again with each reasonable attempt at execution undertaken by the creditor.

Section 5:
Effects of prescription

III. – 7:501: General effect
(1) After expiry of the period of prescription the debtor is entitled to refuse
    performance.
(2) Whatever has been paid or transferred by the debtor in performance of
    the obligation may not be reclaimed merely because the period of pre-
    scription had expired.

III. – 7:502: Effect on ancillary rights
The period of prescription for a right to payment of interest, and other
rights of an ancillary nature, expires not later than the period for the principal right.

III. – 7:503: Effect on set-off

A right in relation to which the period of prescription has expired may nonetheless be set off, unless the debtor has invoked prescription previously or does so within two months of notification of set-off.

Section 6:
Modification by agreement

III. – 7:601: Agreements concerning prescription

(1) The requirements for prescription may be modified by agreement between the parties, in particular by either shortening or lengthening the periods of prescription.

(2) The period of prescription may not, however, be reduced to less than one year or extended to more than thirty years after the time of commencement set out in III. – 7:203 (Commencement)

Book IV
Specific contracts and the rights and obligations arising from them

Part A.
Sales

Chapter 1:
Scope and definitions
Section 1:
Scope

IV. A. – 1:101: Contracts covered

(1) This Part of Book IV applies to contracts for the sale of goods and associated consumer guarantees.
(2) It applies with appropriate adaptations to:
  (a) contracts for the sale of electricity;
  (b) contracts for the sale of stocks, shares, investment securities and negotiable instruments;
  (c) contracts for the sale of other forms of incorporeal property, including rights to the performance of obligations, industrial and intellectual property rights and other transferable rights;
  (d) contracts conferring, in exchange for a price, rights in information or data, including software and databases;
  (e) contracts for the barter of goods or any of the other assets mentioned above.
(3) It does not apply to contracts for the sale or barter of immovable property or rights in immovable property.

IV. A. – 1:102: Goods to be manufactured or produced

A contract under which one party undertakes, for a price, to manufacture or produce goods for the other party and to transfer their ownership to the other party is to be considered as primarily a contract for the sale of the goods.

Section 2:
Definitions

IV. A. – 1:201: Goods

In this Part of Book IV:

(a) the word "goods" includes goods which at the time of the conclusion of the contract do not yet exist; and

(b) references to goods, other than in IV. A. – 1:101 (Contracts covered) itself, are to be taken as referring also to the other assets mentioned in paragraph (2) of that Article.

IV. A. – 1:202: Contract for sale

A contract for the "sale" of goods is a contract under which one party, the seller, undertakes to another party, the buyer, to transfer the ownership of the goods to the buyer, or to a third person, either immediately on conclusion of the contract or at some future time, and the buyer undertakes to pay the price.

IV. A. – 1:203: Contract for barter

(1) A contract for the "barter" of goods is a contract under which each party undertakes to transfer the ownership of goods, either immediately on conclusion of the contract or at some future time, in return for the transfer of ownership of other goods.

(2) Each party is considered to be the buyer with respect to the goods to be received and the seller with respect to the goods or assets to be transferred.

IV. A. – 1:204: Consumer contract for sale

For the purpose of this Part of Book IV, a consumer contract for sale is a contract for sale in which the seller is a business and the buyer is a consumer.

Chapter 2:
Obligations of the seller
Section 1:
Overview

IV. A. – 2:101: Overview of obligations of the seller
The seller must:
(a) transfer the ownership of the goods;
(b) deliver the goods;
(c) transfer such documents representing or relating to the goods as may
    be required by the contract; and
(d) ensure that the goods conform to the contract.

Section 2:
Delivery of the goods

IV. A. – 2:201: Delivery
(1) The seller fulfils the obligation to deliver by making the goods, or
    where it is agreed that the seller need only deliver documents repre-
    senting the goods, the documents, available to the buyer.
(2) If the contract involves carriage of the goods by a carrier or series of
    carriers, the seller fulfils the obligation to deliver by handing over the
    goods to the first carrier for transmission to the buyer and by transfer-
    ring to the buyer any document necessary to enable the buyer to take
    over the goods from the carrier holding the goods.
(3) In this Article, any reference to the buyer includes a third person to
    whom delivery is to be made in accordance with the contract.

IV. A. – 2:202: Place and time for delivery
(1) The place and time for delivery are determined by III. – 2:101 (Place of
    performance) and III. – 2:102 (Time of performance) as modified by
    this Article.
(2) If the performance of the obligation to deliver requires the transfer of
    documents representing the goods, the seller must transfer them at
    such a time and place and in such a form as is required by the contract.

(3) If in a consumer contract for sale the contract involves carriage of goods by a carrier or a series of carriers and the consumer is given a time for delivery, the goods must be received from the last carrier or made available for collection from that carrier by that time.

IV. A. – 2:203: Cure in case of early delivery

(1) If the seller has delivered goods before the time for delivery, the seller may, up to that time, deliver any missing part or make up any deficiency in the quantity of the goods delivered, or deliver goods in replacement of any non-conforming goods delivered or otherwise remedy any lack of conformity in the goods delivered, provided that the exercise of this right does not cause the buyer unreasonable inconvenience or unreasonable expense.

(2) If the seller has transferred documents before the time required by the contract, the seller may, up to that time, cure any lack of conformity in the documents, provided that the exercise of this right does not cause the buyer unreasonable inconvenience or unreasonable expense.

(3) This Article does not preclude the buyer from claiming damages, in accordance with Book III, Chapter 3, Section 7 (Damages and interest), for any loss not remedied by the seller's cure.

IV. A. – 2:204: Carriage of the goods

(1) If the contract requires the seller to arrange for carriage of the goods, the seller must make such contracts as are necessary for carriage to the place fixed by means of transportation appropriate in the circumstances and according to the usual terms for such transportation.

(2) If the seller, in accordance with the contract, hands over the goods to a carrier and if the goods are not clearly identified to the contract by markings on the goods, by shipping documents or otherwise, the seller must give the buyer notice of the consignment specifying the goods.

(3) If the contract does not require the seller to effect insurance in respect of the carriage of the goods, the seller must, at the buyer's request, provide the buyer with all available information necessary to enable the buyer to effect such insurance.

Section 3:
Conformity of the goods

IV. A. – 2:301: Conformity with the contract
The goods do not conform with the contract unless they:
(a) are of the quantity, quality and description required by the contract;
(b) are contained or packaged in the manner required by the contract;
(c) are supplied along with any accessories, installation instructions or other instructions required by the contract; and
(d) comply with the remaining Articles of this Section.

IV. A. – 2:302: Fitness for purpose, qualities, packaging
The goods must:
(a) be fit for any particular purpose made known to the seller at the time of the conclusion of the contract, except where the circumstances show that the buyer did not rely, or that it was unreasonable for the buyer to rely, on the seller's skill and judgement;
(b) be fit for the purposes for which goods of the same description would ordinarily be used;
(c) possess the qualities of goods which the seller held out to the buyer as a sample or model;
(d) be contained or packaged in the manner usual for such goods or, where there is no such manner, in a manner adequate to preserve and protect the goods;
(e) be supplied along with such accessories, installation instructions or other instructions as the buyer may reasonably expect to receive; and
(f) possess such qualities and performance capabilities as the buyer may reasonably expect.

IV. A. – 2:303: Statements by third persons
The goods must possess the qualities and performance capabilities held out in any statement on the specific characteristics of the goods made about them by a person in earlier links of the business chain, the producer or the producer's representative which forms part of the terms of the contract by virtue of II. – 9:102 (Certain pre-contractual statements regarded as contract terms).

IV. A. – 2:304: Incorrect installation under a consumer contract for sale

Where goods supplied under a consumer contract for sale are incorrectly installed, any lack of conformity resulting from the incorrect installation is regarded as a lack of conformity of the goods if:

(a) the goods were installed by the seller or under the seller's responsibility; or

(b) the goods were intended to be installed by the consumer and the incorrect installation was due to a shortcoming in the installation instructions.

IV. A. – 2:305: Third party rights or claims in general

The goods must be free from any right or reasonably well founded claim of a third party. However, if such a right or claim is based on industrial property or other intellectual property, the seller's obligation is governed by the following Article.

IV. A. – 2:306: Third party rights or claims based on industrial property or other intellectual property

(1) The goods must be free from any right or claim of a third party which is based on industrial property or other intellectual property and of which at the time of the conclusion of the contract the seller knew or could reasonably be expected to have known.

(2) However, paragraph (1) does not apply where the right or claim results from the seller's compliance with technical drawings, designs, formulae or other such specifications furnished by the buyer.

IV. A. – 2:307: Buyer's knowledge of lack of conformity

(1) The seller is not liable under IV. A. – 2:302 (Fitness for purpose, qualities, packaging), IV. A. – 2:305 (Third party rights or claims in general) or IV. A. – 2:306 (Third party rights or claims based on industrial property or other intellectual property) if, at the time of the conclusion of the contract, the buyer knew or could reasonably be assumed to have known of the lack of conformity.

(2) The seller is not liable under IV. A. – 2:304 (Incorrect installation under a consumer contract for sale) sub-paragraph (b) if, at the time of the

conclusion of the contract, the buyer knew or could reasonably be assumed to have known of the shortcoming in the installation instructions.

IV. A. – 2:308: Relevant time for establishing conformity
(1) The seller is liable for any lack of conformity which exists at the time when the risk passes to the buyer, even if the lack of conformity becomes apparent only after that time.
(2) In a consumer contract for sale, any lack of conformity which becomes apparent within six months of the time when risk passes to the buyer is presumed to have existed at that time unless this is incompatible with the nature of the goods or the nature of the lack of conformity.
(3) In a case governed by IV. A. – 2:304 (Incorrect installation under a consumer contract for sale) any reference in paragraphs (1) or (2) to the time when risk passes to the buyer is to be read as a reference to the time when the installation is complete.

IV. A. – 2:309: Limits on derogation from conformity rights in a consumer contract for sale
In a consumer contract for sale, any contractual term or agreement concluded with the seller before a lack of conformity is brought to the seller's attention which directly or indirectly waives or restricts the rights resulting from the seller's obligation to ensure that the goods conform to the contract is not binding on the consumer.

Chapter 3:
Obligations of the buyer

IV. A. – 3:101: Main obligations of the buyer
The buyer must:
(a) pay the price;
(b) take delivery of the goods; and
(c) take over documents representing or relating to the goods as may be required by the contract.

IV. A. – 3:102: Determination of form, measurement or other features

(1) If under the contract the buyer is to specify the form, measurement or other features of the goods, or the time or manner of their delivery, and fails to make such specification either within the time agreed upon or within a reasonable time after receipt of a request from the seller, the seller may, without prejudice to any other rights, make the specification in accordance with any requirements of the buyer that may be known to the seller.

(2) A seller who makes such a specification must inform the buyer of the details of the specification and must fix a reasonable time within which the buyer may make a different specification. If, after receipt of such a communication, the buyer fails to do so within the time so fixed, the specification made by the seller is binding.

IV. A. – 3:103: Price fixed by weight

If the price is fixed according to the weight of the goods, in case of doubt it is to be determined by the net weight.

IV. A. – 3:104: Taking delivery

The buyer fulfils the obligation to take delivery by:

(a) doing all the acts which could reasonably be expected in order to enable the seller to perform the obligation to deliver; and

(b) taking over the goods, or the documents representing the goods, as required by the contract.

IV. A. – 3:105: Early delivery and delivery of excess quantity

(1) If the seller delivers all or part of the goods before the time fixed, the buyer may take delivery or, except where acceptance of the tender would not unreasonably prejudice the buyer's interests, refuse to take delivery.

(2) If the seller delivers a quantity of goods greater than that provided for by the contract, the buyer may retain or refuse the excess quantity.

(3) If the buyer retains the excess quantity it is regarded as having been supplied under the contract and must be paid for at the contractual rate.

(4) In a consumer contract for sale paragraph (3) does not apply if the buyer believes on reasonable grounds that the seller has delivered the excess quantity intentionally and without error, knowing that it had not been ordered. In such a case the rules on unsolicited goods apply.

Chapter 4:
Remedies
Section 1:
Limits on derogation

IV. A. – 4:101: Limits on derogation from remedies for non-conformity in a consumer contract for sale

In a consumer contract for sale, any contractual term or agreement concluded with the seller before a lack of conformity is brought to the seller's attention which directly or indirectly waives or restricts the remedies of the buyer provided in Book III, Chapter 3 (Remedies for Non-performance), as modified in this Chapter, in respect of the lack of conformity is not binding on the consumer.

Section 2:
Modifications of buyer's remedies for lack of conformity

IV. A. – 4:201: Termination by consumer for lack of conformity.

In a consumer contract for sale, the buyer may terminate the contractual relationship for non-performance under Book III, Chapter 3, Section 5 (Termination) in the case of any lack of conformity, unless the lack of conformity is minor.

IV. A. – 4:202: Limitation of liability for damages of non-business sellers

(1) If the seller is a natural person acting for purposes not related to that person's trade, business or profession, the buyer is not entitled to damages for lack of conformity exceeding the contract price.

(2) The seller is not entitled to rely on paragraph (1) if the lack of conformity relates to facts of which the seller, at the time when the risk passed to the buyer, knew or could reasonably be expected to have known and which the seller did not disclose to the buyer before that time.

Section 3:
Requirements of examination and notification

IV. A. – 4:301: Examination of the goods

(1) The buyer should examine the goods, or cause them to be examined, within as short a period as is reasonable in the circumstances. Failure to do so may result in the buyer losing, under III. – 3:107 (Failure to notify non-conformity) as supplemented by IV. A. – 4:302 (Notification of lack of conformity), the right to rely on the lack of conformity.

(2) If the contract involves carriage of the goods, examination may be deferred until after the goods have arrived at their destination.

(3) If the goods are redirected in transit, or redispatched by the buyer before the buyer has had a reasonable opportunity to examine them, and at the time of the conclusion of the contract the seller knew or could reasonably be expected to have known of the possibility of such redirection or redispatch, examination may be deferred until after the goods have arrived at the new destination.

(4) This Article does not apply to a consumer contract for sale.

IV. A. – 4:302: Notification of lack of conformity

(1) In a contract between two businesses the rule in III. – 3:107 (Failure to notify non-conformity) requiring notification of a lack of conformity within a reasonable time is supplemented by the following rules.

(2) The buyer in any event loses the right to rely on a lack of conformity if the buyer does not give the seller notice of the lack of conformity at the latest within two years from the time at which the goods were actually handed over to the buyer in accordance with the contract.

(3) If the parties have agreed that the goods must remain fit for a particular purpose or for their ordinary purpose during a fixed period of time, the period for giving notice under paragraph (2) does not expire before the end of the agreed period.

(4) Paragraph (2) does not apply in respect of third party claims or rights pursuant to IV. A. – 2:305 (Third party rights or claims in general) and IV. A. – 2:306 (Third party rights or claims based on industrial property or other intellectual property) .

IV. A. – 4:303: Notification of partial delivery

The buyer does not have to notify the seller that not all the goods have been delivered, if the buyer has reason to believe that the remaining goods will be delivered.

IV. A. – 4:304: Seller's knowledge of lack of conformity

The seller is not entitled to rely on the provisions of IV. A. – 4:301 (Examination of the goods) or IV. A. – 4:302 (Notification of lack of conformity) if the lack of conformity relates to facts of which the seller knew or could reasonably be expected to have known and which the seller did not disclose to the buyer.

Chapter 5:
Passing of risk
Section 1:
General provisions

IV. A. – 5:101: Effect of passing of risk

Loss of, or damage to, the goods after the risk has passed to the buyer does not discharge the buyer from the obligation to pay the price, unless the loss or damage is due to an act or omission of the seller.

IV. A. – 5:102: Time when risk passes

(1) The risk passes when the buyer takes over the goods or the documents representing them.
(2) However, if the contract relates to goods not then identified, the risk does not pass to the buyer until the goods are clearly identified to the contract, whether by markings on the goods, by shipping documents, by notice given to the buyer or otherwise.
(3) The rule in paragraph (1) is subject to the Articles in Section 2 of this Chapter.

IV. A. – 5:103: Passing of risk in a consumer contract for sale

(1) In a consumer contract for sale, the risk does not pass until the buyer takes over the goods.
(2) Paragraph (1) does not apply if the buyer has failed to perform the obligation to take over the goods and the non-performance is not ex-

cused under III. – 3:104 (Excuse due to an impediment) in which case
IV. A. – 5:201 (Goods placed at buyer's disposal) applies.
(3) Except in so far as provided in the preceding paragraph, Section 2 of
this Chapter does not apply to a consumer contract for sale.
(4) The parties may not, to the detriment of the consumer, exclude the
application of this Article or derogate from or vary its effects.

Section 2:
Special rules

IV. A. – 5:201: Goods placed at buyer's disposal
(1) If the goods are placed at the buyer's disposal and the buyer is aware of
this, the risk passes to the buyer from the time when the goods should
have been taken over, unless the buyer was entitled to withhold taking
of delivery under III. – 3:401 (Right to withhold performance of reciprocal obligation).
(2) If the goods are placed at the buyer's disposal at a place other than a
place of business of the seller, the risk passes when delivery is due and
the buyer is aware of the fact that the goods are placed at the buyer's
disposal at that place.

IV. A. – 5:202: Carriage of the goods
(1) This Article applies to any contract of sale which involves carriage of
goods.
(2) If the seller is not bound to hand over the goods at a particular place,
the risk passes to the buyer when the goods are handed over to the first
carrier for transmission to the buyer in accordance with the contract.
(3) If the seller is bound to hand over the goods to a carrier at a particular
place, the risk does not pass to the buyer until the goods are handed
over to the carrier at that place.
(4) The fact that the seller is authorised to retain documents controlling
the disposition of the goods does not affect the passing of the risk.

IV. A. – 5:203: Goods sold in transit
(1) This Article applies to any contract of sale which involves goods sold in
transit.

(2) The risk passes to the buyer at the time the goods are handed over to the first carrier. However, if the circumstances so indicate, the risk passes to the buyer as from the time of the conclusion of the contract.

(3) If at the time of the conclusion of the contract the seller knew or could reasonably be expected to have known that the goods had been lost or damaged and did not disclose this to the buyer, the loss or damage is at the risk of the seller.

Chapter 6:
Consumer goods guarantees

IV. A. – 6:101: Definition of a consumer goods guarantee

(1) A consumer goods guarantee means any undertaking of a type mentioned in the following paragraph given to a consumer in connection with a consumer contract for the sale of goods:

(a) by a producer or a person in later links of the business chain; or

(b) by the seller in addition to the seller's obligations as seller of the goods.

(2) The undertaking may be that:

(a) apart from misuse, mistreatment or accident the goods will remain fit for their ordinary purpose for a specified period of time, or otherwise;

(b) the goods will meet the specifications set out in the guarantee document or in associated advertising; or

(c) subject to any conditions stated in the guarantee,

    (i) the goods will be repaired or replaced;

    (ii) the price paid for the goods will be reimbursed in whole or in part; or

    (iii) some other remedy will be provided.

IV. A. – 6:102: Binding nature of the guarantee

(1) A consumer goods guarantee, whether contractual or in the form of a unilateral undertaking, is binding in favour of the first buyer, and in the case of a unilateral undertaking is so binding without acceptance notwithstanding any provision to the contrary in the guarantee document or the associated advertising.

(2) If not otherwise provided in the guarantee document, the guarantee is also binding without acceptance in favour of every owner of the goods within the duration of the guarantee.

(3) Any requirement in the guarantee whereby it is conditional on the fulfilment by the guarantee holder of any formal requirement, such as registration or notification of purchase, is not binding on the consumer.

IV. A. – 6:103: Guarantee document

(1) A person who gives a consumer goods guarantee must (unless such a document has already been provided to the buyer) provide the buyer with a guarantee document which:

(a) states that the buyer has legal rights which are not affected by the guarantee;

(b) points out the advantages of the guarantee for the buyer in comparison with the conformity rules;

(c) lists all the essential particulars necessary for making claims under the guarantee, notably:

– the name and address of the guarantor;

– the name and address of the person to whom any notification is to be made and the procedure by which the notification is to be made;

– any territorial limitations to the guarantee;

(d) is drafted in plain, intelligible language; and

(e) is drafted in the same language as that in which the goods were offered.

(2) The guarantee document must be in textual form on a durable medium and be available and accessible to the buyer.

(3) The validity of the guarantee is not affected by any failure to comply with paragraphs (1) and (2), and accordingly the guarantee holder can still rely on the guarantee and require it to be honoured.

(4) If the obligations under paragraphs (1) and (2) are not observed the guarantee holder may, without prejudice to any right to damages which may be available, require the guarantor to provide a guarantee document which conforms to those requirements.

(5) The parties may not, to the detriment of the consumer, exclude the application of this Article or derogate from or vary its effects.

IV. A. – 6:104: Coverage of the guarantee

If the guarantee document does not specify otherwise:

(a) the period of the guarantee is 5 years or the estimated life-span of the goods, whichever is shorter;

(b) the guarantor's obligations become effective if, for a reason other than misuse, mistreatment or accident, the goods at any time during the period of the guarantee become unfit for their ordinary purpose or cease to possess such qualities and performance capabilities as the guarantee holder may reasonably expect;

(c) the guarantor is obliged, if the conditions of the guarantee are satisfied, to repair or replace the goods; and

(d) all costs involved in invoking and performing the guarantee are to be borne by the guarantor.

IV. A. – 6:105: Guarantee limited to specific parts

A consumer goods guarantee relating only to a specific part or specific parts of the goods must clearly indicate this limitation in the guarantee document; otherwise the limitation is not binding on the consumer.

IV. A. – 6:106: Exclusion or limitation of the guarantor's liability

The guarantee may exclude or limit the guarantor's liability under the guarantee for any failure of or damage to the goods caused by failure to maintain the goods in accordance with instructions, provided that the exclusion or limitation is clearly set out in the guarantee document.

IV. A. – 6:107: Burden of proof

(1) Where the guarantee holder invokes a consumer goods guarantee within the period covered by the guarantee the burden of proof is on the guarantor that:

(a) the goods met the specifications set out in the guarantee document or in associated advertisements; and

(b) any failure of or damage to the goods is due to misuse, mistreatment, accident, failure to maintain, or other cause for which the guarantor is not responsible.

(2) The parties may not, to the detriment of the consumer, exclude the application of this Article or derogate from or vary its effects.

IV. A. – 6:108: Prolongation of the guarantee period

(1) If any defect or failure in the goods is remedied under the guarantee then the guarantee is prolonged for a period equal to the period during which the guarantee holder could not use the goods due to the defect or failure.

(2) The parties may not, to the detriment of the consumer, exclude the application of this Article or derogate from or vary its effects.

Part B.
Lease of goods

Chapter 1:
Scope of application and general provisions

IV. B. – 1:101: Lease of goods

(1) This Part of Book IV applies to contracts for the lease of goods.

(2) A contract for the lease of goods is a contract under which one party, the lessor, undertakes to provide the other party, the lessee, with a temporary right of use of goods in exchange for rent. The rent may be in the form of money or other value.

(3) This Part of Book IV does not apply to contracts where the parties have agreed that ownership will be transferred after a period with right of use even if the parties have described the contract as a lease.

(4) The application of this Part of Book IV is not excluded by the fact that the contract has a financing purpose, the lessor has the role as a financing party, or the lessee has an option to become owner of the goods.

(5) This Part of Book IV regulates only the contractual relationship arising from a contract for lease.

IV. B. – 1:102: Consumer contract for the lease of goods

For the purpose of this Part of Book IV, a consumer contract for the lease of goods is a contract for the lease of goods in which the lessor is a business and the lessee is a consumer

IV. B. – 1:103: Limits on derogation from conformity rights in a consumer contract for lease

In the case of a consumer contract for the lease of goods, any contractual term or agreement concluded with the lessor before a lack of conformity is brought to the lessor's attention which directly or indirectly waives or restricts the rights resulting from the lessor's obligation to ensure that the goods conform to the contract is not binding on the consumer.

IV. B. – 1:104: Limits on derogation from rules on remedies in a consumer contract for lease

(1) In the case of a consumer contract for the lease of goods the parties may not, to the detriment of the consumer, exclude the application of the rules on remedies in Book III, Chapter 3, as modified in Chapters 3 and 6 of this Part, or derogate from or vary their effects.

(2) Notwithstanding paragraph (1), the parties may agree on a limitation of the lessor's liability for loss related to the lessee's trade, business or profession. Such a term may not, however, be invoked if it would be contrary to good faith and fair dealing to do so.

Chapter 2:
Lease period

IV. B. – 2:101: Start of lease period

(1) The lease period starts:
   (a) at the time determinable from the terms agreed by the parties;
   (b) if a time frame within which the lease period is to start can be determined, at any time chosen by the lessor within that time frame unless the circumstances of the case indicate that the lessee is to choose the time;
   (c) in any other case, a reasonable time after the conclusion of the contract, at the request of either party.

(2) The lease period starts at the time when the lessee takes control of the goods if this is earlier than the starting time under paragraph (1).

IV. B. – 2:102: End of lease period

(1) A definite lease period ends at the time determinable from the terms agreed by the parties. A definite lease period cannot be terminated unilaterally beforehand by giving notice.

(2) An indefinite lease period ends at the time specified in a notice of termination given by either party.

(3) A notice under paragraph (2) is effective only if the time specified in the notice of termination is in compliance with the terms agreed by the parties or, if no period of notice can be determined from such terms, a reasonable time after the notice has reached the other party.

IV. B. – 2:103: Tacit prolongation

(1) Where a contract for the lease of goods for a definite period is tacitly prolonged under III. – 1:111 (Tacit prolongation) and where the rent prior to prolongation was calculated so as to take into account amortisation of the cost of the goods by the lessee, the rent payable following prolongation is limited to what is reasonable having regard to the amount already paid.

(2) In the case of a consumer contract for the lease of goods the parties may not, to the detriment of the consumer, exclude the application of paragraph (1) or derogate from or vary its effects.

Chapter 3:
Obligations of the lessor

IV. B. – 3:101: Availability of the goods

(1) The lessor must make the goods available for the lessee's use at the start of the lease period and at the place determined by III. – 2:101 (Place of performance).

(2) Notwithstanding the rule in the previous paragraph, the lessor must make the goods available for the lessee's use at the lessee's place of business or, as the case may be, at the lessee's habitual residence if the lessor, on the specifications of the lessee, acquires the goods from a supplier selected by the lessee.

(3) The lessor must ensure that the goods remain available for the lessee's use throughout the lease period, free from any right or reasonably based claim of a third party which prevents or is otherwise likely to

interfere with the lessee's use of the goods in accordance with the contract.

(4) The lessor's obligations when the goods are lost or damaged during the lease period are regulated by IV. B. – 3:104 (Conformity of the goods during the lease period).

IV. B. – 3:102: Conformity with the contract at the start of the lease period

(1) The lessor must ensure that the goods conform with the contract at the start of the lease period.

(2) The goods do not conform with the contract unless they:
   (a) are of the quantity, quality and description required by the terms agreed by the parties;
   (b) are contained or packaged in the manner required by the terms agreed by the parties;
   (c) are supplied along with any accessories, installation instructions or other instructions required by the terms agreed by the parties; and
   (d) comply with the following Article .

IV. B. – 3:103: Fitness for purpose, qualities, packaging etc.

The goods do not conform with the contract unless they:

(a) are fit for any particular purpose made known to the lessor at the time of the conclusion of the contract, except where the circumstances show that the lessee did not rely, or that it was unreasonable for the lessee to rely, on the lessor's skill and judgement;

(b) are fit for the purposes for which goods of the same description would ordinarily be used;

(c) possess the qualities of goods which the lessor held out to the lessee as a sample or model;

(d) are contained or packaged in the manner usual for such goods or, where there is no such manner, in a manner adequate to preserve and protect the goods;

(e) are supplied along with such accessories, installation instructions or other instructions as the lessee could reasonably expect to receive; and

(f) possess such qualities and performance capabilities as the lessee may reasonably expect.

IV. B. – 3:104: Conformity of the goods during the lease period

(1) The lessor must ensure that throughout the lease period, and subject to normal wear and tear, the goods:

    (a) remain of the quantity, quality and description required by the contract; and

    (b) remain fit for the purposes of the lease, even where this requires modifications to the goods.

(2) Paragraph (1) does not apply where the rent is calculated so as to take into account the amortisation of the cost of the goods by the lessee.

(3) Nothing in paragraph (1) affects the lessee's obligations under IV. B. – 5:104 (Handling the goods in accordance with the contract) paragraph (1)(c).

IV. B. – 3:105: Incorrect installation under a consumer contract for the lease of goods

Where, under a consumer contract for the lease of goods, the goods are incorrectly installed, any lack of conformity resulting from the incorrect installation is regarded as a lack of conformity of the goods if:

(a) the goods were installed by the lessor or under the lessor's responsibility; or

(b) the goods were intended to be installed by the consumer and the incorrect installation was due to shortcomings in the installation instructions.

IV. B. – 3:106: Obligations on return of the goods

The lessor must:

(a) take all the steps which may reasonably be expected in order to enable the lessee to perform the obligation to return the goods; and

(b) accept return of the goods as required by the contract.

Chapter 4:
Remedies of the lessee: modifications of normal rules

IV. B. – 4:101: Lessee's right to have lack of conformity remedied

(1) The lessee may have any lack of conformity of the goods remedied, and recover any expenses reasonably incurred, to the extent that the lessee

is entitled to enforce specific performance according to III. – 3:302 (Enforcement of non-monetary obligations).

(2) Nothing in the preceding paragraph affects the lessor's right to cure the lack of conformity according to Book III, Chapter 3, Section 2.

IV. B. – 4:102: Rent reduction

(1) The lessee may reduce the rent for a period in which the value of the lessor's performance is decreased due to delay or lack of conformity, to the extent that the reduction in value is not caused by the lessee.

(2) The rent may be reduced even for periods in which the lessor retains the right to perform or cure according to III. – 3:103 (Notice fixing additional time for performance), III. – 3:202 (Cure by debtor: general rules) paragraph (2) and III. – 3:204 (Consequences of allowing debtor opportunity to cure)).

(3) Notwithstanding the rule in paragraph (1), the lessee may lose the right to reduce the rent for a period according to IV. B. – 4:103 (Notification of lack of conformity).

IV. B. – 4:103: Notification of lack of conformity

(1) The lessee cannot resort to remedies for lack of conformity unless notification is given to the lessor. Where notification is not timely, the lack of conformity is disregarded for a period corresponding to the unreasonable delay. Notification is always considered timely where it is given within a reasonable time after the lessee has become, or could reasonably be expected to have become, aware of the lack of conformity.

(2) When the lease period has ended the rules in III. – 3:107 (Failure to notify non-conformity) apply.

(3) The lessor is not entitled to rely on the provisions of paragraphs (1) and (2) if the lack of conformity relates to facts of which the lessor knew or could reasonably be expected to have known and which the lessor did not disclose to the lessee.

IV. B. – 4:104: Remedies to be directed towards supplier of the goods

(1) This Article applies where:
   (a) the lessor, on the specifications of the lessee, acquires the goods from a supplier selected by the lessee;

(b) the lessee, in providing the specifications for the goods and select-
ing the supplier, does not rely primarily on the skill and judgement
of the lessor;

(c) the lessee approves the terms of the supply contract;

(d) the supplier's obligations under the supply contract are owed, by
law or by contract, to the lessee as a party to the supply contract or
as if the lessee were a party to that contract; and

(e) the supplier's obligations owed to the lessee cannot be varied without the consent of the lessee.

(2) The lessee has no right to enforce performance by the lessor, to reduce
the rent or to damages or interest from the lessor, for late delivery or for
lack of conformity, unless non-performance results from an act or omission of the lessor.

(3) The provision in paragraph (2) does not preclude:

(a) any right of the lessee to reject the goods, to terminate the lease
under Book III, Chapter 3, Section 5 (Termination) or, prior to acceptance of the goods, to withhold rent to the extent that the
lessee could have resorted to these remedies as a party to the supply contract; or

(b) any remedy of the lessee where a third party right or reasonably
based claim prevents, or is otherwise likely to interfere with, the
lessee's continuous use of the goods in accordance with the contract.

(4) The lessee cannot terminate the lessee's contractual relationship with
the supplier under the supply contract without the consent of the lessor.

Chapter 5:
Obligations of the lessee

IV. B. – 5:101: Obligation to pay rent

(1) The lessee must pay the rent.

(2) Where the rent cannot be determined from the terms agreed by the
parties, from any other applicable rule of law or from usages or practices, it is a monetary sum determined in accordance with II. – 9:104
(Determination of price).

(3) The rent accrues from the start of the lease period.

IV. B. – 5:102: Time for payment

Rent is payable:

(a) at the end of each period for which the rent is agreed;
(b) if the rent is not agreed for certain periods, at the expiry of a definite lease period; or
(c) if no definite lease period is agreed and the rent is not agreed for certain periods, at the end of reasonable intervals.

IV. B. – 5:103: Acceptance of goods

The lessee must:

(a) take all steps reasonably to be expected in order to enable the lessor to perform the obligation to make the goods available at the start of the lease period; and
(b) take control of the goods as required by the contract.

IV. B. – 5:104: Handling the goods in accordance with the contract

(1) The lessee must:
  (a) observe the requirements and restrictions which follow from the terms agreed by the parties;
  (b) handle the goods with the care which can reasonably be expected in the circumstances, taking into account the duration of the lease period, the purpose of the lease and the character of the goods; and
  (c) take all measures which could ordinarily be expected to become necessary in order to preserve the normal standard and functioning of the goods, in so far as is reasonable, taking into account the duration of the lease period, the purpose of the lease and the character of the goods.

(2) Where the rent is calculated so as to take into account the amortisation of the cost of the goods by the lessee, the lessee must, during the lease period, keep the goods in the condition they were in at the start of the lease period, subject to any wear and tear which is normal for that kind of goods.

IV. B. – 5:105: Intervention to avoid danger or damage to the goods

(1) The lessee must take such measures for the maintenance and repair of the goods as would ordinarily be carried out by the lessor, if the mea-

    sures are necessary to avoid danger or damage to the goods, and it is impossible or impracticable for the lessor, but not for the lessee, to ensure these measures are taken.

(2) The lessee has a right against the lessor to indemnification or, as the case may be, reimbursement in respect of an obligation or expenditure (whether of money or other assets) in so far as reasonably incurred for the purposes of the measures.

IV. B. – 5:106: Compensation for maintenance and improvements

(1) The lessee has no right to compensation for maintenance of or improvements to the goods.

(2) Paragraph (1) does not exclude or restrict any right the lessee may have to damages or any right the lessee may have under IV. B. – 4:101 (Lessee's right to have lack of conformity remedied), IV. B. – 5:105 (Intervention to avoid danger or damage to the goods) or Book VIII (Acquisition and loss of ownership of goods).

IV. B. – 5:107: Obligation to inform

(1) The lessee must inform the lessor of any damage or danger to the goods, and of any right or claim of a third party, if these circumstances would normally give rise to a need for action on the part of the lessor.

(2) The lessee must inform the lessor under paragraph (1) within a reasonable time after the lessee first becomes aware of the circumstances and their character.

(3) The lessee is presumed to be aware of the circumstances and their character if the lessee could reasonably be expected to be so aware.

IV. B. – 5:108: Repairs and inspections of the lessor

(1) The lessee, if given reasonable notice where possible, must tolerate the carrying out by the lessor of repair work and other work on the goods which is necessary in order to preserve the goods, remove defects and prevent danger. This obligation does not preclude the lessee from reducing the rent in accordance with IV. B. – 4:102 (Rent reduction).

(2) The lessee must tolerate the carrying out of work on the goods which does not fall under paragraph (1), unless there is good reason to object.

(3) The lessee must tolerate inspection of the goods for the purposes indicated in paragraph (1). The lessee must also accept inspection of the goods by a prospective lessee during a reasonable period prior to expiry of the lease.

IV. B. – 5:109: Obligation to return the goods
At the end of the lease period the lessee must return the goods to the place where they were made available for the lessee.

Chapter 6:
Remedies of the lessor: modifications of normal rules

IV. B. – 6:101: Limitation of right to enforce payment of future rent
(1) Where the lessee has taken control of the goods, the lessor may not enforce payment of future rent if the lessee wishes to return the goods and it would be reasonable for the lessor to accept their return.
(2) The fact that a right to enforce specific performance is excluded under paragraph (1) does not preclude a claim for damages.

IV. B. – 6:102: Reduction of liability in consumer contract for the lease of goods
(1) In the case of a consumer contract for the lease of goods, the lessor's right to damages may be reduced to the extent that the loss is mitigated by insurance covering the goods, or to the extent that loss would have been mitigated by insurance, in circumstances where it is reasonable to expect the lessor to take out such insurance.
(2) The rule in paragraph (1) applies in addition to the rules in Book III, Chapter 3, Section 7.

Chapter 7:
New parties and sublease

IV. B. – 7:101: Change in ownership and substitution of lessor
(1) Where ownership passes from the lessor to a new owner, the new owner of the goods is substituted as a party to the lease if the lessee has possession of the goods at the time ownership passes. The former

owner remains subsidiarily liable for the non-performance of the obligations under the contract for lease as a personal security provider.
(2) A reversal of the passing of ownership puts the parties back in their original positions except as regards performance already rendered at the time of reversal.
(3) The rules in the preceding paragraphs apply accordingly where the lessor has acted as holder of a right other than ownership.

IV. B. – 7:102: Assignment of lessee's rights to performance
The lessee's rights to performance of the lessor's obligations under the contract for lease cannot be assigned without the lessor's consent.

IV. B. – 7:103: Sublease
(1) The lessee may not sublease the goods without the lessor's consent.
(2) If consent to a sublease is withheld without good reason, the lessee may terminate the lease by giving a reasonable period of notice.
(3) In the case of a sublease, the lessee remains liable for the performance of the lessee's obligations under the contract for lease.

Part C.
Services

Chapter 1:
General provisions

IV. C. – 1:101: Scope
(1) This Part of Book IV applies:
(a) to contracts under which one party, the service provider, undertakes to supply a service to the other party, the client, in exchange for a price; and
(b) with appropriate adaptations, to contracts under which the service provider undertakes to supply a service to the client otherwise than in exchange for a price.
(2) It applies in particular to contracts for construction, processing, storage, design, information or advice, and treatment.

IV. C. – 1:102: Exclusions
This Part does not apply to contracts in so far as they are for transport, insurance, the provision of a security or the supply of a financial product or a financial service.

IV. C. – 1:103: Priority rules
In the case of any conflict:
(a) the rules in Part IV. D. (Mandate) and Part IV. E. (Commercial agency, franchise and distributorship) prevail over the rules in this Part; and
(b) the rules in Chapters 3 to 8 of this Part prevail over the rules in Chapter 2 of this Part.

Chapter 2:
Rules applying to service contracts in general

IV. C. – 2:101: Price
Where the service provider is a business, a price is payable unless the circumstances indicate otherwise.

IV. C. – 2:102: Pre-contractual duties to warn
(1) The service provider is under a pre-contractual duty to warn the client if the service provider becomes aware of a risk that the service requested:
　(a) may not achieve the result stated or envisaged by the client;
　(b) may damage other interests of the client; or
　(c) may become more expensive or take more time than reasonably expected by the client.
(2) The duty to warn in paragraph (1) does not apply if the client:
　(a) already knows of the risks referred to in paragraph (1); or
　(b) could reasonably be expected to know of them.
(3) If a risk referred to in paragraph (1) materialises and the service provider was in breach of the duty to warn of it, a subsequent change of the service by the service provider under IV. C. – 2:109 (Unilateral variation of the service contract) which is based on the materialisation of the risk is of no effect unless the service provider proves that the client, if duly warned, would have entered into a contract anyway. This is without prejudice to any other remedies, including remedies for mistake, which the client may have.

(4) The client is under a pre-contractual duty to warn the service provider if the client becomes aware of unusual facts which are likely to cause the service to become more expensive or time-consuming than expected by the service provider or to cause any danger to the service provider or others when performing the service.

(5) If the facts referred to under paragraph (4) occur and the service provider was not duly warned, the service provider is entitled to:

    (a) damages for the loss the service provider sustained as a consequence of the failure to warn; and

    (b) an adjustment of the time allowed for performance of the service.

(6) For the purpose of paragraph (1), the service provider is presumed to be aware of the risks mentioned if they should be obvious from all the facts and circumstances known to the service provider, considering the information which the service provider must collect about the result stated or envisaged by the client and the circumstances in which the service is to be carried out.

(7) For the purpose of paragraph (2)(b) the client cannot reasonably be expected to know of a risk merely because the client was competent, or was advised by others who were competent, in the relevant field, unless such other person acted as the agent of the client, in which case II. – 1:105 (Imputed knowledge etc.) applies.

(8) For the purpose of paragraph (4), the client is presumed to be aware of the facts mentioned if they should be obvious from all the facts and circumstances known to the client without investigation.

IV. C. – 2:103: Obligation to co-operate

(1) The obligation of co-operation requires in particular:

    (a) the client to answer reasonable requests by the service provider for information in so far as this may reasonably be considered necessary to enable the service provider to perform the obligations under the contract;

    (b) the client to give directions regarding the performance of the service in so far as this may reasonably be considered necessary to enable the service provider to perform the obligations under the contract;

(c) the client, in so far as the client is to obtain permits or licences, to obtain these at such time as may reasonably be considered necessary to enable the service provider to perform the obligations under the contract;

(d) the service provider to give the client a reasonable opportunity to determine whether the service provider is performing the obligations under the contract; and

(e) the parties to co-ordinate their respective efforts in so far as this may reasonably be considered necessary to perform their respective obligations under the contract.

(2) If the client fails to perform the obligations under paragraph (1)(a) or (b), the service provider may either withhold performance or base performance on the expectations, preferences and priorities the client could reasonably be expected to have, given the information and directions which have been gathered, provided that the client is warned in accordance with IV. C. – 2:108 (Contractual obligation of the service provider to warn).

(3) If the client fails to perform the obligations under paragraph (1) causing the service to become more expensive or to take more time than agreed on in the contract, the service provider is entitled to:

(a) damages for the loss the service provider sustained as a consequence of the non-performance; and

(b) an adjustment of the time allowed for supplying the service.

IV. C. – 2:104: Subcontractors, tools and materials

(1) The service provider may subcontract the performance of the service in whole or in part without the client's consent, unless personal performance is required by the contract.

(2) Any subcontractor so engaged by the service provider must be of adequate competence.

(3) The service provider must ensure that any tools and materials used for the performance of the service are in conformity with the contract and the applicable statutory rules, and fit to achieve the particular purpose for which they are to be used.

(4) In so far as subcontractors are nominated by the client or tools and materials are provided by the client, the responsibility of the service provider is governed by IV. C. – 2:107 (Directions of the client) and IV. C. – 2:108 (Contractual obligation of the service provider to warn).

IV. C. – 2:105: Obligation of skill and care

(1) The service provider must perform the service:
- (a) with the care and skill which a reasonable service provider would exercise under the circumstances; and
- (b) in conformity with any statutory or other binding legal rules which are applicable to the service.

(2) If the service provider professes a higher standard of care and skill the provider must exercise that care and skill.

(3) If the service provider is, or purports to be, a member of a group of professional service providers for which standards have been set by a relevant authority or by that group itself, the service provider must exercise the care and skill expressed in those standards.

(4) In determining the care and skill the client is entitled to expect, regard is to be had, among other things, to:
- (a) the nature, the magnitude, the frequency and the foreseeability of the risks involved in the performance of the service for the client;
- (b) if damage has occurred, the costs of any precautions which would have prevented that damage or similar damage from occurring;
- (c) whether the service provider is a business;
- (d) whether a price is payable and, if one is payable, its amount; and
- (e) the time reasonably available for the performance of the service.

(5) The obligations under this Article require in particular the service provider to take reasonable precautions in order to prevent the occurrence of damage as a consequence of the performance of the service.

IV. C. – 2:106: Obligation to achieve result

(1) The supplier of a service must achieve the specific result stated or envisaged by the client at the time of the conclusion of the contract, provided that in the case of a result envisaged but not stated:
- (a) the result envisaged was one which the client could reasonably be expected to have envisaged; and
- (b) the client had no reason to believe that there was a substantial risk that the result would not be achieved by the service.

(2) In so far as ownership of anything is transferred to the client under the service contract, it must be transferred free from any right or reasonably based claim of a third party. IV. A. – 2:305 (Third party rights or claims in general) and IV. A. – 2:306 (Third party rights or claims based on

industrial property or other intellectual property) apply with any appropriate adaptations.

IV. C. – 2:107: Directions of the client

(1) The service provider must follow all timely directions of the client regarding the performance of the service, provided that the directions:

    (a) are part of the contract itself or are specified in any document to which the contract refers; or

    (b) result from the realisation of choices left to the client by the contract; or

    (c) result from the realisation of choices initially left open by the parties.

(2) If non-performance of one or more of the obligations of the service provider under IV. C. – 2:105 (Obligation of skill and care) or IV. C. – 2:106 (Obligation to achieve result) is the consequence of following a direction which the service provider is obliged to follow under paragraph (1), the service provider is not liable under those Articles, provided that the client was duly warned under IV. C. – 2:108 (Contractual obligation of the service provider to warn).

(3) If the service provider perceives a direction falling under paragraph (1) to be a variation of the contract under IV. C. – 2:109 (Unilateral variation of the service contract) the service provider must warn the client accordingly. Unless the client then revokes the direction without undue delay, the service provider must follow the direction and the direction has effect as a variation of the contract.

IV. C. – 2:108: Contractual obligation of the service provider to warn

(1) The service provider must warn the client if the service provider becomes aware of a risk that the service requested:

    (a) may not achieve the result stated or envisaged by the client at the time of conclusion of the contract;

    (b) may damage other interests of the client; or

    (c) may become more expensive or take more time than agreed on in the contract

either as a result of following information or directions given by the client or collected in preparation for performance, or as a result of the occurrence of any other risk.

(2) The service provider must take reasonable measures to ensure that the client understands the content of the warning.

(3) The obligation to warn in paragraph (1) does not apply if the client:
(a) already knows of the risks referred to in paragraph (1); or
(b) could reasonably be expected to know of them.

(4) If a risk referred to in paragraph (1) materialises and the service provider did not perform the obligation to warn the client of it, a notice of variation by the service provider under IV. C. – 2:109 (Unilateral variation of the service contract) based on the materialisation of that risk is without effect.

(5) For the purpose of paragraph (1), the service provider is presumed to be aware of the risks mentioned if they should be obvious from all the facts and circumstances known to the service provider without investigation.

(6) For the purpose of paragraph (3)(b), the client cannot reasonably be expected to know of a risk merely because the client was competent, or was advised by others who were competent, in the relevant field, unless such other person acted as the agent of the client, in which case II. – 1:105 (Imputed knowledge etc.) applies.

IV. C. – 2:109: Unilateral variation of the service contract

(1) Without prejudice to the client's right to terminate under IV. C. – 2:111 (Client's right to terminate), either party may, by notice to the other party, change the service to be provided, if such a change is reasonable taking into account:
(a) the result to be achieved;
(b) the interests of the client;
(c) the interests of the service provider; and
(d) the circumstances at the time of the change.

(2) A change is regarded as reasonable only if it is:
(a) necessary in order to enable the service provider to act in accordance with IV. C. – 2:105 (Obligation of skill and care) or, as the case may be, IV. C. – 2:106 (Obligation to achieve result);
(b) the consequence of a direction given in accordance with paragraph (1) of IV. C. – 2:107 (Directions of the client) and not revoked without undue delay after receipt of a warning in accordance with paragraph (3) of that Article;

(c) a reasonable response to a warning from the service provider under IV. C. – 2:108 (Contractual obligation of the service provider to warn); or

(d) required by a change of circumstances which would justify a variation of the service provider's obligations under III. – 1:110 (Variation or termination by court on a change of circumstances).

(3) Any additional price due as a result of the change has to be reasonable and is to be determined using the same methods of calculation as were used to establish the original price for the service.

(4) In so far as the service is reduced, the loss of profit, the expenses saved and any possibility that the service provider may be able to use the released capacity for other purposes are to be taken into account in the calculation of the price due as a result of the change.

(5) A change of the service may lead to an adjustment of the time of performance proportionate to the extra work required in relation to the work originally required for the performance of the service and the time span determined for performance of the service.

IV. C. – 2:110: Client's obligation to notify anticipated non-conformity

(1) The client must notify the service provider if the client becomes aware during the period for performance of the service that the service provider will fail to perform the obligation under IV. C. – 2:106 (Obligation to achieve result).

(2) The client is presumed to be so aware if from all the facts and circumstances known to the client without investigation the client has reason to be so aware.

(3) If a non-performance of the obligation under paragraph (1) causes the service to become more expensive or to take more time than agreed on in the contract, the service provider is entitled to:

(a) damages for the loss the service provider sustains as a consequence of that failure; and

(b) an adjustment of the time allowed for performance of the service.

IV. C. – 2:111: Client's right to terminate

(1) The client may terminate the contractual relationship at any time by giving notice to the service provider.

(2) The effects of termination are governed by III. – 1:109 (Variation or termination by notice) paragraph (3).

(3) When the client was justified in terminating the relationship no damages are payable for so doing.

(4) When the client was not justified in terminating the relationship, the termination is nevertheless effective but, the service provider has a right to damages in accordance with the rules in Book III.

(5) For the purposes of this Article, the client is justified in terminating the relationship if the client:

    (a) was entitled to terminate the relationship under the express terms of the contract and observed any requirements laid down in the contract for doing so;

    (b) was entitled to terminate the relationship under Book III, Chapter 3, Section 5 (Termination); or

    (c) was entitled to terminate the relationship under III. – 1:109 (Variation or termination by notice) paragraph (2) and gave a reasonable period of notice as required by that provision.

Chapter 3:
Construction

IV. C. – 3:101: Scope

(1) This Chapter applies to contracts under which one party, the constructor, undertakes to construct a building or other immovable structure, or to materially alter an existing building or other immovable structure, following a design provided by the client.

(2) It applies with appropriate adaptations to contracts under which the constructor undertakes:

    (a) to construct a movable or incorporeal thing, following a design provided by the client; or

    (b) to construct a building or other immovable structure, to materially alter an existing building or other immovable structure, or to construct a movable or incorporeal thing, following a design provided by the constructor.

IV. C. – 3:102: Obligation of client to co-operate
The obligation of co-operation requires in particular the client to:
(a) provide access to the site where the construction has to take place in so far as this may reasonably be considered necessary to enable the constructor to perform the obligations under the contract; and
(b) provide the components, materials and tools, in so far as they must be provided by the client, at such time as may reasonably be considered necessary to enable the constructor to perform the obligations under the contract.

IV. C. – 3:103: Obligation to prevent damage to structure
The constructor must take reasonable precautions in order to prevent any damage to the structure.

IV. C. – 3:104: Conformity
(1) The constructor must ensure that the structure is of the quality and description required by the contract. Where more than one structure is to be made, the quantity also must be in conformity with the contract.
(2) The structure does not conform to the contract unless it is:
    (a) fit for any particular purpose expressly or impliedly made known to the constructor at the time of the conclusion of the contract or at the time of any variation in accordance with IV. C. – 2:109 (Unilateral variation of the service contract) pertaining to the issue in question; and
    (b) fit for the particular purpose or purposes for which a structure of the same description would ordinarily be used.
(3) The client is not entitled to invoke a remedy for non-conformity if a direction provided by the client under IV. C. – 2:107 (Directions of the client) is the cause of the non-conformity and the constructor performed the obligation to warn pursuant to IV. C. – 2:108 (Contractual obligation of the service provider to warn).

IV. C. – 3:105: Inspection, supervision and acceptance
(1) The client may inspect or supervise the tools and materials used in the construction process, the process of construction and the resulting structure in a reasonable manner and at any reasonable time, but is not bound to do so.

(2) If the parties agree that the constructor has to present certain elements of the tools and materials used, the process or the resulting structure to the client for acceptance, the constructor may not proceed with the construction before having been allowed by the client to do so.

(3) Absence of, or inadequate, inspection, supervision or acceptance does not relieve the constructor wholly or partially from liability. This rule also applies when the client is under a contractual obligation to inspect, supervise or accept the structure or the construction of it.

IV. C. – 3:106: Handing-over of the structure

(1) If the constructor regards the structure, or any part of it which is fit for independent use, as sufficiently completed and wishes to transfer control over it to the client, the client must accept such control within a reasonable time after being notified. The client may refuse to accept the control when the structure, or the relevant part of it, does not conform to the contract and such non-conformity makes it unfit for use.

(2) Acceptance by the client of the control over the structure does not relieve the constructor wholly or partially from liability. This rule also applies when the client is under a contractual obligation to inspect, supervise or accept the structure or the construction of it.

(3) This Article does not apply if, under the contract, control is not to be transferred to the client.

IV. C. – 3:107: Payment of the price

(1) The price or a proportionate part of it is payable when the constructor transfers the control of the structure or a part of it to the client in accordance with the preceding Article.

(2) However, where work remains to be done under the contract on the structure or relevant part of it after such transfer the client may withhold such part of the price as is reasonable until the work is completed.

(3) If, under the contract, control is not to be transferred to the client, the price is payable when the work has been completed, the constructor has so informed the client and the client has had a chance to inspect the structure.

IV. C. – 3:108: Risks

(1) This Article applies if the structure is destroyed or damaged due to an event which the constructor could not have avoided or overcome and the constructor cannot be held accountable for the destruction or damage.

(2) In this Article the "relevant time" is:
- (a) where the control of the structure is to be transferred to the client, the time when such control has been, or should have been, transferred in accordance with IV. C. – 3:106 (Handing-over of the structure);
- (b) in other cases, the time when the work has been completed and the constructor has so informed the client.

(3) When the situation mentioned in paragraph (1) has been caused by an event occurring before the relevant time and it is still possible to perform:
- (a) the constructor still has to perform or, as the case may be, perform again;
- (b) the client is only obliged to pay for the constructor's performance under (a);
- (c) the time for performance is extended in accordance with paragraph (6) of IV. C. – 2:109 (Unilateral variation of the service contract);
- (d) the rules of III. – 3:104 (Excuse due to an impediment) may apply to the constructor's original performance; and
- (e) the constructor is not obliged to compensate the client for losses to materials provided by the client.

(4) When the situation mentioned in paragraph (1) has been caused by an event occurring before the relevant time, and it is no longer possible to perform:
- (a) the client does not have to pay for the service rendered;
- (b) the rules of III. – 3:104 (Excuse due to an impediment) may apply to the constructor's performance; and
- (c) the constructor is not obliged to compensate the client for losses to materials provided by the client, but is obliged to return the structure or what remains of it to the client.

(5) When the situation mentioned in paragraph (1) has been caused by an event occurring after the relevant time:
- (a) the constructor does not have to perform again; and
- (b) the client remains obliged to pay the price.

Chapter 4:
Processing

IV. C. – 4:101: Scope

(1) This Chapter applies to contracts under which one party, the processor, undertakes to perform a service on an existing movable or incorporeal thing or to an immovable structure for another party, the client. It does not, however, apply to construction work on an existing building or other immovable structure.

(2) This Chapter applies in particular to contracts under which the processor undertakes to repair, maintain or clean an existing movable or incorporeal thing or immovable structure.

IV. C. – 4:102: Obligation of client to co-operate

The obligation to co-operate requires in particular the client to:

(a) hand over the thing or to give the control of it to the processor, or to give access to the site where the service is to be performed in so far as may reasonably be considered necessary to enable the processor to perform the obligations under the contract; and

(b) in so far as they must be provided by the client, provide the components, materials and tools in time to enable the processor to perform the obligations under the contract.

IV. C. – 4:103: Obligation to prevent damage to thing being processed

The processor must take reasonable precautions in order to prevent any damage to the thing being processed.

IV. C. – 4:104: Inspection and supervision

(1) If the service is to be performed at a site provided by the client, the client may inspect or supervise the tools and material used, the performance of the service and the thing on which the service is performed in a reasonable manner and at any reasonable time, but is not bound to do so.

(2) Absence of, or inadequate inspection or supervision does not relieve the processor wholly or partially from liability. This rule also applies

when the client is under a contractual obligation to accept, inspect or supervise the processing of the thing.

IV. C. – 4:105: Return of the thing processed

(1) If the processor regards the service as sufficiently completed and wishes to return the thing or the control of it to the client, the client must accept such return or control within a reasonable time after being notified. The client may refuse to accept the return or control when the thing is not fit for use in accordance with the particular purpose for which the client had the service performed, provided that such purpose was made known to the processor or that the processor otherwise has reason to know of it.

(2) The processor must return the thing or the control of it within a reasonable time after being so requested by the client.

(3) Acceptance by the client of the return of the thing or the control of it does not relieve the processor wholly or partially from liability for non-performance.

(4) If, by virtue of the rules on the acquisition of property, the processor has become the owner of the thing, or a share in it, as a consequence of the performance of the obligations under the contract, the processor must transfer ownership of the thing or share when the thing is returned.

IV. C. – 4:106: Payment of the price

(1) The price is payable when the processor transfers the thing or the control of it to the client in accordance with IV. C. – 4:105 (Return of the thing processed) or the client, without being entitled to do so, refuses to accept the return of the thing.

(2) However, where work remains to be done under the contract on the thing after such transfer or refusal the client may withhold such part of the price as is reasonable until the work is completed.

(3) If, under the contract, the thing or the control of it is not to be transferred to the client, the price is payable when the work has been completed and the processor has so informed the client.

IV. C. – 4:107: Risks

(1) This Article applies if the thing is destroyed or damaged due to an event which the processor could not have avoided or overcome and the processor cannot be held accountable for the destruction or damage.

(2) If, prior to the event mentioned in paragraph (1), the processor had indicated that the processor regarded the service as sufficiently completed and that the processor wished to return the thing or the control of it to the client:

(a) the processor is not required to perform again; and

(b) the client must pay the price.

The price is due when the processor returns the remains of the thing, if any, or the client indicates that the client does not want the remains. In the latter case, the processor may dispose of the remains at the client's expense. This provision does not apply if the client was entitled to refuse the return of the thing under paragraph (1) of IV. C. – 4:105 (Return of the thing processed).

(3) If the parties had agreed that the processor would be paid for each period which has elapsed, the client is obliged to pay the price for each period which has elapsed before the event mentioned in paragraph (1) occurred.

(4) If, after the event mentioned in paragraph (1), performance of the obligations under the contract is still possible for the processor:

(a) the processor still has to perform or, as the case may be, perform again;

(b) the client is only obliged to pay for the processor's performance under (a); the processor's entitlement to a price under paragraph (3) is not affected by this provision;

(c) the client is obliged to compensate the processor for the costs the processor has to incur in order to acquire materials replacing the materials supplied by the client, unless the client on being so requested by the processor supplies these materials; and

(d) if need be, the time for performance is extended in accordance with paragraph (6) of IV. C. – 2:109 (Unilateral variation of the service contract).

This paragraph is without prejudice to the client's right to terminate the contractual relationship under IV. C. – 2:111 (Client's right to terminate).

(5) If, in the situation mentioned in paragraph (1), performance of the obligations under the contract is no longer possible for the processor:

    (a) the client does not have to pay for the service rendered; the processor's entitlement to a price under paragraph (3) is not affected by this provision; and

    (b) the processor is obliged to return to the client the thing and the materials supplied by the client or what remains of them, unless the client indicates that the client does not want the remains. In the latter case, the processor may dispose of the remains at the client's expense.

IV. C. – 4:108: Limitation of liability

In a contract between two businesses, a term restricting the processor's liability for non-performance to the value of the thing, had the service been performed correctly, is presumed to be fair for the purposes of II. – 9:405 (Meaning of "unfair" in contracts between businesses) except to the extent that it restricts liability for damage caused intentionally or by way of grossly negligent behaviour on the part of the processor or any person for whose actions the processor is responsible.

Chapter 5:
Storage

IV. C. – 5:101: Scope

(1) This Chapter applies to contracts under which one party, the storer, undertakes to store a movable or incorporeal thing for another party, the client.

(2) This Chapter does not apply to the storage of:

    (a) immovable structures;

    (b) movable or incorporeal things during transportation; and

    (c) money or securities (except in the circumstances mentioned in paragraph (7) of IV. C. – 5:110 (Liability of the hotel-keeper)) or rights.

IV. C. – 5:102: Storage place and subcontractors

(1) The storer, in so far as the storer provides the storage place, must provide a place fit for storing the thing in such a manner that the thing can be returned in the condition the client may expect.

(2) The storer may not subcontract the performance of the service without the client's consent.

IV. C. – 5:103: Protection and use of the thing stored

(1) The storer must take reasonable precautions in order to prevent unnecessary deterioration, decay or depreciation of the thing stored.

(2) The storer may use the thing handed over for storage only if the client has agreed to such use.

IV. C. – 5:104: Return of the thing stored

(1) Without prejudice to any other obligation to return the thing, the storer must return the thing at the agreed time or, where the contractual relationship is terminated before the agreed time, within a reasonable time after being so requested by the client.

(2) The client must accept the return of the thing when the storage obligation comes to an end and when acceptance of return is properly requested by the storer.

(3) Acceptance by the client of the return of the thing does not relieve the storer wholly or partially from liability for non-performance.

(4) If the client fails to accept the return of the thing at the time provided under paragraph (2), the storer has the right to sell the thing in accordance with III. – 2:111 (Property not accepted), provided that the storer has given the client reasonable warning of the storer's intention to do so.

(5) If, during storage, the thing bears fruit, the storer must hand this fruit over when the thing is returned to the client.

(6) If, by virtue of the rules on the acquisition of ownership, the storer has become the owner of the thing, the storer must return a thing of the same kind and the same quality and quantity and transfer ownership of that thing. This Article applies with appropriate adaptations to the substituted thing.

(7) This Article applies with appropriate adaptations if a third party who has the right or authority to receive the thing requests its return.

IV. C. – 5:105: Conformity

(1) The storage of the thing does not conform with the contract unless the thing is returned in the same condition as it was in when handed over to the storer.

(2) If, given the nature of the thing or the contract, it cannot reasonably be expected that the thing is returned in the same condition, the storage of the thing does not conform with the contract if the thing is not returned in such condition as the client could reasonably expect.

(3) If, given the nature of the thing or the contract, it cannot reasonably be expected that the same thing is returned, the storage of the thing does not conform with the contract if the thing which is returned is not in the same condition as the thing which was handed over for storage, or if it is not of the same kind, quality and quantity, or if ownership of the thing is not transferred in accordance with paragraph (6) of IV. C. – 5:104 (Return of the thing stored).

IV. C. – 5:106: Payment of the price

(1) The price is payable at the time when the thing is returned to the client in accordance with IV. C. – 5:104 (Return of the thing stored) or the client, without being entitled to do so, refuses to accept the return of the thing.

(2) The storer may withhold the thing until the client pays the price. III. – 3:401 (Right to withhold performance of reciprocal obligation) applies accordingly.

IV. C. – 5:107: Post-storage obligation to inform

After the ending of the storage, the storer must inform the client of:

(a) any damage which has occurred to the thing during storage; and

(b) the necessary precautions which the client must take before using or transporting the thing, unless the client could reasonably be expected to be aware of the need for such precautions.

IV. C. – 5:108: Risks

(1) This Article applies if the thing is destroyed or damaged due to an event which the storer could not have avoided or overcome and if the storer cannot be held accountable for the destruction or damage.

(2) If, prior to the event, the storer had notified the client that the client was required to accept the return of the thing, the client must pay the

price. The price is due when the storer returns the remains of the thing, if any, or the client indicates to the storer that the client does not want those remains.

(3) If, prior to the event, the storer had not notified the client that the client was required to accept the return of the thing:

   (a) if the parties had agreed that the storer would be paid for each period of time which has elapsed, the client must pay the price for each period which has elapsed before the event occurred;

   (b) if further performance of the obligations under the contract is still possible for the storer, the storer is required to continue performance, without prejudice to the client's right to terminate the contractual relationship under IV. C. – 2:111 (Client's right to terminate);

   (c) if performance of the obligations under the contract is no longer possible for the storer the client does not have to pay for the service rendered except to the extent that the storer is entitled to a price under subparagraph (a); and the storer must return to the client the remains of the thing unless the client indicates that the client does not want those remains.

(4) If the client indicates to the storer that the client does not want the remains of the thing, the storer may dispose of the remains at the client's expense.

IV. C. – 5:109: Limitation of liability

In a contract between two businesses, a term restricting the storer's liability for non-performance to the value of the thing is presumed to be fair for the purposes of II. – 9:405 (Meaning of "unfair" in contracts between businesses), except to the extent that it restricts liability for damage caused intentionally or by way of grossly negligent conduct on the part of the storer or any person for whose actions the storer is responsible.

IV. C. – 5:110: Liability of the hotel-keeper

(1) A hotel-keeper is liable as a storer for any damage to, or destruction or loss of, a thing brought to the hotel by any guest who stays at the hotel and has sleeping accommodation there.

(2) For the purposes of paragraph (1) a thing is regarded as brought to the hotel:

(a) if it is at the hotel during the time when the guest has the use of sleeping accommodation there;

(b) if the hotel-keeper or a person for whose actions the hotel-keeper is responsible takes charge of it outside the hotel during the period for which the guest has the use of the sleeping accommodation at the hotel; or

(c) if the hotel-keeper or a person for whose actions the hotel-keeper is responsible takes charge of it whether at the hotel or outside it during a reasonable period preceding or following the time when the guest has the use of sleeping accommodation at the hotel.

(3) The hotel-keeper is not liable in so far as the damage, destruction or loss is caused by:

(a) a guest or any person accompanying, employed by or visiting the guest;

(b) an impediment beyond the hotel-keeper's control; or

(c) the nature of the thing.

(4) A term excluding or limiting the liability of the hotel-keeper is unfair for the purposes of Book II, Chapter 9, Section 4 if it excludes or limits liability in a case where the hotel-keeper, or a person for whose actions the hotel-keeper is responsible, causes the damage, destruction or loss intentionally or by way of grossly negligent conduct.

(5) Except where the damage, destruction or loss is caused intentionally or by way of grossly negligent conduct of the hotel-keeper or a person for whose actions the hotel-keeper is responsible, the guest is required to inform the hotel-keeper of the damage, destruction or loss without undue delay. If the guest fails to inform the hotel-keeper without undue delay, the hotel-keeper is not liable.

(6) The hotel-keeper has the right to withhold any thing referred to in paragraph (1) until the guest has satisfied any right the hotel-keeper has against the guest with respect to accommodation, food, drink and solicited services performed for the guest in the hotel-keeper's professional capacity.

(7) This Article does not apply if and to the extent that a separate storage contract is concluded between the hotel-keeper and any guest for any thing brought to the hotel. A separate storage contract is concluded if a thing is handed over for storage to, and accepted for storage by, the hotel-keeper.

Chapter 6:
Design

IV. C. – 6:101: Scope

(1) This Chapter applies to contracts under which one party, the designer, undertakes to design for another party, the client:
   (a) an immovable structure which is to be constructed by or on behalf of the client; or
   (b) a movable or incorporeal thing or service which is to be constructed or performed by or on behalf of the client.
(2) A contract under which one party undertakes to design and to supply a service which consists of carrying out the design is to be considered as primarily a contract for the supply of the subsequent service.

IV. C. – 6:102: Pre-contractual duty to warn

The designer's pre-contractual duty to warn requires in particular the designer to warn the client in so far as the designer lacks special expertise in specific problems which require the involvement of specialists.

IV. C. – 6:103: Obligation of skill and care

The designer's obligation of skill and care requires in particular the designer to:

(a) attune the design work to the work of other designers who contracted with the client, to enable there to be an efficient performance of all services involved;
(b) integrate the work of other designers which is necessary to ensure that the design will conform to the contract;
(c) include any information for the interpretation of the design which is necessary for a user of the design of average competence (or a specific user made known to the designer at the conclusion of the contract) to give effect to the design;
(d) enable the user of the design to give effect to the design without violation of public law rules or interference based on justified third-party rights of which the designer knows or could reasonably be expected to know; and
(e) provide a design which allows economic and technically efficient realisation.

IV. C. – 6:104: Conformity

(1) The design does not conform to the contract unless it enables the user of the design to achieve a specific result by carrying out the design with the skill and care which could reasonably be expected.

(2) The client is not entitled to invoke a remedy for non-conformity if a direction provided by the client under IV. C. – 2:107 (Directions of the client) is the cause of the non-conformity and the designer performed the obligation to warn under IV. C. – 2:108 (Contractual obligation of the service provider to warn).

IV. C. – 6:105: Handing over of the design

(1) In so far as the designer regards the design, or a part of it which is fit for carrying out independently from the completion of the rest of the design, as sufficiently completed and wishes to transfer the design to the client, the client must accept it within a reasonable time after being notified.

(2) The client may refuse to accept the design when it, or the relevant part of it, does not conform to the contract and such non-conformity amounts to a fundamental non-performance.

IV. C. – 6:106: Records

(1) After performance of both parties' other contractual obligations, the designer must, on request by the client, hand over all relevant documents or copies of them.

(2) The designer must store, for a reasonable time, relevant documents which are not handed over. Before destroying the documents, the designer must offer them again to the client.

IV. C. – 6:107: Limitation of liability

In contracts between two businesses, a term restricting the designer's liability for non-performance to the value of the structure, thing or service which is to be constructed or performed by or on behalf of the client following the design, is presumed to be fair for the purposes of II. – 9:405 (Meaning of "unfair" in contracts between businesses) except to the extent that it restricts liability for damage caused intentionally or by grossly negligent conduct on the part of the designer or any person for whose actions the designer is responsible.

Chapter 7:
Information and advice

IV. C. – 7:101: Scope
(1) This Chapter applies to contracts under which one party, the provider, undertakes to provide information or advice to another party, the client.
(2) This Chapter does not apply in relation to treatment in so far as Chapter 8 (Treatment) contains more specific rules on the obligation to inform.
(3) In the remainder of this Chapter any reference to information includes a reference to advice.

IV. C. – 7:102: Obligation to collect preliminary data
(1) The provider must, in so far as this may reasonably be considered necessary for the performance of the service, collect data about:
  (a) the particular purpose for which the client requires the information;
  (b) the client's preferences and priorities in relation to the information;
  (c) the decision the client can be expected to make on the basis of the information; and
  (d) the personal situation of the client.
(2) In case the information is intended to be passed on to a group of persons, the data to be collected must relate to the purposes, preferences, priorities and personal situations that can reasonably be expected from individuals within such a group.
(3) In so far as the provider must obtain data from the client, the provider must explain what the client is required to supply.

IV. C. – 7:103: Obligation to acquire and use expert knowledge
The provider must acquire and use the expert knowledge to which the provider has or should have access as a professional information provider or adviser, in so far as this may reasonably be considered necessary for the performance of the service.

IV. C. – 7:104: Obligation of skill and care

(1) The provider's obligation of skill and care requires in particular the provider to:
  (a) take reasonable measures to ensure that the client understands the content of the information;
  (b) act with the care and skill that a reasonable information provider would demonstrate under the circumstances when providing evaluative information; and
  (c) in any case where the client is expected to make a decision on the basis of the information, inform the client of the risks involved, in so far as such risks could reasonably be expected to influence the client's decision.

(2) When the provider expressly or impliedly undertakes to provide the client with a recommendation to enable the client to make a subsequent decision, the provider must:
  (a) base the recommendation on a skilful analysis of the expert knowledge to be collected in relation to the purposes, priorities, preferences and personal situation of the client;
  (b) inform the client of alternatives the provider can personally provide relating to the subsequent decision and of their advantages and risks, as compared with those of the recommended decision; and
  (c) inform the client of other alternatives the provider cannot personally provide, unless the provider expressly informs the client that only a limited range of alternatives is offered or this is apparent from the situation.

IV. C. – 7:105: Conformity

(1) The provider must provide information which is of the quantity, quality and description required by the contract.
(2) The factual information provided by the information provider to the client must be a correct description of the actual situation described.

IV. C. – 7:106: Records

In so far as this may reasonably be considered necessary, having regard to the interest of the client, the provider must keep records regarding the information provided in accordance with this Chapter and make such records or excerpts from them available to the client on reasonable request.

IV. C. – 7:107: Conflict of interest

(1) When the provider expressly or impliedly undertakes to provide the client with a recommendation to enable the client to make a subsequent decision, the provider must disclose any possible conflict of interest which might influence the performance of the provider's obligations.

(2) So long as the contractual obligations have not been completely performed, the provider may not enter into a relationship with another party which may give rise to a possible conflict with the interests of the client, without full disclosure to the client and the client's explicit or implicit consent.

IV. C. – 7:108: Influence of ability of the client

(1) The involvement in the supply of the service of other persons on the client's behalf or the mere competence of the client does not relieve the provider of any obligation under this Chapter.

(2) The provider is relieved of those obligations if the client already has knowledge of the information or if the client has reason to know of the information.

(3) For the purpose of paragraph (2), the client has reason to know if the information should be obvious to the client without investigation.

IV. C. – 7:109: Causation

If the provider knows or could reasonably be expected to know that a subsequent decision will be based on the information to be provided, and if the client makes such a decision and suffers loss as a result, any non-performance of an obligation under the contract by the provider is presumed to have caused the loss if the client proves that, if the provider had provided all information required, it would have been reasonable for the client to have seriously considered making an alternative decision.

Chapter 8:
Treatment

IV. C. – 8:101: Scope

(1) This Chapter applies to contracts under which one party, the treatment provider, undertakes to provide medical treatment for another party, the patient.

(2) It applies with appropriate adaptations to contracts under which the treatment provider undertakes to provide any other service in order to change the physical or mental condition of a person.

(3) Where the patient is not the contracting party, the patient is regarded as a third party on whom the contract confers rights corresponding to the obligations of the treatment provider imposed by this Chapter.

IV. C. – 8:102: Preliminary assessment

The treatment provider must, in so far as this may reasonably be considered necessary for the performance of the service:

(a) interview the patient about the patient's health condition, symptoms, previous illnesses, allergies, previous or other current treatment and the patient's preferences and priorities in relation to the treatment;

(b) carry out the examinations necessary to diagnose the health condition of the patient; and

(c) consult with any other treatment providers involved in the treatment of the patient.

IV. C. – 8:103: Obligations regarding instruments, medicines, materials, installations and premises

(1) The treatment provider must use instruments, medicines, materials, installations and premises which are of at least the quality demanded by accepted and sound professional practice, which conform to applicable statutory rules, and which are fit to achieve the particular purpose for which they are to be used.

(2) The parties may not, to the detriment of the patient, exclude the application of this Article or derogate from or vary its effects.

IV. C. – 8:104: Obligation of skill and care

(1) The treatment provider's obligation of skill and care requires in particular the treatment provider to provide the patient with the care and skill which a reasonable treatment provider exercising and professing care and skill would demonstrate under the given circumstances.

(2) If the treatment provider lacks the experience or skill to treat the patient with the required degree of skill and care, the treatment provider must refer the patient to a treatment provider who can.

(3) The parties may not, to the detriment of the patient, exclude the application of this Article or derogate from or vary its effects.

IV. C. – 8:105: Obligation to inform

(1) The treatment provider must, in order to give the patient a free choice regarding treatment, inform the patient about, in particular:
    (a) the patient's existing state of health;
    (b) the nature of the proposed treatment;
    (c) the advantages of the proposed treatment;
    (d) the risks of the proposed treatment;
    (e) the alternatives to the proposed treatment, and their advantages and risks as compared to those of the proposed treatment; and
    (f) the consequences of not having treatment.
(2) The treatment provider must, in any case, inform the patient about any risk or alternative which might reasonably influence the patient's decision on whether to give consent to the proposed treatment or not. It is presumed that a risk might reasonably influence that decision if its materialisation would lead to serious detriment to the patient. Unless otherwise provided, the obligation to inform is subject to the provisions of Chapter 7 (Information and Advice).
(3) The information must be provided in a way understandable to the patient.

IV. C. – 8:106: Obligation to inform in case of unnecessary or experimental treatment

(1) If the treatment is not necessary for the preservation or improvement of the patient's health, the treatment provider must disclose all known risks.
(2) If the treatment is experimental, the treatment provider must disclose all information regarding the objectives of the experiment, the nature of the treatment, its advantages and risks and the alternatives, even if only potential.
(3) The parties may not, to the detriment of the patient, exclude the application of this Article or derogate from or vary its effects.

IV. C. – 8:107: Exceptions to the obligation to inform

(1) Information which would normally have to be provided by virtue of the obligation to inform may be withheld from the patient:
    (a) if there are objective reasons to believe that it would seriously and negatively influence the patient's health or life; or

(b) if the patient expressly states a wish not to be informed, provided that the non-disclosure of the information does not endanger the health or safety of third parties.

(2) The obligation to inform need not be performed where treatment must be provided in an emergency. In such a case the treatment provider must, so far as possible, provide the information later.

IV. C. – 8:108: Obligation not to treat without consent

(1) The treatment provider must not carry out treatment unless the patient has given prior informed consent to it.

(2) The patient may revoke consent at any time.

(3) In so far as the patient is incapable of giving consent, the treatment provider must not carry out treatment unless:
   (a) informed consent has been obtained from a person or institution legally entitled to take decisions regarding the treatment on behalf of the patient; or
   (b) any rules or procedures enabling treatment to be lawfully given without such consent have been complied with; or
   (c) the treatment must be provided in an emergency.

(4) In the situation described in paragraph (3), the treatment provider must not carry out treatment without considering, so far as possible, the opinion of the incapable patient with regard to the treatment and any such opinion expressed by the patient before becoming incapable.

(5) In the situation described in paragraph (3), the treatment provider may carry out only such treatment as is intended to improve the health condition of the patient.

(6) In the situation described in paragraph (2) of IV. C. – 8:106 (Obligation to inform in case of unnecessary or experimental treatment), consent must be given in an express and specific way.

(7) The parties may not, to the detriment of the patient, exclude the application of this Article or derogate from or vary its effects.

IV. C. – 8:109: Records

(1) The treatment provider must create adequate records of the treatment. Such records must include, in particular, information collected in any preliminary interviews, examinations or consultations, information regarding the consent of the patient and information regarding the treatment performed.

(2) The treatment provider must, on reasonable request:
- (a) give the patient, or if the patient is incapable of giving consent, the person or institution legally entitled to take decisions on behalf of the patient, access to the records; and
- (b) answer, in so far as reasonable, questions regarding the interpretation of the records.

(3) If the patient has suffered injury and claims that it is a result of non-performance by the treatment provider of the obligation of skill and care and the treatment provider fails to comply with paragraph (2), non-performance of the obligation of skill and care and a causal link between such non-performance and the injury are presumed.

(4) The treatment provider must keep the records, and give information about their interpretation, during a reasonable time of at least 10 years after the treatment has ended, depending on the usefulness of these records for the patient or the patient's heirs or representatives and for future treatments. Records which can reasonably be expected to be important after the reasonable time must be kept by the treatment provider after that time. If for any reason the treatment provider ceases activity, the records must be deposited or delivered to the patient for future consultation.

(5) The parties may not, to the detriment of the patient, exclude the application of paragraphs (1) to (4) or derogate from or vary their effects.

(6) The treatment provider may not disclose information about the patient or other persons involved in the patient's treatment to third parties unless disclosure is necessary in order to protect third parties or the public interest. The treatment provider may use the records in an anonymous way for statistical, educational or scientific purposes.

IV. C. – 8:110: Remedies for non-performance

With regard to any non-performance of an obligation under a contract for treatment, Book III, Chapter 3 (Remedies for Non-performance) and IV. C. – 2:111 (Client's right to terminate) apply with the following adaptations:
- (a) the treatment provider may not withhold performance or terminate the contractual relationship under that Chapter if this would seriously endanger the health of the patient; and

(b) in so far as the treatment provider has the right to withhold performance or to terminate the contractual relationship and is planning to
exercise that right, the treatment provider must refer the patient to
another treatment provider.

IV. C. – 8:111: Obligations of treatment-providing organisations
(1) If, in the process of performance of the obligations under the treatment
contract, activities take place in a hospital or on the premises of another treatment-providing organisation, and the hospital or that other
treatment-providing organisation is not a party to the treatment contract, it must make clear to the patient that it is not the contracting
party.
(2) Where the treatment provider cannot be identified, the hospital or
treatment-providing organisation in which the treatment took place is
treated as the treatment provider unless the hospital or treatment-providing organisation informs the patient, within a reasonable time, of
the identity of the treatment provider.
(3) The parties may not, to the detriment of the patient, exclude the application of this Article or derogate from or vary its effects.

Part D.
Mandate contracts

Chapter 1:
General provisions

IV. D. – 1:101: Scope
(1) This Part of Book IV applies to contracts and other juridical acts under
which a person, the agent, is authorised and instructed (mandated) by
another person, the principal:
  (a) to conclude a contract between the principal and a third party or
  otherwise directly affect the legal position of the principal in relation to a third party;
  (b) to conclude a contract with a third party, or do another juridical act
  in relation to a third party, on behalf of the principal but in such a

way that the agent and not the principal is a party to the contract
or other juridical act; or

    (c) to take steps which are meant to lead to, or facilitate, the conclu-
sion of a contract between the principal and a third party or the
doing of another juridical act which would affect the legal position
of the principal in relation to a third party.

(2) It applies where the agent undertakes to act on behalf of, and in accordance with the instructions of, the principal and, with appropriate
adaptations, where the agent is merely authorised but does not undertake to act, but nevertheless does act.

(3) It applies where the agent is to be paid a price and, with appropriate
adaptations, where the agent is not to be paid a price.

(4) It applies only to the internal relationship between the principal and
the agent (the mandate relationship). It does not apply to the relationship between the principal and the third party or the relationship (if
any) between the agent and the third party.

(5) Contracts to which this Part applies and to which Part C (Services) also
applies are to be regarded as falling primarily under this Part.

(6) This Part does not apply to contracts pertaining to investment services
and activities as defined by Directive 2004/39/EC, OJ L 145/1, as subsequently amended or replaced.

IV. D. – 1:102: Definitions

In this Part;

(a) the 'mandate' of the agent is the authorisation and instruction given by
the principal as modified by any subsequent direction;

(b) the 'mandate contract' is the contract under which the agent is authorised and instructed to act, and any reference to the mandate contract
includes a reference to any other juridical act by which the agent is
authorised and instructed to act;

(c) the 'prospective contract' is the contract the agent is authorised and
instructed to conclude, negotiate or facilitate, and any reference to the
prospective contract includes a reference to any other juridical act
which the agent is authorised and instructed to do, negotiate or facilitate;

(d) a mandate for direct representation is a mandate under which the agent
is to act in the name of the principal, or otherwise in such a way as to
indicate an intention to affect the principal's legal position;

(e) a mandate for indirect representation is a mandate under which the agent is to act in the agent's own name or otherwise in such a way as not to indicate an intention to affect the principal's legal position;

(f) a "direction" is a decision by the principal pertaining to the performance of the obligations under the mandate contract or to the contents of the prospective contract that is given at the time the mandate contract is concluded or, in accordance with the mandate, at a later moment;

(g) the "third party" is the party with whom the prospective contract is to be concluded, negotiated or facilitated by the agent;

(h) the "revocation" of the mandate of the agent is the recall by the principal of the mandate, so that it no longer has effect.

IV. D. – I:103: Duration of the mandate contract

A mandate contract may be concluded:

(a) for an indefinite period of time;

(b) for a fixed period; or

(c) for a particular task.

IV. D. – I:104: Revocation of the mandate

(1) Unless the following Article applies, the mandate of the agent can be revoked by the principal at any time by giving notice to the agent.

(2) The termination of the mandate relationship has the effect of a revocation of the mandate of the agent.

(3) The parties may not, to the detriment of the principal, exclude the application of this Article or derogate from or vary its effects, unless the requirements of the following Article are met.

IV. D. – I:105: Irrevocable mandate

(1) In derogation of the preceding Article, the mandate of the agent cannot be revoked by the principal if the mandate is given:

(a) in order to safeguard a legitimate interest of the agent other than the interest in the payment of the price; or

(b) in the common interest of the parties to another legal relationship, whether or not these parties are all parties to the mandate contract, and the irrevocability of the mandate of the agent is meant to properly safeguard the interest of one or more of these parties.

(2) The mandate may nevertheless be revoked if:
- (a) the mandate is irrevocable under paragraph (1)(a) and:
    - (i) the contractual relationship from which the legitimate interest of the agent originates is terminated for non-performance by the agent; or
    - (ii) there is a fundamental non-performance by the agent of the obligations under the mandate contract; or
    - (iii) there is an extraordinary and serious reason for the principal to terminate under IV. D. – 6:103 (Termination by principal for extraordinary and serious reason); or
- (b) the mandate is irrevocable under paragraph (1)(b) and:
    - (i) the parties in whose interest the mandate is irrevocable have agreed to the revocation of the mandate;
    - (ii) the relationship referred to in paragraph (1)(b) is terminated;
    - (iii) the agent commits a fundamental non-performance of the obligations under the mandate contract, provided that the agent is replaced without undue delay by another agent in conformity with the terms regulating the legal relationship between the principal and the other party or parties; or
    - (iv) there is an extraordinary and serious reason for the principal to terminate under IV. D. – 6:103 (Termination by principal for extraordinary and serious reason), provided that the agent is replaced without undue delay by another agent in conformity with the terms regulating the legal relationship between the principal and the other party or parties.

(3) Where the revocation of the mandate is not allowed under this Article, a notice of revocation is without effect.

(4) This Article does not apply if the mandate relationship is terminated under Chapter 7 of this Part.

Chapter 2:
Main obligations of the principal

IV. D. – 2:101: Obligation to co-operate
The obligation to co-operate under III. – 1:104 (Co-operation) requires the principal in particular to:

(a) answer requests by the agent for information in so far as such information is needed to allow the agent to perform the obligations under the mandate contract;

(b) give a direction regarding the performance of the obligations under the mandate contract in so far as this is required under the mandate contract or follows from a request for a direction under IV. D. – 4:102 (Request for a direction).

IV. D. – 2:102: Price
(1) The principal must pay a price if the agent performs the obligations under the mandate contract in the course of a business, unless the principal expected and could reasonably have expected the agent to perform the obligations otherwise than in exchange for a price.

(2) The price is payable when the mandated task has been completed and the agent has given account of that to the principal.

(3) If the parties had agreed on payment of a price for services rendered, the mandate relationship has terminated and the mandated task has not been completed, the price is payable as of the moment the agent has given account of the performance of the obligations under the mandate contract.

(4) When the mandate is for the conclusion of a prospective contract and the principal has concluded the prospective contract directly or another person appointed by the principal has concluded the prospective contract on the principal's behalf, the agent is entitled to the price or a proportionate part of it if the conclusion of the prospective contract can be attributed in full or in part to the agent's performance of the obligations under the mandate contract.

(5) When the mandate is for the conclusion of a prospective contract and the prospective contract is concluded after the mandate relationship has terminated, the principal must pay the price if payment of a price

based solely on the conclusion of the prospective contract was agreed and:

(a) the conclusion of the prospective contract is mainly the result of the agent's efforts; and

(b) the prospective contract is concluded within a reasonable period after the mandate relationship has terminated.

IV. D. – 2:103: Expenses incurred by agent

(1) When the agent is entitled to a price, the price is presumed to include the reimbursement of the expenses the agent has incurred in the performance of the obligations under the mandate contract.

(2) When the agent is not entitled to a price or when the parties have agreed that the expenses will be paid separately, the principal must reimburse the agent for the expenses the agent has incurred in the performance of the obligations under the mandate contract, when and in so far as the agent acted reasonably when incurring the expenses.

(3) The agent is entitled to reimbursement of expenses under paragraph (2) as from the time when the expenses are incurred and the agent has given account of the expenses.

(4) If the mandate relationship has terminated and the result on which the agent's remuneration is dependent is not achieved, the agent is entitled to reimbursement of reasonable expenses the agent has incurred in the performance of the obligations under the mandate contract. Paragraph (3) applies accordingly.

Chapter 3:
Performance by the agent
Section 1:
Main obligations of agent

IV. D. – 3:101: Obligation to act in accordance with mandate
At all stages of the mandate relationship the agent must act in accordance with the mandate.

IV. D. – 3:102: Obligation to act in interests of principal

(1) The agent must act in accordance with the interests of the principal, in so far as these have been communicated to the agent or the agent could reasonably be expected to be aware of them.

(2) Where the agent is not sufficiently aware of the principal's interests to enable the agent to properly perform the obligations under the mandate contract, the agent must request information from the principal.

IV. D. – 3:103: Obligation of skill and care

(1) The agent has an obligation to perform the obligations under the mandate contract with the care and skill that the principal is entitled to expect under the circumstances.

(2) If the agent professes a higher standard of care and skill the agent has an obligation to exercise that care and skill.

(3) If the agent is, or purports to be, a member of a group of professional agents for which standards exist that have been set by a relevant authority or by that group itself, the agent must exercise the care and skill expressed in these standards.

(4) In determining the care and skill the principal is entitled to expect, regard is to be had, among other things, to:
   (a) the nature, the magnitude, the frequency and the foreseeability of the risks involved in the performance of the obligations;
   (b) whether the obligations are performed by a non-professional or gratuitously;
   (c) the amount of the remuneration for the performance of the obligations; and
   (d) the time reasonably available for the performance of the obligations.

Section 2:
Consequences of acting beyond mandate

IV. D. – 3:201: Acting beyond mandate

(1) The agent may act in a way not covered by the mandate if:
   (a) the agent has reasonable ground for so acting on behalf of the principal;

    (b) the agent does not have a reasonable opportunity to discover the principal's wishes in the particular circumstances; and

    (c) the agent does not know and could not reasonably be expected to know that the act in the particular circumstances is against the principal's wishes.

(2) An act within paragraph (1) has the same consequences as between the agent and the principal as an act covered by the mandate.

IV. D. – 3:202: Consequences of ratification

Where, in circumstances not covered by the preceding Article, an agent has acted beyond the mandate in concluding a contract on behalf of the principal, ratification of that contract by the principal absolves the agent from liability to the principal, unless the principal without undue delay after ratification notifies the agent that the principal reserves remedies for the non-performance by the agent.

Section 3:
Mandate normally not exclusive

IV. D. – 3:301: Exclusivity not presumed

The principal is free to conclude, negotiate or facilitate the prospective contract directly or to appoint another agent to do so.

IV. D. – 3:302: Subcontracting

(1) The agent may subcontract the performance of the obligations under the mandate contract in whole or in part without the principal's consent, unless personal performance is required by the contract.

(2) Any subcontractor so engaged by the agent must be of adequate competence.

(3) In accordance with III. – 2:106 (Performance entrusted to another) the agent remains responsible for performance.

Section 4:
Obligation to inform principal

IV. D. – 3:401: Information about progress of performance
During the performance of the obligations under the mandate contract the agent must in so far as is reasonable under the circumstances inform the principal of the existence of, and the progress in, the negotiations or other steps leading to the possible conclusion or facilitation of the prospective contract.

IV. D. – 3:402: Accounting to the principal
(1) The agent must without undue delay inform the principal of the completion of the mandated task.
(2) The agent must give an account to the principal:
    (a) of the manner in which the obligations under the mandate contract have been performed; and
    (b) of money spent or received or expenses incurred by the agent in performing those obligations.
(3) Paragraph (2) applies with appropriate modifications if the mandate relationship is terminated in accordance with Chapters 6 and 7 and the obligations under the mandate contract have not been fully performed.

IV. D. – 3:403: Communication of identity of third party
(1) An agent who concludes the prospective contract with a third party must communicate the name and address of the third party to the principal on the principal's demand.
(2) In the case of a mandate for indirect representation paragraph (1) applies only if the agent has become insolvent.

Chapter 4:
Directions and changes
Section 1:
Directions

IV. D. – 4:101: Directions given by principal

(1) The principal is entitled to give directions to the agent.

(2) The agent must follow directions by the principal.

(3) The agent must warn the principal if the direction:

    (a) has the effect that the performance of the obligations under the mandate contract would become significantly more expensive or take significantly more time than agreed upon in the mandate contract; or

    (b) is inconsistent with the purpose of the mandate contract or may otherwise be detrimental to the interests of the principal.

(4) Unless the principal revokes the direction without undue delay after having been so warned by the agent, the direction is to be regarded as a change of the mandate contract under IV. D. – 4:201 (Changes of the mandate contract).

IV. D. – 4:102: Request for a direction

(1) The agent must ask for a direction on obtaining information which requires the principal to make a decision pertaining to the performance of the obligations under the mandate contract or the content of the prospective contract.

(2) The agent must ask for a direction if the mandated task is the conclusion of a prospective contract and the mandate contract does not determine whether the mandate is for direct representation or indirect representation.

IV. D. – 4:103: Consequences of failure to give a direction

(1) If the principal fails to give a direction when required to do so under the mandate contract or under paragraph (1) of IV. D. – 4:102 (Request for a direction), the agent may, in so far as relevant, resort to any of the remedies under Book III, Chapter 3 (Remedies for Non-performance) or base performance upon the expectations, preferences and priorities the

principal might reasonably be expected to have, given the information and directions that have been gathered.

(2) Where the agent bases performance upon the expectations, preferences and priorities the principal might reasonably be expected to have, the agent has a right to a proportionate adjustment of the price and of the time allowed or required for the conclusion of the prospective contract.

(3) If the principal fails to give a direction under paragraph (2) of IV. D. – 4:102 (Request for a direction), the agent may choose direct representation or indirect representation or may withhold performance under III. – 3:401 (Right to withhold performance of reciprocal obligation).

(4) The adjusted price that is to be paid under paragraph (2) must be reasonable and is to be determined using the same methods of calculation as were used to establish the original price for the performance of the obligations under the mandate contract.

IV. D. – 4:104: No time to ask or wait for direction

(1) If the agent is required to ask for a direction under IV. D. – 4:102 (Request for a direction) but needs to act before being able to contact the principal and to ask for a direction, or needs to act before the direction is given, the agent may base performance upon the expectations, preferences and priorities the principal might reasonably be expected to have, given the information and directions that have been gathered.

(2) In the situation referred to in paragraph (1), the agent has a right to a proportionate adjustment of the price and of the time allowed or required for the performance of the obligations under the mandate contract in so far as such an adjustment is reasonable given the circumstances of the case.

Section 2:
Changes of the mandate contract

IV. D. – 4:201: Changes of the mandate contract

(1) The mandate contract is changed if the principal:
  (a) significantly changes the mandate of the agent;

(b) does not revoke a direction without undue delay after having been warned in accordance with paragraph (3) of IV. D. – 4:101 (Directions given by principal).

(2) In the case of a change of the mandate contract under paragraph (1) the agent is entitled:

(a) to a proportionate adjustment of the price and of the time allowed or required for the performance of the obligations under the mandate contract; or

(b) to damages in accordance with III. – 3:702 (General measure of damages) to put the agent as nearly as possible into the position in which the agent would have been if the mandate contract had not been changed.

(3) In the case of a change of the mandate contract under paragraph (1) the agent may also terminate the mandate relationship by giving notice of termination for an extraordinary and serious reason under IV. D. – 6:105 (Termination by agent for extraordinary and serious reason), unless the change is minor or is to the agent's advantage.

(4) The adjusted price that is to be paid under paragraph (2)(a) must be reasonable and is to be determined using the same methods of calculation as were used to establish the original price for the performance of the obligations under the mandate contract.

Chapter 5:
Conflicts of interests

IV. D. – 5:101: Self-contracting

(1) The agent may not become the principal's counterparty to the prospective contract.

(2) The agent may nevertheless become the counterparty if:

(a) this is agreed by the parties in the mandate contract;

(b) the agent has disclosed an intention to become the counterparty and:

(i) the principal subsequently expresses consent; or

(ii) the principal does not object to the agent becoming the counterparty after having been requested to indicate consent or a refusal of consent;

    (c) the principal otherwise knew, or could reasonably be expected to have known, of the agent becoming the counterparty and the principal did not object within a reasonable time; or

    (d) the content of the prospective contract is so precisely determined in the mandate contract that there is no risk that the interests of the principal may be disregarded.

(3) If the principal is a consumer, the agent may only become the counterparty if:

    (a) the agent has disclosed that information and the principal has given express consent to the agent becoming the counterparty to the particular prospective contract; or

    (b) the content of the prospective contract is so precisely determined in the mandate contract that there is no risk that the interests of the principal may be disregarded.

(4) The parties may not, to the detriment of the principal, exclude the application of paragraph (3) or derogate from or vary its effects.

(5) If the agent has become the counterparty, the agent is not entitled to a price for services rendered as an agent.

IV. D. – 5:102: Double mandate

(1) The agent may not act as the agent of both the principal and the principal's counterparty to the prospective contract.

(2) The agent may nevertheless act as the agent of both the principal and the counterparty if:

    (a) this is agreed by the parties in the mandate contract;

    (b) the agent has disclosed an intention to act as the agent of the counterparty and the principal:

        (i) subsequently expresses consent; or

        (ii) does not object to the agent acting as the agent of the counterparty after having been requested to indicate consent or a refusal of consent;

    (c) the principal otherwise knew, or could reasonably be expected to have known, of the agent acting as the agent of the counterparty and the principal did not object within a reasonable time; or

    (d) the content of the prospective contract is so precisely determined in the mandate contract that there is no risk that the interests of the principal may be disregarded.

(3) If the principal is a consumer, the agent may only act as the agent of both the principal and of the counterparty if:

    (a) the agent has disclosed that information and the principal has given express consent to the agent acting also as the agent of the counterparty to the particular prospective contract; or

    (b) the content of the prospective contract is so precisely determined in the mandate contract that there is no risk that the interests of the principal may be disregarded.

(4) The parties may not, to the detriment of the principal, exclude the application of paragraph (3) or derogate from or vary its effects.

(5) If and in so far as the agent has acted in accordance with the previous paragraphs, the agent is entitled to the price.

Chapter 6:
Termination by notice other than for non-performance

IV. D. – 6:101: Termination by notice in general

(1) Either party may terminate the mandate relationship at any time by giving notice to the other.

(2) For the purposes of paragraph (1), a revocation of the mandate of the agent is treated as termination.

(3) Termination of the mandate relationship is not effective if the mandate of the agent is irrevocable under IV. D. – 1:105 (Irrevocable mandate).

(4) The effects of termination are governed by III. – 1:109 (Variation or termination by notice) paragraph (3).

(5) When the party giving the notice was justified in terminating the relationship no damages are payable for so doing.

(6) When the party giving the notice was not justified in terminating the relationship, the termination is nevertheless effective but the other party is entitled to damages in accordance with the rules in Book III.

(7) For the purposes of this Article the party giving the notice is justified in terminating the relationship if that party:

    (a) was entitled to terminate the relationship under the express terms of the contract and observed any requirements laid down in the contract for doing so;

    (b) was entitled to terminate the relationship under Book III, Chapter 3, Section 5 (Termination); or

(c) was entitled to terminate the relationship under any other Article of the present Chapter and observed any requirements laid down in such Article for doing so.

IV. D. – 6:102: Termination by principal when relationship is to last for indefinite period or when mandate is for a particular task

(1) The principal may terminate the mandate relationship at any time by giving notice of reasonable length if the mandate contract has been concluded for an indefinite period or for a particular task.
(2) Paragraph (1) does not apply if the mandate is irrevocable.
(3) The parties may not, to the detriment of the principal, exclude the application of this Article or derogate from or vary its effects, unless the conditions set out under IV. D. – 1:105 (Irrevocable mandate) are met.

IV. D. – 6:103: Termination by principal for extraordinary and serious reason

(1) The principal may terminate the mandate relationship by giving notice for extraordinary and serious reason.
(2) No period of notice is required.
(3) For the purposes of this Article, the death or incapacity of the person who, at the time of conclusion of the mandate contract, the parties had intended to perform the agent's obligations under the mandate contract, constitutes an extraordinary and serious reason.
(4) This Article applies with appropriate adaptations if the successors of the principal terminate the mandate relationship in accordance with IV. D. – 7:102 (Death of the principal).
(5) The parties may not, to the detriment of the principal or the principal's successors, exclude the application of this Article or derogate from or vary its effects.

IV. D. – 6:104: Termination by agent when relationship is to last for indefinite period or when it is gratuitous

(1) The agent may terminate the mandate relationship at any time by giving notice of reasonable length if the mandate contract has been concluded for an indefinite period.
(2) The agent may terminate the mandate relationship by giving notice of reasonable length if the agent is to represent the principal otherwise than in exchange for a price.

(3) The parties may not, to the detriment of the agent, exclude the application of paragraph (1) of this Article or derogate from or vary its effects.

IV. D. – 6:105: Termination by agent for extraordinary and serious reason

(1) The agent may terminate the mandate relationship by giving notice for extraordinary and serious reason.
(2) No period of notice is required.
(3) For the purposes of this Article an extraordinary and serious reason includes:
    (a) a change of the mandate contract under IV. D. – 4:201 (Changes of the mandate contract);
    (b) the death or incapacity of the principal; and
    (c) the death or incapacity of the person who, at the time of conclusion of the mandate contract, the parties had intended to perform the agent's obligations under the mandate contract.
(4) The parties may not, to the detriment of the agent, exclude the application of this Article or derogate from or vary its effects.

Chapter 7:
Other grounds for termination

IV. D. – 7:101: Conclusion of prospective contract by principal or other agent

(1) If the mandate contract was concluded solely for the conclusion of a specific prospective contract the mandate relationship terminates when the principal or another agent appointed by the principal has concluded the prospective contract.
(2) In such a case, the conclusion of the prospective contract is treated as a notice under IV. D. – 6:101 (Termination by notice in general).

IV. D. – 7:102: Death of the principal

(1) The death of the principal does not end the mandate relationship.
(2) Both the agent and the successors of the principal may terminate the mandate relationship by giving notice of termination for extraordinary and serious reason under IV. D. – 6:103 (Termination by principal for

extraordinary and serious reason) or IV. D. – 6:105 (Termination by agent for extraordinary and serious reason).

IV. D. – 7:103: Death of the agent
(1) The death of the agent ends the mandate relationship.
(2) The expenses and any other payments due at the time of death remain payable.

Part E.
Commercial agency, franchise and distributorship

Chapter 1:
General provisions
Section 1:
Scope

IV. E. – 1:101: Contracts covered
(1) This Part of Book IV applies to contracts for the establishment and regulation of a commercial agency, franchise or distributorship and with appropriate adaptations to other contracts under which a party engaged in business independently is to use skills and efforts to bring another party's products on to the market.
(2) In this Part, "products" includes goods and services.

Section 2:
Other general provisions

IV. E. – 1:201: Priority rules
In the case of any conflict:
(a) the rules in this Part prevail over the rules in Part D (Mandate); and
(b) the rules in Chapters 3 to 5 of this Part prevail over the rules in Chapter 2 of this Part.

Chapter 2:
**Rules applying to all contracts within the
scope of this part**
Section 1:
Pre-contractual

IV. E. – 2:101: Pre-contractual information duty
A party who is engaged in negotiations for a contract within the scope of
this Part has a duty to provide the other party, a reasonable time before the
contract is concluded and so far as required by good commercial practice,
with such information as is sufficient to enable the other party to decide on
a reasonably informed basis whether or not to enter into a contract of the
type and on the terms under consideration.

Section 2:
Obligations of the parties

IV. E. – 2:201: Co-operation
The parties to a contract within the scope of this Part of Book IV must
collaborate actively and loyally and co-ordinate their respective efforts in
order to achieve the objectives of the contract.

IV. E. – 2:202: Information during the performance
During the period of the contractual relationship each party must provide
the other in due time with all the information which the first party has and
the second party needs in order to achieve the objectives of the contract.

IV. E. – 2:203: Confidentiality
(1) A party who receives confidential information from the other must
    keep such information confidential and must not disclose the informa-
    tion to third parties either during or after the period of the contractual
    relationship.
(2) A party who receives confidential information from the other must not
    use such information for purposes other than the objectives of the
    contract.

(3) Any information which a party already possessed or which has been disclosed to the general public, and any information which must necessarily be disclosed to customers as a result of the operation of the business is not regarded as confidential information for this purpose.

Section 3:
Termination of contractual relationship

IV. E. – 2:301: Contract for a definite period
A party is free not to renew a contract for a definite period. If a party has given notice in due time that it wishes to renew the contract, the contract will be renewed for an indefinite period unless the other party gives that party notice, not later than a reasonable time before the expiry of the contract period, that it is not to be renewed.

IV. E. – 2:302: Contract for an indefinite period
(1) Either party to a contract for an indefinite period may terminate the contractual relationship by giving notice to the other.
(2) If the notice provides for termination after a period of reasonable length no damages are payable under IV. E. – 2:303 (Damages for termination with inadequate notice). If the notice provides for immediate termination or termination after a period which is not of reasonable length damages are payable under that Article.
(3) Whether a period of notice is of reasonable length depends, among other factors, on:
    (a) the time the contractual relationship has lasted;
    (b) reasonable investments made;
    (c) the time it will take to find a reasonable alternative; and
    (d) usages.
(4) A period of notice of one month for each year during which the contractual relationship has lasted, with a maximum of 36 months, is presumed to be reasonable.
(5) The period of notice for the principal, the franchisor or the supplier is to be no shorter than one month for the first year, two months for the second, three months for the third, four months for the fourth, five months for the fifth and six months for the sixth and subsequent years during which the contractual relationship has lasted. Parties may not

exclude the application of this provision or derogate from or vary its
effects.

(6) Agreements on longer periods than those laid down in paragraphs (4)
and (5) are valid provided that the agreed period to be observed by the
principal, franchisor or supplier is no shorter than that to be observed
by the commercial agent, the franchisee or the distributor.

(7) In relation to contracts within the scope of this Part, the rules in this
Article replace those in paragraph (2) of III. – 1:109 (Variation or termination by notice). Paragraph (3) of that Article governs the effects of
termination.

IV. E. – 2:303: Damages for termination with inadequate notice

(1) Where a party terminates a contractual relationship under IV. E. – 2:302
(Contract for an indefinite period) but does not give a reasonable period of notice the other party is entitled to damages.

(2) The general measure of damages is such sum as corresponds to the
benefit which the other party would have obtained during the extra
period for which the relationship would have lasted if a reasonable
period of notice had been given.

(3) The yearly benefit is presumed to be equal to the average benefit which
the aggrieved party has obtained from the contract during the previous
3 years or, if the contractual relationship has lasted for a shorter period,
during that period.

(4) The general rules on damages for non-performance in Book III, Chapter
3, Section 7 apply with any appropriate adaptations.

IV. E. – 2:304: Termination for non-performance

(1) Any term of a contract within the scope of this Part whereby a party
may terminate the contractual relationship for non-performance which
is not fundamental is without effect.

(2) The parties may not exclude the application of this Article or derogate
from or vary its effects.

IV. E. – 2:305: Indemnity for goodwill

(1) When the contractual relationship comes to an end for any reason
(including termination by either party for fundamental non-performance), a party is entitled to an indemnity from the other party for goodwill if and to the extent that:

    (a) the first party has significantly increased the other party's volume of business and the other party continues to derive substantial benefits from that business; and

    (b) the payment of the indemnity is reasonable.

(2) The grant of an indemnity does not prevent a party from seeking damages under IV. E. – 2:303 (Damages for termination with inadequate notice).

IV. E. – 2:306: Stock, spare parts and materials

If the contract is avoided, or the contractual relationship terminated, by either party, the party whose products are being brought on to the market must repurchase the other party's remaining stock, spare parts and materials at a reasonable price, unless the other party can reasonably resell them.

Section 4:
Other general provisions

IV. E. – 2:401: Right of retention

In order to secure its rights to remuneration, compensation, damages and indemnity the party who is bringing the products on to the market has a right of retention over the movables of the other party which are in its possession as a result of the contract, until the other party has performed its obligations.

IV. E. – 2:402: Signed document available on request

(1) Each party is entitled to receive from the other, on request, a signed statement in textual form on a durable medium setting out the terms of the contract.

(2) The parties may not exclude the application of this Article or derogate from or vary its effects.

Chapter 3:
Commercial agency
Section 1:
General

IV. E. – 3:101: Scope
This Chapter applies to contracts under which one party, the commercial agent, agrees to act on a continuing basis as a self-employed intermediary to negotiate or to conclude contracts on behalf of another party, the principal, and the principal agrees to remunerate the agent for those activities.

Section 2:
Obligations of the commercial agent

IV. E. – 3:201: Negotiate and conclude contracts
The commercial agent must make reasonable efforts to negotiate contracts on behalf of the principal and to conclude the contracts which the agent was instructed to conclude.

IV. E. – 3:202: Instructions
The commercial agent must follow the principal's reasonable instructions, provided they do not substantially affect the agent's independence.

IV. E. – 3:203: Information by agent during the performance
The obligation to inform requires the commercial agent in particular to provide the principal with information concerning:
(a) contracts negotiated or concluded;
(b) market conditions;
(c) the solvency of and other characteristics relating to clients.

IV. E. – 3:204: Accounting
(1) The commercial agent must maintain proper accounts relating to the contracts negotiated or concluded on behalf of the principal.
(2) If the agent represents more than one principal, the agent must maintain independent accounts for each principal.

(3) If the principal has important reasons to doubt that the agent maintains proper accounts, the agent must allow an independent accountant to have reasonable access to the agent's books upon the principal's request. The principal must pay for the services of the independent accountant.

Section 3:
Obligations of the principal

IV. E. – 3:301: Commission during the agency

(1) The commercial agent is entitled to commission on any contract concluded with a client during the period covered by the agency, if:
   (a) the contract has been concluded
      (i) as a result of the commercial agent's efforts;
      (ii) with a third party whom the commercial agent has previously acquired as a client for contracts of the same kind; or
      (iii) with a client belonging to a certain geographical area or group of clients with which the commercial agent was entrusted; and
   (b) either
      (i) the principal has or should have performed the principal's obligations under the contract; or
      (ii) the client has performed the client's obligations under the contract or justifiably withholds performance.
(2) The parties may not, to the detriment of the commercial agent, exclude the application of paragraph (1)(b)(ii) or derogate from or vary its effects.

IV. E. – 3:302: Commission after the agency has ended

(1) The commercial agent is entitled to commission on any contract concluded with a client after the agency has ended, if:
   (a) either
      (i) the contract with the client is mainly the result of the commercial agent's efforts during the period covered by the agency contract, and the contract with the client was concluded within a reasonable period after the agency ended; or
      (ii) the requirements of paragraph (1) of IV. E. – 3:301 (Commission during the agency) would have been satisfied except that

the contract with the client was not concluded during the period of the agency, and the client's offer reached the principal or the commercial agent before the agency ended; and

(b) either

    (i) the principal has or should have performed the principal's obligations under the contract; or

    (ii) the client has performed the client's obligations under the contract or justifiably withholds the client's performance.

(2) The parties may not, to the detriment of the commercial agent, exclude the application of paragraph (1)(b)(ii) or derogate from or vary its effects.

IV. E. – 3:303: Conflicting entitlements of successive agents

The commercial agent is not entitled to the commission referred to in IV. E. – 3:301 (Commission during the agency) if a previous commercial agent is entitled to that commission under IV.E–3:302 (Commission after the agency has ended), unless it is reasonable that the commission is shared between the two commercial agents.

IV. E. – 3:304: When commission is to be paid

(1) The principal must pay the commercial agent's commission not later than the last day of the month following the quarter in which the agent became entitled to it.

(2) The parties may not, to the detriment of the commercial agent, exclude the application of this Article or derogate from or vary its effects.

IV. E. – 3:305: Entitlement to commission extinguished

(1) A contract term whereby the commercial agent's entitlement to commission on a contract concluded with a client is extinguished is valid only if and to the extent that it provides for extinction on the basis that the client's contractual obligations are not performed for a reason for which the principal is not accountable.

(2) Upon the extinguishing of the commercial agent's entitlement to commission, the commercial agent must refund any commission already received.

(3) The parties may not, to the detriment of the commercial agent, exclude the application of paragraph (1) or derogate from or vary its effects.

IV. E. – 3:306: Remuneration
Any remuneration which wholly or partially depends upon the number or value of contracts is presumed to be commission within the meaning of this Chapter.

IV. E. – 3:307: Information by principal during the performance
The obligation to inform requires the principal in particular to provide the commercial agent with information concerning:
(a) characteristics of the goods or services; and
(b) prices and conditions of sale or purchase.

IV. E. – 3:308: Information on acceptance, rejection and non-performance
(1) The principal must inform the commercial agent, within a reasonable period, of:
  (a) the principal's acceptance or rejection of a contract which the commercial agent has negotiated on the principal's behalf; and
  (b) any non-performance of obligations under a contract which the commercial agent has negotiated or concluded on the principal's behalf.
(2) The parties may not, to the detriment of the commercial agent, exclude the application of this Article or derogate from or vary its effects.

IV. E. – 3:309: Warning of decreased volume of contracts
(1) The principal must warn the commercial agent within a reasonable time when the principal foresees that the volume of contracts that the principal will be able to conclude will be significantly lower than the commercial agent could reasonably have expected.
(2) For the purpose of paragraph (1) the principal is presumed to foresee what the principal could reasonably be expected to foresee.
(3) The parties may not, to the detriment of the commercial agent, exclude the application of this Article or derogate from or vary its effects.

IV. E. – 3:310: Information on commission
(1) The principal must supply the commercial agent in reasonable time with a statement of the commission to which the commercial agent is entitled. This statement must set out how the amount of the commission has been calculated.

(2) For the purpose of calculating commission, the principal must provide the commercial agent upon request with an extract from the principal's books.

(3) The parties may not, to the detriment of the commercial agent, exclude the application of this Article or derogate from or vary its effects.

IV. E. – 3:311: Accounting

(1) The principal must maintain proper accounts relating to the contracts negotiated or concluded by the commercial agent.

(2) If the principal has more than one commercial agent, the principal must maintain independent accounts for each commercial agent.

(3) The principal must allow an independent accountant to have reasonable access to the principal's books upon the commercial agent's request, if:
  (a) the principal does not comply with the principal's obligations under paragraphs (1) or (2) of IV. E. – 3:310 (Information on commission); or
  (b) the commercial agent has important reasons to doubt that the principal maintains proper accounts.

IV. E. – 3:312: Amount of indemnity

(1) The commercial agent is entitled to an indemnity for goodwill on the basis of IV. E. – 2:305 (Indemnity for goodwill) amounting to:
  (a) the average commission on contracts with new clients and on the increased volume of business with existing clients calculated for the last 12 months, multiplied by:
  (b) the number of years the principal is likely to continue to derive benefits from these contracts in the future.

(2) The resulting indemnity must be amended to take account of:
  (a) the probable attrition of clients, based on the average rate of migration in the commercial agent's territory; and
  (b) the discount required for early payment, based on average interest rates.

(3) In any case, the indemnity must not exceed one year's remuneration, calculated from the commercial agent's average annual remuneration over the preceding five years or, if the contractual relationship has been in existence for less than five years, from the average during the period in question.

(4) The parties may not, to the detriment of the commercial agent, exclude the application of this Article or derogate from or vary its effects.

IV. E. – 3:313: Del credere clause
(1) An agreement whereby the commercial agent guarantees that a client will pay the price of the products forming the subject-matter of the contract which the commercial agent has negotiated or concluded (del credere clause) is valid only if and to the extent that the agreement:
  (a) is in textual form on a durable medium;
  (b) covers particular contracts which were negotiated or concluded by the commercial agent or such contracts with particular clients who are specified in the agreement; and
  (c) is reasonable with regard to the interests of the parties.
(2) The commercial agent is entitled to be paid a commission of a reasonable amount on contracts to which the del credere guarantee applies (del credere commission).

Chapter 4:
Franchise
Section 1:
General

IV. E. – 4:101: Scope
This Chapter applies to contracts under which one party (the franchisor) grants the other party (the franchisee), in exchange for remuneration, the right to conduct a business (franchise business) within the franchisor's network for the purposes of supplying certain products on the franchisee's behalf and in the franchisee's name, and under which the franchisee has the right and the obligation to use the franchisor's tradename or trademark or other intellectual property rights, know-how and business method.

IV. E. – 4:102: Pre-contractual information
(1) The duty under IV. E. – 2:101 (Pre-contractual information duty) requires the franchisor in particular to provide the franchisee with adequate and timely information concerning:
  (a) the franchisor's company and experience;
  (b) the relevant intellectual property rights;

(c) the characteristics of the relevant know-how;

(d) the commercial sector and the market conditions;

(e) the particular franchise method and its operation;

(f) the structure and extent of the franchise network;

(g) the fees, royalties or any other periodical payments; and

(h) the terms of the contract.

(2) Even if the franchisor's non-compliance with paragraph (1) does not give rise to a mistake for which the contract could be avoided under II. – 7:201 (Mistake), the franchisee may recover damages in accordance with paragraphs (2) and (3) of II. – 7:214 (Damages for loss), unless the franchisor had reason to believe that the information was adequate or had been given in reasonable time.

(3) The parties may not exclude the application of this Article or derogate from or vary its effects.

IV. E. – 4:103: Co-operation

The parties to a contract within the scope of this Chapter may not exclude the application of IV. E. – 2:201 (Co-operation) or derogate from or vary its effects.

Section 2:
Obligations of the franchisor

IV. E. – 4:201: Intellectual property rights

(1) The franchisor must grant the franchisee a right to use the intellectual property rights to the extent necessary to operate the franchise business.

(2) The franchisor must make reasonable efforts to ensure the undisturbed and continuous use of the intellectual property rights.

(3) The parties may not exclude the application of this Article or derogate from or vary its effects.

IV. E. – 4:202: Know-how

(1) Throughout the duration of the contractual relationship the franchisor must provide the franchisee with the know-how which is necessary to operate the franchise business.

(2) The parties may not exclude the application of this Article or derogate from or vary its effects.

IV. E. – 4:203: Assistance
(1) The franchisor must provide the franchisee with assistance in the form of training courses, guidance and advice, in so far as necessary for the operation of the franchise business, without additional charge for the franchisee.
(2) The franchisor must provide further assistance, in so far as reasonably requested by the franchisee, at a reasonable cost.

IV. E. – 4:204: Supply
(1) When the franchisee is obliged to obtain the products from the franchisor, or from a supplier designated by the franchisor, the franchisor must ensure that the products ordered by the franchisee are supplied within a reasonable time, in so far as practicable and provided that the order is reasonable.
(2) Paragraph (1) also applies to cases where the franchisee, although not legally obliged to obtain the products from the franchisor or from a supplier designated by the franchisor, is in fact required to do so.
(3) The parties may not exclude the application of this Article or derogate from or vary its effects.

IV. E. – 4:205: Information by franchisor during the performance
The obligation to inform requires the franchisor in particular to provide the franchisee with information concerning:
(a) market conditions;
(b) commercial results of the franchise network;
(c) characteristics of the products;
(d) prices and terms for the supply of products;
(e) any recommended prices and terms for the re-supply of products to customers;
(f) relevant communication between the franchisor and customers in the territory; and
(g) advertising campaigns.

IV. E. – 4:206: Warning of decreased supply capacity

(1) When the franchisee is obliged to obtain the products from the franchisor, or from a supplier designated by the franchisor, the franchisor must warn the franchisee within a reasonable time when the franchisor foresees that the franchisor's supply capacity or the supply capacity of the designated suppliers will be significantly less than the franchisee had reason to expect.

(2) For the purpose of paragraph (1) the franchisor is presumed to foresee what the franchisor could reasonably be expected to foresee.

(3) Paragraph (1) also applies to cases where the franchisee, although not legally obliged to obtain the products from the franchisor or from a supplier designated by the franchisor, is in fact required to do so.

(4) The parties may not, to the detriment of the franchisee, exclude the application of this Article or derogate from or vary its effects.

IV. E. – 4:207: Reputation of network and advertising

(1) The franchisor must make reasonable efforts to promote and maintain the reputation of the franchise network.

(2) In particular, the franchisor must design and co-ordinate the appropriate advertising campaigns aiming at the promotion of the franchise network.

(3) The activities of promotion and maintenance of the reputation of the franchise network are to be carried out without additional charge to the franchisee.

Section 3:
Obligations of the franchisee

IV. E. – 4:301: Fees, royalties and other periodical payments

(1) The franchisee must pay to the franchisor fees, royalties or other periodical payments agreed upon in the contract.

(2) If fees, royalties or any other periodical payments are to be determined unilaterally by the franchisor, II. – 9:105 (Unilateral determination by a party) applies.

IV. E. – 4:302: Information by franchisee during the performance
The obligation under IV. E. – 2:202 ((Information during the performance) requires the franchisee in particular to provide the franchisor with information concerning:
(a) claims brought or threatened by third parties in relation to the franchisor's intellectual property rights; and
(b) infringements by third parties of the franchisor's intellectual property rights.

IV. E. – 4:303: Business method and instructions
(1) The franchisee must make reasonable efforts to operate the franchise business according to the business method of the franchisor.
(2) The franchisee must follow the franchisor's reasonable instructions in relation to the business method and the maintenance of the reputation of the network.
(3) The franchisee must take reasonable care not to harm the franchise network.
(4) The parties may not exclude the application of this Article or derogate from or vary its effects.

IV. E. – 4:304: Inspection
(1) The franchisee must grant the franchisor reasonable access to the franchisee's premises to enable the franchisor to check that the franchisee is complying with the franchisor's business method and instructions.
(2) The franchise must grant the franchisor reasonable access to the accounting books of the franchisee.

Chapter 5:
Distributorship
Section 1:
General

IV. E. – 5:101: Scope and definitions
(1) This Chapter applies to contracts (distribution contracts) under which one party, the supplier, agrees to supply the other party, the distributor, with products on a continuing basis and the distributor agrees to pur-

chase them, or to take and pay for them, and to supply them to others in the distributor's name and on the distributor's behalf.

(2) An exclusive distribution contract is a distribution contract under which the supplier agrees to supply products to only one distributor within a certain territory or to a certain group of customers.

(3) A selective distribution contract is a distribution contract under which the supplier agrees to supply products, either directly or indirectly, only to distributors selected on the basis of specified criteria.

(4) An exclusive purchasing contract is a distribution contract under which the distributor agrees to purchase, or to take and pay for, products only from the supplier or from a party designated by the supplier.

Section 2:
Obligations of the supplier

IV. E. – 5:201: Obligation to supply
The supplier must supply the products ordered by the distributor in so far as it is practicable and provided that the order is reasonable.

IV. E. – 5:202: Information by supplier during the performance
The obligation under IV. E. – 2:202 (Information during the performance) requires the supplier to provide the distributor with information concerning:

(a) the characteristics of the products;
(b) the prices and terms for the supply of the products;
(c) any recommended prices and terms for the re-supply of the products to customers;
(d) any relevant communication between the supplier and customers; and
(e) any advertising campaigns relevant to the operation of the business.

IV. E. – 5:203: Warning by supplier of decreased supply capacity
(1) The supplier must warn the distributor within a reasonable time when the supplier foresees that the supplier's supply capacity will be significantly less than the distributor had reason to expect.

(2) For the purpose of paragraph (1) the supplier is presumed to foresee what the supplier could reasonably be expected to foresee.

(3) In exclusive purchasing contracts, the parties may not exclude the application of this Article or derogate from or vary its effects.

IV. E. – 5:204: Advertising materials
The supplier must provide the distributor at a reasonable price with all the advertising materials the supplier has which are needed for the proper distribution and promotion of the products.

IV. E. – 5:205: The reputation of the products
The supplier must make reasonable efforts not to damage the reputation of the products.

Section 3:
Obligations of the distributor

IV. E. – 5:301: Obligation to distribute
In exclusive distribution contracts and selective distribution contracts the distributor must, so far as practicable, make reasonable efforts to promote the products.

IV. E. – 5:302: Information by distributor during the performance
In exclusive distribution contracts and selective distribution contracts, the obligation under IV. E. – 2:202 (Information during the performance) requires the distributor to provide the supplier with information concerning:
(a) claims brought or threatened by third parties in relation to the supplier's intellectual property rights; and
(b) infringements by third parties of the supplier's intellectual property rights.

IV. E. – 5:303: Warning by distributor of decreased requirements
(1) In exclusive distribution contracts and selective distribution contracts, the distributor must warn the supplier within a reasonable time when the distributor foresees that the distributor's requirements will be significantly less than the supplier had reason to expect.
(2) For the purpose of paragraph (1) the distributor is presumed to foresee what the distributor could reasonably be expected to foresee.

IV. E. – 5:304: Instructions

In exclusive distribution contracts and selective distribution contracts, the distributor must follow reasonable instructions from the supplier which are designed to secure the proper distribution of the products or to maintain the reputation or the distinctiveness of the products.

IV. E. – 5:305: Inspection

In exclusive distribution contracts and selective distribution contracts, the distributor must provide the supplier with reasonable access to the distributor's premises to enable the supplier to check that the distributor is complying with the standards agreed upon in the contract and with reasonable instructions given.

IV. E. – 5:306: The reputation of the products

In exclusive distribution contracts and selective distribution contracts, the distributor must make reasonable efforts not to damage the reputation of the products.

Part F.
Loan contracts

IV.F. – 1:101: Scope

(1) This Part of Book IV applies to loan contracts other than:
    (a) those under which a business lends to a consumer; and
    (b) those where the loan is made for the purchase or maintenance of immovable property.
(2) A loan contract is a contract by which one party, the lender, is obliged to provide the other party, the borrower, with credit of any amount for a definite or indefinite period (the loan period), in the form of a monetary loan or of an overdraft facility and by which the borrower is obliged to repay the money obtained under the credit, whether or not the borrower is obliged to pay interest or any other kind of remuneration the parties have agreed upon.

(3) A monetary loan is a fixed sum of money which is lent to the borrower and which the borrower agrees to repay either by fixed instalments or by paying the whole sum at the end of the loan period.

(4) An overdraft facility is an option for the borrower to withdraw funds on a fluctuating, limited basis from the borrower's current account in excess of the current balance in the account. Unless otherwise determined, an overdraft facility has a revolving character meaning that the borrower has the possibility to use this facility over and over again.

(5) A contract is not a loan contract merely because it provides for the time of payment of an obligation to pay money to be deferred, unless it requires the borrower to pay interest or any other charge in addition to the price.

(6) The parties may however agree that money due under an existing obligation to pay money will in future be due under a loan contract.

IV.F. – 1:102: Main obligation of the lender

(1) The lender is obliged to provide the borrower with credit for the amount, in the manner and for the period determinable from the contract.

(2) If a period of time within which the obligation is to be performed cannot be determined from the terms regulating the obligation, the lender is obliged to make the credit available a reasonable time after the borrower's demand.

IV.F. – 1:103: Obligation of the borrower to take up loan

(1) Where the credit takes the form of a monetary loan, the borrower is obliged to take up the loan in the manner and for the period determinable from the contract.

(2) If the time the borrower is to take up the loan is not determinable from the contract, the borrower is obliged to take up the loan a reasonable time after the lender's demand.

IV.F. – 1:104: Interest

(1) The borrower is obliged to pay interest or any other kind of remuneration according to the terms of the contract.

(2) If the contract does not specify the interest payable, interest is payable unless both parties are consumers.

(3) Interest accrues day by day from the date the borrower takes up the monetary loan or makes use of the overdraft facility but is payable at the end of the loan period or annually, whichever occurs earlier.

(4) Interest payable according to the preceding paragraph is added to the outstanding capital every 12 months.

IV.F. – 1:105: Purpose of the credit
If the contract restricts use of the credit to a specific purpose, the borrower is obliged, within a reasonable time after the lender's demand, to provide information necessary to enable the lender to verify its use.

IV.F. – 1:106: Repayment and termination
(1) The borrower is obliged to repay the money obtained under the credit in the manner and at the time determinable from the loan contract. If the time the borrower is to repay the money is not determinable from the contract, the borrower is obliged to repay it a reasonable time after the lender's demand.

(2) The borrower can, by repayment, terminate an overdraft at will.

(3) The borrower can, by repayment, terminate a loan at any time if under the loan contract the borrower does not have to pay interest or any other kind of remuneration which depends on the duration of the credit.

(4) The borrower can, by repayment, terminate at any time the loan under any other type of loan contract with a specified duration. Parties cannot exclude the application of this rule or derogate from or vary its effects.

(5) Where the loan contract has a specified duration of more than 1 year and provides for a fixed interest rate the borrower can terminate by early repayment under paragraph (4) only on giving the lender three months notice.

(6) On early termination under paragraphs (4) or (5) the borrower is obliged to pay all interest due up to the date of repayment and to indemnify the lender for any loss caused by the early termination.

(7) If the loan contract has an unspecified duration then, without prejudice to the borrower's rights under paragraphs (2) and (3), either party can terminate the relationship by giving the other a reasonable period of notice. II. – 1:109 (Variation or termination by notice) applies.

Part G.
Personal security

Chapter 1:
Common rules

IV. G. – 1:101: Definitions

For the purposes of this Part:

(a) a "dependent personal security" is an obligation by a security provider which is assumed in favour of a creditor in order to secure a right to performance of a present or future obligation of the debtor owed to the creditor and performance of which is due only if, and to the extent that, performance of the latter obligation is due;

(b) an "independent personal security" is an obligation by a security provider which is assumed in favour of a creditor for the purposes of security and which is expressly or impliedly declared not to depend upon another person's obligation owed to the creditor;

(c) the "security provider" is the person who assumes the obligations towards the creditor for the purposes of security;

(d) the "debtor" is the person who owes the secured obligation, if any, to the creditor, and, in provisions relating to purported obligations, includes an apparent debtor;

(e) a "co-debtorship for security purposes" is an obligation owed by two or more debtors in which one of the debtors, the security provider, assumes the obligation primarily for purposes of security towards the creditor;

(f) a "global security" is a dependent personal security which is assumed in order to secure a right to performance of all the debtor's obligations towards the creditor or a right to payment of the debit balance of a current account or a security of a similar extent;

(g) "proprietary security" covers security rights in all kinds of assets, whether movable or immovable, corporeal or incorporeal; and

(h) the "secured obligation" is the obligation the right to the performance of which is secured.

IV. G. – 1:102: Scope

(1) This Part applies to any type of voluntarily assumed personal security and, in particular, to:
- (a) dependent personal securities, including those assumed by binding comfort letters;
- (b) independent personal securities, including those assumed by stand-by letters of credit; and
- (c) co-debtorship for security purposes.

(2) This Part does not apply to insurance contracts. In the case of a guarantee insurance, this Part applies only if and in so far as the insurer has issued a document containing a personal security in favour of the creditor.

(3) This Part does not affect the rules on the aval and the security endorsement of negotiable instruments, but does apply to security for obligations resulting from such an aval or security endorsement.

IV. G. – 1:103: Creditor's acceptance

(1) If the parties intend to create the security by contract, the creditor is regarded as accepting an offer of security as soon as the offer reaches the creditor, unless the offer requires express acceptance, or the creditor without undue delay rejects it or reserves time for consideration.

(2) A personal security can also be assumed by a unilateral undertaking intended to be legally binding without acceptance. The rules of this Part apply with any appropriate adaptations.

IV. G. – 1:104: Co-debtorship for security purposes

A co-debtorship for security purposes is subject to the rules of Chapters 1 and 4 and, subsidiarily, to the rules in Book III, Chapter 4, Section 1 (Plurality of debtors).

IV. G. – 1:105: Several security providers: solidary liability towards creditor

(1) To the extent that several providers of personal security have secured the right to performance of the same obligation or the same part of an obligation or have assumed their undertakings for the same security purpose, each security provider assumes within the limits of that security provider's undertaking to the creditor solidary liability together with the other security providers. This rule also applies if these

security providers in assuming their securities have acted independently.

(2) Paragraph (1) applies with appropriate adaptations if proprietary security has been provided by the debtor or a third person in addition to the personal security.

IV. G. – 1:106: Several security providers: internal recourse

(1) In the cases covered by the preceding Article recourse between several providers of personal security or between providers of personal security and of proprietary security is governed by III. – 4:107 (Recourse between solidary debtors), subject to the following paragraphs.

(2) Subject to paragraph (8), the proportionate share of each security provider for the purposes of that Article is determined according to the rules in paragraphs (3) to (7).

(3) Unless the security providers have otherwise agreed, as between themselves each security provider is liable in the same proportion that the maximum risk assumed by that security provider bore to the total of the maximum risks assumed by all the security providers. The relevant time is that of the creation of the last security.

(4) For personal security, the maximum risk is determined by the agreed maximum amount of the security. In the absence of an agreed maximum amount, the value of the secured right or, if a current account has been secured, the credit limit is decisive. If a secured current account does not have a credit limit, its final balance is decisive.

(5) For proprietary security, the maximum risk is determined by the agreed maximum amount of the security. In the absence of an agreed maximum amount, the value of the assets serving as security is decisive.

(6) If the maximum amount in the case of paragraph (4) first sentence or the maximum amount or the value, respectively, in the case of paragraph (5) is higher than the value of the secured right at the time of creation of the last security, the latter determines the maximum risk.

(7) In the case of an unlimited personal security securing an unlimited credit the maximum risk of other limited personal or proprietary security rights which exceed the final balance of the secured credit is limited to the latter.

(8) The rules in paragraphs (3) to (7) do not apply to proprietary security provided by the debtor and to security providers who, at the time when the creditor was satisfied, were not liable towards the latter.

IV. G. – 1:107: Several security providers: recourse against debtor

(1) Any security provider who has satisfied a right of recourse of another security provider is subrogated to this extent to the other security provider's rights against the debtor as acquired under IV. G. – 2:113 (Security provider's rights after performance) paragraphs (1) and (3), including proprietary security rights granted by the debtor. IV. G. – 2:110 (Reduction of creditor's rights) applies with appropriate adaptations.

(2) Where a security provider has recourse against the debtor by virtue of the rights acquired under IV. G. – 2:113 (Security provider's rights after performance) paragraphs (1) and (3) or under the preceding paragraph, including proprietary security rights granted by the debtor, every security provider is entitled to a proportionate share, as defined in IV. G. – 1:106 (Several security providers: internal recourse) paragraph (2) and III. – 4:107 (Recourse between solidary debtors), of the benefits recovered from the debtor. IV. G. – 2:110 (Reduction of creditor's rights) applies with appropriate adaptations.

(3) Unless expressly stated to the contrary, the preceding rules do not apply to proprietary security provided by the debtor.

IV. G. – 1:108: Subsidiary application of rules on solidary debtors

If and in so far as the provisions of this Part do not apply, the rules on plurality of debtors in III. – 4:107 (Recourse between solidary debtors) to III. – 4:112 (Opposability of other defences in solidary obligations) are subsidiarily applicable.

Chapter 2:
Dependent personal security

IV. G. – 2:101: Presumption for dependent personal security

(1) Any undertaking to pay, to render any other performance or to pay damages to the creditor by way of security is presumed to give rise to a dependent personal security, unless the creditor shows that it was agreed otherwise.

(2) A binding comfort letter is presumed to give rise to a dependent personal security.

IV. G. – 2:102: Dependence of security provider's obligation

(1) Whether and to what extent performance of the obligation of the provider of a dependent personal security is due, depends upon whether and to what extent performance of the debtor's obligation to the creditor is due.

(2) The security provider's obligation does not exceed the debtor's obligation. This rule does not apply if the debtor's obligations are reduced or discharged:

    (a) in an insolvency proceeding;

    (b) in any other way caused by the debtor's inability to perform because of insolvency; or

    (c) by virtue of law due to events affecting the person of the debtor.

(3) Except in the case of a global security, if an amount has not been fixed for the security and cannot be determined from the agreement of the parties, the security provider's obligation is limited to the value of the secured right at the time the security became effective.

(4) Except in the case of a global security, any agreement between the creditor and the debtor to make performance of the secured obligation due earlier, or to make the obligation more onerous by changing the conditions on which performance is due, or to increase its amount, does not affect the security provider's obligation if the agreement was concluded after the security provider's obligation became effective.

IV. G. – 2:103: Debtor's defences available to the security provider

(1) As against the creditor, the security provider may invoke any defence of the debtor with respect to the secured obligation, even if the defence is no longer available to the debtor due to acts or omissions of the debtor occurring after the security became effective.

(2) The security provider is entitled to refuse to perform the security obligation if:

    (a) the debtor is entitled to withdraw from the contract with the creditor under Book II, Chapter 5 (Right of withdrawal).

    (b) the debtor has a right to withhold performance under III. – 3:401 (Right to withhold performance of reciprocal obligation); or

    (c) the debtor is entitled to terminate the debtor's contractual relationship with the creditor under Book III, Chapter 3, Section 5 (Termination).

(3) The security provider may not invoke the lack of capacity of the debtor, whether a natural person or a legal entity, or the non-existence of the debtor, if a legal entity, if the relevant facts were known to the security provider at the time when the security became effective.

(4) As long as the debtor is entitled to avoid the contract from which the secured obligation arises on a ground other than those mentioned in the preceding paragraph and has not exercised that right, the security provider is entitled to refuse performance.

(5) The preceding paragraph applies with appropriate adaptations if the secured obligation is subject to set-off.

IV. G. – 2:104: Coverage of security

(1) The security covers, within its maximum amount, if any, not only the principal secured obligation, but also the debtor's ancillary obligations towards the creditor, especially:

    (a) contractual interest and interest due by law on delay in payment;

    (b) damages, a penalty or an agreed payment for non-performance by the debtor; and

    (c) the reasonable costs of extra-judicial recovery of those items.

(2) The costs of legal proceedings and enforcement proceedings against the debtor are covered, provided the security provider had been informed about the creditor's intention to undertake such proceedings in sufficient time to enable the security provider to avert those costs.

(3) A global security covers only obligations which originated in contracts between the debtor and the creditor.

IV. G. – 2:105: Solidary liability of security provider

Unless otherwise agreed, the liability of the debtor and the security provider is solidary and, accordingly, the creditor has the choice of claiming solidary performance from the debtor or, within the limits of the security, from the security provider.

IV. G. – 2:106: Subsidiary liability of security provider

(1) If so agreed, the security provider may invoke as against the creditor the subsidiary character of the security provider's liability. A binding comfort letter is presumed to establish only subsidiary liability.

(2) Subject to paragraph (3), before demanding performance from the security provider, the creditor must have undertaken appropriate attempts

to obtain satisfaction from the debtor and other security providers, if any, securing the same obligation under a personal or proprietary security establishing solidary liability.

(3) The creditor is not required to attempt to obtain satisfaction from the debtor and any other security provider according to the preceding paragraph if and in so far as it is obviously impossible or exceedingly difficult to obtain satisfaction from the person concerned. This exception applies, in particular, if and in so far as an insolvency or equivalent proceeding has been opened against the person concerned or opening of such a proceeding has failed due to insufficient assets, unless a proprietary security provided by that person and for the same obligation is available.

IV. G. – 2:107: Requirement of notification by creditor

(1) The creditor is required to notify the security provider without undue delay in case of a non-performance by, or inability to pay of, the debtor as well as of an extension of maturity; this notification must include information about the secured amounts of the principal obligation, interest and other ancillary obligations owed by the debtor on the date of the notification. An additional notification of a new event of non-performance need not be given before three months have expired since the previous notification. No notification is required if an event of non-performance merely relates to ancillary obligations of the debtor, unless the total amount of all non-performed secured obligations has reached five percent of the outstanding amount of the secured obligation.

(2) In addition, in the case of a global security, the creditor is required to notify the security provider of any agreed increase:
  (a) whenever such increase, starting from the creation of the security, reaches 20 percent of the amount that was so secured at that time; and
  (b) whenever the secured amount is further increased by 20 percent compared with the secured amount at the date when the last information according to this paragraph was or should have been given.

(3) Paragraphs (1) and (2) do not apply, if and in so far as the security provider knows or could reasonably be expected to know the required information.

(4) If the creditor omits or delays any notification required by this Article the creditor's rights against the security provider are reduced by the extent necessary to prevent the latter from suffering any loss as a result of the omission or delay.

IV. G. – 2:108: Time limit for resort to security

(1) If a time limit has been agreed, directly or indirectly, for resort to a security establishing solidary liability for the security provider, the latter is no longer liable after expiration of the agreed time limit. However, the security provider remains liable if the creditor had requested performance from the security provider after maturity of the secured obligation but before expiration of the time limit for the security.

(2) If a time limit has been agreed, directly or indirectly, for resort to a security establishing subsidiary liability for the security provider, the latter is no longer liable after the expiration of the agreed time limit. However, the security provider remains liable if the creditor:

    (a) after maturity of the secured obligation, but before expiration of the time limit, has informed the security provider of an intention to demand performance of the security and of the commencement of appropriate attempts to obtain satisfaction as required according to IV. G. – 2:106 (Subsidiary liability of security provider) paragraphs (2) and (3); and

    (b) informs the security provider every six months about the status of these attempts, if so demanded by the security provider.

(3) If performance of the secured obligations falls due upon, or within 14 days before, expiration of the time limit of the security, the request for performance or the information according to paragraphs (1) and (2) may be given earlier than provided for in paragraphs (1) and (2), but no more than 14 days before expiration of the time limit of the security.

(4) If the creditor has taken due measures according to the preceding paragraphs, the security provider's maximum liability is restricted to the amount of the secured obligations as defined in IV. G. – 2:104 (Coverage of security) paragraphs (1) and (2). The relevant time is that at which the agreed time limit expires.

IV. G. – 2:109: Limiting security without time limit

(1) Where the scope of a security is not limited to obligations arising, or obligations performance of which falls due, within an agreed time limit, the scope of the security may be limited by any party giving notice of at least three months to the other party. The preceding sentence does not apply if the security is restricted to cover specific obligations or obligations arising from specific contracts.

(2) By virtue of the notice, the scope of the security is limited to the secured principal obligations performance of which is due at the date at which the limitation becomes effective and any secured ancillary obligations as defined in IV. G. – 2:104 (Coverage of security) paragraphs (1) and (2).

IV. G. – 2:110: Reduction of creditor's rights

(1) If and in so far as due to the creditor's conduct the security provider cannot be subrogated to the creditor's rights against the debtor and to the creditor's personal and proprietary security rights granted by third persons, or cannot be fully reimbursed from the debtor or from third party security providers, if any, the creditor's rights against the security provider are reduced by the extent necessary to prevent the latter from suffering any loss as a result of the creditor's conduct. The security provider has a corresponding right to recover from the creditor if the security provider has already performed.

(2) Paragraph (1) applies only if the creditor's conduct falls short of the standard of care which could be expected of persons managing their affairs with reasonable prudence.

IV. G. – 2:111: Debtor's relief for the security provider

(1) A security provider who has provided a security at the debtor's request or with the debtor's express or presumed consent may request relief by the debtor:

    (a) if the debtor has not performed the secured obligation when performance became due;

    (b) if the debtor is unable to pay or has suffered a substantial diminution of assets; or

    (c) if the creditor has brought an action on the security against the security provider.

(2) Relief may be granted by furnishing adequate security.

IV. G. – 2:112: Notification and request by security provider before performance

(1) Before performance to the creditor, the security provider is required to notify the debtor and request information about the outstanding amount of the secured obligation and any defences or counterclaims against it.

(2) If the security provider fails to comply with the requirements in paragraph (1) or neglects to raise defences communicated by the debtor or known to the security provider from other sources, the security provider's rights to recover from the debtor under IV. G. – 2:113 (Security provider's rights after performance) are reduced by the extent necessary to prevent loss to the debtor as a result of such failure or neglect.

(3) The security provider's rights against the creditor remain unaffected.

IV. G. – 2:113: Security provider's rights after performance

(1) The security provider has a right to reimbursement from the debtor if and in so far as the security provider has performed the security obligation. In addition the security provider is subrogated to the extent indicated in the preceding sentence to the creditor's rights against the debtor. The right to reimbursement and rights acquired by subrogation are concurrent.

(2) In case of part performance, the creditor's remaining partial rights against the debtor have priority over the rights to which the security provider has been subrogated.

(3) By virtue of the subrogation under paragraph (1), dependent and independent personal and proprietary security rights are transferred by operation of law to the security provider notwithstanding any contractual restriction or exclusion of transferability agreed by the debtor. Rights against other security providers can be exercised only within the limits of IV. G. – 1:106 (Several security providers: internal recourse).

(4) Where the debtor due to incapacity is not liable to the creditor but the security provider is nonetheless bound by, and performs, the security obligation, the security provider's right to reimbursement from the debtor is limited to the extent of the debtor's enrichment by the transaction with the creditor. This rule applies also if a debtor legal entity has not come into existence.

Chapter 3:
Independent personal security

IV. G. – 3:101: Scope
(1) The independence of a security is not prejudiced by a mere general reference to an underlying obligation (including a personal security).
(2) The provisions of this Chapter also apply to standby letters of credit.

IV. G. – 3:102: Notification to debtor by security provider
(1) The security provider is required:
    (a) to notify the debtor immediately if a demand for performance is received and to state whether or not, in the view of the security provider, performance falls to be made;
    (b) to notify the debtor immediately if performance has been made in accordance with a demand; and
    (c) to notify the debtor immediately if performance has been refused notwithstanding a demand and to state the reasons for the refusal.
(2) If the security provider fails to comply with the requirements in paragraph (1) the security provider's rights against the debtor under IV. G. – 3:109 (Security provider's rights after performance) are reduced by the extent necessary to prevent loss to the debtor as a result of such failure.

IV. G. – 3:103: Performance by security provider
(1) The security provider is obliged to perform only if there is, in textual form, a demand for performance which complies exactly with the terms set out in the contract or other juridical act creating the security.
(2) Unless otherwise agreed, the security provider may invoke defences which the security provider has against the creditor.
(3) The security provider must without undue delay and at the latest within seven days of receipt, in textual form, of a demand for performance:
    (a) perform in accordance with the demand; or
    (b) inform the creditor of a refusal to perform, stating the reasons for the refusal.

IV. G. – 3:104: Independent personal security on first demand

(1) An independent personal security which is expressed as being due upon first demand or which is in such terms that this can unequivocally be inferred, is governed by the rules in the preceding Article, except as provided in the two following paragraphs.

(2) The security provider is obliged to perform only if the creditor's demand is supported by a declaration in textual form by the creditor which expressly confirms that any condition upon which performance of the security becomes due is fulfilled.

(3) Paragraph (2) of the preceding Article does not apply.

IV. G. – 3:105: Manifestly abusive or fraudulent demand

(1) A security provider is not obliged to comply with a demand for performance if it is proved by present evidence that the demand is manifestly abusive or fraudulent.

(2) If the requirements of the preceding paragraph are fulfilled, the debtor may prohibit:

    (a) performance by the security provider; and

    (b) issuance or utilisation of a demand for performance by the creditor.

IV. G. – 3:106: Security provider's right to reclaim

(1) The security provider has the right to reclaim the benefits received by the creditor if:

    (a) the conditions for the creditor's demand were not or subsequently ceased to be fulfilled; or

    (b) the creditor's demand was manifestly abusive or fraudulent.

(2) The security provider's right to reclaim benefits is subject to the rules in Book VII (Unjustified Enrichment).

IV. G. – 3:107: Security with or without time limits

(1) If a time limit has been agreed, directly or indirectly, for the resort to a security, the security provider exceptionally remains liable even after expiration of the time limit, provided the creditor had demanded performance according to IV. G. – 3:103 (Performance by security provider) paragraph (1) or IV. G. – 3:104 (Independent personal security on first demand) at a time when the creditor was entitled to do so and before expiration of the time limit for the security. IV. G. – 2:108 (Time limit for resort to security) paragraph (3) applies with appropriate adap-

tations. The security provider's maximum liability is restricted to the amount which the creditor could have demanded as of the date when the time limit expired.

(2) Where a security does not have an agreed time limit, the security provider may set such a time limit by giving notice of at least three months to the other party. The security provider's liability is restricted to the amount which the creditor could have demanded as of the date set by the security provider. The preceding sentences do not apply if the security is given for specific purposes.

IV. G. – 3:108: Transfer of security right

(1) The creditor's right to performance by the security provider can be assigned or otherwise transferred.

(2) However, in the case of an independent personal security on first demand, the right to performance cannot be assigned or otherwise transferred and the demand for performance can be made only by the original creditor, unless the security provides otherwise. This does not prevent transfer of the proceeds of the security.

IV. G. – 3:109: Security provider's rights after performance

IV. G. – 2:113 (Security provider's rights after performance) applies with appropriate adaptations to the rights which the security provider may exercise after performance.

Chapter 4:
Special rules for personal security of consumers

IV. G. – 4:101: Scope of application

(1) Subject to paragraph (2), this Chapter applies when a security is provided by a consumer.

(2) This Chapter is not applicable if:
  (a) the creditor is also a consumer; or
  (b) the consumer security provider is able to exercise substantial influence upon the debtor where the debtor is not a natural person.

IV. G. – 4:102: Applicable rules

(1) A personal security subject to this Chapter is governed by the rules of Chapters 1 and 2, except as otherwise provided in this Chapter.

(2) The parties may not, to the detriment of a security provider, exclude the application of the rules of this Chapter or derogate from or vary their effects.

IV. G. – 4:103: Creditor's pre-contractual duties

(1) Before a security is granted, the creditor has a duty to explain to the intending security provider:

    (a) the general effect of the intended security; and

    (b) the special risks to which the security provider may according to the information accessible to the creditor be exposed in view of the financial situation of the debtor.

(2) If the creditor knows or has reason to know that due to a relationship of trust and confidence between the debtor and the security provider there is a significant risk that the security provider is not acting freely or with adequate information, the creditor has a duty to ascertain that the security provider has received independent advice.

(3) If the information or independent advice required by the preceding paragraphs is not given at least five days before the security provider signs the offer of security or the contract creating the security, the offer can be revoked or the contract avoided by the security provider within a reasonable time after receipt of the information or the independent advice. For this purpose five days is regarded as a reasonable time unless the circumstances suggest otherwise.

(4) If contrary to paragraph (1) or (2) no information or independent advice is given, the offer can be revoked or the contract avoided by the security provider at any time.

(5) If the security provider revokes the offer or avoids the contract according to the preceding paragraphs, the return of benefits received by the parties is governed by Book VII (Unjustified Enrichment).

IV. G. – 4:104: Form

The contract of security must be in textual form on a durable medium and must be signed by the security provider. A contract of security which does not comply with the requirements of the preceding sentence is void.

IV. G. – 4:105: Nature of security provider's liability
Where this Chapter applies:
(a) an agreement purporting to create a security without a maximum amount, whether a global security or not, is considered as creating a dependent security with a fixed amount to be determined according to IV. G. – 2:102 (Dependence of security provider's obligation) paragraph (3);
(b) the liability of a provider of dependent security is subsidiary within the meaning of IV. G. – 2:106 (Subsidiary liability of security provider), unless expressly agreed otherwise; and
(c) in an agreement purporting to create an independent security, the declaration that it does not depend upon another person's obligation owed to the creditor is disregarded, and accordingly a dependent security is considered as having been created, provided the other requirements of such a security are met.

IV. G. – 4:106: Creditor's obligations of annual information
(1) Subject to the debtor's consent, the creditor has to inform the security provider annually about the secured amounts of the principal obligation, interest and other ancillary obligations owed by the debtor on the date of the information. The debtor's consent, once given, is irrevocable.
(2) IV. G. – 2:107 (Requirement of notification by creditor) paragraphs (3) and (4) apply with appropriate adaptations.

IV. G. – 4:107: Limiting security with time limit
(1) A security provider who has provided a security whose scope is limited to obligations arising, or obligations performance of which falls due, within an agreed time limit may three years after the security became effective limit its effects by giving notice of at least three months to the creditor. The preceding sentence does not apply if the security is restricted to cover specific obligations or obligations arising from specific contracts. The creditor has to inform the debtor immediately on receipt of a notice of limitation of the security by the security provider.
(2) By virtue of the notice, the scope of the security is limited according to IV. G. – 2:109 (Limiting security without time limit) paragraph (2).

Part H.
Donation

Chapter 1:
Scope and general provisions
Section 1:
Scope and definitions

IV. H. – 1:101: Contracts covered

(1) This Part of Book IV applies to contracts for the donation of goods.

(2) A contract for the donation of goods is a contract under which one party, the donor, gratuitously undertakes to transfer the ownership of goods to another party, the donee, and does so with an intention to benefit the donee.

IV. H. – 1:102: Future goods and goods to be manufactured or produced

(1) In this Part of Book IV the word "goods" includes goods which at the time of the conclusion of the contract do not yet exist or are to be acquired by the donor.

(2) A contract under which one party undertakes gratuitously, and with an intention to benefit the other party, to manufacture or produce goods for the other party and to transfer their ownership to the other party is to be regarded as primarily a contract for the donation of the goods.

IV. H. – 1:103: Application to other assets

(1) This Part applies with appropriate adaptations to:

    (a) contracts for the donation of money;

    (b) contracts for the donation of electricity;

    (c) contracts for the donation of stocks, shares, investment securities and negotiable instruments;

    (d) contracts for the donation of other forms of incorporeal property, including rights to the performance of obligations, industrial and intellectual property rights and other transferable rights;

    (e) contracts gratuitously conferring rights in information or data, including software and databases.

(2) This Part does not apply to contracts for the donation of immovable property or rights in immovable property.

IV. H. – 1:104: Application to unilateral undertakings and immediate donations

This Part applies with appropriate adaptations where the donor gratuitously, with an intention to benefit the donee:

(a) unilaterally undertakes to transfer the ownership of goods to the donee; or

(b) immediately transfers the ownership of goods to the donee.

IV. H. – 1:105: Donations due or conditional on death

(1) This Part does not apply where:

    (a) performance of the obligation to transfer is due only on the donor's death;

    (b) the transfer or obligation to transfer is subject to the suspensive condition of the donor's death; or

    (c) the transfer or obligation to transfer is made subject to the resolutive condition of the donee predeceasing the donor.

(2) Paragraph (1) does not apply if the donor renders performance or waives the condition before the donor's death.

Section 2:
Gratuitousness and intention to benefit

IV. H. – 1:201: Gratuitousness

An undertaking to transfer is gratuitous if it is done without reward.

IV. H. – 1:202: Transactions which are not entirely gratuitous

(1) If the party undertaking to transfer receives or is entitled to some reward and the transaction is thereby not entirely gratuitous the contract is regarded primarily as a contract for the donation of goods if:

    (a) this party undertakes to transfer with an intention inter alia to benefit the other party; and

    (b) the values to be conferred by the performances are regarded by both parties as not substantially equivalent.

(2) If the contract coming under paragraph (1) is void or avoided under these rules but would not be under general rules, III. – 1:110 (Variation or termination by court on a change of circumstances) applies with appropriate adaptations.

(3) If in a case within paragraph (1) a party exercises a right to revoke under this Part, IV. H. – 4:103 (Consequences of revocation) applies to the whole contractual relationship. The other party may prevent the effects of revocation by offering a reasonable reward within a reasonable time after revocation.

IV. H. – 1:203: Intention to benefit

A donor may be regarded as intending to benefit the donee notwithstanding that the donor:

(a) is under a moral obligation to transfer; or

(b) has a promotional purpose.

Chapter 2:
Formation and validity

IV. H. – 2:101: Form requirements

A contract for the donation of goods is not valid unless the undertaking of the donor is in textual form on a durable medium signed by the donor. An electronic signature which is not an advanced signature in the sense of I. – 1:107 ("Signature" and similar expressions) paragraph 4, does not suffice in this regard.

IV. H. – 2:102: Exceptions to the form requirements

The preceding Article does not apply:

(a) in the case of an immediate delivery of the goods to the donee or an equivalent to such delivery, regardless of whether ownership is transferred;

(b) if the donation is made by a business;

(c) if the undertaking of the donor is declared in a public statement broadcast in the radio or television or published in print and is not excessive in the circumstances.

IV. H. – 2:103: Mistake

A donor may avoid the contract if it was concluded because of a mistake of fact or law although the requirements of II. – 7:201 (Mistake) paragraph (1)(b) are not satisfied.

IV. H. – 2:104: Unfair exploitation

A donor, who was dependent on, or was the more vulnerable party in a relationship of trust with, the donee, may avoid the contract under II. – 7:207 (Unfair exploitation) unless the donee proves that the donee did not exploit the donor's situation by taking an excessive benefit or grossly unfair advantage.

Chapter 3:
Obligations and remedies
Section 1:
Obligations of the donor

IV. H. – 3:101: Obligations in general

(1) The donor must:
    (a) deliver goods which conform with the contract; and
    (b) transfer the ownership in the goods as required by the contract.
(2) This Section applies with appropriate adaptations to fruits acquired from the time when the obligation to deliver is due.

IV. H. – 3:102: Conformity of the goods

(1) The goods do not conform with the contract if they do not possess the qualities which the donee could reasonably expect unless the donee knew of the lack of quality or could reasonably be expected to have known of it when the contract was concluded.
(2) In determining what qualities the donee could reasonably expect, regard is to be had, among other things, to:
    (a) the gratuitous nature of the contract;
    (b) the purpose of the contract of donation known by, or obvious to, the donee;
    (c) whether the transfer or delivery of the goods was immediate;
    (d) the value of the goods; and
    (e) whether the donor was a business.

(3) The goods do not conform to the contract if they are not of a quantity, quality or description provided for by the terms of the contract.

IV. H. – 3:103: Third party rights or claims
The goods do not conform with the contract if they are not free from any right or reasonably well founded claim of a third party unless the donee knew or could reasonably expected to have known of the third party's right or claim.

Section 2:
Remedies of the donee

IV. H. – 3:201: Application of general rules
If the donor fails to perform any of the donor's obligations under the contract, the donee has the remedies provided for in Book III, Chapter 3 (Remedies for non-performance) unless otherwise provided in this Section.

IV. H. – 3:202: Restricted right to enforce performance
(1) If the goods do not conform with the contract, the donee may not require replacement or repair under III. – 3:302 (Enforcement of non-monetary obligations).
(2) The donee may not enforce performance under III. – 3:302 (Enforcement of non-monetary obligations) in the case of goods which are to be acquired by the donor.

IV. H. – 3:203: Restitution in case of termination
If the donee terminates the contract under Book III, Chapter 3, Section 5 (Termination), III. – 3:511 (When restitution not required) paragraph (3) does not apply.

IV. H. – 3:204: Exclusion of the right to damages in case of impediment
(1) A donee's right to damages is excluded if the donor's non-performance is due to an impediment and if the donor could not reasonably be expected to have avoided or overcome the impediment or its consequences.

(2) III. – 3:104 (Excuse due to an impediment) paragraphs (3) and (5) apply correspondingly.
(3) In determining what impediment or consequences the donor could reasonably be expected to have avoided or overcome regard is to be had to the gratuitous nature of the contract.
(4) This Article does not affect liability under Book VI (Non-contractual liability arising out of damage caused to another).

IV. H. – 3:205: Measure of damages
(1) Damages cover loss suffered by the donee acting in the reasonable belief that the donor would fulfil the obligations.
(2) A supplementary sum of damages may be awarded by the court if it is seen as just and reasonable in the circumstances.
(3) In determining what is just and reasonable under paragraph (2), regard is to be had, among other things and apart from the gratuitous nature of the contract:
    (a) the declarations and acts of the parties;
    (b) the donor's purpose in making the donation; and
    (c) the reasonable expectations of the donee.
(4) The total amount of damages under this Article may not exceed such a sum as will put the aggrieved party as nearly as possible into the position in which it would have been if the donor's obligations under the contract had been duly performed.
(5) This Article does not affect liability under Book VI (Non-contractual liability arising out of damage caused to another).

IV. H. – 3:206: Delay in payment of money
If payment of a sum of money is delayed, the donee is entitled to interest under III. – 3:708 (Interest on late payments) unless the non-performance is excused under III. – 3:104 (Excuse due to an impediment) or the donee's right to damages is excluded under IV. H. – 3:204 (Exclusion of the right to damages in case of impediment).

Section 3:
Obligations of the donee

IV. H. – 3:301: Obligations to take delivery and accept transfer
(1) The donee must take delivery and accept the transfer of ownership.
(2) The donee performs the obligation to take delivery and accept transfer by carrying out all the acts which could reasonably be expected of the donee in order to enable the donor to perform the obligations to deliver and transfer.

Section 4:
Remedies of the donor

IV. H. – 3:401: Application of general rules
If the donee fails to perform any of the donee's obligations under the contract, the donor has the remedies provided for in III. – 2:111 (Property not accepted), III. – 2:112 (Money not accepted) and Book III, Chapter 3 (Remedies for non-performance).

Chapter 4:
Revocation by the donor
Section 1:
Revocation in general

IV. H. – 4:101: Irrevocability and its exceptions
Contracts for the donation of goods are revocable only if a right to revoke is
(a) conferred by the terms of the contract; or
(b) provided for under the rules in this Chapter.

IV. H. – 4:102: Exercise and scope of the right to revoke
(1) The donor's right to revoke is to be exercised by giving notice to the donee.
(2) A declaration of partial revocation is to be understood as a revocation of the whole contract for the donation of goods, if, giving due con-

sideration to all the circumstances of the case, it is unreasonable to uphold the remaining parts.

IV. H. – 4:103: Consequences of revocation
(1) On revocation under this Chapter, the outstanding obligations of the parties under the contract come to an end. In the case of a partial revocation, the relevant part of the outstanding obligations comes to an end.
(2) On revocation under this Chapter, the donee is obliged to return the goods. Chapters 5 and 6 of Book VII (Unjustified enrichment) apply with appropriate adaptations, unless otherwise provided in this Chapter.

IV. H. – 4:104: Time limits
The right to revoke under this Chapter expires if notice of revocation is not given within a reasonable time, with due regard to the circumstances, after the donor knew or could reasonably be expected to have known of the relevant facts.

Section 2:
Rights of the donor to revoke

IV. H. – 4:201: Ingratitude of the donee
(1) A contract for the donation of goods may be revoked if the donee is guilty of gross ingratitude by intentionally committing a serious wrong against the donor.
(2) Revocation under this Article is excluded if the donor knowing the relevant facts forgives the donee.
(3) For the purpose of paragraph (1) a reasonable time under IV.H–4:104 (Time limits) is at least one year. If the donor dies before the reasonable time has expired, the running of the period is suspended until the person entitled to revoke knows or can reasonably be expected to know of the relevant facts.
(4) For the purpose of paragraph (1) the defence of disenrichment under VII. – 6:101 (Disenrichment) does not apply.

IV. H. – 4:202: Impoverishment of the donor

(1) A contract for the donation of goods may be revoked if the donor is not in a position to maintain himself or herself out of his or her own patrimony or income.

(2) The donor is not in a position to maintain himself or herself if:
  (a) he or she would be entitled to maintenance from another if that other were in a position to provide the maintenance; or
  (b) he or she is entitled to social assistance.

(3) The right to revoke is suspended if the donee maintains the donor to the extent that the latter is or would be entitled to under paragraph (2).

(4) A donor who is not in a position to maintain himself or herself in the sense of paragraph (1) or who will imminently be in that situation may withhold performance of any obligations under the contract which have not yet been performed. Paragraph (3) applies correspondingly to the right to withhold performance. If the donor withholds performance, the donee may terminate the contractual relationship.

(5) This Article applies also when the donor's ability to meet maintenance obligations established by rule of law or by court order, or the existence of those obligations, is dependent on effective revocation of a donation.

(6) The right to revoke under this Article may not be restricted or excluded by the parties.

IV. H. – 4:203: Residual right to revoke

(1) A contract for the donation of goods may also be revoked to the extent that other essential circumstances upon which it was based have materially changed after the conclusion of the contract, provided that as a result of that change:
  (a) the benefit to the donee is manifestly inappropriate or excessive; or
  (b) it is manifestly unjust to hold the donor to the donation.

(2) Paragraph (1) applies only if:
  (a) the change of circumstances was not so foreseeable at the time of the conclusion of the contract that the donor could reasonably have been expected to provide for it; and
  (b) the risk of that change of circumstances was not assumed by the donor.

Book V
Benevolent intervention in another's affairs

Chapter 1:
Scope

V. – 1:101: Intervention to benefit another
(1) This Book applies where a person, the intervener, acts with the pre-dominant intention of benefiting another, the principal, and:
   (a) the intervener has a reasonable ground for acting; or
   (b) the principal approves the act without such undue delay as would adversely affect the intervener.
(2) The intervener does not have a reasonable ground for acting if the intervener:
   (a) has a reasonable opportunity to discover the principal's wishes but does not do so; or
   (b) knows or can reasonably be expected to know that the interven-tion is against the principal's wishes.

V. – 1:102: Intervention to perform another's duty
Where an intervener acts to perform another person's duty, the perform-ance of which is due and urgently required as a matter of overriding public interest, and the intervener acts with the predominant intention of bene-fiting the recipient of the performance, the person whose duty the inter-vener acts to perform is a principal to whom this Book applies.

V. – 1:103: Exclusions
This Book does not apply where the intervener:
(a) is authorised to act under a contractual or other obligation to the prin-cipal;
(b) is authorised, other than under this Book, to act independently of the principal's consent; or
(c) is under an obligation to a third party to act.

Chapter 2:
Duties of intervener

V. – 2:101: Duties during intervention
(1) During the intervention, the intervener must:
   (a) act with reasonable care;
   (b) except in relation to a principal within V. – 1:102 (Intervention to perform another's duty), act in a manner which the intervener knows or can reasonably be expected to assume accords with the principal's wishes; and
   (c) so far as possible and reasonable, inform the principal about the intervention and seek the principal's consent to further acts.
(2) The intervention may not be discontinued without good reason.

V. – 2:102: Reparation for damage caused by breach of duty
(1) The intervener is liable to make reparation to the principal for damage caused by breach of a duty set out in this Chapter if the damage resulted from a risk which the intervener created, increased or intentionally perpetuated.
(2) The intervener's liability is reduced or excluded in so far as this is fair and reasonable, having regard to, among other things, the intervener's reasons for acting.
(3) An intervener who at the time of intervening lacks full legal capacity is liable to make reparation only in so far as that intervener is also liable to make reparation under Book VI (Non-contractual liability arising out of damage caused to another).

V. – 2:103: Obligations after intervention
(1) After intervening the intervener must without undue delay report and account to the principal and hand over anything obtained as a result of the intervention.
(2) If at the time of intervening the intervener lacks full legal capacity, the obligation to hand over is subject to the defence which would be available under VII. – 6:101 (Disenrichment).

(3) The remedies for non-performance in Book III, Chapter 3 apply but with the modification that any liability to pay damages or interest is subject to the qualifications in paragraphs (2) and (3) of the preceding Article.

Chapter 3:
Rights and authority of intervener

V. – 3:101: Right to indemnification or reimbursement
The intervener has a right against the principal for indemnification or, as the case may be, reimbursement in respect of an obligation or expenditure (whether of money or other assets) in so far as reasonably incurred for the purposes of the intervention.

V. – 3:102: Right to remuneration
(1) The intervener has a right to remuneration in so far as the intervention is reasonable and undertaken in the course of the intervener's profession or trade.
(2) The remuneration due is the amount, so far as reasonable, which is ordinarily paid at the time and place of intervention in order to obtain a performance of the kind undertaken. If there is no such amount a reasonable remuneration is due.

V. – 3:103: Right to reparation
An intervener who acts to protect the principal, or the principal's property or interests, against danger has a right against the principal for reparation for loss caused as a result of personal injury or property damage suffered in acting, if:
(a) the intervention created or significantly increased the risk of such injury or damage; and
(b) that risk, so far as foreseeable, was in reasonable proportion to the risk to the principal.

V. – 3:104: Reduction or exclusion of intervener's rights

(1) The intervener's rights are reduced or excluded in so far as the intervener at the time of acting did not want to demand indemnification, reimbursement, remuneration or reparation, as the case may be.

(2) These rights are also reduced or excluded in so far as this is fair and reasonable, having regard among other things to whether the intervener acted to protect the principal in a situation of joint danger, whether the liability of the principal would be excessive and whether the intervener could reasonably be expected to obtain appropriate redress from another.

V. – 3:105: Obligation of third person to indemnify or reimburse the principal

If the intervener acts to protect the principal from damage, a person who would be accountable under Book VI (Non-contractual liability arising out of damage caused to another) for the causation of such damage to the principal is obliged to indemnify or, as the case may be, reimburse the principal's liability to the intervener.

V. – 3:106: Authority of intervener to act as representative of the principal

(1) The intervener may conclude legal transactions or perform other juridical acts as a representative of the principal in so far as this may reasonably be expected to benefit the principal.

(2) However, a unilateral juridical act by the intervener as a representative of the principal has no effect if the person to whom it is addressed rejects the act without undue delay.

Book VI
Non-contractual liability arising out of damage caused to another

Chapter 1:
Fundamental provisions

VI. – 1:101: Basic rule
(1) A person who suffers legally relevant damage has a right to reparation from a person who caused the damage intentionally or negligently or is otherwise accountable for the causation of the damage.
(2) Where a person has not caused legally relevant damage intentionally or negligently that person is accountable for the causation of legally relevant damage only if Chapter 3 so provides.

VI. – 1:102: Prevention
Where legally relevant damage is impending, this Book confers on a person who would suffer the damage a right to prevent it. This right is against a person who would be accountable for the causation of the damage if it occurred.

VI. – 1:103: Scope of application
VI. – 1:101 (Basic rule) and VI. – 1:102 (Prevention):
(a) apply only in accordance with the following provisions of this Book;
(b) apply to both legal and natural persons, unless otherwise stated;
(c) do not apply in so far as their application would contradict the purpose of other private law rules; and
(d) do not affect remedies available on other legal grounds.

Chapter 2:
Legally relevant damage
Section 1:
General

VI. – 2:101: Meaning of legally relevant damage

(1) Loss, whether economic or non-economic, or injury is legally relevant damage if:

  (a) one of the following rules of this Chapter so provides;

  (b) the loss or injury results from a violation of a right otherwise conferred by the law; or

  (c) the loss or injury results from a violation of an interest worthy of legal protection.

(2) In any case covered only by sub-paragraphs (b) or (c) of paragraph (1) loss or injury constitutes legally relevant damage only if it would be fair and reasonable for there to be a right to reparation or prevention, as the case may be, under VI. – 1:101 (Basic rule) or VI. – 1:102 (Prevention).

(3) In considering whether it would be fair and reasonable for there to be a right to reparation or prevention regard is to be had to the ground of accountability, to the nature and proximity of the damage or impending damage, to the reasonable expectations of the person who suffers or would suffer the damage, and to considerations of public policy.

(4) In this Book:

  (a) economic loss includes loss of income or profit, burdens incurred and a reduction in the value of property;

  (b) non-economic loss includes pain and suffering and impairment of the quality of life.

Section 2:
Particular instances of legally relevant damage

VI. – 2:201: Personal injury and consequential loss

(1) Loss caused to a natural person as a result of injury to his or her body or health and the injury as such are legally relevant damage.

(2) In this Book:

(a) such loss includes the costs of health care including expenses reasonably incurred for the care of the injured person by those close to him or her; and

(b) personal injury includes injury to mental health only if it amounts to a medical condition.

VI. – 2:202: Loss suffered by third persons as a result of another's personal injury or death

(1) Non-economic loss caused to a natural person as a result of another's personal injury or death is legally relevant damage if at the time of injury that person is in a particularly close personal relationship to the injured person.

(2) Where a person has been fatally injured:

(a) legally relevant damage caused to the deceased on account of the injury to the time of death becomes legally relevant damage to the deceased's successors;

(b) reasonable funeral expenses are legally relevant damage to the person incurring them; and

(c) loss of maintenance is legally relevant damage to a natural person whom the deceased maintained or, had death not occurred, would have maintained under statutory provisions or to whom the deceased provided care and financial support.

VI. – 2:203: Infringement of dignity, liberty and privacy

(1) Loss caused to a natural person as a result of infringement of his or her right to respect for his or her dignity, such as the rights to liberty and privacy, and the injury as such are legally relevant damage.

(2) Loss caused to a person as a result of injury to that person's reputation and the injury as such are also legally relevant damage if national law so provides.

VI. – 2:204: Loss upon communication of incorrect information about another

Loss caused to a person as a result of the communication of information about that person which the person communicating the information knows or could reasonably be expected to know is incorrect is legally relevant damage.

VI. – 2:205: Loss upon breach of confidence

Loss caused to a person as a result of the communication of information
which, either from its nature or the circumstances in which it was obtained, the person communicating the information knows or could reasonably be expected to know is confidential to the person suffering the loss is
legally relevant damage.

VI. – 2:206: Loss upon infringement of property or lawful possession

(1) Loss caused to a person as a result of an infringement of that person's
    property right or lawful possession of a movable or immovable thing is
    legally relevant damage.
(2) In this Article:
    (a) loss includes being deprived of the use of property;
    (b) infringement of a property right includes destruction of or physical
        damage to the subject-matter of the right (property damage), dis-
        position of the right, interference with its use and other distur-
        bance of the exercise of the right.

VI. – 2:207: Loss upon reliance on incorrect advice or information

Loss caused to a person as a result of making a decision in reasonable
reliance on incorrect advice or information is legally relevant damage if:

(a) the advice or information is provided by a person in pursuit of a pro-
    fession or in the course of trade; and
(b) the provider knew or could reasonably be expected to have known that
    the recipient would rely on the advice or information in making a de-
    cision of the kind made.

VI. – 2:208: Loss upon unlawful impairment of business

(1) Loss caused to a person as a result of an unlawful impairment of that
    person's exercise of a profession or conduct of a trade is legally relevant
    damage.
(2) Loss caused to a consumer as a result of unfair competition is also
    legally relevant damage if Community or national law so provides.

VI. – 2:209: Burdens incurred by the state upon environmental impairment

Burdens incurred by the State or designated competent authorities in restoring substantially impaired natural elements constituting the environment, such as air, water, soil, flora and fauna, are legally relevant damage to the State or the authorities concerned.

VI. – 2:210: Loss upon fraudulent misrepresentation

(1) Without prejudice to the other provisions of this Section loss caused to a person as a result of another's fraudulent misrepresentation, whether by words or conduct, is legally relevant damage.

(2) A misrepresentation is fraudulent if it is made with knowledge or belief that the representation is false and it is intended to induce the recipient to make a mistake.

VI. – 2:211: Loss upon inducement of non-performance of obligation

Without prejudice to the other provisions of this Section, loss caused to a person as a result of another's inducement of the non-performance of an obligation by a third person is legally relevant damage only if:

(a) the obligation was owed to the person sustaining the loss; and

(b) the person inducing the non-performance:

    (i) intended the third person to fail to perform the obligation, and

    (ii) did not act in legitimate protection of the inducing person's own interest.

Chapter 3:
Accountability
Section 1:
Intention and negligence

VI. – 3:101: Intention

A person causes legally relevant damage intentionally when that person causes such damage either:

(a) meaning to cause damage of the type caused; or

(b) by conduct which that person means to do, knowing that such damage, or damage of that type, will or will almost certainly be caused.

VI. – 3:102: Negligence

A person causes legally relevant damage negligently when that person causes the damage by conduct which either:

(a) does not meet the particular standard of care provided by a statutory provision whose purpose is the protection of the person suffering the damage from that damage; or

(b) does not otherwise amount to such care as could be expected from a reasonably careful person in the circumstances of the case.

VI. – 3:103: Persons under eighteen

(1) A person under eighteen years of age is accountable for causing legally relevant damage according to VI. – 3:102 (Negligence) sub-paragraph (b) only in so far as that person does not exercise such care as could be expected from a reasonably careful person of the same age in the circumstances of the case.

(2) A person under seven years of age is not accountable for causing damage intentionally or negligently.

(3) However, paragraphs (1) and (2) do not apply to the extent that:

(a) the person suffering the damage cannot obtain reparation under this Book from another; and

(b) liability to make reparation would be equitable having regard to the financial means of the parties and all other circumstances of the case.

VI. – 3:104: Accountability for damage caused by children or supervised persons

(1) Parents or other persons obliged by law to provide parental care for a person under fourteen years of age are accountable for the causation of legally relevant damage where that person under age caused the damage by conduct that would constitute intentional or negligent conduct if it were the conduct of an adult.

(2) An institution or other body obliged to supervise a person is accountable for the causation of legally relevant damage suffered by a third party when:

(a) the damage is personal injury, loss within VI. – 2:202 (Loss suffered by third persons as a result of another's personal injury or death) or property damage;

    (b) the person whom the institution or other body is obliged to super-
        vise caused that damage intentionally or negligently or, in the case
        of a person under eighteen, by conduct that would constitute in-
        tention or negligence if it were the conduct of an adult; and
    (c) the person whom the institution or other body is obliged to super-
        vise is a person likely to cause damage of that type.
(3) However, a person is not accountable under this Article for the causa-
    tion of damage if that person shows that there was no defective super-
    vision of the person causing the damage.

Section 2:
Accountability without intention or negligence

VI. – 3:201: Accountability for damage caused by employees and representatives

(1) A person who employs or similarly engages another is accountable for
    the causation of legally relevant damage suffered by a third person
    when the person employed or engaged:
    (a) caused the damage in the course of the employment or engage-
        ment; and
    (b) caused the damage intentionally or negligently, or is otherwise ac-
        countable for the causation of the damage.
(2) Paragraph (1) applies correspondingly to a legal person in relation to a
    representative causing damage in the course of their engagement. A
    representative is a person who is authorised to effect juridical acts on
    behalf of the legal person by its constitution.

VI. – 3:202: Accountability for damage caused by the unsafe state of an immovable

(1) A person who independently exercises control over an immovable is
    accountable for the causation of personal injury and consequential
    loss, loss within VI. – 2:202 (Loss suffered by third persons as a result
    of another's personal injury or death), and loss resulting from property
    damage (other than to the immovable itself) by a state of the immo-
    vable which does not ensure such safety as a person in or near the
    immovable is entitled to expect having regard to the circumstances
    including:

    (a) the nature of the immovable;

    (b) the access to the immovable; and

    (c) the cost of avoiding the immovable being in that state.

(2) A person exercises independent control over an immovable if that person exercises such control that it is reasonable to impose a duty on that person to prevent legally relevant damage within the scope of this Article.

(3) The owner of the immovable is to be regarded as independently exercising control, unless the owner shows that another independently exercises control.

VI. – 3:203: Accountability for damage caused by animals

A keeper of an animal is accountable for the causation by the animal of personal injury and consequential loss, loss within VI. – 2:202 (Loss suffered by third persons as a result of another's personal injury or death), and loss resulting from property damage.

VI. – 3:204: Accountability for damage caused by defective products

(1) The producer of a product is accountable for the causation of personal injury and consequential loss, loss within VI. – 2:202 (Loss suffered by third persons as a result of another's personal injury or death), and, in relation to consumers, loss resulting from property damage (other than to the product itself) by a defect in the product.

(2) A person who imported the product into the European Economic Area for sale, hire, leasing or distribution in the course of that person's business is accountable correspondingly.

(3) A supplier of the product is accountable correspondingly if:

    (a) the producer cannot be identified; or

    (b) in the case of an imported product, the product does not indicate the identity of the importer (whether or not the producer's name is indicated), unless the supplier informs the person suffering the damage, within a reasonable time, of the identity of the producer or the person who supplied that supplier with the product.

(4) A person is not accountable under this Article for the causation of damage if that person shows that:

    (a) that person did not put the product into circulation;

(b) it is probable that the defect which caused the damage did not exist at the time when that person put the product into circulation;

(c) that person neither manufactured the product for sale or distribution for economic purpose nor manufactured or distributed it in the course of business;

(d) the defect is due to the product's compliance with mandatory regulations issued by public authorities;

(e) the state of scientific and technical knowledge at the time that person put the product into circulation did not enable the existence of the defect to be discovered; or

(f) in the case of a manufacturer of a component, the defect is attributable to:

(i) the design of the product into which the component has been fitted; or

(ii) instructions given by the manufacturer of the product.

(5) "Producer" means:

(a) in the case of a finished product or a component, the manufacturer;

(b) in the case of raw material, the person who abstracts or wins it; and

(c) any person who, by putting a name, trade mark or other distinguishing feature on the product, gives the impression of being its producer.

(6) "Product" means a movable, even if incorporated into another movable or an immovable, or electricity.

(7) A product is defective if it does not provide the safety which a person is entitled to expect, having regard to the circumstances including:

(a) the presentation of the product;

(b) the use to which it could reasonably be expected that the product would be put; and

(c) the time when the product was put into circulation,

but a product is not defective merely because a better product is subsequently put into circulation.

VI. – 3:205: Accountability for damage caused by motor vehicles

(1) A keeper of a motor vehicle is accountable for the causation of personal injury and consequential loss, loss within VI. – 2:202 (Loss suffered by third persons as a result of another's personal injury or death), and loss

resulting from property damage (other than to the vehicle and its freight) in a traffic accident which results from the use of the vehicle.

(2) "Motor vehicle" means any vehicle intended for travel on land and propelled by mechanical power, but not running on rails, and any trailer, whether or not coupled.

VI. – 3:206: Accountability for damage caused by dangerous substances or emissions

(1) A keeper of a substance or an operator of an installation is accountable for the causation by that substance or by emissions from that installation of personal injury and consequential loss, loss within VI. – 2:202 (Loss suffered by third persons as a result of another's personal injury or death), loss resulting from property damage, and burdens within VI. – 2:209 (Burdens incurred by the State upon environmental impairment), if:

(a) having regard to their quantity and attributes, at the time of the emission, or, failing an emission, at the time of contact with the substance it is very likely that the substance or emission will cause such damage unless adequately controlled; and

(b) the damage results from the realisation of that danger.

(2) "Substance" includes chemicals (whether solid, liquid or gaseous). Microorganisms are to be treated like substances.

(3) "Emission" includes:

(a) the release or escape of substances;

(b) the conduction of electricity;

(c) heat, light and other radiation;

(d) noise and other vibrations; and

(e) other incorporeal impact on the environment.

(4) "Installation" includes a mobile installation and an installation under construction or not in use.

(5) However, a person is not accountable for the causation of damage under this Article if that person:

(a) does not keep the substance or operate the installation for purposes related to that person's trade, business or profession; or

(b) shows that there was no failure to comply with statutory standards of control of the substance or management of the installation.

VI. – 3:207: Other accountability for the causation of legally relevant damage

A person is also accountable for the causation of legally relevant damage if national law so provides where it:

(a) relates to a source of danger which is not within VI. – 3:104 (Accountability for damage caused by children or supervised persons) to VI. – 3:205 (Accountability for damage caused by motor vehicles);

(b) relates to substances or emissions; or

(c) disapplies VI. – 3:204 (Accountability for damage caused by defective products) paragraph (4)(e).

VI. – 3:208: Abandonment

For the purposes of this section, a person remains accountable for an immovable, vehicle, substance or installation which that person abandons until another exercises independent control over it or becomes its keeper or operator. This applies correspondingly, so far as reasonable, in respect of a keeper of an animal.

Chapter 4:
Causation

VI. – 4:101: General rule

(1) A person causes legally relevant damage to another if the damage is to be regarded as a consequence of that person's conduct or the source of danger for which that person is responsible.

(2) In cases of personal injury or death the injured person's predisposition with respect to the type or extent of the injury sustained is to be disregarded.

VI. – 4:102: Collaboration

A person who participates with, instigates or materially assists another in causing legally relevant damage is to be regarded as causing that damage.

VI. – 4:103: Alternative causes

Where legally relevant damage may have been caused by any one or more of a number of occurrences for which different persons are accountable and it is established that the damage was caused by one of these occurrences but not which one, each person who is accountable for any of the occurrences is rebuttably presumed to have caused that damage.

Chapter 5:
Defences
Section 1:
Consent or conduct of the person suffering the damage

VI. – 5:101: Consent and acting at own risk
(1) A person has a defence if the person suffering the damage validly consents to the legally relevant damage and is aware or could reasonably be expected to be aware of the consequences of that consent.
(2) The same applies if the person suffering the damage, knowing the risk of damage of the type caused, voluntarily takes that risk and is to be regarded as accepting it.

VI. – 5:102: Contributory fault and accountability
(1) Where the fault of the person suffering the damage contributes to the occurrence or extent of legally relevant damage, reparation is to be reduced according to the degree of such fault.
(2) However, no regard is to be had to:
    (a) an insubstantial fault of the person suffering the damage;
    (b) fault or accountability whose contribution to the causation of the damage is insubstantial;
    (c) the injured person's want of care contributing to that person's personal injury caused by a motor vehicle in a traffic accident, unless that want of care constitutes profound failure to take such care as is manifestly required in the circumstances.
(3) Paragraphs (1) and (2) apply correspondingly where the fault of a person for whom the person suffering the damage is responsible within the scope of VI. – 3:201 (Accountability for damage caused by employees and representatives) contributes to the occurrence or extent of the damage.
(4) Compensation is to be reduced likewise if and in so far as any other source of danger for which the person suffering the damage is responsible under Chapter 3 (Accountability) contributes to the occurrence or extent of the damage.

VI. – 5:103: Damage caused by a criminal to a collaborator
Legally relevant damage caused unintentionally in the course of committing a criminal offence to another person participating or otherwise collaborating in the offence does not give rise to a right to reparation if this would be contrary to public policy.

Section 2:
Interests of accountable persons or third parties

VI. – 5:201: Authority conferred by law
A person has a defence if legally relevant damage is caused with authority conferred by law.

VI. – 5:202: Self-defence, benevolent intervention and necessity
(1) A person has a defence if that person causes legally relevant damage in reasonable protection of a right or of an interest worthy of legal protection of that person or a third person if the person suffering the legally relevant damage is accountable for endangering the right or interest protected. For the purposes of this paragraph VI. – 3:103 (Persons under eighteen) is to be disregarded.
(2) The same applies to legally relevant damage caused by a benevolent intervener to a principal without breach of the intervener's duties.
(3) Where a person causes legally relevant damage to the patrimony of another in a situation of imminent danger to life, body, health or liberty in order to save the person causing the damage or a third person from that danger and the danger could not be eliminated without causing the damage, the person causing the damage is not liable to make reparation beyond providing reasonable recompense.

VI. – 5:203: Protection of public interest
A person has a defence if legally relevant damage is caused in necessary protection of values fundamental to a democratic society, in particular where damage is caused by dissemination of information in the media.

Section 3:
Inability to control

VI. – 5:301: Mental incompetence
(1) A person who is mentally incompetent at the time of conduct causing
legally relevant damage is liable only if this is equitable, having regard
to the mentally incompetent person's financial means and all the other
circumstances of the case. Liability is limited to reasonable recompense.
(2) A person is to be regarded as mentally incompetent if that person lacks
sufficient insight into the nature of his or her conduct, unless the lack
of sufficient insight is the temporary result of his or her own miscon-
duct.

VI. – 5:302: Event beyond control
A person has a defence if legally relevant damage is caused by an abnormal
event which cannot be averted by any reasonable measure and which is not
to be regarded as that person's risk.

Section 4:
Contractual exclusion and restriction of liability

VI. – 5:401: Contractual exclusion and restriction of liability
(1) Liability for causing legally relevant damage intentionally cannot be
excluded or restricted.
(2) Liability for causing legally relevant damage as a result of a profound
failure to take such care as is manifestly required in the circumstances
cannot be excluded or restricted:
  (a) in respect of personal injury (including fatal injury); or
  (b) if the exclusion or restriction is otherwise illegal or contrary to
      good faith and fair dealing.
(3) Liability for damage for the causation of which a person is accountable
under VI. – 3:204 (Accountability for damage caused by defective products) cannot be restricted or excluded.
(4) Other liability under this Book can be excluded or restricted unless
statute provides otherwise.

Section 5:
Loss within VI. – 2:202 (Loss suffered by third persons as a result of another's personal injury or death)

VI. – 5:501: Extension of defences against the injured person to third persons

A defence which may be asserted against a person's right of reparation in respect of that person's personal injury or, if death had not occurred, could have been asserted, may also be asserted against a person suffering loss within VI. – 2:202 (Loss suffered by third persons as a result of another's personal injury or death).

Chapter 6:
Remedies
Section 1:
Reparation in general

VI. – 6:101: Aim and forms of reparation

(1) Reparation is to reinstate the person suffering the legally relevant damage in the position that person would have been in had the legally relevant damage not occurred.

(2) Reparation may be in money (compensation) or otherwise, as is most appropriate, having regard to the kind and extent of damage suffered and all the other circumstances of the case.

(3) Where a tangible object is damaged, compensation equal to its depreciation of value is to be awarded instead of the cost of its repair if the cost of repair unreasonably exceeds the depreciation of value. This rule applies to animals only if appropriate, having regard to the purpose for which the animal was kept.

(4) As an alternative to reinstatement under paragraph (1), but only where this is reasonable, reparation may take the form of recovery from the person accountable for the causation of the legally relevant damage of any advantage obtained by the latter in connection with causing the damage.

VI. – 6:102: De minimis rule

Trivial damage is to be disregarded.

VI. – 6:103: Equalisation of benefits

(1) Benefits arising to the person suffering legally relevant damage as a result of the damaging event are to be disregarded unless it would be fair and reasonable to take them into account.

(2) In deciding whether it would be fair and reasonable to take the benefits into account, regard shall be had to the kind of damage sustained, the nature of the accountability of the person causing the damage and, where the benefits are conferred by a third person, the purpose of conferring those benefits.

VI. – 6:104: Multiple persons suffering damage

Where multiple persons suffer legally relevant damage and reparation to one person will also make reparation to another, Book III, Chapter 4, Section 2 (Plurality of creditors) applies with appropriate adaptation to their rights to reparation.

VI. – 6:105: Solidary liability

Where several persons are liable for the same legally relevant damage, they are liable solidarily.

VI. – 6:106: Assignment of right to reparation

The person suffering the damage may assign a right to reparation, including a right to reparation for non-economic loss.

Section 2:
Compensation

VI. – 6:201: Right of election

The person suffering the damage may choose whether or not to spend compensation on the reinstatement of the damaged interest.

VI. – 6:202: Reduction of liability

Where it is fair and reasonable to do so, a person may be relieved of liability to compensate, either wholly or in part, if, where the damage is not caused intentionally, liability in full would be disproportionate to the accountability of the person causing the damage or the extent of the damage or the means to prevent it.

VI. – 6:203: Capitalisation and quantification

(1) Compensation is to be awarded as a lump sum unless a good reason requires periodical payment.

(2) National law determines how compensation for personal injury and non-economic loss is to be quantified.

VI. – 6:204: Compensation for injury as such

Injury as such is to be compensated independent of compensation for economic or non-economic loss.

Section 3:
Prevention

VI. – 6:301: Right to prevention

(1) The right to prevention exists only in so far as:

(a) reparation would not be an adequate alternative remedy; and

(b) it is reasonable for the person who would be accountable for the causation of the damage to prevent it from occurring.

(2) Where the source of danger is an object or an animal and it is not reasonably possible for the endangered person to avoid the danger the right to prevention includes a right to have the source of danger removed.

VI. – 6:302: Liability for loss in preventing damage

A person who has reasonably incurred expenditure or sustained other loss in order to prevent that person from suffering an impending damage, or in order to limit the extent or severity of damage suffered, has a right to compensation from the person who would have been accountable for the causation of the damage.

Chapter 7:
Ancillary rules

VI. – 7:101: National constitutional laws
The provisions of this Book are to be interpreted and applied in a manner compatible with the constitutional law of the court.

VI. – 7:102: Statutory provisions
National law determines what legal provisions are statutory provisions.

VI. – 7:103: Public law functions and court proceedings
This Book does not govern the liability of a person or body arising from the exercise or omission to exercise public law functions or from performing duties during court proceedings.

VI. – 7:104: Liability of employees, employers, trade unions and employers' associations
This Book does not govern the liability of:
(a) employees (whether to co-employees, employers or third parties) arising in the course of employment;
(b) employers to employees arising in the course of employment; and
(c) trade unions and employers' associations arising in the course of an industrial dispute.

VI. – 7:105: Reduction or exclusion of liability to indemnified persons
If a person is entitled from another source to reparation, whether in full or in part, for that person's damage, in particular from an insurer, fund or other body, national law determines whether or not by virtue of that entitlement liability under this Book is limited or excluded.

Book VII
Unjustified enrichment

Chapter 1:
General

VII. – 1:101: Basic rule

(1) A person who obtains an unjustified enrichment which is attributable to another's disadvantage is obliged to that other to reverse the enrichment.

(2) This rule applies only in accordance with the following provisions of this Book.

Chapter 2:
When enrichment unjustified

VII. – 2:101: Circumstances in which an enrichment is unjustified

(1) An enrichment is unjustified unless:
  (a) the enriched person is entitled as against the disadvantaged person to the enrichment by virtue of a contract or other juridical act, a court order or a rule of law; or
  (b) the disadvantaged person consented freely and without error to the disadvantage.

(2) If the contract or other juridical act, court order or rule of law referred to in paragraph (1)(a) is void or avoided or otherwise rendered ineffective retrospectively, the enriched person is not entitled to the enrichment on that basis.

(3) However, the enriched person is to be regarded as entitled to an enrichment by virtue of a rule of law only if the policy of that rule is that the enriched person is to retain the value of the enrichment.

(4) An enrichment is also unjustified if:
  (a) the disadvantaged person conferred it:

(i) for a purpose which is not achieved; or

(ii) with an expectation which is not realised;

(b) the enriched person knew of, or could reasonably be expected to know of, the purpose or expectation; and

(c) the enriched person accepted or could reasonably be assumed to have accepted that the enrichment must be reversed in such circumstances.

VII. – 2:102: Performance of obligation to third person

Where the enriched person obtains the enrichment as a result of the disadvantaged person performing an obligation or a supposed obligation owed by the disadvantaged person to a third person, the enrichment is justified if:

(a) the disadvantaged person performed freely; or

(b) the enrichment was merely the incidental result of performance of the obligation.

VII. – 2:103: Consenting or performing freely

(1) If the disadvantaged person's consent is affected by incapacity, fraud, coercion, threats or unfair exploitation, the disadvantaged person does not consent freely.

(2) If the obligation which is performed is ineffective because of incapacity, fraud, coercion threats or unfair exploitation, the disadvantaged person does not perform freely.

Chapter 3:
Enrichment and disadvantage

VII. – 3:101: Enrichment

(1) A person is enriched by:

(a) an increase in assets or a decrease in liabilities;

(b) receiving a service or having work done; or

(c) use of another's assets.

(2) In determining whether and to what extent a person obtains an enrichment, no regard is to be had to any disadvantage which that person sustains in exchange for or after the enrichment.

VII. – 3:102: Disadvantage

(1) A person is disadvantaged by:
  (a) a decrease in assets or an increase in liabilities;
  (b) rendering a service or doing work; or
  (c) another's use of that person's assets.
(2) In determining whether and to what extent a person sustains a disadvantage, no regard is to be had to any enrichment which that person obtains in exchange for or after the disadvantage.

Chapter 4:
Attribution

VII. – 4:101: Instances of attribution

An enrichment is attributable to another's disadvantage in particular where:
(a) an asset of that other is transferred to the enriched person by that other;
(b) a service is rendered to or work is done for the enriched person by that other;
(c) the enriched person uses that other's asset, especially where the enriched person infringes the disadvantaged person's rights or legally protected interests;
(d) an asset of the enriched person is improved by that other; or
(e) the enriched person is discharged from a liability by that other.

VII. – 4:102: Intermediaries

Where one party to a juridical act is an authorised intermediary indirectly representing a principal, any enrichment or disadvantage of the principal which results from the juridical act, or from a performance of obligations under it, is to be regarded as an enrichment or disadvantage of the intermediary.

VII. – 4:103: Debtor's performance to a non-creditor; onward transfer in good faith

(1) An enrichment is also attributable to another's disadvantage where a debtor confers the enrichment on the enriched person and as a result the disadvantaged person loses a right against the debtor to the same or a like enrichment.

(2) Paragraph (1) applies in particular where a person who is obliged to the disadvantaged person to reverse an unjustified enrichment transfers it to a third person in circumstances in which the debtor has a defence under VII. – 6:101 (Disenrichment).

VII. – 4:104: Ratification of debtor's performance to a non-creditor

(1) Where a debtor purports to discharge a debt by paying a third person, the creditor may ratify that act.

(2) Ratification extinguishes the creditor's right against the debtor to the extent of the payment with the effect that the third person's enrichment is attributable to the creditor's loss of the claim against the debtor.

(3) As between the creditor and the third person, ratification does not amount to consent to the loss of the creditor's right against the debtor.

(4) This Article applies correspondingly to performances of non-monetary obligations.

(5) Other rules may exclude the application of this Article if an insolvency or equivalent proceeding has been opened against the debtor before the creditor ratifies.

VII. – 4:105: Attribution resulting from an act of an intervener

(1) An enrichment is also attributable to another's disadvantage where a third person uses an asset of the disadvantaged person without authority so that the disadvantaged person is deprived of the asset and it accrues to the enriched person.

(2) Paragraph (1) applies in particular where, as a result of an intervener's interference with or disposition of goods, the disadvantaged person ceases to be owner of the goods and the enriched person becomes owner, whether by juridical act or rule of law.

VII. – 4:106: Ratification of intervener's acts

(1) A person entitled to an asset may ratify the act of an intervener who purports to dispose of or otherwise uses that asset in a juridical act with a third person.

(2) The ratified act has the same effect as a juridical act by an authorised intermediary. As between the person ratifying and the intervener, ratification does not amount to consent to the intervener's use of the asset.

VII. – 4:107: Where type or value not identical

An enrichment may be attributable to another's disadvantage even though the enrichment and disadvantage are not of the same type or value.

Chapter 5:
Reversal of enrichment

VII. – 5:101: Transferable enrichment

(1) Where the enrichment consists of a transferable asset, the enriched person reverses the enrichment by transferring the asset to the disadvantaged person.

(2) Instead of transferring the asset, the enriched person may choose to reverse the enrichment by paying its monetary value to the disadvantaged person if a transfer would cause the enriched person unreasonable effort or expense.

(3) If the enriched person is no longer able to transfer the asset, the enriched person reverses the enrichment by paying its monetary value to the disadvantaged person.

(4) However, to the extent that the enriched person has obtained a substitute in exchange, the substitute is the enrichment to be reversed if:

   (a) the enriched person is in good faith at the time of disposal or loss and the enriched person so chooses; or

   (b) the enriched person is not in good faith at the time of disposal or loss, the disadvantaged person so chooses and the choice is not inequitable.

(5) The enriched person is in good faith if that person neither knew nor could reasonably be expected to know that the enrichment was or was likely to become unjustified.

VII. – 5:102: Non-transferable enrichment

(1) Where the enrichment does not consist of a transferable asset, the enriched person reverses the enrichment by paying its monetary value to the disadvantaged person.

(2) The enriched person is not liable to pay more than any saving if the enriched person:
   (a) did not consent to the enrichment; or
   (b) was in good faith.

(3) However, where the enrichment was obtained under an agreement which fixed a price or value for the enrichment, the enriched person is at least liable to pay that sum if the agreement was void or voidable for reasons which were not material to the fixing of the price.

(4) Paragraph (3) does not apply so as to increase liability beyond the monetary value of the enrichment.

VII. – 5:103: Monetary value of an enrichment; saving

(1) The monetary value of an enrichment is the sum of money which a provider and a recipient with a real intention of reaching an agreement would lawfully have agreed as its price. Expenditure of a service provider which the agreement would require the recipient to reimburse is to be regarded as part of the price.

(2) A saving is the decrease in assets or increase in liabilities which the enriched person would have sustained if the enrichment had not been obtained.

VII. – 5:104: Fruits and use of an enrichment

(1) Reversal of the enrichment extends to the fruits and use of the enrichment or, if less, any saving resulting from the fruits or use.

(2) However, if the enriched person obtains the fruits or use in bad faith, reversal of the enrichment extends to the fruits and use even if the saving is less than the value of the fruits or use.

Chapter 6:
Defences

VII. – 6:101: Disenrichment
(1) The enriched person is not liable to reverse the enrichment to the extent that the enriched person has sustained a disadvantage by disposing of the enrichment or otherwise (disenrichment), unless the enriched person would have been disenriched even if the enrichment had not been obtained.
(2) However, a disenrichment is to be disregarded to the extent that:
    (a) the enriched person has obtained a substitute;
    (b) the enriched person was not in good faith at the time of disenrichment, unless:
        (i) the disadvantaged person would also have been disenriched even if the enrichment had been reversed; or
        (ii) the enriched person was in good faith at the time of enrichment, the disenrichment was sustained before performance of the obligation to reverse the enrichment was due and the disenrichment resulted from the realisation of a risk for which the enriched person is not to be regarded as responsible;

    or
    (c) paragraph (3) of VII. – 5:102 (Non-transferable enrichment) applies.
(3) Where the enriched person has a defence under this Article as against the disadvantaged person as a result of a disposal to a third person, any right of the disadvantaged person against that third person is unaffected.

VII. – 6:102: Juridical acts in good faith with third parties
The enriched person is also not liable to reverse the enrichment if:
(a) in exchange for that enrichment the enriched person confers another enrichment on a third person; and
(b) the enriched person is still in good faith at that time.

VII. – 6:103: Illegality
Where a contract or other juridical act under which an enrichment is obtained is void or avoided because of an infringement of a fundamental principle (II. – 7:301 (Contracts infringing fundamental principles)) or

mandatory rule of law, the enriched person is not liable to reverse the enrichment to the extent that the reversal would contravene the policy underlying the principle or rule.

Chapter 7:
Relation to other legal rules

VII. – 7:101: Other private law rights to recover
(1) The legal consequences of an enrichment which is obtained by virtue of a contract or other juridical act are governed by other rules if those rules grant or exclude a right to reversal of an enrichment, whether on withdrawal, termination, price reduction or otherwise.
(2) This Book does not address the proprietary effect of a right to reversal of an enrichment.
(3) This Book does not affect any other right to recover arising under contractual or other rules of private law.

VII. – 7:102: Concurrent obligations
(1) Where the disadvantaged person has both:
>   (a) a claim under this Book for reversal of an unjustified enrichment; and
>   (b) (i) a claim for reparation for the disadvantage (whether against the enriched person or a third party); or
>   (ii) a right to recover under other rules of private law as a result of the unjustified enrichment,

the satisfaction of one of the claims reduces the other claim by the same amount.
(2) The same applies where a person uses an asset of the disadvantaged person so that it accrues to another and under this Book:
>   (a) the user is liable to the disadvantaged person in respect of the use of the asset; and
>   (b) the recipient is liable to the disadvantaged person in respect of the increase in assets.

VII. – 7:103: Public law claims
This Book does not determine whether it applies to enrichments which a person or body obtains or confers in the exercise of public law functions.

Book VIII
Acquisition and loss of ownership of goods

Chapter 1:
General provisions
Section 1:
Scope of application and relation to other provisions

VIII. – 1:101: Scope of application
(1) This Book applies to the acquisition, loss and protection of ownership of goods and to specific related issues.
(2) This Book does not apply to the acquisition or loss of ownership of goods by:
  (a) universal succession, in particular under the law of succession and under company law;
  (b) expropriation and forfeiture;
  (c) separation from movable or immovable property;
  (d) division of co-ownership, unless provided by VIII. – 2:306 (Delivery out of the bulk) or VIII. – 5:202 (Commingling);
  (e) survivorship or accrual, unless covered by Chapter 5 of this Book;
  (f) real subrogation, unless covered by Chapter 5 of this Book;
  (g) occupation;
  (h) finding; or
  (i) abandonment.
(3) This Book applies to the acquisition and loss of ownership of goods by extrajudicial enforcement in the sense of Book IX or the equivalent. It may be applied, with appropriate adaptations, to the acquisition and loss of ownership of goods by judicial or equivalent enforcement.
(4) This Book does not apply to:
  (a) company shares or documents embodying the right to an asset or to the performance of an obligation, except documents containing the undertaking to deliver goods for the purposes of VIII. – 2:105 (Equivalents to delivery) paragraph (4); or
  (b) electricity.

(5) This Book applies, with appropriate adaptations, to banknotes and coins that are current legal tender.

VIII. – 1:102: Registration of goods

(1) Whether ownership and the transfer of ownership in certain categories of goods may be or have to be registered in a public register is determined by national law.

(2) The effects of such registration, as determined by national law, have priority over the respective rules of this Book.

VIII. – 1:103: Priority of other provisions

(1) In relation to a transfer, or retention, of ownership for purposes of security, the provisions of Book IX apply and have priority over the provisions in this Book.

(2) In relation to a transfer of ownership for purposes of a trust, or to or from a trust, the provisions of Book X apply and have priority over the provisions in this Book.

VIII. – 1:104: Application of rules of Books I to III

Where, under the provisions of this Book, proprietary effects are determined by an agreement, Books I to III apply, where appropriate.

Section 2:
Definitions

VIII. – 1:201: Goods

"Goods" means corporeal movables. It includes ships, vessels, hovercraft or aircraft, space objects, animals, liquids and gases.

VIII. – 1:202: Ownership

"Ownership" is the most comprehensive right a person, the "owner", can have over property, including the exclusive right, so far as consistent with applicable laws or rights granted by the owner, to use, enjoy, modify, destroy, dispose of and recover the property.

VIII. – I:203: Co-ownership
Where "co-ownership" is created under this Book, this means that two or more co-owners own undivided shares in the whole goods and each co-owner can dispose of that co-owner's share by acting alone, unless otherwise provided by the parties.

VIII. – I:204: Limited proprietary rights
Limited proprietary rights in the sense of this Book are:
(a) security rights if characterised or treated as proprietary rights by Book IX or by national law;
(b) rights to use if characterised or treated as proprietary rights by other provisions of these model rules or by national law;
(c) rights to acquire in the sense of VIII. – 2:307 (Contingent right of transferee under retention of ownership) or if characterised or treated as proprietary rights by other provisions of these model rules or by national law;
(d) trust-related rights if characterised or treated as proprietary rights by Book X or by national law.

VIII. – I:205: Possession
(1) Possession, in relation to goods, means having direct physical control or indirect physical control over the goods.
(2) Direct physical control is physical control which is exercised by the possessor personally or through a possession-agent exercising such control on behalf of the possessor (direct possession).
(3) Indirect physical control is physical control which is exercised by means of another person, a limited-right-possessor (indirect possession).

VIII. – I:206: Possession by owner-possessor
An "owner-possessor" is a person who exercises direct or indirect physical control over the goods with the intention of doing so as, or as if, an owner.

VIII. – I:207: Possession by limited-right-possessor
(1) A "limited-right-possessor" is a person who exercises physical control over the goods either:

(a) with the intention of doing so in that person's own interest, and under a specific legal relationship with the owner-possessor which gives the limited-right-possessor the right to possess the goods; or

(b) with the intention of doing so to the order of the owner-possessor, and under a specific contractual relationship with the owner-possessor which gives the limited-right-possessor a right to retain the goods until any charges or costs have been paid by the owner-possessor.

(2) A limited-right-possessor may have direct physical control or indirect physical control over the goods.

VIII. – 1:208: Possession through a possession-agent

(1) A "possession-agent" is a person:

(a) who exercises direct physical control over the goods on behalf of an owner-possessor or limited-right-possessor without the intention and specific legal relationship required under VIII. – 1:207 (Possession by limited-right-possessor) paragraph (1); and

(b) to whom the owner-possessor or limited-right-possessor may give binding instructions as to the use of the goods in the interest of the owner-possessor or limited-right-possessor.

(2) A possession-agent may, in particular, be:

(a) an employee of the owner-possessor or limited-right-possessor or a person exercising a similar function; or

(b) a person who is given physical control over the goods by the owner-possessor or limited-right-possessor for practical reasons.

(3) A person is also a possession-agent where that person is accidentally in a position to exercise, and does exercise, direct physical control over the goods for an owner-possessor or limited-right-possessor.

Section 3:
Further general rules

VIII. – 1:301: Transferability

(1) All goods are transferable except where provided otherwise by law. A limitation or prohibition of the transfer of goods by a contract or other juridical act does not affect the transferability of the goods.

(2) Whether or to what extent uncollected fruits of, and accessories or appurtenances to, goods or immovable assets are transferable separately is regulated by national law. Chapter 5 remains unaffected.

Chapter 2:
Transfer of ownership based on the transferor's right or authority
Section 1:
Requirements for transfer under this chapter

VIII. – 2:101: Requirements for the transfer of ownership in general

(1) The transfer of ownership of goods under this Chapter requires that:
    (a) the goods exist;
    (b) the goods are transferable;
    (c) the transferor has the right or authority to transfer the ownership;
    (d) the transferee is entitled as against the transferor to the transfer of ownership by virtue of a contract or other juridical act, a court order or a rule of law; and
    (e) there is an agreement as to the time ownership is to pass and the conditions of this agreement are met, or, in the absence of such agreement, delivery or an equivalent to delivery.

(2) For the purposes of paragraph (1)(e) the delivery or equivalent to delivery must be based on, or referable to, the entitlement under the contract or other juridical act, court order or rule of law.

(3) Where the contract or other juridical act, court order or rule of law defines the goods in generic terms, ownership can pass only when the goods are identified to it. Where goods form part of an identified bulk, VIII. – 2:305 (Transfer of goods forming part of a bulk) applies.

(4) Paragraph (1)(e) does not apply where ownership passes under a court order or rule of law at the time determined in it.

VIII. – 2:102: Transferor's right or authority

(1) Where the transferor lacks a right or authority to transfer ownership at the time ownership is to pass, the transfer takes place when the right is obtained or the person having the right or authority to transfer has ratified the transfer at a later time.

(2) Upon ratification the transfer produces the same effects as if it had initially been carried out with authority. However, proprietary rights acquired by other persons before ratification remain unaffected.

VIII. – 2:103: Agreement as to the time ownership is to pass
The point in time when ownership passes may be determined by party agreement, except where registration is necessary to acquire ownership under national law.

VIII. – 2:104: Delivery
(1) For the purposes of this Book, delivery of the goods takes place when the transferor gives up and the transferee obtains possession of the goods in the sense of VIII. – 1:205 (Possession).
(2) If the contract or other juridical act, court order or rule of law involves carriage of the goods by a carrier or a series of carriers, delivery of the goods takes place when the transferor's obligation to deliver is fulfilled and the carrier or the transferee obtains possession of the goods.

VIII. – 2:105: Equivalents to delivery
(1) Where the goods are already in the possession of the transferee, the retention of the goods on the coming into effect of the entitlement under the contract or other juridical act, court order or rule of law has the same effect as delivery.
(2) Where a third person possesses the goods for the transferor, the same effect as delivery is achieved when the third party receives the transferor's notice of the ownership being transferred to the transferee, or at a later time if so stated in the notice. The same applies where notice is given to a possession-agent in the sense of VIII. – 1:208 (Possession through possession-agent).
(3) The same effect as delivery of the goods is achieved when the transferor gives up and the transferee obtains possession of means enabling the transferee to obtain possession of the goods.
(4) Where a person exercising physical control over goods issues a document containing an undertaking to deliver the goods to the current holder of the document, the transfer of that document is equivalent to delivery of the goods. The document may be an electronic one.

Section 2:
Effects

VIII. – 2:201: Effects of the transfer of ownership

(1) At the time determined by Section 1, ownership passes within the limits of the transferor's right or authority to dispose, with effect between the parties and with effect against third persons.

(2) The transfer of ownership does not affect rights and obligations between the parties based on the terms of a contract or other juridical act, court order or rule of law, such as:

(a) a right resulting from the passing of risk;

(b) a right to withhold performance;

(c) a right to fruits or benefits, or an obligation to cover costs and charges; or

(d) a right to use or an obligation not to use or otherwise deal with the goods.

(3) The transfer of ownership does not affect rights of or against third parties under other rules of law, such as:

(a) any right of the transferor's creditors to treat the transfer as ineffective arising from the law of insolvency or similar provisions; or

(b) a right to claim reparation under Book VI (Non-contractual liability arising out of damage caused to another) from a third party damaging the goods.

(4) Where ownership has been transferred but the transferor still has a right to withhold delivery of the goods (paragraph (2)(b)), terminating the contractual relationship while exercising the right to withhold performance has retroactive proprietary effect in the sense of the following Article.

VIII. – 2:202: Effect of initial invalidity, subsequent avoidance, withdrawal, termination and revocation

(1) Where the underlying contract or other juridical act is invalid from the beginning, a transfer of ownership does not take place.

(2) Where, after ownership has been transferred, the underlying contract or other juridical act is avoided under Book II, Chapter 7, ownership is treated as never having passed to the transferee (retroactive proprietary effect).

(3) Where ownership must be re-transferred as a consequence of withdrawal in the sense of Book II, Chapter 5, or termination in the sense of Book III, Chapter 3, or revocation of a donation in the sense of Book IV.H, there is no retroactive proprietary effect nor is ownership re-transferred immediately. VIII. – 2:201 (Effects of the transfer of ownership) paragraph (4) remains unaffected.

(4) This Article does not affect any right to recover the goods based on other provisions of these model rules.

VIII. – 2:203: Transfer subject to condition

(1) Where the parties agreed on a transfer subject to a resolutive condition, ownership is re-transferred immediately upon the fulfilment of that condition, subject to the limits of the re-transferor's right or authority to dispose at that time. A retroactive proprietary effect of the re-transfer cannot be achieved by party agreement.

(2) Where the contract or other juridical act entitling to the transfer of ownership is subject to a suspensive condition, ownership passes when the condition is fulfilled.

Section 3:
Special constellations

VIII. – 2:301: Multiple transfers

(1) Where there are several purported transfers of the same goods by the transferor, ownership is acquired by the transferee who first fulfils all the requirements of Section 1 and, in the case of a later transferee, who neither knew nor could reasonably be expected to know of the earlier entitlement of the other transferee.

(2) A later transferee who first fulfils all the requirements of Section 1 but is not in good faith in the sense of paragraph (1) must restore the goods to the transferor. The transferor's entitlement to recovery of the goods from that transferee may also be exercised by the first transferee.

VIII. – 2:302: Indirect representation

(1) Where an agent acting under a mandate for indirect representation within the meaning of IV. D. – 1:102 (Definitions) acquires goods from

a third party on behalf of the principal, the principal directly acquires the ownership of the goods (representation for acquisition).

(2) Where an agent acting under a mandate for indirect representation within the meaning of IV. D. – 1:102 (Definitions) transfers goods on behalf of the principal to a third party, the third party directly acquires the ownership of the goods (representation for alienation).

(3) The acquisition of ownership of the goods by the principal (paragraph (1)) or by the third party (paragraph (2)) takes place when:
   (a) the agent has authority to transfer or receive the goods on behalf of the principal;
   (b) there is an entitlement to transfer by virtue of a contract or other juridical act, a court order or a rule of law between the agent and the third party; and
   (c) there has been an agreement as to the time ownership is to pass or delivery or an equivalent to delivery in the sense of VIII. – 2:101 (Requirements for the transfer of ownership in general) paragraph (1)(e) between the third party and the agent.

VIII. – 2:303: Passing of ownership in case of direct delivery in a chain of transactions

Where there is a chain of contracts or other juridical acts, court orders or entitlements based on a rule of law for the transfer of ownership of the same goods and delivery or an equivalent to delivery is effected directly between two parties within this chain, ownership passes to the recipient with effect as if it had been transferred from each preceding member of the chain to the next.

VIII. – 2:304: Passing of ownership of unsolicited goods

(1) If a business delivers unsolicited goods to a consumer, the consumer acquires ownership subject to the business's right or authority to transfer ownership. The consumer may reject the acquisition of ownership; for these purposes, II. – 4:303 (Right or benefit may be rejected) applies by way of analogy.

(2) The exceptions provided for in II. – 3:401 (No obligation arising from failure to respond) paragraphs (2) and (3) apply accordingly.

(3) For the purposes of this Article delivery occurs when the consumer obtains physical control over the goods.

VIII. – 2:305: Transfer of goods forming part of a bulk

(1) For the purposes of this Chapter, "bulk" means a mass or mixture of fungible goods which is identified as contained in a defined space or area.

(2) If the transfer of a specified quantity of an identified bulk fails to take effect because the goods have not yet been identified in the sense of VIII. – 2:101 (Requirements for the transfer of ownership in general) paragraph (3), the transferee acquires co-ownership in the bulk.

(3) The undivided share of the transferee in the bulk at any time is such share as the quantity of goods to which the transferee is entitled out of the bulk as against the transferor bears to the quantity of the goods in the bulk at that time.

(4) Where the sum of the quantities to which the transferees are entitled as against the transferor and, if relevant, of the quantity of the transferor exceeds the total quantity contained in the bulk because the bulk has diminished, the diminution of the bulk is first attributed to the transferor, before being attributed to the transferees in proportion to their individual shares.

(5) Where the transferor purports to transfer more than the total quantity contained in the bulk, the quantity in excess of the total quantity of the bulk to which a transferee is entitled as against the transferor is reflected in the transferee's undivided share in the bulk only if the transferee, acquiring for value, neither knew nor could reasonably be expected to know of this excess. Where, as a result of such purported transfer of a quantity in excess of the bulk to a transferee in good faith and for value, the sum of the quantities to which the transferees are entitled as against the transferor exceeds the total quantity contained in the bulk, the lack of quantity is attributed to the transferees in proportion to their individual shares.

VIII. – 2:306: Delivery out of the bulk

(1) Each transferee can take delivery of a quantity corresponding to the transferee's undivided share and acquires ownership of that quantity by taking delivery.

(2) Where the delivered quantity exceeds the quantity corresponding to the transferee's undivided share, the transferee acquires ownership of the excess quantity only if the transferee, acquiring for value, neither knew nor could reasonably be expected to know of possible negative consequences of this excess for the other transferees.

VIII. – 2:307: Contingent right of transferee under retention of ownership

Where the transferor retains ownership of the goods for the purposes of a "retention of ownership device" in the sense of IX. – 1:103 (Retention of ownership devices: scope), the transferee's right to pay the price under the terms of the contract and the transferee's right to acquire ownership upon payment have effect against the transferor's creditors.

Chapter 3:
Good faith acquisition of ownership

VIII. – 3:101: Good faith acquisition through a person without right or authority to transfer ownership

(1) Where the person purporting to transfer the ownership (the transferor) has no right or authority to transfer ownership of the goods, the transferee nevertheless acquires and the former owner loses ownership provided that:
- (a) the requirements set out in VIII. – 2:101 (Requirements for the transfer of ownership in general) paragraphs (1)(a), (1)(b), (1)(d), (2) and (3) are fulfilled;
- (b) the requirement of delivery or an equivalent to delivery as set out in VIII. – 2:101 (Requirements for the transfer of ownership in general) paragraph (1)(e) is fulfilled;
- (c) the transferee acquires the goods for value; and
- (d) the transferee neither knew nor could reasonably be expected to know that the transferor had no right or authority to transfer ownership of the goods at the time ownership would pass under VIII. – 2:101 (Requirements for the transfer of ownership in general). The facts from which it follows that the transferee could not reasonably be expected to know of the transferor's lack of right or authority have to be proved by the transferee.

(2) Good faith acquisition in the sense of paragraph (1) does not take place with regard to stolen goods, unless the transferee acquired the goods from a transferor acting in the ordinary course of business. Good faith acquisition of stolen cultural objects in the sense of VIII. – 4:102 (Cultural objects) is impossible.

(3) Where the transferee is already in possession of the goods, good faith acquisition will take place only if the transferee obtained possession from the transferor.

VIII. – 3:102: Good faith acquisition of ownership free of limited proprietary rights

(1) Where the goods are encumbered with a limited proprietary right of a third person and the transferor has no right or authority to dispose of the goods free of the third person's right, the transferee nevertheless acquires ownership free of this right provided that:
   (a) the transferee acquires ownership in a manner provided for in Chapter 2 or the preceding Article;
   (b) the requirement of delivery or an equivalent to delivery as set out in VIII. – 2:101 (Requirements for the transfer of ownership in general) paragraph (1)(e) is fulfilled;
   (c) the transferee acquires the goods for value; and
   (d) the transferee neither knew nor could reasonably be expected to know that the transferor had no right or authority to transfer ownership of the goods free of the third person's right at the time ownership passes. The facts from which it follows that the transferee could not reasonably be expected to know of the transferor's lack of right or authority have to be proved by the transferee.

(2) Paragraphs (2) and (3) of the preceding Article apply for the purposes of this Article.

(3) Where the goods are transferred by notice as provided for in VIII. – 2:105 (Equivalents to delivery) paragraph (2), the notified person's limited proprietary rights in the goods are not extinguished.

(4) For the purposes of the application of this Article to proprietary security rights, IX. – 6:102 (Loss of proprietary security due to good faith acquisition of ownership) paragraph (2) applies in addition to this Article.

Chapter 4:
Acquisition of ownership by continuous possession
Section 1:
Requirements for acquisition
of ownership by continuous possession

VIII. – 4:101: Basic rule

(1) An owner-possessor acquires ownership by continuous possession of goods:
   (a) for a period of ten years, provided that the possessor, throughout the whole period, possesses in good faith; or
   (b) for a period of thirty years.
(2) For the purposes of paragraph (1)(a):
   (a) a person possesses in good faith if, and only if, the person possesses in the belief of being the owner and is reasonably justified in that belief; and
   (b) good faith of the possessor is presumed.
(3) Acquisition of ownership by continuous possession is excluded for a person who obtained possession by stealing the goods.

VIII. – 4:102: Cultural objects

(1) Under this Chapter, acquisition of ownership of goods qualifying as a "cultural object" in the sense of Article 1 (1) of Council Directive 93/7/EEC, regardless of whether the cultural object has been unlawfully removed before or after 1 January 1993, or not removed from the territory of a Member State at all, requires continuous possession of the goods:
   (a) for a period of 30 years, provided that the possessor, throughout the whole period, possesses in good faith; or
   (b) for a period of 50 years.
(2) Member States may adopt or maintain in force more stringent provisions to ensure a higher level of protection for the owner of cultural objects in the sense of this paragraph or in the sense of national or international regulations.

VIII. – 4:103: Continuous possession

(1) Involuntary loss of possession does not exclude continuous possession for the purpose of VIII. – 4:101 (Basic rule), provided that posses-

sion is recovered within one year or an action which leads to such recovery is instituted within one year.

(2) Where the owner-possessor is in possession of the goods at the beginning and at the end of the period there is a presumption of continuous possession for the whole period.

Section 2:
Additional provisions as to the period required for acquisition of ownership

VIII. – 4:201: Extension in case of incapacity

(1) If an owner who is subject to an incapacity is without a representative when the period required for the acquisition of ownership by another by continuous possession would begin to run, the commencement of the period against that person is suspended until either the incapacity has ended or a representative has been appointed.

(2) If the running of the period has already begun before incapacity occurred, the period does not expire before one year has passed after either incapacity has ended or a representative has been appointed.

(3) The running of the period is suspended where the owner is a person subject to an incapacity and the owner-possessor is that person's representative, as long as this relationship lasts. The period does not expire before one year has passed after either the incapacity has ended or a new representative has been appointed.

VIII. – 4:202: Extension in case of impediment beyond owner's control

(1) The running of the period is suspended as long as the owner is prevented from exercising the right to recover the goods by an impediment which is beyond the owner's control and which the owner could not reasonably have been expected to avoid or overcome. The mere fact that the owner does not know where the goods are does not cause suspension under this Article.

(2) Paragraph (1) applies only if the impediment arises, or subsists, within the last six months of the period.

(3) Where the duration or nature of the impediment is such that it would be unreasonable to expect the owner to take proceedings to assert the right to recover the goods within the part of the period which has still to run after the suspension comes to an end, the period does not expire before six months have passed after the time when the impediment was removed.

VIII. – 4:203: Extension and renewal in case of judicial and other proceedings

(1) The running of the period is suspended from the time when judicial proceedings are begun against the owner-possessor or a person exercising physical control for the owner-possessor, by or on behalf of the owner, contesting the owner-possessor's ownership or possession. Suspension lasts until a decision has been made which has the effect of res judicata or until the case has otherwise been disposed of. Suspension has effect only in relation to the parties to the judicial proceedings and persons on whose behalf the parties act.

(2) Suspension under paragraph (1) is to be disregarded when the action is dismissed or otherwise unsuccessful. Where the action is dismissed because of incompetence of the court, the period does not expire before six months have passed from this decision.

(3) Where the action is successful, a new period begins to run from the day when the effect of res judicata occurs or the case has otherwise been disposed of in favour of the owner.

(4) These provisions apply, with appropriate adaptations, to arbitration proceedings and to all other proceedings initiated with the aim of obtaining an instrument which is enforceable as if it were a judgment.

VIII. – 4:204: Postponement of expiry in case of negotiations

If the owner and the owner-possessor or a person exercising physical control for the owner-possessor negotiate about the right of ownership, or about circumstances from which acquisition of ownership by the owner-possessor may arise, the period does not expire before six months have passed since the last communication made in the negotiations.

VIII. – 4:205: Ending of period in case of acknowledgement
The period ends when the owner-possessor, or a person exercising physical control for the owner-possessor, acknowledges the owner's right to the goods. A new period begins to run when the former owner-possessor continues to exercise direct or indirect physical control with the intention of doing so as, or as if, an owner.

VIII. – 4:206: Period of a predecessor to be taken into account
(1) Where one person succeeds another in owner-possession and the requirements set out in this Chapter are fulfilled cumulatively by the predecessor and the successor in possession, the period of the predecessor is taken into account in favour of the successor.
(2) A successor in good faith may take into account the period of a predecessor in bad faith only for acquisition under VIII. – 4:101 (Basic rule) paragraph (1)(b).

Section 3:
Effects of acquisition
of ownership by continuous possession

VIII. – 4:301: Acquisition of ownership
(1) Upon expiry of the period required for the acquisition of ownership by continuous possession the original owner loses and the owner-possessor acquires ownership.
(2) When the owner-possessor knows or can reasonably be expected to know that the goods are encumbered with a limited proprietary right of a third person, this right continues to exist as long as this right is not itself extinguished by expiry of the respective period, or a period of 30 years (VIII. – 4:101 (Basic rule) paragraph (1)(b)) or 50 years (VIII. – 4:102 (Cultural objects) paragraph (1)(b)) has passed.

VIII. – 4:302: Extinction of rights under rules on unjustified enrichment and non-contractual liability for damage
Upon acquisition of ownership, the original owner loses all rights to recover the goods and all rights to payment of the monetary value of the goods or for any future use of the goods under the provisions on unjustified enrichment (Book VII) and non-contractual liability for damage (Book VI).

Chapter 5:
Production, combination and commingling
Section 1:
General provisions

VIII. – 5:101: Party autonomy and relation to other provisions

(1) The consequences of production, combination or commingling can be regulated by party agreement. The provisions of Section 2 apply where production, combination or commingling takes place:

    (a) without the consent of the owner of the material; or

    (b) with the consent of the owner of the material, but without a party agreement as to the proprietary consequences.

(2) An agreement in the sense of paragraph (1) may provide for:

    (a) proprietary rights as recognised by this Book; and

    (b) a right to payment or other performance.

(3) The effects of production, combination and commingling as to goods subject to a retention of ownership device are regulated by Book IX.

(4) Proprietary security rights created under Section 2 of this Chapter are subject to the provisions on proprietary security rights in Book IX, unless provided otherwise in Section 2. Proprietary security rights created by a party agreement under paragraph (1) are subject to the provisions on proprietary security rights in Book IX except as provided otherwise by VIII. – 5:204 (Additional provisions as to proprietary security rights) paragraph (3).

(5) This Chapter does not affect the applicability of the rules on non-contractual liability for damage (Book VI). The rules on benevolent intervention in another's affairs (Book V) have priority over the provisions of this Chapter.

Section 2:
Default rules and supplementary provisions

VIII. – 5:201: Production

(1) Where one person, by contributing labour, produces new goods out of
material owned by another person, the producer becomes owner of the
new goods and the owner of the material is entitled, against the producer, to payment equal to the value of the material at the moment of
production, secured by a proprietary security right in the new goods.

(2) Paragraph (1) does not apply where:
   (a) the labour contribution is of minor importance; or
   (b) the producer knows that the material is owned by another person
   and that the owner of the material does not consent to the production, unless the value of the labour is much higher than the
   value of the material.

(3) In the cases covered by paragraph (2) and in cases where no new
goods are produced, ownership remains with the owner of the material
or, where there is more than one such owner, the attribution of ownership is determined by application of VIII. – 5:202 (Commingling) or
VIII. – 5:203 (Combination). The person contributing labour is entitled
to the reversal of any enrichment subject to the provisions of Book VII.
For the purposes of this paragraph, VII. – 2:101 (Circumstances in
which an enrichment is unjustified) paragraph (1)(b) does not exclude
the entitlement of a person contributing labour to a reversal of the
enrichment.

VIII. – 5:202: Commingling

(1) Where goods owned by different persons are commingled in the sense
that it is impossible or economically unreasonable to separate the resulting mass or mixture into its original constituents, but it is possible
and economically reasonable to separate the mass or mixture into proportionate quantities, these persons become co-owners of the resulting
mass or mixture, each for a share proportionate to the value of the
respective part at the moment of commingling.

(2) Each co-owner can separate a quantity equivalent to that co-owner's
undivided share out of the mass or mixture.

VIII. – 5:203: Combination

(1) This Article applies where goods owned by different persons are combined in the sense that separation would be impossible or economically unreasonable.

(2) Where one of the component parts is to be regarded as the principal part, the owner of that part acquires sole ownership of the whole, and the owner or the owners of the subordinate parts are entitled, against the sole owner, to payment subject to sentence 2, secured by a proprietary security right in the combined goods. The amount due under sentence 1 is calculated according to the rules on unjustified enrichment (Book VII); or, where the owner of the principal part effects the combination, is equal to the value of the respective subordinate part at the moment of combination.

(3) Where none of the component parts is to be regarded as the principal part, the owners of the component parts become co-owners of the whole, each for a share proportionate to the value of the respective part at the moment of combination. If, in the case of more than two component parts, one component part is of minimal importance in relation to other parts, the owner of this part is entitled, against the co-owners, only to payment proportionate to the value of the respective part at the moment of combination, secured by a proprietary security right in the combined goods.

(4) Paragraph (2) does not apply where the person who owns the principal part effects the combination, knowing that a subordinate part is owned by another person and that the owner of the subordinate part does not consent to combination, unless the value of the principal part is much higher than the value of the subordinate part. The owners of the component parts become co-owners, the shares of the owners of subordinate parts being equal to the value of their respective parts at the moment of combination.

VIII. – 5:204: Additional provisions as to proprietary security rights

(1) A proprietary security right created under the preceding Articles on production and combination is effective against third persons without requiring possession by, or registration of, the former owner of the material or of the component part.

(2) If the proprietary security right in the new or combined goods is extinguished by a third party's good faith acquisition (Chapter 3), the security right extends to the proceeds of the sale. Paragraph (1) applies accordingly.

(3) A proprietary security right created under the preceding Articles on production and combination takes priority over any other security right which has previously been created, by the producer or by the owner of the principal part, in the new or combined goods. The same applies to equivalent security rights created by agreement between the former owner of the material and the producer, or between the former owner of the subordinate part and the owner of the principal part.

Chapter 6:
Protection of ownership and protection of possession
Section 1:
Protection of ownership

VIII. – 6:101: Protection of ownership

(1) The owner is entitled to obtain or recover possession of the goods from any person exercising physical control over these goods, unless this person has a right to possess the goods in the sense of VIII. – 1:207 (Possession by limited-right-possessor) in relation to the owner.

(2) Where another person interferes with the owner's rights as owner or where such interference is imminent, the owner is entitled to a declaration of ownership and to a protection order.

(3) A protection order is an order which, as the circumstances may require:
    (a) prohibits imminent future interference;
    (b) orders the cessation of existing interference;
    (c) orders the removal of traces of past interference.

VIII. – 6:102: Recovery of goods after transfer based on invalid or avoided contract or other juridical act

(1) Where goods are or have been transferred based on a contract or other juridical act which is invalid or avoided, the transferor may exercise the right of recovery under paragraph (1) of the preceding Article in order to recover physical control of the goods.

(2) Where the obligation of the transferee to restore the goods to the transferor, after a transfer based on an invalid or avoided contract or other
juridical act, is one of two reciprocal obligations which have to be
performed simultaneously, the transferee may, in accordance with
III. – 3:401 (Right to withhold performance of reciprocal obligation),
withhold performance of the obligation to restore the goods until the
transferor has tendered performance of, or has performed, the transfer-
or's reciprocal obligation.

(3) The preceding paragraphs also apply where the transfer was based on a
contract or other juridical act subject to a resolutive condition in the
sense of VIII. – 2:203 (Transfer subject to condition) paragraph (1) and
this condition is fulfilled.

Section 2:
Protection of mere possession

VIII. – 6:201: Definition of unlawful dispossession and interference
A person depriving the possessor of possession or interfering with that
possession acts "unlawfully" under this Section if the person acts without
the consent of the possessor and the dispossession or interference is not
permitted by law.

VIII. – 6:202: Self-help of possessor
(1) A possessor or a third person may resort to self-help against another
person who unlawfully deprives the possessor of possession of the
goods, or who otherwise unlawfully interferes with that possession,
or whose act of unlawful dispossession or interference is imminent.

(2) The means of self-help are limited to such immediate and proportionate action as is necessary to regain the goods or to stop or prevent the
dispossession or interference.

(3) Under the restrictions of paragraphs (1) and (2) self-help may also be
directed against an indirect owner-possessor who unlawfully deprives
the limited-right-possessor of possession or interferes with that possession in violation of the specific legal relationship between owner-
possessor and limited-right-possessor. This rule applies equally to an

indirect limited-right-possessor who unlawfully deprives the other limited-right-possessor of possession or interferes with that possession.

(4) Where a person in the exercise of a right of self-help conferred by this Article causes legally relevant damage to the person depriving the possessor of possession or interfering with that possession, VI. – 5:202 (Self-defence, benevolent intervention and necessity) applies.

VIII. – 6:203: Entitlement to recover as protection of mere possession

(1) Where another person unlawfully deprives an owner-possessor or a limited-right-possessor of possession, the possessor is, within the period of one year, entitled to recover the goods, irrespective of who has the right or better position in terms of VIII. – 6:301 (Entitlement to recover in case of better possession) to possess the goods. The period of one year starts to run at the time of dispossession.

(2) The right to recover may also be directed against an indirect owner-possessor who unlawfully deprives the limited-right-possessor of possession in violation of the specific legal relationship between them. This rule applies equally to an indirect limited-right-possessor who unlawfully deprives the other limited-right-possessor of possession.

(3) The right to recover is excluded if the person seeking to exercise it unlawfully deprived the other person of possession within the last year.

(4) Where the other person in the sense of paragraph (1) invokes an alleged right or better position in terms of VIII. – 6:301 (Entitlement to recover in case of better possession) to possess the goods as a defence or counter-claim, the obligation to return the goods according to paragraph (1) may be replaced by an obligation to hand the goods over to the court or other competent public authority, or to a third person pursuant to an order of the competent authority.

VIII. – 6:204: Entitlement to protection order to protect mere possession

(1) Where another person unlawfully interferes with the possession of goods or such interference or an unlawful dispossession is imminent, the owner-possessor or the limited-right-possessor is, within the period of one year, entitled to a protection order under VIII. – 6:101 (Protection of ownership) paragraph (3), irrespective of who has the right or better position in terms of VIII. – 6:301 (Entitlement to recover in

case of better possession) to possess, use or otherwise deal with the goods. The period of one year starts to run from the time when the interference began or, in cases of repeated interferences, from the time when the last interference began.

(2) The protection order may also be directed against an indirect owner-possessor who unlawfully interferes with the possession of a limited-right-possessor in violation of the specific legal relationship between them. This rule applies equally to an indirect limited-right-possessor who unlawfully interferes with the possession of a subsidiary limited-right-possessor in violation of the specific legal relationship between them.

(3) Where the other person in the sense of paragraph (1) invokes an alleged right or better position to possess, use or otherwise deal with the goods as a defence or counter-claim, the court order may be suspended until, or replaced by, a decision on the existence of such alleged right or better position.

Section 3:
Protection of better possession

VIII. – 6:301: Entitlement to recover in case of better possession

(1) A former owner-possessor or former limited-right possessor is entitled to recover possession of the goods from another person exercising physical control over them if the former possession was "better" than the current possession of the other person in the sense of paragraph (2).

(2) The former possession is "better" than the current possession if the former possessor is in good faith and has a right to possess, while the other person has no right to possess, the goods. Where both persons are in good faith and have a right to possess the goods, the right derived from the owner prevails over a right derived from an owner-possessor who is not the owner; if this does not apply, the older rightful possession prevails. Where both persons are in good faith, but neither has a right to possess the goods, the current possession prevails.

VIII. – 6:302: Entitlement to protection order in case of better possession

Where another person interferes with the possession, or such interference or a dispossession is imminent, the owner-possessor or the limited-right-possessor who is in good faith is entitled to a protection order under VIII. – 6:101 (Protection of ownership) paragraph (3), unless the other person would, in case of dispossession, have a better possession in the sense of VIII. – 6:301 (Entitlement to recover in case of better possession) paragraph (2), or the third person has a better right to use or otherwise deal with the goods than the owner-possessor or limited-right-possessor.

Section 4:
Other remedies

VIII. – 6:401: Non-contractual liability

The owner and the limited-right-possessor are entitled to reparation for an infringement of their right of ownership or their right to possess the goods under the terms of VI. – 2:206 (Loss upon infringement of property or lawful possession).

Chapter 7:
Consequential questions on restitution of goods

VIII. – 7:101: Scope

(1) This Chapter applies where the situations covered by the subsequent Articles occur while the goods are possessed by a person against whom, at that time, the owner is entitled to obtain or recover possession of the goods.

(2) Where the requirements for the application of Book V are fulfilled, the provisions of that Book apply and have priority over the provisions of this Chapter.

(3) The provisions of Chapter 5 have priority over the provisions of this Chapter.

VIII. – 7:102: Loss of, or damage to, the goods during possession

(1) Where the goods are lost, are destroyed or deteriorate during possession in the sense of VIII. – 7:101 (Scope of application), the rights of
the owner resulting from such loss or damage are determined by Book
VI.

(2) For the purposes of this Article, intention or negligence as to posses-
sing the goods despite the owner's entitlement to obtain or recover
possession suffice to establish accountability in the sense of Book VI,
Chapter 3.

VIII. – 7:103: Fruits from, use of, and other benefits derived from the goods during possession

Where the possessor obtains fruits from, makes use of, or derives other
benefits from the goods during possession in the sense of VIII. – 7:101
(Scope of application), the rights of the owner resulting from such benefits
are determined by Book VII.

VIII. – 7:104: Expenditure on, or parts added to, the goods during possession

(1) Where the possessor incurs expenditure on, or adds parts to, the goods
during possession in the sense of VIII. – 7:101 (Scope of application),
the rights of the possessor to reimbursement of such expenditure or for
such addition are determined by Book VII.

(2) The possessor is entitled to retain the goods in order to secure the
rights referred to in paragraph (1). Sentence 1 does not apply where
the possessor knows of the owner's entitlement to obtain or recover
possession at the time when expenditure is incurred on, or parts are
added to, the goods.

Book IX
Proprietary security in movable assets

Chapter 1:
General rules
Section 1:
Scope

IX. – 1:101: General rule
(1) This Book applies to the following rights in movable property based upon contracts for proprietary security:
  (a) security rights; and
  (b) ownership retained under retention of ownership devices.
(2) The rules of this Book on security rights apply with appropriate adaptations to:
  (a) rights under a trust for security purposes;
  (b) security rights in movable assets created by unilateral juridical acts; and
  (c) security rights in movable assets implied by patrimonial law, if and in so far as this is compatible with the purpose of the law.

IX. – 1:102: Security right in movable asset
(1) A security right in a movable asset is any limited proprietary right in the asset which entitles the secured creditor to preferential satisfaction of the secured right from the encumbered asset.
(2) The term security right includes:
  (a) limited proprietary rights of a type which is generally recognised as designed to serve as proprietary security, especially the pledge;
  (b) limited proprietary rights, however named, that are based upon a contract for proprietary security and that are either intended by the parties to entitle the secured creditor to preferential satisfaction of the secured right from the encumbered asset or have this effect under the contract; and

     (c) other rights which are regarded as security rights under the rules of this Book, such as the right referred to in IX. – 2:114 (Right of retention of possession) and the rights covered by paragraph (3).

(3) A transfer or purported transfer of ownership of a movable asset which is made, on the basis of a contract for proprietary security, with the intention or the effect of securing satisfaction of a secured right can create only a security right in the asset for the transferee.

(4) Paragraph (3) applies in particular to:

     (a) a security transfer of ownership of corporeal assets;

     (b) a security assignment;

     (c) a sale and lease-back; and

     (d) a sale and resale.

IX. – 1:103: Retention of ownership devices: scope

(1) There is a "retention of ownership device" when ownership is retained by the owner of supplied assets in order to secure a right to performance of an obligation.

(2) The term retention of ownership device includes:

     (a) retention of ownership by a seller under a contract of sale;

     (b) ownership of the supplier under a contract of hire-purchase;

     (c) ownership of the leased assets under a contract of leasing, provided that according to the terms of the contract the lessee at the expiration of the lease period has an option to acquire ownership of, or a right to continue to use, the leased asset without payment or for merely nominal payment (financial leasing); and

     (d) ownership of the supplier under a contract of consignment with the intention or the effect of fulfilling a security purpose.

IX. – 1:104: Retention of ownership devices: applicable rules

(1) Retention of ownership devices are subject to the following rules on security rights, unless specifically provided otherwise:

     (a) IX. – 2:104 (Specific issues of transferability, existence and specification) paragraphs (2) to (4);

     (b) Chapter 2, Sections 3 and 4;

     (c) Chapters 3 to 6; and

     (d) Chapter 7, Section 1.

(2) When applying rules on security rights to retention of ownership devices, the following adaptations apply:

(a) references to the encumbered assets refer to the assets supplied under a contract of sale, hire-purchase, leasing or consignment, respectively;

(b) in retention of ownership under contracts of sale, references to the secured creditor are to be understood as referring to the seller, and references to the security provider as referring to the buyer;

(c) in retention of ownership devices under contracts of hire-purchase, references to the secured creditor are to be understood as referring to the supplier, and references to the security provider as referring to the hire-purchaser;

(d) in retention of ownership devices under contracts of financial leasing, references to the secured creditor are to be understood as referring to the lessor, and references to the security provider as referring to the lessee; and

(e) in retention of ownership devices under contracts of consignment, references to the secured creditor are to be understood as referring to the supplier, and references to the security provider as referring to the consignee.

IX. – 1:105: Exclusions
(1) This Book does not apply to security rights for micro-credits, if and in so far as national legislation of the place where the security provider's business or residence is located contains specific protective rules for the security provider.

(2) The rules of an international Convention dealing with a subject-matter regulated in this Book and binding upon a member state are presumed to have for that member state precedence over the rules of this Book.

Section 2:
Definitions

IX. – 1:201: Definitions
(1) For the purposes of this Book the following definitions apply.

(2) An "accessory" is a corporeal asset that is or becomes closely connected with or part of a movable or an immovable, provided it is possible

and economically reasonable to separate the accessory without dam-age from the movable or immovable.
(3) "Acquisition finance devices" cover:
    (a) retention of ownership devices;
    (b) where ownership of the sold assets has been transferred to the buyer, those security rights in the sold asset which secure the right:
        (i) of the seller to payment of the purchase price for the encum-bered asset under a contract of sale;
        (ii) of a lender to repayment of a loan granted to the buyer for payment of the purchase price for the encumbered asset, if and in so far as this payment is actually made to the seller; and
    (c) rights of third persons to whom any of the rights under sub-para-graph (a) or (b) has been transferred as security for a credit covered by sub-paragraphs (a) or (b).
(4) A "contract for proprietary security" is a contract under which:
    (a) a security provider undertakes to grant a security right to the se-cured creditor;
    (b) a secured creditor is entitled to retain a security right when trans-ferring ownership to the transferee who is regarded as security pro-vider; or
    (c) a seller, lessor or other supplier of assets is entitled to retain own-ership of the supplied assets in order to secure its rights to per-formance.
(5) "Default" means:
    (a) any non-performance by the debtor of the obligation covered by the security; and
    (b) any other event or set of circumstances agreed by the secured cred-itor and the security provider as entitling the secured creditor to have recourse to the security.
(6) "Financial assets" are financial instruments and rights to the payment of money.
(7) "Financial instruments" are:
    (a) share certificates and equivalent securities as well as bonds and equivalent debt instruments, if these are negotiable;
    (b) any other securities which are dealt in and which give the right to acquire any such financial instruments or which give rise to cash settlements, except instruments of payment;
    (c) share rights in collective investment undertakings;

  (d) money market instruments; and
  (e) rights in or relating to the instruments covered by sub-paragraphs
      (a) to (d).
 (8) "Intangibles" means incorporeal assets and includes uncertificated
     and indirectly held securities and the undivided share of a co-owner
     in corporeal assets or in a bulk or a fund.
 (9) "Ownership" for the purposes of these rules covers ownership of
     movable corporeal assets and of intangible assets.
(10) A "possessory security right" is a security right that requires posses-
     sion of the encumbered corporeal asset by the secured creditor or an-
     other person (except the debtor) holding for the secured creditor.
(11) "Proceeds" is every value derived from an encumbered asset, such as:
      (a) value realised by sale or other disposition or by collection;
      (b) damages or insurance payments in respect of defects, damage or
          loss;
      (c) civil and natural fruits, including distributions; and
      (d) proceeds of proceeds.
(12) The "secured creditor" may be the creditor of the secured right or a
     third person who may hold the security right in that person's own
     name for the creditor, especially as a trustee.
(13) The "security provider" may be the debtor of the obligation to be
     covered by the security right or a third person.

Chapter 2:
Creation and coverage
Section 1:
Creation of security rights
Subsection 1:
General provisions

IX. – 2:101: Methods of creation of security rights
A security right in a movable asset may be created:
(a) by the security provider granting the security right to the secured cred-
    itor;
(b) by the secured creditor retaining the security right when transferring
    ownership of the asset to the security provider; or
(c) by the secured creditor relying on a right of retention of possession.

IX. – 2:102: Requirements for creation of security rights in general

The creation of a security right in a movable asset requires that:

(a) the asset exists;

(b) the asset is transferable;

(c) the secured right exists; and

(d) the additional requirements for the creation of a security right by granting, by retention or on the basis of a right of retention of possession are fulfilled.

IX. – 2:103: Possessory and non-possessory security rights

Unless otherwise agreed by the parties, the creation of a security right by contract does not require possession of the encumbered asset by the secured creditor.

IX. – 2:104: Specific issues of transferability, existence and specification

(1) A security right can be created in a right to performance other than a right to the payment of money, even if this right is not transferable, provided that it can be transformed into a right to the payment of money.

(2) A security right can be created in an asset, even if its owner had agreed not to transfer or to encumber the asset. This rule applies also to a right to performance, whether contractual or not, unless it is non-assignable by virtue of III. – 5:109 (Assignability: rights personal to the creditor) paragraph (1)).

(3) If the parties purport to create a security right in a future, generic or untransferable asset, the security right arises only if and when the asset comes into existence, is specified or becomes transferable. Paragraph (2) remains unaffected.

(4) Paragraph (3) sentence 1 applies with appropriate adaptations to the creation of security rights in a conditional right, including the rights covered by that paragraph. A security right may be created in a present conditional right, especially in the right of a transferee under a conditional transfer of ownership.

(5) Paragraph (3) sentence 1 applies with appropriate adaptations to the creation of security rights for secured rights which are future or only conditional.

Subsection 2:
Granting of security right

IX. – 2:105: Requirements for granting of security right
In addition to the requirements under Subsection 1, the creation of a security right in a movable asset by granting requires that:
(a) the asset to be encumbered is specified by the parties;
(b) the security provider has the right or authority to grant a security right in the asset;
(c) the secured creditor is entitled as against the security provider to the granting of a security right on the basis of the contract for proprietary security; and
(d) the secured creditor and the security provider agree on the granting of a security right to the secured creditor.

IX. – 2:106: Time when security right is created by granting
Subject to IX. – 2:110 (Delayed creation), the security right is created by granting at the time when the requirements set out in the preceding Article are fulfilled, unless the parties have agreed on another time of creation.

IX. – 2:107: Granting of security right by consumer
(1) The creation of a security right by a consumer security provider by granting is only valid within the following limits:
(a) the assets to be encumbered must be identified individually; and
(b) an asset not yet owned by the consumer upon conclusion of the contract for proprietary security (apart from the rights to payment covered by paragraph (2)) can only be encumbered as security for a credit to be used for the acquisition of the asset by the consumer.
(2) Rights to payment of future salary, pensions or equivalent income cannot be encumbered in so far as they serve the satisfaction of the living expenses of the consumer security provider and his or her family.

IX. – 2:108: Good faith acquisition of security right
(1) Even where the security provider has no right or authority to dispose of a corporeal asset, the secured creditor nevertheless acquires a security right in it, provided that:

(a) the asset or a negotiable document to bearer on the asset is in the security provider's possession or, if so required, the asset is registered in an international or national register of ownership as owned by the security provider at the time the security right is to be created; and

(b) the secured creditor does not know and cannot reasonably be expected to know that the security provider has no right or authority to grant a security right in the asset at the time the security right is to be created.

(2) For the purposes of paragraph (1)(b), a secured creditor acquiring a security right in an asset that is subject to a retention of ownership device which is registered under Chapter 3 Section 3 against the security provider is regarded as knowing that the latter has no right or authority to grant a security right in the asset.

(3) Good faith acquisition of a security right is excluded for an asset that was stolen from the owner or the person holding for the owner.

IX. – 2:109: Good faith acquisition of security right in encumbered corporeal asset

(1) Where a corporeal asset is encumbered with a security right or another limited proprietary right and the security provider has no right or authority to dispose of the asset free from the third person's limited proprietary right, a secured creditor nevertheless acquires a security right free from that other right, provided that:

(a) the requirements of paragraph (1)(a) of the preceding Article are met; and

(b) the secured creditor does not know nor can reasonably be expected to know that the security provider has no right or authority to grant a security right in disregard of the third person's limited proprietary right at the time the security right is to be created.

(2) For the purposes of paragraph (1)(b), a secured creditor acquiring a security right in the encumbered asset is regarded as knowing that the security provider has no right or authority to grant a security right in the asset in disregard of the existing security right if this right is registered under Chapter 3, Section 3 against the security provider.

(3) Where the requirements of paragraph (1) are not met but the requirements of the preceding Article are met, the secured creditor obtains a

security right in the encumbered assets. The priority between this security right and the prior encumbrance is determined according to the general provisions.

IX. – 2:110: Delayed creation
In assets for which at the time when the security right would have been created according to IX. – 2:106 (Time when security right is created by granting) the requirements of IX. – 2:107 (Granting of security right by consumer) and IX. – 2:108 (Good faith acquisition of security right) have not yet been met, a security right automatically arises as soon as the events indicated in the preceding provisions have occurred.

IX. – 2:111: Security right in cash, negotiable instruments and documents
A security right in cash, negotiable instruments and documents to bearer may be created free from any earlier rights, even if the requirements of IX. – 2:105 (Requirements for granting of security right) sub-paragraph (b), IX. – 2:108 (Good faith acquisition of security right) and IX. – 2:109 (Good faith acquisition of security right in an encumbered corporeal asset) are not met, provided that direct possession of these assets is transferred to the secured creditor.

IX. – 2:112: General matters of property law
Rules on general matters of property law in Book VIII, Chapter 2 apply for the purposes of this Book with appropriate adaptations.

Subsection 3:
Retention of security right

IX. – 2:113: Requirements for retention of security right
(1) In addition to the requirements under Subsection 1, the creation of a security right in a movable asset by retention requires that:
  (a) the secured creditor is entitled as against the transferee to the retention of a security right by virtue of the contract for proprietary security; and
  (b) the secured creditor transfers its ownership in the asset to be encumbered by the retained security right to the transferee.

(2) The security right is created by retention at the time when all the requirements set out in the preceding paragraph are fulfilled.

(3) The transferee is regarded as the security provider for the purposes of the application of the rules of this Book.

Subsection 4:
Right of retention of possession

IX. – 2:114: Right of retention of possession

Where under a contract or rule of law a person is entitled as against the owner of an asset to retain possession of the asset as security for a right to performance, this right of retention of possession gives rise to a possessory security right.

Section 2:
Creation of retention of ownership devices

IX. – 2:201: Retention of ownership devices

(1) A retention of ownership device arises in the cases set out in IX. – 1:103 (Retention of ownership devices: scope) paragraph (2) if:
   (a) the seller, supplier or lessor is the owner of the supplied asset or acts with authority in relation to this asset;
   (b) the asset is specified in the contract for proprietary security;
   (c) the secured right exists; and
   (d) the seller, supplier or lessor retains ownership.

(2) Ownership is also retained for the purposes of paragraph (1)(d) where there is a transfer subject to the suspensive condition that the obligation covered is performed.

Section 3:
Creation of security rights in specific types of assets

IX. – 2:301: Encumbrance of right to payment of money

(1) The encumbrance of a right to payment of money is also subject to the following special rules.

(2) The provisions of Book III, Chapter 5 apply with appropriate adaptations, except III. – 5:108 (Assignability: effect of contractual prohibition) paragraphs (2) and (3) and III. – 5:121 (Competition between successive assignees).

(3) A right to payment held by the security provider against the secured creditor may be encumbered by the security provider also in favour of the secured creditor.

(4) A security right encumbering a right to payment extends to any personal or proprietary security right securing this right to payment.

IX. – 2:302: Security rights in shares of a company

(1) Possession of negotiable certificates of shares of a company which are directly held is regarded as possession of the shares.

(2) Shares of companies which do not meet the requirements of paragraph (1), whether or not they are registered, cannot be subject to a possessory security right.

(3) Security rights in shares of companies extend to dividends, bonus shares and other assets which the shareholder derives from the shares but are limited to the financial value of the shares and such assets.

IX. – 2:303: Security rights in bonds

Paragraphs (1) and (2) of the preceding Article apply also to bonds.

IX. – 2:304: Negotiable documents of title and negotiable instruments

(1) If and as long as a negotiable document of title covers goods, a security right in the document covers also the goods.

(2) For negotiable instruments, a security right in the instrument covers also the right embodied in the instrument.

(3) Possession of a negotiable document of title or a negotiable instrument is regarded as possession of the goods covered by the document of title or the right embodied in the instrument.

IX. – 2:305: Security right in an accessory

(1) A security right may be created in an asset that, at the time of creation, is an accessory to a movable or an immovable. If the rules applicable to immovable property so provide, the security right may also be created according to the rules governing immovable property.

(2) A security right in goods continues even if the encumbered asset subsequently becomes an accessory to a movable or an immovable.

IX. – 2:306: Proceeds of the originally encumbered assets

(1) A security right extends to rights to payment due to a defect in, damage to, or loss of the originally encumbered asset, including insurance proceeds.

(2) A possessory security right extends to civil and natural fruits of the originally encumbered assets unless the parties agree otherwise.

(3) Other proceeds of the originally encumbered assets are covered only if the parties so agree.

IX. – 2:307: Use of encumbered goods
for production or combination

(1) Where encumbered materials owned by the security provider are used for the production of new goods, the secured creditor's security right may be extended by party agreement:
   (a) to the products; and
   (b) to the right to payment to which the security provider as former owner of the material is entitled by virtue of the production against the producer according to VIII. – 5:201 (Production).

(2) The preceding paragraph applies accordingly if goods are combined in such a way that separation would be impossible or economically unreasonable for the purposes of VIII. – 5:203 (Combination).

(3) The issue whether a former owner of material other than the holder of a retention of ownership device acquires a security right by operation of law as the result of production or combination involving the material, and the effectiveness and priority of this security right are governed by Book VIII, Chapter 5. If these security rights are created by party agreement, they are subject to the provisions of Book IX, but enjoy superpriority according to VIII. – 5:204 (Additional provisions as to proprietary security rights) paragraph (3).

(4) In the case of paragraph (1)(b), the right of the secured creditor, as the former holder of an encumbrance in the material, extends to the security rights mentioned in paragraph (3).

IX. – 2:308: Use of goods subject to a retention of ownership device for production or combination

(1) The rules of Book VIII, Chapter 5 (Production, combination and commingling) apply to the consequences of production or combination of goods subject to a retention of ownership device; references to the owner of these goods are to be understood as references to the buyer, hire-purchaser, lessee or consignee.

(2) Where materials subject to a retention of ownership device are used for the production of new goods, the seller, supplier or lessor may acquire a security right by party agreement:

(a) in the products; and

(b) in the right to payment to which the buyer, hire-purchaser, lessee or consignee is entitled against the producer according to VIII. – 5:201 (Production) on the basis of being regarded as the former owner of the material according to paragraph (1).

(3) The preceding paragraph applies accordingly if the goods are combined.

(4) In the case of paragraph (2)(b), the right of the seller, supplier or lessor extends to the security rights in the products or combined goods acquired by the buyer, hire-purchaser, lessee or consignee as a result of the production or combination.

IX. – 2:309: Commingling of assets subject to proprietary security

(1) Where encumbered goods are commingled in such a way that it is impossible or economically unreasonable to separate the resulting mass or mixture into its original constituents, but it is possible and economically reasonable to separate the mass or mixture into proportionate quantities, the security rights that had encumbered the goods continue as encumbrances of the rights which the former owners of the goods have in the resulting mass or mixture by virtue of VIII. – 5:202 (Commingling) paragraph (1)); this encumbrance is limited to a share proportionate to the value of the respective goods at the moment of commingling.

(2) Where the goods that are commingled as set out in the preceding paragraph were subject to a retention of ownership device, VIII. – 5:202 (Commingling) paragraph (1) applies with the proviso that the rights of the holder of the retention of ownership device are continued

in a share of the resulting mass or mixture proportionate to the value of the respective goods at the moment of commingling.

(3) Any secured creditor is entitled to exercise the security provider's right to separate a quantity equivalent to that co-owner's undivided share out of the mass or mixture (VIII. – 5:202 (Commingling) paragraph (2)).

(4) If encumbered financial assets held by the secured creditor are commingled by the latter in a fund, the security provider is entitled to a share in the fund. Paragraph (1) applies with appropriate adaptations.

(5) If in the cases covered by paragraphs (1), (2) and (4) the assets of the mass or fund do not suffice to satisfy all co-owners, VIII. – 2:305 (Transfer of goods forming part of a bulk) paragraphs (4) and (5) apply accordingly.

Section 4:
Coverage of security

IX. – 2:401: Secured rights

(1) The security covers, within its maximum amount, if any, not only the principal secured right, but also the ancillary rights of the creditor against the debtor, especially rights to payment of:

(a) contractual and default interest;

(b) damages, a penalty or an agreed sum for non-performance by the debtor; and

(c) the reasonable costs of extra-judicial recovery of those items.

(2) The right to payment of the reasonable costs of legal proceedings and enforcement proceedings against the security provider and against the debtor, if different from the security provider, is covered, provided the security provider had been informed about the creditor's intention to undertake such proceedings in sufficient time to enable the security provider to avert those costs.

(3) A global security covers only rights which originated in contracts between the debtor and the creditor.

Chapter 3:
Effectiveness as against third persons
Section 1:
General rules

IX. – 3:101: Effectiveness as against third persons
(1) A security right created according to Chapter 2 has no effects against the following classes of third persons:
  (a) holders of proprietary rights, including effective security rights, in the encumbered asset;
  (b) a creditor who has started to bring execution against those assets and who, under the applicable law, has obtained a position providing protection against a subsequent execution; and
  (c) the insolvency administrator of the security provider,
  unless, subject to exceptions, the requirements of this Chapter are met.
(2) Where a security right that is effective against third persons according to the provisions of this Chapter is extended by virtue of the provisions of this Book without a need for an agreement to this effect to assets other than the assets that were originally encumbered, the extension of the security right is not subject to the requirements of this Chapter.
(3) A security right that had been acquired by a good faith acquisition in disregard of a retention of ownership device or an earlier security right in the asset to be encumbered is effective against the holder of the retention of ownership device or the holder of the earlier security right even if the requirements of this Chapter are not met. The effectiveness of the security right that had been acquired by a good faith acquisition against other third persons remains subject to the other rules of this Chapter.

IX. – 3:102: Methods of achieving effectiveness
(1) For security rights in all types of assets, effectiveness may be achieved by registration of the security right pursuant to Section 3.
(2) Effectiveness can also be achieved pursuant to Section 2:
  (a) in the case of corporeal assets, by the secured creditor holding possession of the encumbered assets; or
  (b) in the case of certain intangible assets, by the secured creditor exercising control over the encumbered assets.

IX. – 3:103: Security right made effective by several methods

(1) If a security right has been made effective by registration, possession or control, it may be made effective also by any of the other methods. Where the effects diverge, the stronger effects of a chosen method prevail.

(2) The preceding rules also apply if a security right that is exempted from the requirements of this Chapter is also made effective by registration, possession or control.

IX. – 3:104: Change of method

If the method for achieving effectiveness is changed, effectiveness is continuous, provided the requirements of the new method are met immediately upon termination of the preceding method.

IX. – 3:105: Security right in an accessory to an immovable

A security right in an accessory to an immovable may upon accession also be made effective by registration or annotation in a land register, provided this is authorised by the law governing the land register.

IX. – 3:106: Security right in commingled assets

(1) Where a corporeal asset, which is encumbered with an effective security right, is commingled, the security right in the corresponding share of the bulk according to IX. – 2:309 (Commingling of assets subject to proprietary security) remains effective.

(2) The preceding paragraph applies with appropriate adaptations if financial assets are commingled in a fund.

IX. – 3:107: Registration of acquisition finance devices

(1) An acquisition finance device is effective only if registered.

(2) If registration is effected within 35 days after delivery of the supplied asset, the acquisition finance device is effective from the date of creation.

(3) If registration takes place later than 35 days after delivery, the acquisition finance device becomes effective only at the time of registration and does not enjoy superpriority under IX. – 4:102 (Superpriority).

(4) Where a credit for assets supplied to a consumer is secured by an acquisition finance device, this proprietary security is effective without registration. This exception does not apply to security rights in proceeds and other assets different from the supplied asset.

IX. – 3:108: Importation of encumbered asset
If an encumbered asset is brought from a country outside the European Union into this area, any pre-existing security right which is effective remains effective if the requirements laid down in this Chapter are fulfilled within three months.

Section 2:
Possession or control by creditor

IX. – 3:201: Possession
Security rights in encumbered corporeal assets can be made effective by the secured creditor holding possession:
(a) if the secured creditor or an agent (other than the security provider) acting for the secured creditor exercises direct physical control over the encumbered assets;
(b) where the encumbered assets are held by a third person (other than the security provider), if the third person has agreed with the secured creditor to hold the encumbered assets only for the latter; or
(c) where the encumbered assets are jointly held by the secured creditor and the security provider or where a third person holds the encumbered assets for both parties, if in either case the security provider has no access to the encumbered assets without the secured creditor's express consent.

IX. – 3:202: Negotiable documents of title and negotiable instruments
(1) Possession of a negotiable document of title or negotiable instrument is also sufficient for the effectiveness of a security right in the goods covered by the document of title or in the right embodied in the instrument.
(2) The security right in the goods covered by the document of title according to paragraph (1) is not affected if the covered assets are relinquished to the security provider or another person for a period of up to ten days against a duly dated formal trust receipt and for the purpose of loading or unloading, sale or exchange or other dealing with the goods except the creation of a competing security right.

IX. – 3:203: Certificated shares and bonds

Paragraph (1) of the preceding Article applies with appropriate adaptations to possession of directly held certificates of shares of companies, if negotiable, and directly held bond certificates.

IX. – 3:204: Control over financial assets

(1) Security rights can be made effective by the secured creditor exercising control over:
- (a) financial assets which are entered into book accounts held by a financial institution (intermediated financial assets); and
- (b) non-intermediated financial instruments registered in a register maintained by or for the issuer or which under national law is determinative of title.

(2) The secured creditor exercises control over the assets mentioned in paragraph (1)(a), if:
- (a) the secured creditor with the assent of the security provider has instructed the financial institution administering the book account not to admit dispositions by the security provider without the secured creditor's consent;
- (b) the assets are held by the financial institution for the secured creditor in a special account; or
- (c) the financial institution is the secured creditor.

(3) The preceding paragraph applies with appropriate adaptations to the exercise of control by the secured creditor over the assets mentioned in paragraph (1)(b).

(4) The satisfaction of the requirements of paragraphs (2) and (3) must be evidenced in writing or recording by electronic means or any other durable medium.

Section 3:
Registration
Subsection 1:
Operation of the register of proprietary security

IX. – 3:301: European register of proprietary security; other systems of registration or notation

(1) A registration that is required or allowed for any security right or retention of ownership device under the rules of this Book is to be effected in a European register of proprietary security, subject to paragraph (2).

(2) Where systems of registration or notation on title certificates for security rights in specific types of assets exist, the effectiveness of a security right to be registered or noted in these systems depends upon compliance with any mandatory rules applicable for these systems. For systems established under the national law of a member state, this rule is subject to IX. – 3:312 (Transitional provision in relation to entries in other systems of registration or notation under national law).

(3) An entry of security rights in financial instruments into a register maintained by or for the issuer of financial instruments or which under national law is determinative of title is not regarded as registration for the purposes of this Section but may constitute control if the requirements of IX. – 3:204 (Control over financial assets) paragraph (3) are complied with.

IX. – 3:302: Structure and operation of the register

(1) The European register of proprietary security is to operate as a personal folio system, allowing entries concerning security rights to be filed against identified security providers.

(2) The register is to operate electronically and to be directly accessible for its users in an online format.

IX. – 3:303: Retention of ownership devices and security rights

(1) For the purposes of the European register of proprietary security no distinction is made between retention of ownership devices and security rights.

(2) Any reference in this Section to security rights includes retention of ownership devices.

IX. – 3:304: Authentication as requirement for declarations to the register

(1) Any declaration to the online register, such as filing, amending or deleting an entry in the register or a declaration of consent, requires authentication by the person making the declaration.

(2) Authentication requires:

(a) the use of log-in information which is issued to individual users of the online register after an initial enrolment in the register during which the identity and the contact details of the user are verified; or

(b) the use of secure online identity verification systems of general application, if such systems are brought into operation at a European or member state level.

Subsection 2:
Entries in the register

IX. – 3:305: Entries to be made by secured creditor and advance filing

(1) Entries in the register can be made directly by the secured creditor.

(2) Entries can be made before or after the security right referred to has been created or the contract for proprietary security has been concluded.

IX. – 3:306: Minimum content of the entry in the register

(1) An entry can be entered into the register only if:

(a) it is made in respect of an identified security provider;

(b) it contains a minimum declaration as to the encumbered assets;

(c) it is indicated by one or several references to a list of categories of assets to which category the encumbered assets belong;

(d) the requirements of consent are fulfilled; and

(e) it is accompanied by a declaration of the creditor that the latter assumes liability for damage caused to the security provider or third persons by a wrongful registration.

(2) For the purposes of paragraph (1)(b) a declaration that the creditor is to take security over the security provider's assets or is to retain ownership as security is sufficient.

IX. – 3:307: Additional content of the entry

An entry in the register may include the following additional content:

(a) additional information provided by the creditor in relation to the encumbered assets or the content of the security right;

(b) a date at which the entry is to expire provided that it is before the end of the regular period of expiry of five years; and

(c) a maximum amount of the security.

IX. – 3:308: Information appearing on the register

In respect of each entry the following information appears on the register and is accessible to any user:

(a) the name and contact details of the security provider;

(b) the name and contact details of the creditor;

(c) the time the entry was made;

(d) the minimum content of the entry under IX. – 3:306 (Minimum content of the entry in the register) paragraph (1)(b) and (c); and

(e) any additional content of the entry under IX. – 3:307 (Additional content of the entry) sub-paragraphs (a) to (c).

IX. – 3:309: Required consent of the security provider

(1) An entry in the register can be made only if the security provider has consented to it by declaration to the register. Any such consent can be freely terminated by the security provider by declaration to the register. A termination of consent does not affect entries that have been entered before the termination of the consent is declared to the register.

(2) The secured creditor may demand from the security provider a declaration of consent to an entry to the extent that such a consent is necessary to cover the security rights created in the contract for proprietary security.

(3) This Article does not affect the validity, terms and effects of any of the security provider's agreements with the secured creditor other than the declaration of consent to the register.

IX. – 3:310: Identity of security provider, description of encumbered assets and effectiveness of registration

(1) If under the rules in this Book the effectiveness or priority of a security right encumbering assets of a certain security provider depends upon registration, an entry in the register according to this Subsection suffices only if:

    (a) the entry is filed against the correct security provider;

    (b) the creditor's declaration as to the encumbered assets as appearing on the register covers the assets encumbered by the security right;

    (c) the encumbered assets actually belong to the category or categories of assets indicated in the entry; and

    (d) the creditor's declaration is in an official language of the European Union. The creditor may add translations.

(2) For the purposes of paragraph (1)(b):

    (a) the entry is effective in respect of fruits, products, proceeds and any other assets different from the original assets serving as security only if these assets are also covered by the creditor's declaration as to the encumbered assets; and

    (b) a description identifying individual assets is not necessary.

(3) The creditor making the entry bears the risk that:

    (a) the description of the encumbered assets, the translation of this description or the indication of the category or categories of encumbered assets is wrong; and

    (b) the entry is filed against a wrong person.

IX. – 3:311: Amendments of entries

(1) The creditor may amend any of the creditor's entries after filing.

(2) An amendment to an entry can only be entered into the register if:

    (a) it is made in respect of a specific entry;

    (b) it contains a declaration as to the content of the amendment; and

    (c) it is accompanied by a declaration of the creditor that the latter assumes liability for damage caused to the security provider or third persons by a wrongful amendment to the original entry.

(3) In case of an amendment, the register preserves and shows both the original text and the amendment as such, including the time the amendment was made.

(4) An amendment to an entry is effective only if it does not extend the creditor's rights. In particular, an amendment can have the effect of

limiting the creditor's rights, especially by subordinating the creditor's rights to another creditor's rights, by indicating a transfer of the security right to another creditor, by limiting the scope of assets covered according to the content of the creditor's declaration as to the encumbered assets or by setting or predating a date of expiry of the entry.

(5) An extension of the creditor's rights is effective only if contained in a new entry.

IX. – 3:312: Transitional provision in relation to entries in other systems of registration or notation under national law

(1) Where a security right is registered or noted in another system of registration or notation on title certificates under the national law of a member state, as long as such systems are still in operation for security rights in specific types of assets, an entry reiterating the content of that registration or notation, including the time of the registration or notation, is to be entered into the European register of proprietary security against the security provider by the body operating the other system. An entry in the European register of proprietary security is required for the effectiveness of the registration or notation under this Book.

(2) For purposes of priority according to Chapter 4, the time of registration or notation in the national system is decisive.

IX. – 3:313: Automated certification of entry to creditor and security provider

After an entry or an amendment to an entry has been filed, a certificate to that effect is to be communicated automatically to the creditor and the security provider.

IX. – 3:314: Third person acting as agent of the creditor

(1) As an additional content of the entry made by the secured creditor, the latter may identify a third person acting as agent of the creditor, whose name and contact details will appear on the register instead of those of the creditor. In such a situation, the entry can be entered into the register only if in addition to the requirements of the preceding Articles being satisfied this third person has also consented to it according to IX. – 3:309 (Required consent of the security provider) paragraphs (1) and (3), applied with appropriate adaptations.

(2) By a declaration to the register that is subject to IX. – 3:309 (Required consent of the security provider) paragraphs (1) and (3), applied with appropriate adaptations, a secured creditor may authorise a third person to make declarations to the register on the secured creditor's behalf.

(3) Where a third person acting as agent for the secured creditor is identified in the entry, the secured creditor and the third person are liable as solidary debtors for all obligations of secured creditors under this Section.

Subsection 3:
Protection of the security provider

IX. – 3:315: Security provider's right to deletion or amendment of entry

The security provider is entitled against the secured creditor to deletion or amendment of an entry if and in so far as no corresponding security right exists.

IX. – 3:316: Review of contested entries by registration office

(1) The security provider may apply for the assistance of the registration office in the assertion of the right to demand deletion or amendment of an entry from the secured creditor.

(2) On the security provider's application, the registration office asks the secured creditor whether the latter agrees to the security provider's demand.

(3) If the secured creditor does not object within two months of being asked by the registration office according to paragraph (2), the entry is deleted or amended according to the security provider's demand.

(4) If the secured creditor objects within the time limit of paragraph (3), the entry is marked as contested to the extent of the security provider's demand.

(5) The entry remains marked as contested until:
  (a) the security provider withdraws the application by declaration to the registration office;
  (b) the secured creditor agrees to the security provider's demand by declaration made to the registration office;

(c) the secured creditor deletes the entry; or
(d) a final decision is rendered on the security provider's demand by a
    competent court.

Subsection 4:
Accessing and searching the register

IX. – 3:317: Access to the register for searching purposes
Access to the register for searching purposes is open to anyone, subject to
the payment of fees; it does not depend upon a consent by the security
provider or the secured creditor.

IX. – 3:318: Searching the register
The register can be searched for entries filed against individual security
providers or for entries containing specified descriptions of the encumbered
assets.

Subsection 5: Registered creditors' duty
to answer requests for information
IX. – 3:319: Duty to give information
(1) Any registered secured creditor has a duty to answer requests for in-
    formation by inquirers concerning the security right covered by the
    entry and the encumbered assets if these requests are made with the
    security provider's approval.
(2) The request must be in an official language of the member state of the
    European Union where the place of business or incorporation or the
    residence of the secured creditor is situated or in English.
(3) The request must be answered within fourteen days after the request,
    including the security provider's approval, has been received by the
    secured creditor.
(4) The secured creditor's duty to answer requests for information by in-
    quirers according to the preceding paragraphs is owed both to the in-
    quirer and to the security provider. To both parties, the secured creditor
    is liable in damages for any loss caused by breach of the duty.

IX. – 3:320: Content of the information

(1) Requests for information under the preceding Article must be answered by the secured creditor giving information concerning the existence of a security right in specific assets at the time when the information is given.

(2) The information may be given by:

(a) stating specifically whether the assets concerned are encumbered in favour of the secured creditor; or

(b) forwarding the relevant parts of the agreements between security provider and secured creditor covering the providing or retention of proprietary security.

(3) Where the security right has been transferred, the person registered as the secured creditor must disclose the name and contact details of the transferee.

(4) The information must be given in an official language of the member state of the European Union where the place of business or incorporation or the residence of the secured creditor is situated or in English.

(5) No information needs to be given:

(a) if it is apparent directly from the entry that the asset concerned is not encumbered, provided that the entry complies with the requirements of paragraph (4); or

(b) if the secured creditor had already answered a request for information by the same inquirer in relation to the same asset within the past three months and the information given is still correct.

(6) These provisions do not affect the secured creditor's obligation to give information concerning the obligation covered by the security under IX. – 5:401 (Secured creditor's obligation to give information about secured right) or any equivalent obligation owed to the debtor of the obligation covered by the security and the consequences of a non-performance of these obligations.

IX. – 3:321: Consequences of correct information given by secured creditor

(1) If the secured creditor correctly informs the inquirer under this Subsection that the assets concerned are not encumbered, a security right in these assets which is subsequently created in favour of the secured creditor cannot enjoy priority conferred by the original entry over security rights of the inquirer. This rule applies only if the security rights

of the inquirer are acquired by the latter within three months after the request for information had been made.

(2) If the secured creditor correctly informs the inquirer under this Subsection that the assets concerned are encumbered, the inquirer cannot acquire a proprietary right in the encumbered assets free of the encumbrance in favour of the secured creditor even if that would otherwise be possible under the principles of good faith acquisition.

IX. – 3:322: Consequences of incorrect information given by secured creditor

(1) If the secured creditor incorrectly informs the inquirer under this Subsection that the assets concerned are not encumbered, the inquirer may within three months acquire a proprietary right in these assets free of any encumbrance in favour of the secured creditor on the basis of a good faith acquisition in spite of the entry in the register covering the secured creditor's rights.

(2) If the secured creditor incorrectly informs the inquirer under this Subsection that the assets concerned are encumbered, and the inquirer nevertheless acquires a proprietary security right in the assets concerned from the security provider, IX. – 3:321 (Consequences of correct information given by secured creditor) paragraph (1) first sentence applies with appropriate adaptations.

IX. – 3:323: Consequences of failure to give information

(1) If the secured creditor fails to answer the request for information under IX. – 3:319 (Duty to give information) and IX. – 3:320 (Content of the information) or incorrectly answers that its security rights in the assets concerned have been transferred, the inquirer is to be treated as if the secured creditor had given the information that the assets concerned are not encumbered. IX. – 3:321 (Consequences of correct information given by secured creditor) paragraph (1) or IX. – 3:322 (Consequences of incorrect information given by secured creditor) paragraph (1), respectively, apply with appropriate adaptations.

(2) If the secured creditor delays in answering the request for information under IX. – 3:319 (Duty to give information) and IX. – 3:320 (Content of the information), the preceding paragraph applies if a proprietary right is created in favour of or acquired by the inquirer before the secured creditor answers the request for information.

IX. – 3:324: Form of requests and information

The request for information under this Subsection and the answer must be in textual form. Both may be made via an electronic means of communication provided by the register, in which case a certification of the inquiry or the answer is to be communicated by the register to the inquirer or the secured creditor, respectively, serving as proof of receipt of the inquiry or of the answer by the other party.

Subsection 6:
Duration, renewal and deletion of entries

IX. – 3:325: Duration

(1) An entry expires five years after it has been entered into the register or at the date of expiry indicated in the entry.

(2) Once an entry expires, it no longer appears on the register and is no longer directly accessible for any user. It ceases to have any effect under this Section. The content of the entry is kept for reference purposes in the archives of the registration office.

IX. – 3:326: Renewal

(1) Unless a date of expiry has been included in the entry, an entry may be renewed before the end of the regular period of expiry for an additional period of five years.

(2) The renewal of an entry is effected by a declaration of the secured creditor to the register.

IX. – 3:327: Deletion

(1) The secured creditor may at any time delete the entry by declaration to the register.

(2) For the consequences of a declaration according to the preceding paragraph, IX. – 3:325 (Duration) paragraph (2) is applicable with appropriate adaptations.

Subsection 7:
Transfer of the security right or of the encumbered asset

IX. – 3:328: Transfer of the security right:
general rules
(1) Where the security right is transferred, it remains effective by virtue of the original entry.
(2) Even if there is no declaration indicating the transfer under IX. – 3:329 (Transfer of the security right: declaration indicating the transfer), the transferee is bound under Subsection 5 in the same way as a secured creditor from the moment of the transfer.
(3) The transferor is liable towards the transferee for any damage caused by its conduct in relation to the entry, as well as to amendments and deletions thereof from the moment of the transfer of the security right until a declaration indicating the transfer is filed or until the transferor declares its consent to such a declaration under IX. – 3:329 (Transfer of the security right: declaration indicating the transfer) paragraph (4)).

IX. – 3:329: Transfer of the security right:
declaration indicating the transfer
(1) Where the security right is transferred, the original entry may be amended by a declaration indicating the transfer.
(2) The declaration indicating the transfer is subject to IX. – 3:311 (Amendments of entries) and any additional rules as laid down in this Article.
(3) The declaration indicating the transfer can be entered into the register only if:
  (a) it is made in respect of a specific entry;
  (b) it indicates the security rights to be transferred;
  (c) it identifies the transferee; and
  (d) it is accompanied by a declaration of the person making the amendment that the latter assumes liability for damage caused to the secured creditor or third persons by a wrongful entry.
(4) The declaration indicating the transfer may be filed by the transferor or, with the transferor's consent, by the transferee.
(5) On the basis and to the extent of the transfer of the security right, the security provider is entitled as against the transferor to the filing of a

declaration indicating the transfer and the transferee is entitled to a declaration of consent by the transferor according to the preceding paragraph. IX. – 3:316 (Review of contested entries by registration office) applies with appropriate adaptations to the assertion of these rights.

(6) Once the declaration indicating the transfer is filed, the original entry is amended accordingly and is no longer regarded as covering the security rights indicated as having been transferred.

(7) Once the declaration indicating the transfer is filed, a new entry is automatically filed against the security provider reiterating the content of the original entry and stating that the security rights indicated are transferred to the transferee.

(8) The transferee assumes the position of the secured creditor in respect of the new entry for all purposes under this Section. In respect of the security rights indicated as transferred, the new entry preserves the priority conferred by the original entry.

IX. – 3:330: Transfer of the encumbered asset: general rules

(1) Ownership of the encumbered asset may be transferred subject to the existing security right without a new entry being filed in the register.

(2) The continuation of effectiveness and the priority of the security right in the encumbered asset by virtue of the original entry in the register are governed by IX. – 5:303 (Transfer of encumbered asset).

(3) For the purposes of this Section, the transferee assumes the position of the security provider in respect of the security right in the transferred assets from the moment of the transfer.

(4) The preceding paragraphs apply with appropriate adaptations where the rights of a buyer, hire-purchaser, lessee or consignee in or relating to the supplied assets are transferred subject to an existing retention of ownership device.

IX. – 3:331: Transfer of the encumbered asset: declaration of transfer

(1) A transferee acquiring ownership of an encumbered asset subject to an existing security right has a duty to enter in the register an entry against itself indicating the transfer, unless such a declaration has already been entered by the secured creditor.

(2) The transferee is liable towards the secured creditor holding a security right in the transferred asset for damage resulting from a breach of the duty under the preceding paragraph.

(3) The declaration of transfer can be entered by the transferee or the secured creditor if:

    (a) it is made in respect of an identified security provider as transferee;

    (b) it indicates the identity of an identified security provider as transferor;

    (c) it contains a minimum declaration as to the transferred asset;

    (d) it is indicated by one or several references to a list of categories of assets to which category the transferred asset belongs; and

    (e) it is accompanied by a declaration of the person making the declaration of transfer that the latter assumes liability for any damage caused to the transferee, the secured creditor or third persons by a wrongful entry.

(4) The preceding paragraphs apply with appropriate adaptations where the rights of a buyer, hire-purchaser, lessee or consignee in or relating to the supplied assets are transferred subject to an existing retention of ownership device.

Subsection 8:
Costs

IX. – 3:332: Distribution of costs

(1) As between the parties:

    (a) each party has to bear the costs of its enrolment or admission to a secure online identity verification system; and

    (b) the security provider has to bear any other costs reasonably incurred by the secured creditor in connection with the registration.

(2) The costs of inquiries and of answers to such inquires are to be borne by the inquirer.

Subsection 9:
Security rights created before establishment of register

IX. – 3:333: Security rights created before establishment of register

(1) Security rights that were effective before the European register of proprietary security started to operate do not require registration under this Section in order to remain effective thereafter.

(2) If the security rights were registered or noted in any system of registration or notation on title certificates under the national law of a member state, an entry reiterating the content of that registration or notation, including the date of registration or notation, is to be entered in the European register of proprietary security against the security provider by the body operating the other register once this register is established.

Chapter 4:
Priority

IX. – 4:101: Priority: general rules

(1) Subject to exceptions, the priority between several security rights and between a security right and other limited proprietary rights in the same asset is determined according to the order of the relevant time.

(2) The relevant time is:

    (a) for security rights, the time of registration according to Chapter 3, Section 3, if any, or the time at which the security right has otherwise become effective according to the other rules of Chapter 3, whichever is earlier;

    (b) for other limited proprietary rights, the time of creation.

(3) An effective security right has priority over an ineffective security right, even if the latter was created earlier.

(4) The ranking of two or more security rights which are ineffective is determined by the time of their creation.

(5) Subject to IX. – 4:108 (Change of ranking), a security right that had been acquired by a good faith acquisition in an asset subject to a retention of ownership device or in disregard of an earlier encumbrance in the same asset always has priority over the retention of ownership device or earlier security right.

IX. – 4:102: Superpriority

(1) An acquisition finance device that is effective against third persons according to the rules of Chapter 3 takes priority over any security right or other limited proprietary right created by the security provider.

(2) A security right in financial assets made effective by control according to IX. – 3:204 (Control over financial assets) or by possession takes priority over any other security right or other limited proprietary right in the same asset. If control is created for different secured creditors, IX. – 4:101 (Priority: general rules) paragraphs (1) and (2)(a) apply.

(3) A security right based upon a right of retention of possession according to IX. – 2:114 (Right of retention of possession) takes priority over any other right in the retained asset.

(4) The preceding paragraphs are subject to IX. – 4:101 (Priority: general rules) paragraph (5) and IX. – 4:108 (Change of ranking).

IX. – 4:103: Continuation of priority

(1) Priority is not affected if the encumbered asset:
   (a) becomes an accessory to a movable asset; or
   (b) is used for the production of new goods, or is commingled or combined with other assets, provided that the security right extends to the security provider's rights in the asset resulting from the production, commingling or combination.

(2) Paragraph (1)(a) also applies if a movable asset becomes an accessory to an immovable, unless the law governing the immovable determines otherwise.

IX. – 4:104: Fruits and proceeds: general rules

(1) Security rights in fruits and proceeds of the following types of assets preserve the priority of the security right in the encumbered original assets:
   (a) fruits and proceeds of the same kind as the assets that were originally encumbered;
   (b) rights to payment due to defects in, damage to, or loss of the assets that were originally encumbered, including insurance proceeds; and
   (c) fruits and proceeds that are covered by the registration of the security right in the assets that were originally encumbered.

(2) In cases not covered by paragraph (1), the priority of security rights in fruits and proceeds is determined according to the general rules laid down in IX. – 4:101 (Priority: general rules) and IX. – 4:102 (Superpriority).

IX. – 4:105: Fruits and proceeds: exceptions

(1) Security rights in fruits and proceeds of assets that are subject to an acquisition finance device or are covered by VIII. – 5:204 (Additional provisions as to proprietary security rights) paragraph (3) do not enjoy the superpriority of the security right in the assets that were originally encumbered.

(2) The preceding paragraph does not affect the superpriority of security rights in:

   (a) rights to payment due to defects in, damage to, or loss of the assets that were originally encumbered, including insurance proceeds; and

   (b) proceeds of the sale of the assets that were originally encumbered.

IX. – 4:106: Importation of encumbered asset

If an encumbered asset is brought from a country outside the European Union into this area, the priority of a security right which was effective before removal of the encumbered asset into the European Union and which fulfils the conditions of IX. – 3:108 (Importation of encumbered asset) is preserved.

IX. – 4:107: Priority of execution creditor

For the purpose of determining priority, an execution creditor is regarded as holding an effective security right as from the moment of bringing an execution against specific assets if all preconditions for execution proceedings against these assets according to the procedural rules of the place of execution are fulfilled.

IX. – 4:108: Change of ranking

(1) The priority between a security right and other security rights as well as other limited proprietary rights in the same asset may be changed by an agreement in textual form between the holders of all rights that would be affected by the change of ranking.

(2) A third person acquiring a security right or a limited proprietary right that has been negatively affected by a change of ranking is bound only if the entry for the security right in the European register of proprietary security has been amended accordingly or if the third person at the time of the transfer knew or had reason to know of the change of ranking.

Chapter 5:
Predefault rules
Section I:
General principles

IX. – 5:101: General principles

(1) The security provider and the secured creditor are free to determine their mutual relationship with respect to the encumbered asset, except as otherwise provided in these rules.
(2) Any agreement concluded before default and providing for the appropriation of the encumbered assets by the secured creditor or having this effect, is void, unless expressly provided otherwise. This paragraph does not apply to retention of ownership devices.

Section 2:
Encumbered assets

IX. – 5:201: Care and insurance of the encumbered assets

(1) The party who is in possession of the encumbered assets has an obligation to keep them identifiable from assets owned by others and must preserve and maintain them with reasonable care.
(2) The other party is entitled to inspect the encumbered assets at any reasonable time.
(3) The security provider has an obligation to insure the encumbered assets against such risks as are usually insured against by a prudent owner at the location of the assets. Upon request of the secured creditor, the security provider must furnish proof of the insurance coverage. If there is no or only insufficient insurance coverage or no proof of it, the secured creditor is entitled to take out sufficient insurance and to add any expenses to the obligation covered by the security.

Subsection 1:
Security provider's rights and obligations

IX. – 5:202: Rights in general
If and as long as the security provider is entitled to possession of the encumbered assets, the security provider is entitled to make use of them in a reasonable manner.

IX. – 5:203: Use of encumbered industrial material
A security provider in possession of encumbered industrial material, such as raw material or semi-finished products, may apply such material for production, unless expressly prohibited.

IX. – 5:204: Dispositions of encumbered assets by traders and manufacturers
(1) A security provider acting in the ordinary course of its business as a trader or manufacturer may dispose of the following types of encumbered assets free of any security right if they are in the security provider's possession:
  (a) assets designated for sale and lease and industrial material (inventory); and
  (b) products of industrial material.
(2) A trader or manufacturer may not dispose of items of its encumbered equipment, unless expressly so authorised by the secured creditor.

IX. – 5:205: Unauthorised use or disposition
(1) A security provider in possession of the encumbered assets has an obligation to the secured creditor not to use or dispose of them in breach of the limits imposed by the preceding Articles of this Subsection.
(2) In addition to liability for damages for non-performance of the obligation referred to in paragraph (1), the security provider who is in breach of those limits is obliged to account to the secured creditor for the value derived from the use or the proceeds of the disposition and to pay the resulting amount, but only up to the amount of the secured right that would otherwise remain unsatisfied.

Subsection 2:
Secured creditor's rights and obligations

IX. – 5:206: Limited right of use

A secured creditor who is in possession or control of the encumbered assets is not entitled to use the assets, unless and in so far as proper use is indispensable for their up-keep and preservation.

IX. – 5:207: Banks entitled to dispose of financial assets

(1) Banks and equivalent financial institutions holding financial assets as secured creditors are entitled to use, appropriate and dispose of the encumbered assets, provided this is expressly agreed.
(2) Upon satisfaction of the secured right, the secured creditor is only obliged to transfer financial assets of the same kind, quality and value to the security provider.

IX. – 5:208: Appropriation of civil fruits

If the security right extends to civil fruits of the assets that were originally encumbered, the secured creditor is entitled to collect and to apply money received as civil fruits to reduce the secured right even before it has become due.

Section 3:
Change of parties

IX. – 5:301: Transfer of the secured right

(1) If a secured right is transferred to another creditor, the security right also passes to that creditor.
(2) The transferor is obliged to inform the transferee of any security right securing the transferred right.
(3) Effectiveness of the security right against third persons is achieved:
   (a) by virtue of the original registration according to IX. – 3:328 (Transfer of the security right: general rules) paragraph (1);
   (b) if either possession or control of the encumbered asset is transferred to the transferee;

   (c) if the transferor agrees to hold possession or control for the transferee; or

   (d) if the security right had been effective without observation of any requirements under Chapter 3.

(4) If the security right remains effective, its priority is not affected by the transfer.

IX. – 5:302: Partial transfer of the secured right

If the secured right is divided into parts held by different persons as the result of a transfer of a part of the secured right or of a transfer of the whole secured right to different transferees each acquiring a part only:

(a) each holder of a part of the secured right is entitled to a part of the security right in proportion to the nominal amount of its part of the secured right; and

(b) the effectiveness of the security rights of each holder of a part of the secured right is to be determined individually; possession or control of the encumbered asset may be held by one holder of a part of the secured right for the others also.

IX. – 5:303: Transfer of encumbered asset

(1) Where ownership of an encumbered asset is transferred to another person, neither the existence nor the effectiveness against third persons of a security right in the asset is affected. As of the time of the transfer, the transferee is regarded as the security provider.

(2) The preceding paragraph does not apply if the transferor acted with authority to dispose of the encumbered asset free of the encumbrance or if the transferee acquires the asset free of the encumbrance on the basis of a good faith acquisition.

(3) Security rights which before transfer of ownership of the encumbered asset had been created for secured creditors in future assets of the new owner do not have priority over security rights encumbering the transferred asset at the time of the transfer.

(4) The preceding paragraphs apply with appropriate adaptations where there is a transfer of the rights of a buyer, hire-purchaser, lessee or consignee in or relating to the supplied assets subject to an existing retention of ownership device.

Section 4:
Secured creditor's obligation to give information about secured right

IX. – 5:401: Secured creditor's obligation to give information about secured right

(1) The security provider has a right to, and the secured creditor has an obligation to provide on request by the security provider, information concerning the amount of the obligation covered by the security. The security provider can require this information to be given to a third person.
(2) If the security provider is not the debtor of the obligation covered by the security, the security provider's right under the preceding Article depends upon the debtor's approval.

Chapter 6:
Termination

IX. – 6:101: Instances of termination of proprietary security

(1) A security right is terminated if, and in so far as:
  (a) the security provider and secured creditor so agree;
  (b) the secured creditor waives the security right, such a waiver being presumed where the secured creditor returns possession of the encumbered asset to the security provider;
  (c) the encumbered asset ceases to exist;
  (d) ownership of the encumbered asset is acquired by the secured creditor;
  (e) ownership in the encumbered asset is acquired by a third person free from the security right; or
  (f) any other provision so provides or this consequence is implied, such as where the debtor and creditor of the secured right become identical, especially by inheritance or merger.
(2) A security right is also terminated if the secured right ceases to exist entirely, especially if a right to payment is fully satisfied by payment to the secured creditor, unless the security right with the secured right passes to another person who has made payment to the secured creditor.

(3) Paragraph (1)(a) to (c), (e) and (f) and paragraph (2) apply with appropriate adaptations to the termination of a retention of ownership device. A retention of ownership device is also terminated if the rights of the buyer, hire-purchaser, lessee or consignee in or relating to the supplied assets under the contract of sale, hire-purchase, financial leasing or consignment cease to exist.

IX. – 6:102: Loss of proprietary security due to good faith acquisition of ownership

(1) Whether a security right is lost due to good faith acquisition of ownership of the encumbered asset by a third person free from a security right is determined by VIII. – 3:102 (Good faith acquisition of ownership free of limited proprietary rights).

(2) For the purposes of VIII. – 3:102 (Good faith acquisition of ownership free of limited proprietary rights) paragraph (1)(d) sentence 1, a transferee is regarded as knowing that the transferor has no right or authority to transfer ownership free from the security right if this right is registered under Chapter 3, Section 3 unless:

    (a) the transferor acts in the ordinary course of its business; or

    (b) the entry is filed against a security provider different from the transferor.

(3) Whether a retention of ownership device is lost due to good faith acquisition of ownership of the supplied asset by a third person is determined by VIII. – 3:101 (Good faith acquisition through a person without right or authority to transfer ownership). Paragraph (2) above applies with appropriate adaptations.

IX. – 6:103: Prescription of the secured right

A security right can be enforced even if the secured right is prescribed and up to two years after the debtor of the secured right has invoked this prescription as against its creditor.

IX. – 6:104: Consequences of termination

(1) The full or partial termination of a security right implies the corresponding termination of the encumbrance of the asset concerned.

(2) If and in so far as a security right is terminated, the secured creditor is no longer entitled to possession or control of the asset that was encumbered as against its owner. For the right to deletion of an entry in

the European register of proprietary security, IX. – 3:315 (Security provider's right to have entry deleted or amended) applies.

(3) The secured creditor is obliged to inform any third person holding the encumbered assets of the removal of the encumbrance and, if the third person holds the assets for the secured creditor's account, to ask the security provider for instructions.

(4) Where in the case of an encumbered right to payment notice of the encumbrance had been given to the third party debtor, the secured creditor is obliged to notify the debtor of the removal of the encumbrance.

(5) If and in so far as a retention of ownership device is terminated, the seller's, supplier's or lessor's ownership of the supplied assets is no longer subject to the rules of this Book. An acquisition of ownership of the supplied assets by the buyer, hire-purchaser, lessee or consignee or the latter's right to use the supplied assets is subject to an agreement of the parties. For the right to deletion of an entry in the European register of proprietary security, paragraph (2) second sentence applies.

IX. – 6:105: Secured creditor liable to account for proceeds
Upon termination of the security right, the secured creditor is liable to account for any proceeds from the encumbered assets, whether or not it has received, used or consumed them, and to transfer them to the security provider.

IX. – 6:106: Recourse of third party security provider
(1) If a security provider who is not the debtor of the secured right (a third party security provider), pays the outstanding amount of the obligation covered by the security, IV. G. – 2:113 (Security provider's rights after performance), IV. G. – 1:106 (Several security providers: internal recourse) and IV. G. – 1:107 (Several security providers: recourse against debtor) apply with appropriate adaptations.

(2) A security provider other than the debtor has as against the debtor the same position as a person who has provided dependent personal security.

Chapter 7:
Default and enforcement
Section 1:
General rules

IX. – 7:101: Secured creditor's rights after default

(1) After an event of default, and provided that any additional conditions agreed by the parties are fulfilled, a secured creditor may exercise the rights under this Chapter.

(2) If a third person listed in IX. – 3:101 (Effectiveness as against third persons) paragraph (1) and fulfilling the requirements of that provision is involved, a secured creditor may exercise the rights under this Chapter only if the security right is effective according to the rules of Book IX Chapter 3. If no such third person is involved, it is sufficient that the security right has been validly created. The provisions on priority remain unaffected.

IX. – 7:102: Mandatory rules

As between the enforcing secured creditor and the security provider, the rules of this Chapter are mandatory, unless otherwise provided.

IX. – 7:103: Extra-judicial and judicial enforcement

(1) Unless otherwise agreed, the secured creditor may carry out extra-judicial enforcement of the security right.

(2) A security right in an asset of a consumer can only be enforced by a court or other competent authority, unless after default the consumer security provider has agreed to extra-judicial enforcement.

(3) In the case of retention of ownership devices the parties may not agree to exclude extra-judicial enforcement and paragraph (2) does not apply.

(4) Enforcement is to be undertaken by the secured creditor in a commercially reasonable way and as far as possible in cooperation with the security provider and, where applicable, any third person involved.

IX. – 7:104: Right to seek court assistance and damages

Any party or third person whose rights are violated by enforcement measures or by resistance to justified enforcement measures may:

(a) call upon a competent court or other authority, which must decide expeditiously, to order the party responsible to act in accordance with the provisions of this Chapter; and

(b) claim damages from the party responsible.

IX. – 7:105: Predefault agreement on appropriation of encumbered assets

(1) Any agreement concluded before default providing for the transfer of ownership of the encumbered assets to the secured creditor after default, or having this effect, is void.

(2) Paragraph (1) does not apply:
    (a) if the encumbered asset is a fungible asset that is traded on a recognised market with published prices; or
    (b) if the parties agree in advance on some other method which allows a ready determination of a reasonable market price.

(3) Paragraph (2)(b) does not apply to a consumer security provider.

(4) Where appropriation is allowed, the secured creditor is entitled to appropriate encumbered assets only for the value of their recognised or agreed market price at the date of appropriation. The security provider is entitled to any surplus over the obligations covered by the security right. The debtor remains liable for any deficit.

(5) This Article does not apply to retention of ownership devices.

IX. – 7:106: Security provider's right of redemption

(1) Even after default, if the outstanding amount of the obligation covered by the security right is paid, the security provider may require the secured creditor to terminate the exercise of the rights under this Chapter and to return possession of the encumbered asset.

(2) The security provider's rights under paragraph (1) may no longer be exercised if:
    (a) in the case of an enforcement under Section 2, the encumbered asset has been appropriated or sold or the secured creditor has concluded a binding contract to sell the asset to a third person; or
    (b) in the case of exercising the rights under Section 3, the holder of the retention of ownership device has terminated the relationship arising under the contract of sale, hire-purchase, financial leasing or consignment.

IX. – 7:107: Enforcement notice to consumer

(1) A secured creditor may exercise the rights under this Chapter against a consumer security provider only if the secured creditor delivers at least ten days before enforcement is to begin an enforcement notice in textual form to the security provider and, if the latter is not the debtor, also to the debtor, if the debtor also is a consumer.

(2) The enforcement notice must:

    (a) unequivocally designate the obligation covered by the security right and state the amount that is due by the end of the day before the notice is sent;

    (b) state that any other condition for enforcement agreed by the parties has been fulfilled;

    (c) state that the secured creditor intends to enforce the security and identify those encumbered assets against which the secured creditor intends to enforce it; and

    (d) be signed by or on behalf of the secured creditor.

(3) The notice must be in an official language of the consumer's place of residence.

IX. – 7:108: Solidary liability of several security providers

(1) To the extent that several proprietary security rights have been created covering the same obligation or same part of an obligation, the creditor may seek satisfaction from any, several or all of these security rights. IV. G. – 1:105 (Several security providers: solidary liability towards creditor) applies accordingly.

(2) Paragraph (1) applies with appropriate adaptations if, in addition to one or more proprietary security rights, personal security has been granted by one or more persons.

IX. – 7:109: Rights of recourse of third party security provider

If the obligation covered by the security right is satisfied by enforcement against the assets of a security provider who is not the debtor, the rights of recourse between several providers of proprietary security or between providers of proprietary security and personal security as well as recourse against the debtor are governed by IV. G. – 2:113 (Security provider's rights after performance), IV. G. – 1:106 (Several security providers: internal recourse) and IV. G. – 1:107 (Several security providers: recourse against debtor), applied with appropriate adaptations.

Section 2:
Enforcement of security rights
Subsection 1:
Extra-judicial enforcement: rules preparatory to realisation

IX. – 7:201: Creditor's right to possession of corporeal asset
(1) The secured creditor is not entitled to take possession of an encumbered corporeal asset, unless:
   (a) the security provider consents at the time when the secured creditor exercises this right; or
   (b) the security provider had agreed to the secured creditor's right to take possession and neither the security provider nor the actual holder objects at the time when the secured creditor exercises this right.
(2) In enforcements against a consumer, the right to take possession according to paragraph (1) does not arise until ten days have elapsed since an enforcement notice has been served.
(3) Unless it indicates otherwise, a consent or agreement to the taking of possession according to paragraph (1) covers the right to enter the security provider's or other holder's premises for the purpose of exercising the right to take possession.

IX. – 7:202: Creditor's right to immobilise and to preserve encumbered asset
(1) The secured creditor is entitled to take any steps necessary to immobilise the encumbered asset, to prevent unauthorised use or disposition of it, and to protect it physically. Paragraphs (1) to (3) of the preceding Article apply with appropriate adaptations.
(2) The secured creditor is entitled:
   (a) to take reasonable steps to preserve, maintain and insure the encumbered asset and to obtain reimbursement for such actions from the security provider;
   (b) to lease the encumbered asset to a third party for the purpose of preserving its value; or
   (c) to take any other protective measures agreed with the security provider.

IX. – 7:203: Intervention of court or other authority

(1) The secured creditor may apply to the competent court or other authority for an order to obtain possession of or access to the encumbered asset, if the security provider or a third person in possession of the asset refuses delivery to or access by the secured creditor.

(2) Upon application by either party, a court or other authority may order the taking of any of the protective measures mentioned in the preceding Article.

IX. – 7:204: Encumbrance of a right to payment

(1) Where the encumbered asset is a right entitling the security provider to payment from a third party debtor, the secured creditor may exercise the rights under this Chapter only if the secured creditor:
    (a) sends to the third party debtor:
        (i) where the security provider is a consumer, a copy of an enforcement notice complying with all the requirements of IX. – 7:107 (Enforcement notice to consumer); and
        (ii) in other cases, an enforcement notice complying with paragraph (2)(a) and (d) of that Article; and
    (b) informs the third party debtor as precisely as possible in the circumstances of the nature, amount and maturity of the security provider's right to payment against the third party debtor.

(2) The third party debtor is obliged to inform the enforcing secured creditor about the amount and maturity of competing rights of other secured creditors known to the third party debtor.

IX. – 7:205: Negotiable instrument

(1) IX. – 7:201 (Creditor's right to possession of corporeal asset), IX. – 7:202 (Creditor's right to immobilise and to preserve encumbered asset) and IX. – 7:203 (Intervention of court or other authority) apply to the taking of possession of a negotiable instrument as such.

(2) IX. – 7:204 (Encumbrance of a right to payment) does not apply to negotiable instruments.

IX. – 7:206: Negotiable document of title

The preceding Article applies also to the taking of possession of a negotiable document of title.

Subsection 2:
Extra-judicial enforcement: realisation of encumbered asset

IX. – 7:207: General rule on realisation
(1) The secured creditor is entitled to realise the encumbered asset in order
to apply the proceeds towards satisfaction of the secured right:
    (a) by sale of the encumbered asset according to IX. – 7:211 (Sale by
    public or private auction or by private sale), unless agreed other-
    wise by the parties;
    (b) by leasing the encumbered asset to a third person and collecting
    the fruits;
    (c) by appropriation according to IX. – 7:216 (Appropriation of encum-
    bered asset by secured creditor); or
    (d) by exercising the methods of realisation (collection, sale or appro-
    priation) for rights to payment and negotiable instruments accord-
    ing to IX. – 7:214 (Realisation of security in right to payment or in
    negotiable instrument).
(2) Where an enforcement notice is required under IX. – 7:107 (Enforcement notice to consumer), paragraph (1) applies only if ten days have
elapsed since the delivery of that notice.
(3) The secured creditor may appoint a private agent or apply to a competent court officer to undertake all or some of the steps for realisation of
the encumbered assets.

IX. – 7:208: Notice of extra-judicial disposition
(1) A secured creditor may exercise its right to dispose of the encumbered
asset only if the secured creditor gives notice of its intention to do so.
(2) Paragraph (1) does not apply if the encumbered asset is perishable or
may otherwise speedily decline in value or is a fungible asset that is
traded on a recognised market with published prices.

IX. – 7:209: Addressees of the notice
The notice required by the preceding Article must be given:
(a) to the security provider, the debtor (if different from the security provider) and other persons who, to the knowledge of the secured creditor, are liable for the obligation covered by the security; and
(b) to the following persons with rights in the encumbered asset:

(i) other secured creditors who have registered such rights;

(ii) persons who were in possession or control of the encumbered asset when enforcement commenced; and

(iii) other persons who were actually known to the secured creditor to have a right in the encumbered asset.

IX. – 7:210: Time and contents of notice

(1) The notice required by IX. – 7:208 (Notice of extra-judicial disposition) must be given in due time. A notice that reaches its addressees at least ten days before the disposition is regarded as given in due time.

(2) The notice must indicate:

(a) the place and time of the planned disposition;

(b) a reasonable description of the encumbered asset to be disposed of;

(c) any minimum price for the disposition of the encumbered asset and payment terms; and

(d) the right of the security provider, of the debtor and of other interested persons to avert disposition of the encumbered asset by payment of the outstanding amount of the obligation covered by the security.

(3) The notice must be in a language that can be expected to inform its addressees.

IX. – 7:211: Sale by public or private auction or by private sale

(1) Realisation of all or parts of the encumbered assets by sale may be by an officially supervised auction (public auction) or by an auction to which the public is invited (private auction).

(2) Realisation of all or parts of the encumbered assets by sale may be by private sale, if so agreed by the parties or if there is a published market price for the encumbered asset.

(3) The details of the arrangements to be made under the preceding paragraphs can be fixed by the secured creditor.

(4) If the transfer is subject to pre-existing prior rights and upon demand, the secured creditor must disclose to the purchaser the relevant details.

(5) If the secured creditor acquires the encumbered asset in a sale by public or private auction, the sale may be set aside by the security provider within a period of ten days after the auction.

(6) Where the owner of the encumbered asset participates as buyer in a realisation of the encumbered asset according to this Article, the sale operates as an agreement to release encumbrances of the asset.

IX. – 7:212: Commercially reasonable price

(1) The secured creditor must realise a commercially reasonable price for the encumbered asset.

(2) If there is a recognised market which is easily accessible for the secured creditor, a price is commercially reasonable if it corresponds to the market price at the time of the sale, having due regard to any special features of the encumbered asset.

(3) If the preceding paragraph does not apply, a price is commercially reasonable if the secured creditor took such steps as could be expected to be taken in the circumstances.

(4) If the sale is by private sale, the security provider may demand that the creditor communicates to the security provider the expected price or price range. If the security provider can show that it is likely that this price range is significantly below what might reasonably be achieved at a private or public auction, the security provider may demand that the secured creditor arrange for a private or a public auction. Subject to paragraph (5) of the preceding Article, a price achieved in this way is binding upon the parties.

IX. – 7:213: Buyer's rights in the assets after realisation by sale

(1) The buyer acquires rights in the sold assets free of the rights of:
   (a) the security provider;
   (b) the enforcing secured creditor;
   (c) junior secured creditors, whether holders of security rights or retention of ownership devices; and
   (d) holders of other limited proprietary rights with lower priority than the enforcing secured creditor's rights.

(2) The following rights in the sold assets remain in existence after the transfer, unless the enforcing secured creditor acted with authority to dispose of the encumbered assets free of these rights or the buyer acquires in good faith according to IX. – 6:102 (Loss of proprietary security due to good faith acquisition of ownership):
   (a) rights of senior secured creditors, whether holders of security rights or retention of ownership devices; and
   (b) other limited proprietary rights with higher priority.

(3) The buyer's position is not affected by any failure to comply with notice requirements under this Chapter or by any other violation of procedural provisions under this Chapter for the auction or private
sale.
(4) If the secured creditor or the security provider participates in the realisation by sale as buyer, the preceding paragraphs apply with appropriate adaptations with respect to the effects of the sale.

IX. – 7:214: Realisation of security in right to payment
or in negotiable instrument

(1) Where the encumbered asset is a right to payment or a negotiable
instrument, the secured creditor may collect the outstanding performance from the third party debtor or may sell and assign or appropriate
the right to payment or the negotiable instrument.
(2) If there are other security rights in the encumbered right to payment or
the negotiable instrument which enjoy priority, the secured creditor is
not entitled as against these senior secured creditors to collect the encumbered right to payment or to the negotiable instrument.
(3) The third party debtor, except a debtor under a negotiable instrument,
may refuse to pay unless the secured creditor sends a notice indicating
the amount duet, supported by adequate proof.
(4) The secured creditor may also collect or otherwise enforce any personal
or proprietary security right to which the security in the right to payment extends according to IX. – 2:301 (Encumbrance of right to payment of money) paragraph (4).

IX. – 7:215: Distribution of proceeds

(1) The proceeds of any extra-judicial enforcement of an encumbered asset
according to the preceding provisions are to be distributed by the secured creditor in the following order.
(2) First, the secured creditor who has enforced may apply the proceeds for
the satisfaction of the secured right including the expenses incurred for
enforcement.
(3) Second, any secured creditor whose proprietary security has a lower
priority than the enforcing secured creditor's right is entitled to receive
any remaining proceeds after any deductions according to paragraph

(2) up to the amount of the obligation covered by this secured creditor's security. If there are several junior secured creditors, the remaining proceeds are distributed in accordance with the order of priority between their rights. The preceding sentences apply with appropriate adaptations to holders of other limited proprietary rights with lower priority than the enforcing secured creditor's rights; instead of an obligation covered by the security, the value of these limited proprietary rights is decisive.

(4) Third, any remaining proceeds after any deductions according to paragraphs (2) and (3) must be repaid to the security provider.

(5) No secured creditor may receive more than any maximum amount that has been agreed or registered for that creditor's security right. This limit does not apply to reasonable expenses incurred for enforcement.

IX. – 7:216: Appropriation of encumbered asset by secured creditor

The secured creditor may accept the encumbered assets in total or partial satisfaction of the secured right under the following conditions:

(a) the secured creditor must give advance notice of the intention to acquire all or parts of the encumbered assets in total or partial satisfaction of the secured right, specifying the relevant details;

(b) the proposal must be sent to the persons specified in IX. – 7:209 (Addressees of the notice);

(c) the conditions of IX. – 7:210 (Time and contents of notice) paragraphs (1), (2) (b) and (d) and (3) and IX. – 7:212 (Commercially reasonable price) paragraph (1), applied with appropriate adaptations, must be fulfilled;

(d) the proposal must indicate the secured amount owed as of the end of business on the day before the proposal is sent and the amount of the right that is proposed to be satisfied by accepting the encumbered asset; and

(e) no addressee objects to this proposal in writing within ten days after the proposal has been received by every addressee.

Subsection 3:
Judicial enforcement

IX. – 7:217: Applicable rules

(1) Judicial enforcement is to be undertaken according to the procedural rules of the member state where enforcement by a court or other competent authority is sought by the secured creditor.

(2) The secured creditor may apply to the court or other competent authority to exercise any of the rights under the preceding Subsections. These rights may be exercised by the court or other competent authority regardless of whether they are under the preceding Subsections dependent upon or excluded by a party agreement or a consent or the absence of an objection of the security provider or other persons.

Section 3:
Rules for retention of ownership devices

IX. – 7:301: Consequences of default
under retention of ownership devices

(1) The holder of a retention of ownership device exercises the rights under the retention of ownership device by termination of the contractual relationship under a contract of sale, hire-purchase, financial leasing or consignment according to the general rules of Book III, Chapter 3, Section 5.

(2) Any rights in the supplied asset that were transferred or created by the buyer, hire-purchaser, lessee or consignee will terminate, unless:
   (a) the latter had been authorised to create or transfer such rights;
   (b) the transferee is protected by IX. – 2:108 (Good faith acquisition of security right) to IX. – 2:111 (Security right in cash, negotiable instruments and documents) or IX. – 6:102 (Loss of proprietary security due to good faith acquisition of ownership); or
   (c) the rights of the transferee exceptionally enjoy priority over the rights of the holder of the retention of ownership device.

(3) On resale or re-leasing, the holder of the retention of ownership device is entitled to any surplus over the original price for the supplied assets which may be realised.

(4) A third party to whom the retention of ownership device has been transferred by agreement or by law is entitled to the rights under paragraphs (1) to (3).

IX. – 7:302: Possession, immobilisation and preservation

IX. – 7:201 (Creditor's right to possession of corporeal asset), IX. – 7:202 (Creditor's right to immobilise and to preserve encumbered asset) and IX. – 7:203 (Intervention of court or other authority) apply in relation to retention of ownership devices with the adaptations set out in IX. – 1:104 (Retention of ownership devices: applicable rules) paragraph (2).

Book X
Trusts

Chapter 1:
Fundamental provisions
Section 1:
Scope and relation to other rules

X. – 1:101: Trusts to which this Book applies
(1) This Book applies to trusts created under Chapter 2 (Constitution of trusts).
(2) With appropriate modifications this Book also applies to trusts:
    (a) constituted by:
        (i) a declaration to that effect set out in an enactment; or
        (ii) a court order with prospective effect; or
    (b) arising by operation of law set out in an enactment relating to a matter not determined by these rules.
(3) In this Book, "court" includes a public officer or body, if authorised to act under the applicable national law, but does not include an arbitral tribunal.

X. – 1:102: Priority of the law of proprietary securities
In relation to trusts for security purposes, this Book is subject to the application of the rules in Book IX (Proprietary security in movable assets).

Section 2:
Definition, special legal effects and parties

X. – 1:201: Definition of a trust
A trust is a legal relationship in which a trustee is obliged to administer or dispose of one or more assets (the trust fund) in accordance with the terms governing the relationship (trust terms) to benefit a beneficiary or advance public benefit purposes.

X. – 1:202: Special legal effects of a trust

(1) A trust takes effect in accordance with the rules in Chapter 10 (Relations to third parties) with the effect that the trust fund is to be regarded as a patrimony distinct from the personal patrimony of the trustee and any other patrimonies vested in or managed by the trustee.

(2) In particular (and except for some reason other than merely that the trust fund is vested in the trustee):

    (a) the personal creditors of the trustee may not have recourse to the trust fund, whether by execution or by means of insolvency proceedings;

    (b) the trust fund is not subject to rules allocating property rights on the basis of matrimonial or family relationships; and

    (c) the trustee's successors are not entitled to benefit from the trust fund on the trustee's death.

X. – 1:203: Parties to a trust

(1) The truster is a person who constitutes or intends to constitute a trust by juridical act.

(2) The trustee is the person in whom the trust fund becomes or remains vested when the trust is created or subsequently on or after appointment and who has the obligation set out in X. – 1:201 (Definition of a trust).

(3) A beneficiary is a person who, according to the trust terms, has either a right to benefit or an eligibility for benefit from the trust fund.

(4) A trust auxiliary is a person who, according to the trust terms, has a power to appoint or remove a trustee or to consent to a trustee's resignation.

(5) Except as otherwise provided for by this Book:

    (a) a truster may also be a trustee or a beneficiary;

    (b) a trustee may also be a beneficiary; and

    (c) any of those parties to a trust may also be a trust auxiliary.

(6) In this Book a person's "successor" is the heir or representative who under the law of succession becomes entitled to that person's personal patrimony on that person's death. Where the context permits, a reference to a party (or former party) to a trust is a reference to that person's successor if that person has died.

X. – 1:204: Plurality of trustees

(1) Where there are several trustees, the trust is solidary.

(2) Where trust assets are vested in several trustees together, their co-ownership is joint.

X. – 1:205: Persons entitled to enforce
performance of trustee's obligations

(1) A beneficiary has a right to performance of the trustee's obligations so far as they relate to that beneficiary's right to benefit or eligibility for benefit.

(2) The persons who may enforce performance of the trustee's obligations under a trust to advance public benefit purposes are:

    (a) any public officer or body having that function; and

    (b) any other person having sufficient interest in the performance of the obligations.

(3) A trustee may enforce performance of the obligations of a co-trustee.

X. – 1:206: Right to benefit and eligibility for benefit

(1) A person has a right to benefit if the trust terms require the trustee in given circumstances to dispose of all or part of the trust fund so as to confer a benefit on that person.

(2) A person has an eligibility for benefit if the trust terms permit the trustee in given circumstances to dispose of all or part of the trust fund so as to confer a benefit on that person, but whether or not that person is to obtain a benefit depends on an exercise of discretion by the trustee or another.

(3) A beneficiary's eligibility for benefit becomes a right to benefit if the trustee gives the beneficiary notice of a decision to confer benefit on that beneficiary in accordance with the trust terms governing that eligibility.

(4) In this Book "benefit" does not include the exercise by a trustee of a right of recourse to the trust fund.

Section 3:
Modifications of and additions to general rules

X. – 1:301: Extended meaning of gratuitous
(1) In this Book "gratuitous" means done or provided without reward.
(2) A juridical act or a benefit is also regarded as gratuitous in this Book if, considering the value of the rights created by the juridical act or the benefit provided, the value of the reward is so trivial that fairness requires it to be disregarded.

X. – 1:302: Notice
(1) Where this Book requires notice to be given to a person, but it is not reasonably practical to do so, notice may be given instead to the court.
(2) Where there are several trustees, a requirement to give notice to the trustees is satisfied by giving notice to any one of them, but a notice relating to a change in trustees must be given to a trustee who will continue to be a trustee after the change takes effect.

X. – 1:303: Mandatory nature of rules
The rules of this Book are mandatory, except as otherwise provided.

Chapter 2:
Constitution of trusts
Section 1:
Basic rules on constitution by juridical act

X. – 2:101: Requirements for constitution
A trust is constituted in relation to a fund vested in the truster, without any further requirement, if:
(a) the truster declares an intention to constitute a trust in relation to that fund;
(b) the declaration satisfies the requirements set out in X. – 2:201 (Requirements for a declaration); and
(c) either X. – 2:102 (Constitution by transfer) or X. – 2:103 (Constitution without transfer) applies.

X. – 2:102: Constitution by transfer

(1) If the other requirements for constitution are satisfied, a trust is constituted when in implementation of the declaration the fund is transferred to a person who agrees to be a trustee or is identified in the declaration as a person who is or is to be a trustee.

(2) The rules on contracts for donation apply analogously to an agreement between truster and intended trustee for the transfer of the fund in the truster's lifetime.

(3) Where the truster has made a binding unilateral undertaking to constitute a trust to a person who is intended to be a trustee of the fund, that person is a trustee of the right to performance of the obligation created by the undertaking, unless that right is rejected.

X. – 2:103: Constitution without transfer

(1) If the other requirements for constitution are satisfied, a trust is constituted by the declaration alone, without a transfer, if:
  (a) the declaration indicates that the truster is to be a sole trustee;
  (b) the declaration is testamentary and does not provide for a trustee; or
  (c) (i) the truster does all of the acts required of the truster to transfer the fund to the intended trustee,
     (ii) the intended trustee does not or cannot accept the fund, and
     (iii) the declaration does not provide otherwise.

(2) When a trust is constituted under paragraph (1), the truster becomes a trustee.

Section 2:
Declaration

X. – 2:201: Requirements for a declaration

(1) The requirements referred to in Section 1 (Basic rules on constitution by juridical act) for a declaration of an intention to constitute a trust are that:
  (a) the declaration is made by the truster or a person who has authority to make it on the truster's behalf; and
  (b) the declaration complies with any requirement as to form set out in X. – 2:203 (Formal requirements for declaration).

(2) No notice or publication of the declaration to any party is required.

X. – 2:202: Mode of declaration

(1) A person declares an intention to constitute a trust when that person by statements or conduct indicates an intention that the person in whom the fund is or is to be vested is to be legally bound as a trustee.

(2) In determining whether one or more statements contained in a testamentary or other instrument determining rights over an asset amount to a declaration of an intention to constitute a trust in relation to that asset, an interpretation of those statements which gives effect to their entirety is to be preferred.

X. – 2:203: Formal requirements for declaration

(1) Where the transfer of a fund requires the making of an instrument by the transferor, the declaration of an intention to constitute a trust is of no effect unless contained in the instrument of transfer or made in the same or an equivalent form.

(2) A declaration that the truster is to be the sole trustee is of no effect unless made in the same form as a unilateral undertaking to donate.

(3) Where the trust is to be created on the death of the maker of the declaration, the declaration is of no effect unless made by testamentary instrument.

X. – 2:204: Revocation or variation of declaration

(1) The maker of a declaration may revoke or vary the declaration or a term of the declaration at any time before the trust is constituted.

(2) A revocation or variation is of no effect unless it satisfies the formality requirements, if any, which applied to the declaration.

(3) However, a declaration or term set out in an instrument may be revoked by substantially destroying or defacing that instrument, so far as it relates to that declaration or term, if the applicable national rules permit a statement intended to have legal effect contained in such an instrument to be revoked by that means.

X. – 2:205: Effects when declaration does not satisfy requirements

If the fund is transferred to the intended trustee in implementation of a declaration which does not satisfy the requirements of X. – 2:201 (Requirements for a declaration), the transferee takes the fund on the terms of a trust to re-transfer the fund to the truster.

Section 3:
Refusal of trust and rejection of right to benefit

X. – 2:301: Right of trustee to refuse the trust
(1) If a person has become a trustee without agreeing to act when a trust is constituted, that person may refuse to act as a trustee by notice to:
  (a) the truster; or
  (b) any co-trustee who has full legal capacity and agrees to act as a trustee.
(2) Refusal may take the form of either a rejection of all the rights which have vested or a disclaimer of the whole trust, but operates as both a rejection and a disclaimer.
(3) A refusal may not be revoked.
(4) Where a person reasonably incurs costs in order to refuse, that person has a right to be reimbursed by any co-trustees who accept the trust fund and agree to act or, if there are no such co-trustees, the truster.
(5) Where a sole trustee refuses or there is no co-trustee who accepts the trust fund and agrees to act, the truster becomes a trustee of the fund in accordance with X. – 2:103 (Constitution without transfer) paragraph (1)(c), unless the declaration of the intention to constitute a trust provides otherwise.
(6) Subject to the previous paragraphs of this Article, the requirements for a refusal and its effects are determined by the application or analogous application of II. – 4:303 (Right or benefit may be rejected).

X. – 2:302: Rejection of right to benefit or eligibility for benefit
A beneficiary's right under II. – 4:303 (Right or benefit may be rejected) to reject a right to benefit or an eligibility for benefit is exercised by giving notice to the trustees.

Section 4:
Additional rules for particular instances

X. – 2:401: Whether donation or trust
(1) Where a person transfers an asset to another gratuitously and it is uncertain whether or to what extent the transferor intends to donate

the asset or to constitute a trust in respect of it for the benefit of the transferor, it is presumed that the transferor intends:

(a) to donate to the transferee, if this would be consistent with the relationship between the parties and past or concurrent dealings of the transferor;

(b) in any other case, that the transferee be a trustee for the benefit of the transferor.

(2) A presumption in paragraph (1) may be rebutted (and the alternative intention in paragraph (1) established) by showing that at the time of transfer the transferor did not or, as the case may be, did intend to dispose of the asset for the exclusive benefit of the transferee.

(3) Paragraphs (1) and (2) apply correspondingly where the transfer is to several transferees (including where the transfer is to the transferor and another).

(4) Where it is shown or presumed that the transferor intends to dispose of the fund for the benefit of a transferee only in part, or for the benefit of one transferee, but not a co–transferee, the transferor is to be regarded as intending to constitute a trust for the benefit of the transferee to that extent.

X. – 2:402: Priority of rules of succession law

Where the trust is to take effect on the truster's death, the trust is subject to the prior application of those rules of succession law which determine:

(a) how the deceased's estate is to be disposed of in satisfaction of the funeral costs and debts of the deceased; and

(b) (i) whether the truster was free to dispose of any part of the fund,

    (ii) whether any person has a claim in respect of any part of the fund by reason of a family or other connection to the deceased, and

    (iii) how such claims are to be satisfied.

X. – 2:403: Trust in respect of right to legacy pending transfer of legacy

Where a truster declares that a legatee is to be a trustee in relation to a legacy from the truster and that declaration satisfies the requirements set out in X. – 2:201 (Requirements for a declaration), but the legacy has not yet been transferred, the legatee is a trustee of the right against the truster's successor which arises in respect of the legacy on the truster's death.

Chapter 3:
Trust fund
Section I:
Requirements for the initial trust fund

X. – 3:101: Trust fund

(1) Trust assets, whether or not of the same kind, form a single trust fund if
    they are vested in the same trustees and either:
- (a) the trust terms relating to the assets indicate that they form a single
    fund or require them to be administered together; or
- (b) separate trusts relating to the assets are merged in performance of
    the obligations under those trusts.

(2) Where trusts are constituted at the same time, on the same terms, and
    with the same trustees, the trust assets form a single trust fund unless
    the trust terms provide otherwise.

(3) In this Book "part of the trust fund" means a share of the trust fund, a
    specific asset or share of an asset in the fund, or a specific amount to
    be provided out of the fund.

X. – 3:102: Permissible trust assets

Trust assets may consist of proprietary or other rights, so far as these are
transferable.

X. – 3:103: Ascertainability and segregation of the trust fund

(1) A trust is only created in relation to a fund in so far as, at the time the
    trust is to come into effect,
- (a) the fund is sufficiently defined in the trust terms or the assets
    forming the fund are otherwise ascertainable; and
- (b) the fund is segregated from other assets.

(2) A declaration of intention to create a trust in relation to an unsegre-
    gated fund is to be regarded, so far as the other terms of the declaration
    permit, as a declaration of an intention to create a trust of the entire
    mixture containing the fund on the terms that:
- (a) the trustee is obliged to segregate the intended trust fund; and
- (b) until the fund is segregated, the rights and obligations envisaged
    by the terms of the declaration apply in relation to a corresponding
    part of the mixture.

Section 2:
Changes to the trust fund

X. – 3:201: Additions to the trust fund
(1) After a trust is created, an asset which is capable of being a trust asset
becomes part of the trust fund if it is acquired by a trustee:
  (a) in performance of the obligations under the trust;
  (b) as an addition to or by making use of the trust fund;
  (c) by making use of information or an opportunity obtained in the
      capacity of trustee, if the use is not in accordance with the terms of
      the trust; or
  (d) when or after the trustee disposed of that asset otherwise than in
      accordance with the terms of the trust.
(2) Where there are several trustees, an asset may become part of the trust
    fund in accordance with this Article without being acquired by all of
    them.

X. – 3:202: Subtractions from the trust fund
(1) An asset ceases to be part of the trust fund when it ceases to be vested
    in a person who is under the obligation set out in X. – 1:201 (Definition
    of a trust).
(2) Where there are several trustees, an asset remains part of the trust fund
    so long as it is vested in at least one of the trustees in that capacity.

X. – 3:203: Mixing of the trust fund with other assets
(1) If trust assets are mixed with other assets vested in the trustee in such a
    way that the trust assets cease to be identifiable, a trust arises in re-
    spect of the mixture and VIII. – 5:202 (Commingling) applies analo-
    gously, as if each patrimony had a different owner, so as to determine
    the share of the mixture which is to be administered and disposed of in
    accordance with the original trust.
(2) If the other assets are the personal patrimony of the trustee, any di-
    minution in the mixture is to be allocated to the trustee's personal
    share.

X. – 3:204: Loss or exhaustion of trust fund
(1) A trust ends when the trust fund has been completely disposed of in performance of the obligations under the trust or for any other reason there ceases to be a trust fund.
(2) Where the trustee is liable to reinstate the trust fund as a result of non-performance of obligations under the trust, the trust revives if the trust fund is reinstated.

Chapter 4:
Trust terms and invalidity
Section 1:
Trust terms

X. – 4:101: Interpretation
Without prejudice to the other rules on the interpretation of unilateral juridical acts, if the meaning of a trust term cannot otherwise be established, interpretations to be preferred are those which:
(a) give effect to the entirety of the words and expressions used;
(b) prevent reasonable conduct of a trustee from amounting to a non-performance;
(c) prevent or best reduce any incompleteness in provision for disposal of the trust fund; and
(d) confer on the truster a right to benefit or enlarge such right, if the trust is constituted gratuitously in the truster's lifetime and the truster has or may have reserved such a right.

X. – 4:102: Incomplete disposal of the trust fund
(1) To the extent that the trust terms and the rules of this Book do not otherwise dispose of the trust fund in circumstances which have arisen, the trust fund is to be disposed of for the benefit of the truster.
(2) However, if the incomplete disposal of the trust fund arises because effect cannot be given to a trust for advancement of a public benefit purpose or because performance of the obligations under such a trust does not exhaust the trust fund, the trust fund is to be disposed of for the advancement of the public benefit purpose which most closely resembles the original purpose.

X. – 4:103: Ascertainability of beneficiaries

(1) A trust term which purports to confer a right to benefit is valid only if
the beneficiary is sufficiently identified by the truster or is otherwise
ascertainable at the time the benefit is due.

(2) A trust term which permits a trustee to benefit those members of a
class of persons which the trustee or a third person selects is valid only
if, at the time the selection is permitted, it can be determined with
reasonable certainty whether any given person is a member of that
class.

(3) A person may be a beneficiary notwithstanding that that person comes
into existence only after the trust is created.

X. – 4:104: Ascertainability of right to benefit or eligibility for benefit

(1) A right to benefit or eligibility for benefit is valid only in so far as the
benefit is sufficiently defined in the trust terms or is otherwise ascertainable at the time the benefit is due or to be conferred.

(2) If the benefit to be conferred is not ascertainable only because a third
party cannot or does not make a choice, the trustees may make that
choice unless the trust terms provide otherwise.

X. – 4:105: Trusts to pay creditors

A trust for the purpose of paying a debt, or for the benefit of a creditor as
such, takes effect as a trust to benefit the debtor by a performance of the
debtor's obligation discharging the debtor.

Section 2:
Invalidity

X. – 4:201: Avoidance by the truster

Without prejudice to other necessary adaptations, Book II Chapter 7
(Grounds of invalidity) is modified as follows in its application to trusts
constituted gratuitously in the truster's lifetime:

(a) the truster may avoid the trust or a trust term if the trust was constituted or the term included because of a mistake of fact or law, regardless of whether the requirements of II. – 7:201 (Mistake) paragraph
(1)(b) are satisfied;

(b) a truster who was dependent on, or was the more vulnerable party in a relationship of trust with, a beneficiary may avoid the trust or a trust term in so far as it provides for benefit to that beneficiary unless that beneficiary proves that the beneficiary did not exploit the truster's situation by taking an excessive benefit or grossly unfair advantage;

(c) the reasonable time for giving notice of avoidance (II. – 7:210 (Time)) does not commence so long as:

    (i) the truster exercises an exclusive right to benefit from the income; or

    (ii) the trust fund consists of one or more rights to benefit which are not yet due; and

(d) where sub-paragraph (c)(i) applies, acceptance of benefit is not to be regarded as an implied confirmation of the trust.

X. – 4:202: Protection of trustees and third parties after avoidance

(1) The trustee's title to the trust fund is unaffected by avoidance.

(2) Unless the trustee knew or could reasonably be expected to know that the trust or trust term might be avoided:

    (a) a trustee is not liable in respect of any administration or disposition of the trust fund which was in accordance with the terms of the trust before the trust was avoided;

    (b) a trustee may invoke against the person entitled to benefit as a result of avoidance defences which the trustee could have invoked against the beneficiary who had a right to that benefit before avoidance; and

    (c) a trustee retains any right of recourse to the trust fund which arose before avoidance.

(3) Avoidance of the trust does not affect the rights of a third party who before avoidance acquired a beneficiary's right to benefit, or a security right or other limited right in that right to benefit, if:

    (a) the third party neither knew nor had reason to know that the trust or trust term could be avoided; and

    (b) the disposition is not gratuitous.

X. – 4:203: Unenforceable trust purposes

(1) A trust which is for a purpose other than to benefit beneficiaries or to advance public benefit purposes takes effect as a trust for the truster.

(2) The trustee has a revocable authority to dispose of the trust fund in accordance with the original trust for the advancement of the unenforceable purpose in so far as:

    (a) advancement of that purpose does not infringe a fundamental principle or mandatory rule and is not contrary to the public interest;

    (b) it can be determined with reasonable certainty whether any given disposal of the trust fund is or is not for its advancement; and

    (c) the disposal is not manifestly disproportionate to any likely benefit from that disposal.

Chapter 5:
Trustee decision-making and powers
Section 1:
Trustee decision-making

X. – 5:101: Trustee discretion

(1) Subject to the obligations of a trustee under this Book and exceptions provided for by other rules, the trustees are free to determine whether, when and how the exercise of their powers and discretions is best suited to performing their obligations under the trust.

(2) Except in so far as the trust terms or other rules provide otherwise, the trustees are not bound by, and are not to regard themselves as bound by, any directions or wishes of any of the parties to the trust or other persons.

(3) The trustees are not obliged to disclose the reasons for the exercise of their discretion unless the trust is for the advancement of a public benefit purpose or the trust terms provide otherwise.

X. – 5:102: Decision-making by several trustees

If there are several trustees, their powers and discretions are exercised by simple majority decision unless the trust terms or other rules of this Book provide otherwise.

X. – 5:103: Conflict of interest in exercise of power or discretion
Unless the trust terms provide otherwise, a trustee may not participate in a decision to exercise or not to exercise a power or discretion if the effect of the decision is to confer, confirm, or enlarge a right to benefit or eligibility for benefit in favour of the trustee.

Section 2:
Powers of a trustee
Sub-section 1:
General rules

X. – 5:201: Powers in general
(1) Except where restricted by the trust terms or other rules of this Book, a trustee may do any act in performance of the obligations under the trust which:
  (a) an owner of the fund might lawfully do; or
  (b) a person might be authorised to do on behalf of another.
(2) Subject to restrictions or modifications in the trust terms, the other Articles of this Section provide for the powers of a trustee in particular cases.

X. – 5:202: Restriction in case of minimum number of trustees
(1) Where there are fewer trustees than a minimum required by the trust terms or these rules, the trustees may only exercise:
  (a) a power to appoint trustees;
  (b) the right to apply to court for assistance;
  (c) a right under X. – 6:201 (Right of reimbursement and indemnification out of the trust fund); and
  (d) any other right or power of a trustee to the extent that its exercise is:
    (i) expressly provided for in the circumstances by the trust terms;
    (ii) necessary for the preservation of the trust fund; or
    (iii) necessary for the satisfaction of trust debts whose performance is due or impending.
(2) If the trust is constituted by a transfer to at least two trustees the minimum number of trustees is two, unless the trust terms provide otherwise.

Sub-section 2:
Particular powers of a trustee

X. – 5:203: Power to authorise agent

(1) The trustees may authorise an agent to act on behalf of the trustees and, subject to the restrictions set out in the following Articles of this Section, may entrust to another performance of obligations under the trust.

(2) Several trustees may authorise one of them to act on their behalf.

(3) However, personal performance by a trustee is required for decisions as to whether or how to exercise:
   (a) a discretion to confer benefit on a beneficiary or to choose a public benefit purpose to be advanced or its manner of advancement;
   (b) a power to change the trustees; or
   (c) a power to delegate performance of obligations under the trust.

(4) A person to whom performance of an obligation is entrusted has the same obligations as a trustee, so far as they relate to that performance.

(5) A trustee is obliged not to conclude, without good reason, a contract of mandate which is not in writing or which includes the following terms:
   (a) a term conferring an irrevocable mandate;
   (b) terms excluding the obligations of an agent set out in Book IV. D., Chapter 3, Section 1 (Main obligations of agent) or modifying them to the detriment of the principal;
   (c) a term permitting the agent to subcontract;
   (d) terms permitting a conflict of interest on the part of the agent;
   (e) a term excluding or restricting the agent's liability to the principal for non-performance.

(6) The trustees are obliged to keep the performance of the agent under review and, if required in the circumstances, give a direction to the agent or terminate the mandate relationship.

X. – 5:204: Power to transfer title to person undertaking to be a trustee

(1) The trustees may transfer trust assets to a person who undertakes to be a trustee in relation to the assets and to dispose of them as the original trustees direct and in default of any such direction to transfer them back to the original trustees on demand.

(2) The recipient must be:
    (a) a person who gives such undertakings in the course of business;
    (b) a legal person controlled by the trustees; or
    (c) a legal person designated in an enactment as eligible to carry out such a trust obligation or satisfying requirements set out therein for this purpose
(3) X. – 5:203 (Power to authorise agent) paragraphs (5) and (6) apply correspondingly.

X. – 5:205: Power to transfer physical control to a storer
(1) The trustees may place trust assets and documents relating to those assets in the physical control of a person who undertakes to keep the trust assets safe and to deliver them back to the trustees on demand.
(2) X. – 5:204 (Power to transfer title to person undertaking to be a trustee) paragraphs (2) and (3) apply correspondingly.

X. – 5:206: Power to delegate
A trustee may entrust to another the performance of any of the trustee's obligations under the trust and the exercise of any of the trustee's powers, including the exercise of a discretion, authority to dispose of trust assets and the power to delegate, but remains responsible for performance in accordance with III. – 2:106 (Performance entrusted to another).

X. – 5:207: Power to select investments
In so far as the trustees are obliged to invest the trust fund, the trustees may invest in any form of investment and determine the particular manner of investment which is best suited to fulfil that obligation.

X. – 5:208: Power to submit trust accounts for audit
Where appropriate, a trustee may submit the trust accounts for an audit by an independent and competent auditor.

Chapter 6:
Obligations and rights of trustees and trust auxiliaries
Section 1:
Obligations of a trustee
Sub-section 1:
General rules

X. – 6:101: General obligation of a trustee

(1) A trustee is obliged to administer the trust fund and exercise any power to dispose of the fund as a prudent manager of another's affairs for the benefit of the beneficiaries or the advancement of the public benefit purposes, in accordance with the law and the trust terms.

(2) In particular, a trustee is obliged to act with the required care and skill, fairly and in good faith.

(3) Except in so far as the trust terms provide otherwise:
  (a) these obligations include the particular obligations set out in X. – 6:102 (Required care and skill) and the following sub-section; and
  (b) an administration or disposal of the trust fund is of benefit to a beneficiary only if it is for that person's economic benefit.

X. – 6:102: Required care and skill

(1) A trustee is required to act with the care and skill which can be expected of a reasonably competent and careful person managing another's affairs, having regard to whether the trustee has a right to remuneration.

(2) If the trustee is acting in the course of a profession, the trustee must act with the care and skill that is expected of a member of that profession.

Sub-section 2:
Particular obligations of a trustee

X. – 6:103: Obligations to segregate, safeguard and insure

(1) A trustee is obliged to keep the trust fund segregated from other patrimony and to keep the trust assets safe.

(2) In particular, a trustee may not invest in assets which are especially at risk of misappropriation unless particular care is taken for their safe-

keeping. Where the asset is a document embodying a right to a performance which is owed to whoever is the holder of the document, such care is taken if the document is placed in a storer's safekeeping in accordance with X. – 5:205 (Power to transfer physical control to a storer).

(3) So far as it is possible and appropriate to do so, the trustee is obliged to insure the trust assets against loss.

X. – 6:104: Obligation to inform and report

(1) A trustee is obliged to inform a beneficiary who has a right to benefit of the existence of the trust and that beneficiary's right.

(2) A trustee is obliged to make reasonable efforts to inform a beneficiary who has an eligibility for benefit of the existence of the trust and that beneficiary's eligibility.

(3) In determining what efforts are reasonable for the purposes of paragraph (2), regard is to be had to:
  (a) whether the expense required is proportionate to the value of the benefit which might be conferred on that beneficiary;
  (b) whether the beneficiary is a member of a class whose members the trustee is required to benefit; and
  (c) the practicalities of identifying and communicating with the beneficiary.

(4) So far as appropriate, a trustee is obliged to make available information about the state and investment of the trust fund, trust debts, and disposals of trust assets and their proceeds.

X. – 6:105: Obligation to keep trust accounts

A trustee is obliged to keep accounts in respect of the trust funds (trust accounts).

X. – 6:106: Obligation to permit inspection and copying of trust documents

(1) A trustee must permit a beneficiary or other person entitled to enforce performance of the obligations under the trust to inspect the trust documents and to make copies of them at that person's own expense.

(2) Paragraph (1) does not apply to:
  (a) the opinions of a legal adviser relating to actual or contemplated legal proceedings by the trustees in that capacity against the per-

son seeking inspection; and evidence gathered for such proceedings;

(b) communications between the trustees and other beneficiaries and any other communications whose disclosure would result in a breach of confidence owed by the trustees in that capacity to another.

(3) The trustees may refuse inspection and copying of trust documents so far as these relate to information which is confidential to the trustees in that capacity if the beneficiary does not provide adequate assurance that the confidentiality will be maintained.

(4) Unless the trust is for the advancement of public benefit purposes, the trustees may also refuse inspection and copying of documents so far as the documents disclose the reasons for the trustees' decision to exercise or not to exercise a discretion, the deliberations of the trustees which preceded that decision, and material relevant to the deliberations.

(5) The trust terms may enlarge the rights of inspection and copying which are provided for by this Article.

(6) In this Book "trust documents" are:

(a) any documents containing the truster's declaration of intentions relating to the trust (whether or not intended to be binding) and any juridical act or court order varying the trust terms;

(b) minutes of meetings of the trustees;

(c) records made and notices and other communications in writing received by a trustee in that capacity, including the opinions of a legal adviser engaged by a trustee at the trust fund's expense;

(d) any documents containing juridical acts concluded or made by the trustees;

(e) receipts for disposal of trust assets; and

(f) the trust accounts.

X. – 6:107: Obligation to invest

(1) A trustee is obliged to invest the trust fund, so far as available for investment, and in particular:

(a) to dispose of assets which ordinarily neither produce income nor increase in value and to invest the proceeds;

> (b) to take professional advice on investment of the fund, if the trustees lack the expertise required for the efficient and prudent investment of funds of the size and nature of the trust fund;
> (c) to make a spread of investments in which overall:
>> (i) the risks of failure or loss of particular investments are diversified; and
>> (ii) the expected gain significantly outweighs the potential failure or loss;

unless the trust fund is so small that a spread of investments is inappropriate; and

> (d) to review at appropriate intervals the suitableness of retaining or changing the investments.

(2) A trustee is not obliged to invest assets:
> (a) which are imminently required for transfer to or use by a beneficiary or for satisfaction of a trust debt; or
> (b) whose investment would otherwise impede the trustees in carrying out their other obligations under this Book.

(3) The obligation to invest does not authorise a trustee to dispose of trust assets which according to the trust terms are to be retained by the trustees or transferred in kind to a beneficiary.

X. – 6:108: Obligation not to acquire trust assets or trust creditors' rights

(1) A trustee is obliged not to purchase a trust asset or the right of a trust creditor against the trustees, whether personally or by means of an agent.

(2) A contract for the sale of a trust asset which is concluded as a result of non-performance of this obligation may be avoided by any other party to the trust or any person entitled to enforce performance of the obligations under the trust.

(3) The right to avoid is in addition to any remedy for non-performance.

(4) This Article applies with appropriate modifications to other contracts for the acquisition or use of a trust asset or a right corresponding to a trust debt.

X. – 6:109: Obligation not to obtain unauthorised enrichment or advantage

(1) A trustee is obliged not to make use of the trust fund, or information or an opportunity obtained in the capacity of trustee, to obtain an enrichment unless that use is authorised by the trust terms.

(2) A trustee may not set off a right to performance from a beneficiary, which is owed to the trustee in a personal capacity, against that beneficiary's right to benefit.

X. – 6:110: Obligations regarding co-trustees

A trustee is obliged to:

(a) cooperate with co-trustees in performing the obligations under the trust; and

(b) take appropriate action if a trustee knows or has reason to suspect that:

(i) a co-trustee has failed to perform any obligation under, or arising out of, the trust, or such non-performance is impending; and

(ii) the non-performance is likely to result or have resulted in loss to the trust fund.

Section 2:
Rights of a trustee

X. – 6:201: Right to reimbursement and indemnification out of the trust fund

A trustee has a right to reimbursement or indemnification out of the trust fund in respect of expenditure and trust debts which the trustee incurs in performance of the obligations under the trust.

X. – 6:202: Right to remuneration out of the trust fund

(1) A trustee has a right to such remuneration out of the trust fund as is provided for by the trust terms.

(2) Unless this is inconsistent with the trust terms, a trustee who acts as a trustee in the course of a profession has a right to reasonable remuneration out of the trust fund for work done in performance of the obligations under the trust.

(3) Paragraph (2) does not apply if:
- (a) the trustee, in the capacity of beneficiary, is entitled to significant benefit from the trust fund; or
- (b) the trust was created as a result of a contract between the trustee and the truster; or
- (c) the trust is for the advancement of public benefit purposes.

X. – 6:203: Rights in respect of unauthorised acquisitions

(1) This Article applies where:
- (a) a trustee acquires an asset or other enrichment as a result of a non-performance of an obligation under the trust; and
- (b) the asset becomes part of the trust fund or the enrichment is added to the trust fund in performance of an obligation to disgorge.

(2) The trustee has a right to reimbursement or indemnification for any expenditure or obligation which it was necessary to incur to make the acquisition. If the trustee previously satisfied in full or in part a liability under X. – 7:201 (Liability of trustee to reinstate the trust fund), the trustee has a right to reimbursement from the trust fund to the extent that after the acquisition the trust fund is more than reinstated.

(3) The trustee also has a right to reasonable remuneration if:
- (a) the acquisition was made in good faith to increase the trust fund; and
- (b) the trustee would be entitled to remuneration under X. – 6:202 (Right to remuneration out of the trust fund) paragraph (2)(b) if the acquisition had been in performance of an obligation under the trust.

(4) If the acquisition resulted from a non-performance of the obligation under X. – 6:109 (Obligation not to obtain unauthorised enrichment or advantage) to which a beneficiary validly consented, the trustee may waive the rights under paragraphs (2) and (3) and take over the consenting beneficiary's right to benefit from the acquisition.

(5) A trustee is not entitled under this Article to more than the value of the acquisition.

X. – 6:204: Corresponding rights against beneficiaries

(1) Where the right of a trustee under X. – 6:201 (Right to reimbursement and indemnification out of the trust fund) exceeds the trust fund, the trustee may recover the excess from the beneficiaries.

(2) The liability of a beneficiary under paragraph (1) is:
  (a) limited to the enrichment which that beneficiary has obtained in accordance with the trust terms; and
  (b) subject to the defence of disenrichment, VII. – 6:101 (Disenrichment) applying with appropriate adaptations.

(3) The right to recover under paragraph (1) ends six months after the right to reimbursement or indemnification has arisen.

X. – 6:205: Right to insure against personal liability at trust fund's expense

(1) A trustee has a right to reimbursement or indemnification out of the trust fund in respect of expenditure or a debt which the trustee reasonably incurs to obtain insurance against liability under X. – 7:201 (Liability of trustee to reinstate the trust fund).

(2) Paragraph (1) does not apply in so far as:
  (a) the trustee has a right to remuneration for performing the obligations under the trust; or
  (b) the insurance is against liability arising out of a non-performance which is intentional or grossly negligent.

Section 3:
Obligations of a trust auxiliary

X. – 6:301: Obligations of a trust auxiliary

(1) A trust auxiliary is obliged to disclose the identity of the trustees if this information is known to the trust auxiliary and is not otherwise apparent.

(2) In deciding whether to exercise a power a trust auxiliary is obliged:
  (a) to act in good faith; and
  (b) not to obtain an enrichment which is not authorised by the trust terms.

Chapter 7:
Remedies for non-performance
Section 1:
Specific performance, judicial review and ancillary remedies

X. – 7:101: Specific performance
(1) The enforcement of specific performance of an obligation under the trust includes the prevention of a trustee from disposing of or otherwise dealing with a trust asset otherwise than in accordance with the terms of the trust.
(2) Specific performance cannot be enforced if performance requires a trustee to exercise a discretion.

X. – 7:102: Judicial review
(1) On the application of a party to the trust or a person entitled to enforce performance of an obligation under the trust, a court may review a decision of the trustees or a trust auxiliary whether or how to exercise a power or discretion conferred on them by the trust terms or this Book.
(2) A former trustee who has been removed by the trustees or a trust auxiliary without the trustee's consent has a corresponding right to judicial review of that decision.
(3) A court may avoid a decision of the trustees or a trust auxiliary which is irrational or grossly unreasonable, motivated by irrelevant or improper considerations, or otherwise an abuse of power or outside the powers of the trustees or the trust auxiliary.

X. – 7:103: Further remedies
Other rules may provide for:
(a) accounts and inquiries concerning the trust fund and its administration and disposal, as directed by court order;
(b) payment or transfer into court of money or other assets in the trust fund;
(c) the appointment by court order of a receiver to administer a trust fund;
(d) the exercise of rights and powers of a trustee by a public officer or body, in particular in relation to trusts to advance public benefit purposes;
(e) suspension of the rights and powers of the trustees to administer and dispose of the fund;
in cases of actual or suspected non-performance of the obligations under the trust.

Section 2:
Reparation and disgorgement of unauthorised enrichment

X. – 7:201: Liability of trustee to reinstate the trust fund

(1) A trustee is liable to reinstate the trust fund in respect of loss caused to the trust fund by non-performance of any obligation under, or arising out of, the trust, if the non-performance:

    (a) is not excused; and

    (b) results from the trustee's failure to exercise the required care and skill.

(2) However, a person is liable under paragraph (1) only if that person knew, or it was manifest, that that person was a trustee.

(3) A trustee is not liable merely because a co-trustee, an agent or other person entrusted with performance, or an authorised recipient of trust assets has caused loss to the trust fund.

(4) Paragraph (3) does not prejudice any liability of the trustee arising:

    (a) under paragraph (1) out of the trustee's own non-performance of an obligation under the trust, in particular:

        (i) an obligation to act with the required care and skill when choosing to appoint or engage that person and agreeing the terms of the engagement; or

        (ii) the obligation to keep the performance of that person under review and, if required in the circumstances, to take measures to protect the trust fund; or

    (b) out of delegation of performance (X. – 5:206 (Power to delegate));

    (c) under VI. – 3:201 (Accountability for damage caused by employees and representatives); or

    (d) because the trustee induced, assisted or collaborated in that person's non-performance.

(5) III. – 3:702 (General measure of damages) applies with appropriate adaptations to determine the measure of reinstatement.

(6) The following rights of a trustee are suspended until the trustee has completely reinstated the trust fund:

    (a) any right of recourse to the trust fund; and

    (b) any right to benefit which the trustee has in the capacity of beneficiary.

(7) This Article is subject to the trust terms.

X. – 7:202: Liability of trustee to compensate a beneficiary

(1) A trustee who is liable under X. – 7:201 (Liability of trustee to reinstate the trust fund) is also obliged to compensate a beneficiary who, despite reinstatement of the trust fund, does not obtain a benefit to which that beneficiary was entitled or, if there had been no failure of performance, would have been entitled under the trust terms.

(2) The beneficiary has the same right to compensation as arises from non-performance of a contractual obligation.

(3) This Article is subject to the trust terms.

X. – 7:203: Disgorgement of unauthorised enrichment

Where a trustee obtains an enrichment as a result of non-performance of the obligation under X. – 6:109 (Obligation not to obtain unauthorised enrichment or advantage) and that enrichment does not become part of the trust fund under X. – 3:201 (Additions to the trust fund), the trustee is obliged to add the enrichment to the trust fund or, if that is not possible, to add its monetary value.

Section 3:
Defences

X. – 7:301: Consent of beneficiary to non-performance

(1) A trustee has a defence to liability to the extent that reinstatement, compensation or disgorgement would benefit a beneficiary who validly consented to the non-performance.

(2) A beneficiary consents to a non-performance when that beneficiary agrees to conduct of the trustee which amounts to a non-performance and either:

(a) the beneficiary knew that such conduct would amount to a non-performance; or

(b) it was manifest that such conduct would amount to a non-performance.

(3) Paragraph (1) applies whether or not the non-performance enriched or disadvantaged the beneficiary who consented.

(4) Where a beneficiary participates in the non-performance in the capacity of trustee, paragraph (1) applies in relation to any co-trustees who are liable. A right of recourse between the solidary debtors as regards

any residual liability to reinstate the trust fund or compensate a beneficiary is unaffected.

(5) A consent is not valid if it results from a mistake which was caused by false information given by the trustee or the trustee's non-performance of an obligation to inform.

X. – 7:302: Prescription

The general period of prescription for a right to performance of an obligation under a trust does not begin to run against a beneficiary until benefit to that beneficiary is due.

X. – 7:303 Protection of the trustee

(1) A trustee is discharged by performing to a person who, after reasonable inquiry, appears to be entitled to the benefit conferred.

(2) The right of the beneficiary who was entitled to the benefit against the recipient of the benefit arising under Book VII (Unjustified enrichment) is unaffected.

Section 4:
Solidary liability and forfeiture

X. – 7:401: Solidary liability

(1) Where several trustees are liable in respect of the same non-performance, their liability is solidary.

(2) As between the solidary debtors themselves, the shares of liability are in proportion to each debtor's relative responsibility for the non-performance, having regard to each debtor's skills and experience as a trustee.

(3) A debtor's relative responsibility for a non-performance to which that debtor consented is not reduced merely because that debtor took no active part in bringing it about.

X. – 7:402: Forfeiture of collaborating beneficiary's right to benefit

(1) Where a beneficiary collaborated in a trustee's non-performance, a court may order on the application of that trustee or another beneficiary that the right to benefit of the beneficiary who collaborated be forfeited.

(2) The right to benefit of a beneficiary who validly consented to the non-performance, but did not collaborate in it, may be forfeited only to the extent that the beneficiary has been enriched by the non-performance.

(3) To the extent that a beneficiary's right to benefit is forfeited under this Article, benefit which is otherwise due to that beneficiary is to be applied so as to satisfy the trustee's liability until either the liability is extinguished or the right to benefit is exhausted.

Chapter 8:
Change of trustees or trust auxiliary
Section 1:
General rules on change of trustees

X. – 8:101: Powers to change trustees in general

(1) After the creation of a trust, a person may be appointed a trustee and a trustee may resign or be removed:
- (a) in accordance with a power:
  - (i) under the trust terms or
  - (ii) conferred on the trustees by this Section; or
- (b) by court order under this Section.

(2) The exercise of a power within paragraph (1)(a) is of no effect unless it is in writing. The same applies to a binding direction to trustees regarding the exercise of such a power.

(3) An exercise of a power under the trust terms by a person who is not also a continuing trustee does not take effect until notice is given to the continuing trustees.

(4) The resignation or removal of a sole trustee is effective only if a substitute trustee is appointed at the same time.

X. – 8:102: Powers to change trustees conferred on trustees

(1) The powers conferred by this Section on trustees may only be exercised:
- (a) by unanimous decision; and
- (b) if in the circumstances a trust auxiliary does not have a corresponding power or the trust auxiliary cannot or does not exercise such a power within a reasonable period after a request to do so by the trustees.

(2) Subject to paragraph (1), the trustees are obliged to exercise their powers under this Section in accordance with any joint direction by the

beneficiaries if the beneficiaries have a joint right to terminate the trust in respect of the whole fund.

(3) The trust terms may modify or exclude the powers conferred by this Section on trustees.

Section 2:
Appointment of trustees

X. – 8:201: General restrictions on appointments

(1) An appointment of a person as trustee is of no effect if:
  (a) it is manifest that the co-trustees would have power to remove that person, if appointed, on grounds of that person's inability, refusal to act, or unsuitability;
  (b) the person appointed does not agree to act as trustee; or
  (c) the appointment exceeds a maximum number of trustees provided for by the trust terms.

(2) A provision in the trust terms that there is to be only one trustee takes effect as a maximum of two.

X. – 8:202: Appointment by trust auxiliary or trustees

(1) The trustees may appoint one or more additional trustees.
(2) The continuing trustees may appoint a substitute trustee for a person who has ceased to be a trustee.
(3) Unless the trust terms provide otherwise, a self-appointment by a trust auxiliary is of no effect.

X. – 8:203: Appointment by court order

On the application of any party to the trust or any person entitled to enforce performance of an obligation under the trust, a court may appoint:

(a) a substitute trustee for a person who has ceased to be a trustee, or
(b) one or more additional trustees,
  if in the circumstances:
    (i) no one else is able and willing to exercise a power to appoint; and
    (ii) the appointment is likely to promote the efficient and prudent administration and disposal of the trust fund in accordance with the trust terms.

Section 3:
Resignation of trustees

X. – 8:301: Resignation with consent of trust auxiliary or co-trustees

(1) A trust auxiliary who may appoint a substitute trustee in the event of the trustee's resignation may consent to a resignation.

(2) A trust auxiliary may consent to a resignation without the consent of the continuing trustees only if a substitute trustee is appointed at the same time.

(3) The continuing trustees may consent to a resignation.

(4) A trustee may only resign with the consent of a trust auxiliary or co-trustees if after resignation there will be at least two continuing trustees or a special trustee.

(5) Special trustees, for the purposes of this Book, are:
  (a) any public officer or body having the function of acting as a trustee; and
  (b) any legal persons designated as such in an enactment or satisfying requirements set out in an enactment for this purpose.

X. – 8:302: Resignation with approval of court

A court may approve the resignation of a trustee who cannot otherwise resign if it is fair to release the trustee from obligations under the trust, having regard in particular to whether after resignation an efficient and prudent administration and disposal of the trust fund in accordance with the trust terms can be secured.

Section 4:
Removal of trustees

X. – 8:401: Removal by trust auxiliary or co-trustees

(1) Where a court might remove a trustee on grounds of inability, refusal to act, or unsuitability, the continuing trustees may remove that trustee.

(2) The removal of a trustee by a trust auxiliary or the trustees does not take effect until notice of the removal is given to the trustee who is to be removed.

X. – 8:402: Removal by court order

(1) On the application of any party to the trust, a court may remove a trustee without that trustee's consent and regardless of the trust terms if it is inappropriate for the trustee to remain a trustee, in particular on grounds of the trustee's:

(a) inability;

(b) actual or anticipated material non-performance of any obligation under, or arising out of, the trust;

(c) unsuitability;

(d) permanent or recurrent fundamental disagreement with co-trustees on a matter requiring a unanimous decision of the trustees; or

(e) other interests which substantially conflict with performance of the obligations under, or arising out of, the trust.

Section 5:
Effect of change of trustees

X. – 8:501: Effect on trustees' obligations and rights

(1) A person who is appointed a trustee becomes bound by the trust and acquires the corresponding rights and powers. Subject to the following paragraphs of this Article, a trustee who resigns or is removed is released from the trust and loses those rights and powers.

(2) The obligation to cooperate with co-trustees does not end until the expiry of a reasonable period after resignation or removal.

(3) A former trustee's right of recourse to the trust fund takes effect as a right against the continuing trustees. A right to reimbursement, indemnification or remuneration by a beneficiary is unaffected.

(4) A former trustee remains bound by:

(a) the obligation in X. – 6:109 (Obligation not to obtain unauthorised enrichment or advantage);

(b) trust debts; and

(c) obligations arising from non-performance.

X. – 8:502: Vesting and divesting of trust assets

(1) Title to a trust asset vests in a person on appointment as a trustee, without a court order to that effect, if that title is:

- (a) capable of transfer by agreement between a transferor and a transferee without the necessity for any further act of transfer or formality; or
- (b) regarded under the applicable national law as vested in the trustees as a body.
(2) The vesting of an asset in a person who is appointed a trustee does not divest any continuing trustees.
(3) A person who resigns or is removed as a trustee is divested correspondingly.

X. – 8:503: Transmission of trust documents

A continuing or substitute trustee is entitled to the delivery up of trust documents in the possession of a former trustee. The person in possession has the right to make and retain copies at that person's own expense.

X. – 8:504: Effect of death or dissolution of trustee

(1) Where one of several trustees dies or a corporate trustee is dissolved, the trust fund remains vested in the continuing trustees. This applies to the exclusion of any person succeeding to a deceased or dissolved trustee's other patrimony.
(2) Where a sole trustee dies, the deceased trustee's successors become trustees and accordingly:
- (a) the trustee's successors become subject to the trust and acquire the corresponding rights and powers;
- (b) the trustee's successors become liable for trust debts incurred by the deceased trustee to the extent of the deceased trustee's estate; and
- (c) the trust fund vests in the trustee's successors,
but the trustee's successors may only exercise the powers set out in X. – 5:202 (Restriction in case of minimum number of trustees) paragraph (1), regardless of the number of successors.
(3) A trustee's testamentary disposition of the trust fund is of no effect, but the trust terms may confer a testamentary power to appoint a trustee.
(4) Obligations arising from non-performance devolve on the deceased trustee's successor.

Section 6:
Death or dissolution of trust auxiliary

X. – 8:601: Effect of death or dissolution of trust auxiliary
A power of a trust auxiliary ends when the trust auxiliary dies or is dissolved, but the trust terms may permit a testamentary exercise of the power.

Chapter 9:
Termination and variation of trusts and transfer of rights to benefit
Section 1:
Termination
Sub-section 1:
General rules on termination

X. – 9:101: Modes of termination
A trust in respect of a fund or part of a fund may be terminated:
(a) by a truster or beneficiaries in accordance with a right provided for by the trust terms;
(b) by a truster in accordance with X. – 9:103 (Right of truster to terminate a gratuitous trust);
(c) by a beneficiary in accordance with X. – 9:104 (Right of beneficiaries to terminate);
(d) by a trustee under X. – 9:108 (Termination by trustee);
(e) by merger of rights and obligations under X. – 9:109 (Merger of right and obligation).

X. – 9:102: Effect of termination on trustee's liabilities
(1) To the extent that the trust is terminated the trustee is discharged.
(2) Unless the parties concerned agree otherwise, termination of the trust does not release a trustee from liability:
   (a) to a beneficiary arising out of the trustee's non-performance of any obligation under, or arising out of, the trust; or
   (b) to a trust creditor.

Sub-section 2:
Termination by truster or beneficiaries

X. – 9:103: Right of truster to terminate a gratuitous trust

(1) Except as provided for by paragraphs (2) and (3), a truster has no implied right to terminate a trust or a trust term merely because the trust was constituted gratuitously, irrespective of whether:

(a) the trust was constituted without a transfer by the truster;

(b) the truster reserved a right to benefit during the truster's lifetime.

(2) A truster may terminate a gratuitously constituted trust, or a term of such a trust, which is for the benefit of a person who does not yet exist.

(3) A truster may terminate a gratuitously constituted trust for the benefit of another to the same extent that the truster might have revoked a donation to that beneficiary if the benefit had been conferred by way of donation.

X. – 9:104: Right of beneficiaries to terminate

(1) A beneficiary of full legal capacity may terminate the trust in respect of a fund or part of the fund which is for that beneficiary's exclusive benefit.

(2) If each is of full legal capacity, several beneficiaries have a corresponding joint right to terminate the trust in respect of a fund or part of the fund which is for the exclusive benefit of those beneficiaries.

(3) A trust may not be terminated in respect of part of the fund if this would adversely affect the trust in respect of the rest of the fund for the benefit of other beneficiaries or for the advancement of public benefit purposes.

X. – 9:105: Meaning of "exclusive benefit"

(1) A fund or part of a fund is to be regarded as for a beneficiary's exclusive benefit if all of that capital and all of the future income from that capital can only be disposed of in accordance with the trust terms for the benefit of that beneficiary or that beneficiary's estate.

(2) For the purposes of paragraph (1) the possibility that the beneficiary might give a consent, or might fail to exercise a right adverse to that beneficiary's own benefit, is to be disregarded.

X. – 9:106: Notice of termination and its effects

(1) A truster or beneficiary exercises a right to terminate by giving notice in writing to the trustees.

(2) A trust or part of a trust which is terminated by the truster takes effect from that time as a trust for the benefit of the truster.

(3) Where a beneficiary, exercising a right to terminate, instructs the trustee to transfer to someone other than the beneficiary, notice of termination vests in that person the right to benefit from the fund or part of the fund which is to be transferred.

(4) Unless the transfer is impossible or unlawful, the trustee is obliged to transfer the fund or part of the fund in accordance with the notice of termination and without delay. The obligation to transfer supersedes the obligation to administer and dispose of the fund or part in accordance with the trust terms.

(5) If a transfer is impossible because it would require the grant of an undivided share in an asset for which undivided shares are not allowed, the trustee is obliged:

    (a) to divide the asset and transfer the divided share, so far as this is possible and reasonable; and otherwise

    (b) to sell the asset, if this is possible, and transfer the corresponding share of the proceeds.

(5) The trust is terminated when and to the extent that the required transfer is made.

X. – 9:107: Trustee's right to withhold

(1) A trustee may withhold such part of the fund which is to be transferred as is needed to satisfy:

    (a) trust debts;

    (b) the trustee's accrued rights of recourse to the fund; and

    (c) the costs of transfer and of any required division or sale of an asset,

so far as those debts, rights and costs are allocated to the part of the fund which is to be transferred.

(2) The right to withhold ends if the person exercising the right to terminate pays compensation for the debts, rights and costs allocated to the part of the fund which is to be transferred.

Sub-section 3:
Other modes of termination

X. – 9:108: Termination by trustee
(1) Where a beneficiary has a right to terminate a trust under X. – 9:104 (Right of beneficiaries to terminate) paragraph (1), a trustee may give a notice to that beneficiary requiring that beneficiary to exercise that right within a period of reasonable length fixed by the notice. If the beneficiary fails to do so within that period, the trustee may terminate the trust by a transfer to that beneficiary. The beneficiary is obliged to accept the transfer.
(2) A trustee may also terminate the trust by payment of money or transfer of other assets of the trust fund into court where other rules so provide.

X. – 9:109: Merger of right and obligation
(1) A trust ends when the sole trustee is also the sole beneficiary and the trust fund is for that beneficiary's exclusive benefit.
(2) Where there are several trustees, paragraph (1) applies correspondingly only if they have a joint right to benefit.
(3) If a trust subsists in relation to the beneficiary's right to benefit or the right to benefit is encumbered with a security right or other limited right, the trustee remains bound by that trust or encumbrance.

Section 2:
Variation

X. – 9:201: Variation by truster or beneficiary
(1) The trust terms may be varied by a truster or beneficiary in accordance with:
    (a) a right provided for by the trust terms;
    (b) the right provided for by paragraph (2).
(2) A truster or beneficiary who has a right to terminate a trust has a corresponding right to vary the trust terms so far as they relate to the fund or part of the fund in respect of which the trust might be terminated.
(3) The exercise by several beneficiaries of a joint right to vary the trust terms requires their agreement to that effect.

(4) A variation which is to take effect from the death of the person exercising the right to vary is of no effect unless it is made by testamentary instrument.

(5) A variation does not take effect until notice in writing is given to the trustees.

X. – 9:202: Variation by court order of administrative trust terms

(1) On the application of any party to the trust or any person entitled to enforce performance of obligations under the trust, a court may vary a trust term relating to the administration of the trust fund if the variation is likely to promote a more efficient and prudent administration of the fund.

(2) A variation under paragraph (1) may not significantly affect the operation of the trust terms governing its disposal unless the court also has power to vary those terms under one of the following Articles.

X. – 9:203: Variation by court order of trusts for beneficiaries

(1) On the application of any party to the trust or any person who would benefit if the term to be varied were removed, a court may vary a trust term which confers a right to benefit or eligibility for benefit on a person who:

(a) does not yet exist; or

(b) does not presently conform to a description, such as membership of a class, on which the right depends.

(2) The same applies where the trust term confers a right to benefit or eligibility for benefit at a remote time in the future or which is conditional on the occurrence of an improbable event.

X. – 9:204: Variation by court order of trusts for public benefit purposes

(1) On the application of any party to the trust or any person entitled to enforce performance of obligations under the trust, a court may vary a trust term which provides for the advancement of a public benefit purpose if, as a result of a change of circumstances, the advancement of the particular purpose provided for by the trust term cannot be regarded as a suitable and effective use of resources.

(2) A variation under paragraph (2) must be in favour of such general or particular public benefit purposes as the truster would probably have

chosen if the truster had constituted the trust after the change in circumstances.

Section 3:
Transfer of right to benefit

X. – 9:301: Transfer by juridical act of right to benefit
(1) Subject to the other paragraphs of this Article, the transfer by juridical act of a right to benefit is governed by Book III Chapter 5 Section 1 (Assignment of rights).
(2) A gratuitous transfer is of no effect unless it is made in writing.
(3) A transfer which is to take effect on the death of the transferor takes effect only in accordance with the applicable law of succession.

Chapter 10:
Relations to third parties
Section 1:
General provisions on creditors

X.–10:101: Basic rule on creditors
(1) A person to whom a trustee owes a trust debt (a trust creditor) may satisfy that person's right out of the trust fund (in accordance with X. – 10:202 (Rights of trust creditors in relation to the trust fund)), but other creditors may not except in so far as these rules provide otherwise.
(2) Paragraph (1) does not affect any right of a creditor of a party to a trust to invoke a right of that party relating to the trust fund.

X.–10:102: Definition of trust debt
(1) An obligation is a trust debt if it is incurred by the trustee:
    (a) as the owner for the time being of a trust asset;
    (b) for the purposes of, and in accordance with the terms of, the trust;
    (c) in the capacity of trustee and by a contract or other juridical act which is not gratuitous, unless the creditor knew or could reasonably be expected to know that the obligation was not incurred in accordance with the terms of the trust;

(d) as a result of an act or omission in the administration or disposition of the trust fund or the performance of a trust debt; or

(e) otherwise materially in connection with the trust patrimony.

(2) The obligations of trustees to reimburse, indemnify or remunerate a former trustee or an intended trustee who has exercised a right of refusal are also trust debts.

(3) Other obligations of a trustee are not trust debts.

Section 2:
Trust creditors

X.–10:201: Rights of trust creditors against the trustee

(1) A trustee is personally liable to satisfy trust debts.

(2) Unless the trustee and the trust creditor agree otherwise:

(a) liability is not limited to the value of the trust fund at the time the trust creditor's right to performance is enforced; and

(b) subject to the rules on change of trustees, liability does not end if the trust fund ceases to be vested in the trustee.

(3) A party to a contract is not to be treated as agreeing to exclude or limit liability merely because the other party discloses that that other party is concluding the contract in the capacity of trustee.

X.–10:202: Rights of trust creditors in relation to the trust fund

A trust creditor may satisfy a right out of the trust fund:

(a) to enforce performance of a trustee's personal liability under X.–10:201 (Rights of trust creditors against the trustee); or

(b) in the exercise of a security right in trust assets.

X.–10:203: Protection of the truster and beneficiaries

A truster or beneficiary is not in that capacity liable to a trust creditor.

Section 3:
Trust debtors

X.–10:301: Right to enforce performance of trust debtor's obligation

(1) Where a trustee has a right to performance and that right is a trust asset, the right to enforce performance of the obligation of the debtor (the trust debtor) accrues to the trustee.

(2) Paragraph (1) does not affect:

    (a) a beneficiary's right to performance by the trustee of obligations under the trust in respect of the right against the trust debtor; or

    (b) procedural rules which allow a beneficiary to be a party to legal proceedings against the trust debtor to which the trustee is also a party.

X.–10:302: Set-off

A trustee's right against a trust debtor may only be set off against:

(a) a right corresponding to a trust debt; or

(b) a beneficiary's right to benefit out of the trust fund.

X.–10:303: Discharge of trust debtor

The discharge of a trust debtor by a trustee is of no effect if:

(a) the discharge is not in performance of the trustee's obligations under the trust; and

(b) (i) the discharge is gratuitous; or

    (ii) the debtor knows or has reason to know that the discharge is not in performance of the trustee's obligations under the trust.

Section 4:
Acquirers of trust assets and rights encumbering trust assets

X.–10:401: Liability of donees and bad faith acquirers

(1) Where a trustee transfers a trust asset to another and the transfer is not in accordance with the terms of the trust, the transferee takes the asset subject to the trust if:

      (a) the transfer is gratuitous; or

      (b) the transferee knows or could reasonably be expected to know that the transfer is by a trustee and is not in accordance with the terms of the trust.

(2) A transferee on whom a trust is imposed under paragraph (1) has a corresponding right to a return of any benefit conferred in exchange.

(3) The trust imposed under paragraph (1) is extinguished if:

      (a) benefit which was provided by the transferee in exchange is disposed of in performance of an obligation under the trust; or

      (b) the trustee or a third party satisfies an obligation to reinstate the trust fund.

(4) A transferee can reasonably be expected to know a matter if:

      (a) it would have been apparent from a reasonably careful investigation; and

      (b) having regard to the nature and value of the asset, the nature and costs of such investigation, and commercial practice, it is fair and reasonable to expect a transferee in the circumstances to make that investigation.

(5) This Article applies correspondingly where a trustee creates a security right or other limited right in a trust asset in favour of another.

Section 5:
Other rules on liability and protection of third parties

X.–10:501: Liability for inducing or assisting misapplication of the trust fund

(1) Non-contractual liability arising out of damage caused to another by virtue of VI. – 2:211 (Loss upon inducement of non-performance of obligation) is modified as provided for by paragraph (2).

(2) A person who intentionally induces a trustee's non-performance of an obligation under the trust, or intentionally assists such non-performance, is solidarily liable with that trustee, if the trustee is liable to reinstate the trust fund.

X.–10:502: Protection of third parties dealing with trustees

(1) A contract which a trustee concludes as a result of a non-performance of an obligation under the trust with a person who is not a party to a trust is not void or avoidable for that reason.

(2) In favour of a person who is not a party to the trust and as against a trustee, a person who has no knowledge of the true facts may rely on the apparent effect of a trust document and the truth of a statement contained in it.

Annex
Definitions

(**General notes.** These definitions are introduced by I. – 1:108 (Definitions in Annex) which provides that they apply for all the purposes of these rules unless the context otherwise requires and that, where a word is defined, other grammatical forms of the word have a corresponding meaning. For the convenience of the user, where a definition is taken from or derived from a particular Article a reference to that Article is added in brackets after the definition. The list also includes some terms which are frequently used in the rules but which are not defined in any Article. It does not include definitions which do not contain any legal concept but which are only drafting devices for the purposes of a particular Article or group of Articles.)

Accessory
An "accessory", in relation to proprietary security, is a corporeal asset that is or becomes closely connected with, or part of, a movable or an immovable, provided it is possible and economically reasonable to separate the accessory without damage from the movable or immovable. (IX. – 1:201)

Acquisition finance device
An "acquisition finance device" is (a) a retention of ownership device; (b) where ownership of a sold asset has been transferred to the buyer, those security rights in the asset which secure the right (i) of the seller to payment of the purchase price or (ii) of a lender to repayment of a loan granted to the buyer for payment of the purchase price, if and in so far as this payment is actually made to the seller; and (c) a right of a third person to whom any of the rights under (a) or (b) has been transferred as security for a credit covered by (a) or (b). (IX. – 1:201(3))

Advanced electronic signature
An "advanced electronic signature" is an electronic signature which is (a) uniquely linked to the signatory (b) capable of identifying the signatory (c) created using means which can be maintained under the signatory's sole control; and (d) linked to the data to which it relates in such a manner that any subsequent change of the data is detectable. (I. – 1:108(4))

Act of assignment
An "act of assignment" of a right is a contract or other juridical act which is intended to effect a transfer of the right. (III. – 5:102(2))

Agent
An "agent" is a person who is authorised to act for another.

Assets
"Assets" means anything of economic value, including property; rights having a monetary value; and goodwill.

Assignment
"Assignment", in relation to a right, means the transfer of the right by one person, the "assignor", to another, "the assignee". (III. – 5:102(1))

Authorisation
"Authorisation" is the granting or maintaining of authority. (II. – 6:102(3))

Authority
"Authority", in relation to a representative acting for a principal, is the power to affect the principal's legal position. (II. – 6:102(2))

Avoidance
"Avoidance" of a juridical act or legal relationship is the process whereby a party or, as the case may be, a court invokes a ground of invalidity so as to make the act or relationship, which has been valid until that point, retrospectively ineffective from the beginning.

Barter, contract for

A contract for the "barter" of goods is a contract under which each party undertakes to transfer the ownership of goods, either immediately on conclusion of the contract or at some future time, in return for the transfer of ownership of other goods. (IV. A. – 1:203)

Beneficiary

A "beneficiary", in relation to a trust, is a person who, according to the trust terms, has either a right to benefit or an eligibility for benefit from the trust fund. (X. – 1:203(3))

Benevolent intervention in another's affairs

"Benevolent intervention in another's affairs" is the process whereby a person, the intervener, acts with the predominant intention of benefiting another, the principal, but without being authorised or bound to do so. (V. – 1:101)

Business

"Business" means any natural or legal person, irrespective of whether publicly or privately owned, who is acting for purposes relating to the person's self-employed trade, work or profession, even if the person does not intend to make a profit in the course of the activity. (I. – 1:106(2))

Claim

A "claim" is a demand for something based on the assertion of a right.

Claimant

A "claimant" is a person who makes, or who has grounds for making, a claim.

Co-debtorship for security purposes

A "co-debtorship for security purposes" is an obligation owed by two or more debtors in which one of the debtors, the security provider, assumes the obligation primarily for purposes of security towards the creditor. (IV. G. – 1:101(e))

Commercial agency

A "commercial agency" is the legal relationship arising from a contract under which one party, the commercial agent, agrees to act on a continuing basis as a self-employed intermediary to negotiate or to conclude contracts on behalf of another party, the principal, and the principal agrees to remunerate the agent for those activities. (IV. E. – 3:101)

Compensation

"Compensation" means reparation in money. (VI. – 6:101(2))

Complete substitution of debtor

There is complete substitution of a debtor when a third person is substituted as debtor with the effect that the original debtor is discharged. (III. – 5:203)

Condition

A "condition" is a provision which makes a legal relationship or effect depend on the occurrence or non-occurrence of an uncertain future event. A condition may be suspensive or resolutive. (III. – 1:106)

Conduct

"Conduct" means voluntary behaviour of any kind, verbal or non-verbal: it includes a single act or a number of acts, behaviour of a negative or passive nature (such as accepting something without protest or not doing something) and behaviour of a continuing or intermittent nature (such as exercising control over something).

Confidential information

"Confidential information" means information which, either from its nature or the circumstances in which it was obtained, the party receiving the information knows or could reasonably be expected to know is confidential to the other party. (II. – 2:302(2))

Construction, contract for

A contract for construction is a contract under which one party, the constructor, undertakes to construct something for another party, the client, or to materially alter an existing building or other immovable structure for a client. (IV.C–3:101)

Consumer
A "consumer" means any natural person who is acting primarily for purposes which are not related to his or her trade, business or profession. (I. – 1:106(1))

Consumer contract for sale
A "consumer contract for sale" is a contract for sale in which the seller is a business and the buyer is a consumer. (IV. A. – 1:204)

Contract
A "contract" is an agreement which is intended to give rise to a binding legal relationship or to have some other legal effect. It is a bilateral or multilateral juridical act. (II. – 1:101(1))

Contractual obligation
A "contractual obligation" is an obligation which arises from a contract, whether from an express term or an implied term or by operation of a rule of law imposing an obligation on a contracting party as such.

Contractual relationship
A "contractual relationship" is a legal relationship resulting from a contract.

Co-ownership
"Co-ownership", when created under Book VIII, means that two or more co-owners own undivided shares in the whole and each co-owner can dispose of that co-owner's share by acting alone, unless otherwise provided by the parties. (Cf. VIII. – 1:203)

Corporeal
"Corporeal", in relation to property, means having a physical existence in solid, liquid or gaseous form.

Costs
"Costs" includes expenses.

Counter-performance
A "counter-performance" is a performance which is due in exchange for another performance.

Court
"Court" includes an arbitral tribunal.

Creditor
A "creditor" is a person who has a right to performance of an obligation, whether monetary or non-monetary, by another person, the debtor.

Damage
"Damage" means any type of detrimental effect.

Damages
"Damages" means a sum of money to which a person may be entitled, or which a person may be awarded by a court, as compensation for some specified type of damage.

Debtor
A "debtor" is a person who has an obligation, whether monetary or non-monetary, to another person, the creditor.

Default
"Default", in relation to proprietary security, means any non-performance by the debtor of the obligation covered by the security; and any other event or set of circumstances agreed by the secured creditor and the security provider as entitling the secured creditor to have recourse to the security. (IX. – 1:201(5))

Defence
A "defence" to a claim is a legal objection or a factual argument, other than a mere denial of an element which the claimant has to prove which, if well-founded, defeats the claim in whole or in part.

Delivery

"Delivery" to a person, for the purposes of any obligation to deliver goods, means transferring possession of the goods to that person or taking such steps to transfer possession as are required by the terms regulating the obligation. For the purposes of Book VIII (Acquisition and loss of ownership of goods) delivery of the goods takes place only when the transferor gives up and the transferee obtains possession of the goods: if the contract or other juridical act, court order or rule of law under which the transferee is entitled to the transfer of ownership involves carriage of the goods by a carrier or a series of carriers, delivery of the goods takes place when the transferor's obligation to deliver is fulfilled and the carrier or the transferee obtains possession of the goods. (VIII. – 2:104)

Dependent personal security

A "dependent personal security" is an obligation by a security provider which is assumed in favour of a creditor in order to secure a present or future obligation of the debtor owed to the creditor and performance of which is due only if, and to the extent that, performance of the latter obligation is due. (IV. G. – 1:101(a))

Design, contract for

A contract for design is a contract under which one party, the designer, undertakes to design for another party, the client, an immovable structure which is to be constructed by or on behalf of the client or a movable or incorporeal thing or service which is to be constructed or performed by or on behalf of the client. (IV. C.-6:101)

Direct physical control

Direct physical control is physical control which is exercised by the possessor personally or through a possession-agent exercising such control on behalf of the possessor (direct possession). (VIII. – 1:205)

Discrimination

"Discrimination" means any conduct whereby, or situation where, on grounds such as sex or ethnic or racial origin, (a) one person is treated less favourably than another person is, has been or would be treated in a comparable situation; or (b) an apparently neutral provision, criterion or practice would place one group of persons at a particular disadvantage when compared to a different group of persons. (II. – 2:102(1))

Distribution contract

A "distribution contract" is a contract under which one party, the supplier, agrees to supply the other party, the distributor, with products on a continuing basis and the distributor agrees to purchase them, or to take and pay for them, and to supply them to others in the distributor's name and on the distributor's behalf. (IV. E. – 5:101(1))

Distributorship

A "distributorship" is the legal relationship arising from a distribution contract.

Divided obligation

An obligation owed by two or more debtors is a "divided obligation" when each debtor is bound to render only part of the performance and the creditor may require from each debtor only that debtor's part. (III. – 4:102(2))

Divided right

A right to performance held by two or more creditors is a "divided right" when the debtor owes each creditor only that creditor's share and each creditor may require performance only of that creditor's share. (III. – 4:202(2))

Donation, contract for

A contract for the donation of goods is a contract under which one party, the donor, gratuitously undertakes to transfer the ownership of goods to another party, the donee, and does so with an intention to benefit the donee. (IV. H. – 1:101)

Durable medium

A "durable medium" means any material on which information is stored so that it is accessible for future reference for a period of time adequate to the purposes of the information, and which allows the unchanged reproduction of this information. (I. – 1:107(3))

Duty

A person has a "duty" to do something if the person is bound to do it or expected to do it according to an applicable normative standard of conduct. A duty may or may not be owed to a specific creditor. A duty is not necessarily an aspect of a legal relationship. There is not necessarily a sanction for breach of a duty. All obligations are duties, but not all duties are obligations.

Economic loss

See "Loss".

Electronic

"Electronic" means relating to technology with electrical, digital, magnetic, wireless, optical, electromagnetic, or similar capabilities.

Electronic signature

An "electronic signature" means data in electronic form which are attached to, or logically associated with, other data and which serve as a method of authentication. (I. – 1:108(3))

Financial assets

"Financial assets" are financial instruments and rights to the payment of money. (IX. – 1:201(6))

Financial instruments

"Financial instruments" are (a) share certificates and equivalent securities as well as bonds and equivalent debt instruments, if these are negotiable (b) any other securities which are dealt in and which give the right to acquire any such financial instruments or which give rise to cash settlements, except instruments of payment (c) share rights in collective investment undertakings (d) money market instruments and (e) rights in or relating to the foregoing instruments. (IX. – 1:201(7))

Franchise

A "franchise" is the legal relationship arising from a contract under which one party, the franchisor, grants the other party, the franchisee, in exchange for remuneration, the right to conduct a business (franchise business) within the franchisor's network for the purposes of supplying certain products on the franchisee's behalf and in the franchisee's name, and whereby the franchisee has the right and the obligation to use the franchisor's trade name or trademark or other intellectual property rights, know-how and business method. (IV.E. – 4:101)

Fraudulent

A misrepresentation is fraudulent if it is made with knowledge or belief that it is false and is intended to induce the recipient to make a mistake to the recipient's prejudice. A non-disclosure is fraudulent if it is intended to induce the person from whom the information is withheld to make a mistake to that person's prejudice. (II. – 7:205(2))

Fundamental non-performance

A non-performance of a contractual obligation is fundamental if (a) it substantially deprives the creditor of what the creditor was entitled to expect under the contract, as applied to the whole or relevant part of the performance, unless at the time of conclusion of the contract the debtor did not foresee and could not reasonably be expected to have foreseen that result or (b) it is intentional or reckless and gives the creditor reason to believe that the debtor's future performance cannot be relied on. (III. – 3:502(2))

Global security

A "global security" is a security which is assumed in order to secure all the debtor's obligations towards the creditor or the debit balance of a current account or a security of a similar extent. (IV. G. – 1:101(f)

Good faith

"Good faith" is a mental attitude characterised by honesty and an absence of knowledge that an apparent situation is not the true situation.

Good faith and fair dealing

"Good faith and fair dealing" is a standard of conduct characterised by honesty, openness and consideration for the interests of the other party to the transaction or relationship in question. (I. – 1:103)

Goods

"Goods" means corporeal movables. It includes ships, vessels, hovercraft or aircraft, space objects, animals, liquids and gases. See also "movables".

Gross negligence

There is "gross negligence" if a person is guilty of a profound failure to take such care as is self-evidently required in the circumstances.

Handwritten signature

A "handwritten signature" means the name of, or sign representing, a person written by that person's own hand for the purpose of authentication. (I. – 1:108(2))

Harassment

"Harassment" means unwanted conduct (including conduct of a sexual nature) which violates a person's dignity, particularly when such conduct creates an intimidating, hostile, degrading, humiliating or offensive environment, or which aims to do so. (II. – 2:102(2))

Immovable property

"Immovable property" means land and anything so attached to land as not to be subject to change of place by usual human action.

Incomplete substitution of debtor

There is incomplete substitution of a debtor when a third person is substituted as debtor with the effect that the original debtor is retained as a debtor in case the original debtor does not perform properly. (III. – 5:205)

Incorporeal
"Incorporeal", in relation to property, means not having a physical existence in solid, liquid or gaseous form.

Indemnify
To "indemnify" means to make such payment to a person as will ensure that that person suffers no loss.

Independent personal security
An "independent personal security" is an obligation by a security provider which is assumed in favour of a creditor for the purposes of security and which is expressly or impliedly declared not to depend upon another person's obligation owed to the creditor. (IV. G. – 1:101(b))

Indirect physical control
Indirect physical control is physical control which is exercised by means of another person, a limited-right-possessor (indirect possession). (VIII. – 1:205)

Individually negotiated
See "not individually negotiated" and II. – 1:110.

Ineffective
"Ineffective" in relation to a contract or other juridical act means having no effect, whether that state of affairs is temporary or permanent, general or restricted.

Insolvency proceeding
An "insolvency proceeding" means a collective judicial or administrative proceeding, including an interim proceeding, in which the assets and affairs of a person who is, or who is believed to be, insolvent are subject to control or supervision by a court or other competent authority for the purpose of reorganisation or liquidation.

Intangibles
"Intangibles", in relation to proprietary security, means incorporeal assets and includes uncertificated and indirectly held securities and the undivided share of a co-owner in corporeal assets or in a bulk or a fund. (IX. – 1:201(8))

Interest
"Interest" means simple interest without any assumption that it will be capitalised from time to time.

Invalid
"Invalid" in relation to a juridical act or legal relationship means that the act or relationship is void or has been avoided.

Joint obligation
An obligation owed by two or more debtors is a "joint obligation" when all the debtors are bound to render the performance together and the creditor may require it only from all of them. (III. – 4:102(3))

Joint right
A right to performance held by two or more creditors is a "joint right" when the debtor must perform to all the creditors and any creditor may require performance only for the benefit of all. (III. – 4:202(3))

Juridical act
A "juridical act" is any statement or agreement, whether express or implied from conduct, which is intended to have legal effect as such. It may be unilateral, bilateral or multilateral. (II. – 1:101(2))

Keeper
A keeper, in relation to an animal, vehicle or substance, is the person who has the beneficial use or physical control of it for that person's own benefit and who exercises the right to control it or its use.

Lease

A "lease" is the legal relationship arising from a contract under which one party, the lessor, undertakes to provide the other party, the lessee, with a temporary right of use in exchange for rent. (IV. B. – 1:101)

Limited proprietary rights

Limited proprietary rights are such rights of the following character as are characterised or treated as proprietary rights by any provision of these model rules or by national law:– (a) security rights (b) rights to use (c) rights to acquire (including a right to acquire in the sense of VIII. – 2:307 (Contingent right of transferee under retention of ownership)) and (d) trust-related rights. (VIII. – 1:204)

Limited-right-possessor

A "limited-right-possessor", in relation to goods, is a person who exercises physical control over the goods either (a) with the intention of doing so in that person's own interest, and under a specific legal relationship with the owner-possessor which gives the limited-right-possessor the right to possess the goods or (b) with the intention of doing so to the order of the owner-possessor, and under a specific contractual relationship with the owner-possessor which gives the limited-right-possessor a right to retain the goods until any charges or costs have been paid by the owner-possessor. (VIII. – 1:207)

Loan contract

A loan contract is a contract by which one party, the lender, is obliged to provide the other party, the borrower, with credit of any amount for a definite or indefinite period (the loan period), in the form of a monetary loan or of an overdraft facility and by which the borrower is obliged to repay the money obtained under the credit, whether or not the borrower is obliged to pay interest or any other kind of remuneration the parties have agreed upon. (IV. F. – 1:101(2))

Loss

"Loss" includes economic and non-economic loss. "Economic loss" includes loss of income or profit, burdens incurred and a reduction in the value of property. "Non-economic loss" includes pain and suffering and impairment of the quality of life. (III. – 3:701(3) and VI. – 2:101(4))

Mandate

The "mandate" of an agent is the authorisation and instruction given by the principal, as modified by any subsequent direction, in relation to the facilitation, negotiation or conclusion of a contract or other juridical act with a third party. (IV. D. – 1:102(1)(a))

Mandate for direct representation

A "mandate for direct representation" is a mandate under which the agent is to act in the name of the principal, or otherwise in such a way as to indicate an intention to affect the principal's legal position directly. (IV. D. – 1:102(1)(d))

Mandate for indirect representation

A "mandate for indirect representation" is a mandate under which the agent is to act in the agent's own name or otherwise in such a way as not to indicate an intention to affect the principal's legal position directly. (IV. D. – 1:102(1)(e))

Merger of debts

A "merger of debts" means that the attributes of debtor and creditor are united in the same person in the same capacity. (III. – 6:201)

Merger clause

A "merger clause" is a term in a contract document stating that the document embodies all the terms of the contract. (II. – 4:104)

Monetary loan

A monetary loan is a fixed sum of money which is lent to the borrower and which the borrower agrees to repay either by fixed instalments or by paying the whole sum at the end of the loan period. (IV. F. – 1:101(3))

Motor vehicle

"Motor vehicle" means any vehicle intended for travel on land and propelled by mechanical power, but not running on rails, and any trailer, whether or not coupled. (VI. – 3:205(2))

Movables

"Movables" means corporeal and incorporeal property other than immovable property.

Negligence

There is "negligence" if a person does not meet the standard of care which could reasonably be expected in the circumstances.

Non-economic loss

See "Loss".

Non-performance

"Non-performance", in relation to an obligation, means any failure to perform the obligation, whether or not excused. It includes delayed performance and defective performance. (III. – 1:101(3))

Notice

"Notice" includes the communication of information or of a juridical act. (I. – 1:105)

Not individually negotiated

A term supplied by one party is not individually negotiated if the other party has not been able to influence its content, in particular because it has been drafted in advance, whether or not as part of standard terms. (II. – 1:110)

Obligation

An obligation is a duty to perform which one party to a legal relationship, the debtor, owes to another party, the creditor. (III. – 1:101(1))

Overdraft facility
An "overdraft facility" is an option for the borrower to withdraw funds on a fluctuating, limited basis from the borrower's current account in excess of the current balance in the account. (IV. F. – 1:101(4))

Owner-possessor
An "owner-possessor", in relation to goods, is a person who exercises physical control over the goods with the intention of doing so as, or as if, an owner. ((VIII. – 1:206)

Ownership
"Ownership" is the most comprehensive right a person, the owner, can have over property, including the exclusive right, so far as consistent with applicable laws or rights granted by the owner, to use, enjoy, modify, destroy, dispose of and recover the property. (VIII. – 1:202)

Performance
"Performance", in relation to an obligation, is the doing by the debtor of what is to be done under the obligation or the not doing by the debtor of what is not to be done. (III. – 1:101(2))

Person
"Person" means a natural or legal person.

Physical control
"Physical control", in relation to goods, means direct physical control or indirect physical control. (Cf. VIII. – 1:205)

Possession
Possession, in relation to goods, means having physical control over the goods. (VIII. – 1:205)

Possession-agent
A "possession-agent", in relation to goods, is a person (such as an employee) who exercises direct physical control over the goods on behalf of an owner-possessor or limited-right-possessor (without the

intention and specific legal relationship required for that person to be a limited-right-possessor); and to whom the owner-possessor or limited-right-possessor may give binding instructions as to the use of the goods in the interest of the owner-possessor or limited-right-possessor. A person is also a possession-agent where that person is accidentally in a position to exercise, and does exercise, direct physical control over the goods for an owner-possessor or limited-right-possessor. (VIII. – 1:208)

Possessory security right
A "possessory security right" is a security right that requires possession of the encumbered corporeal asset by the secured creditor or another person (except the debtor) holding for the secured creditor. (IX. – 1:201(10))

Prescription
"Prescription", in relation to the right to performance of an obligation, is the legal effect whereby the lapse of a prescribed period of time entitles the debtor to refuse performance.

Presumption
A "presumption" means that the existence of a known fact or state of affairs allows the deduction that something else should be held true, until the contrary is demonstrated.

Price
The "price" is what is due by the debtor under a monetary obligation, in exchange for something supplied or provided, expressed in a currency which the law recognises as such.

Proceeds
"Proceeds", in relation to proprietary security, is every value derived from an encumbered asset, such as value realised by sale, collection or other disposition; damages or insurance payments in respect of defects, damage or loss; civil and natural fruits, including distributions; and proceeds of proceeds. (IX. – 1:201(11))

Processing, contract for

A contract for processing is a contract under which one party, the processor, undertakes to perform a service on an existing movable or incorporeal thing or to an immovable structure for another party, the client (except where the service is construction work on an existing building or other immovable structure). (IV. C. – 4:101)

Producer

"Producer" includes, in the case of something made, the maker or manufacturer; in the case of raw material, the person who abstracts or wins it; and in the case of something grown, bred or raised, the grower, breeder or raiser. A special definition applies for the purposes of VI. – 3:204.

Property

"Property" means anything which can be owned: it may be movable or immovable, corporeal or incorporeal.

Proprietary security

A "proprietary security" covers security rights in all kinds of assets, whether movable or immovable, corporeal or incorporeal. (IV. G. – 1:101(g))

Proprietary security, contract for

A "contract for proprietary security" is a contract under which a security provider undertakes to grant a security right to the secured creditor; or a secured creditor is entitled to retain a security right when transferring ownership; or a seller, lessor or other supplier of assets is entitled to retain ownership of the supplied assets in order to secure its rights to performance. (IX. – 1:201(4))

Public holiday

A "public holiday" with reference to a member state, or part of a member state, of the European Union means any day designated as such for that state or part in a list published in the official journal. (I. – 1:110(9))

Ratify
"Ratify" means confirm with legal effect.

Reasonable
What is "reasonable" is to be objectively ascertained, having regard to the nature and purpose of what is being done, to the circumstances of the case and to any relevant usages and practices. (I. – 1:104)

Reciprocal
An obligation is reciprocal in relation to another obligation if (a) performance of the obligation is due in exchange for performance of the other obligation; (b) it is an obligation to facilitate or accept performance of the other obligation; or (c) it is so clearly connected to the other obligation or its subject matter that performance of the one can reasonably be regarded as dependent on performance of the other. (III. – 1:101(4))

Recklessness
A person is "reckless" if the person knows of an obvious and serious risk of proceeding in a certain way but nonetheless voluntarily proceeds without caring whether or not the risk materialises.

Rent
"Rent" is the money or other value which is due in exchange for a temporary right of use. (IV. B. – 1:101)

Reparation
"Reparation" means compensation or another appropriate measure to reinstate the person suffering damage in the position that person would have been in had the damage not occurred. (VI. – 6:101)

Representative
A "representative" is a person who has authority to affect the legal position of another person, the principal, in relation to a third party by acting in the name of the principal or otherwise in such a way as to indicate an intention to affect the principal's legal position directly. (II. – 6:102(1))

Requirement
A "requirement" is something which is needed before a particular result follows or a particular right can be exercised.

Resolutive
A condition is "resolutive" if it causes a legal relationship or effect to come to an end when the condition is satisfied. (III. – 1:106)

Retention of ownership device
There is a retention of ownership device when ownership is retained by the owner of supplied assets in order to secure a right to performance of an obligation. (IX. – 1:103)

Revocation
"Revocation", means (a) in relation to a juridical act, its recall by a person or persons having the power to recall it, so that it no longer has effect and (b) in relation to something conferred or transferred, its recall, by a person or persons having power to recall it, so that it comes back or must be returned to the person who conferred it or transferred it.

Right
"Right", depending on the context, may mean (a) the correlative of an obligation or liability (as in "a significant imbalance in the parties' rights and obligations arising under the contract"); (b) a proprietary right (such as the right of ownership); (c) a personality right (as in a right to respect for dignity, or a right to liberty and privacy); (d) a legally conferred power to bring about a particular result (as in "the right to avoid" a contract); (e) an entitlement to a particular remedy (as in a right to have performance of a contractual obligation judicially ordered) or (f) an entitlement to do or not to do something affecting another person's legal position without exposure to adverse consequences (as in a "right to withhold performance of the reciprocal obligation").

Sale, contract for
A contract for the "sale" of goods or other assets is a contract under which one party, the seller, undertakes to another party, the buyer, to

transfer the ownership of the goods or other assets to the buyer, or to a third person, either immediately on conclusion of the contract or at some future time, and the buyer undertakes to pay the price. (IV. A. – 1:202)

Security right in movable asset

A security right in a movable asset is any limited proprietary right in the asset which entitles the secured creditor to preferential satisfaction of the secured right from the encumbered asset. (IX. – 1:102(1))

Services, contract for

A contract for services is a contract under which one party, the service provider, undertakes to supply a service to the other party, the client. (IV. C. – 1:101)

Set-off

"Set-off" is the process by which a person may use a right to performance held against another person to extinguish in whole or in part an obligation owed to that person. (III. – 6:101)

Signature

"Signature" includes a handwritten signature, an electronic signature or an advanced electronic signature. (I. – 1:108(2))

Solidary obligation

An obligation owed by two or more debtors is a "solidary obligation" when all the debtors are bound to render one and the same performance and the creditor may require it from any one of them until there has been full performance. (III. – 4:102(1))

Solidary right

A right to performance held by two or more creditors is a "solidary right" when any of the creditors may require full performance from the debtor and the debtor may render performance to any of the creditors. (III. – 4:202(1))

Standard terms

"Standard terms" are terms which have been formulated in advance for several transactions involving different parties, and which have not been individually negotiated by the parties. (II. – 1:109)

Storage, contract for

A contract for storage is a contract under which one party, the storer, undertakes to store a movable or incorporeal thing for another party, the client. (IV. C. – 5:101)

Subrogation

"Subrogation", in relation to rights, is the process by which a person who has made a payment or other performance to another person acquires by operation of law that person's rights against a third person.

Substitution of debtor

"Substitution" of a debtor is the process whereby, with the agreement of the creditor, a third party is substituted completely or incompletely for the debtor, the contract remaining in force. (III. – 5:202) See also "complete substitution of debtor" and "incomplete substitution of debtor".

Supply

To "supply" goods or other assets means to make them available to another person, whether by sale, gift, barter, lease or other means: to "supply" services means to provide them to another person, whether or not for a price. Unless otherwise stated, "supply" covers the supply of goods, other assets and services.

Suspensive

A condition is "suspensive" if it prevents a legal relationship or effect from coming into existence until the condition is satisfied. (III. – 1:106)

Tacit prolongation

"Tacit prolongation" is the process whereby, when a contract provides for continuous or repeated performance of obligations for a definite period and the obligations continue to be performed by both parties after that period has expired, the contract becomes a contract for an indefinite period, unless the circumstances are inconsistent with the tacit consent of the parties to such prolongation. (III.–1:111)

Term
"Term" means any provision, express or implied, of a contract or other juridical act, of a law, of a court order or of a legally binding usage or practice: it includes a condition.

Termination
"Termination", in relation to an existing right, obligation or legal relationship, means bringing it to an end with prospective effect except in so far as otherwise provided.

Textual form
In "textual form", in relation to a statement, means expressed in alphabetical or other intelligible characters by means of any support which permits reading, recording of the information contained in the statement and its reproduction in tangible form. (I.–1:107(2))

Transfer of contractual position
"Transfer of contractual position" is the process whereby, with the agreement of all three parties, a new party replaces an existing party to a contract, taking over the rights, obligations and entire contractual position of that party. (III.–5:302)

Treatment, contract for
A contract for treatment is a contract under which one party, the treatment provider, undertakes to provide medical treatment for another party, the patient, or to provide any other service in order to change the physical or mental condition of a person. (IV.C.–8:101)

Trust
A "trust" is a legal relationship in which a trustee is obliged to administer or dispose of one or more assets (the trust fund) in ac-

cordance with the terms governing the relationship (trust terms) to benefit a beneficiary or advance public benefit purposes. (X. – 1:201)

Trustee
A "trustee" is a person in whom a trust fund becomes or remains vested when the trust is created or subsequently on or after appointment and who has the obligation set out in the definition of "trust" above. (X. – 1:203(2))

Truster
A "truster" is a person who constitutes or intends to constitute a trust by juridical act. (X. – 1:203(1))

Unjustified enrichment
An "unjustified enrichment" is an enrichment which is not legally justified.

Valid
"Valid", in relation to a juridical act or legal relationship, means that the act or relationship is not void and has not been avoided.

Void
"Void", in relation to a juridical act or legal relationship, means that the act or relationship is automatically of no effect from the beginning.

Voidable
"Voidable", in relation to a juridical act or legal relationship, means that the act or relationship is subject to a defect which renders it liable to be avoided and hence rendered retrospectively of no effect.

Withdraw
A right to "withdraw" from a contract or other juridical act is a right, exercisable only within a limited period, to terminate the legal relationship arising from the contract or other juridical act, without having to give any reason for so doing and without incurring any

liability for non-performance of the obligations arising from that contract or juridical act. (II. – 5:101 to II. – 5:105)

Withholding performance
"Withholding performance", as a remedy for non-performance of a contractual obligation, means that one party to a contract may decline to render due counter-performance until the other party has tendered performance or has performed. (III. – 3:401)

Working days
"Working days" means all days other than Saturdays, Sundays and public holidays. (I. – 1:110(9)(b))

Writing
In "writing" means in textual form, on paper or another durable medium and in directly legible characters. (I. – 1:107(1))

Index

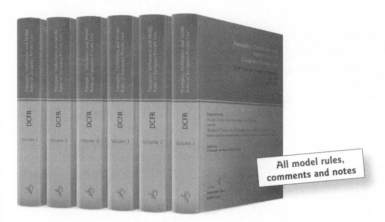

Steps towards a common European private law

The Study Group on a European Civil Code has taken upon itself the task of drafting common European principles for the most important aspects of the law of obligations and for certain parts of the law of property in movables.

The results seek to advance the process of Europeanisation of private law. Among other topics the series covers

- sales,
- service contracts,
- distribution contracts,
- personal security,
- lease of goods,
- benevolent intervention in another's affairs,
- non-contractual liability arising out of damage caused to another,
- unjustified enrichment,
- acquisition and loss of ownership in movables,
- proprietary security rights in movable assets,
- and trust law.

These principles furnish each of the national jurisdictions a grid reference. They could be agreed upon by the parties within the framework of the rules of private international law. They may provide a stimulus to both the national and European legislator for moulding private law.

sellier.elp · Geibelstraße 8 · D–81679 München · Tel + 49 · 89 · 451 084 58-0 · Fax + 49 · 89 · 451 084 58-9 · www.sellier.de

sellier.
european law
publishers

Yes, I would like to order:

Complete Series
App. 14 volumes

**Benevolent Intervention
in Another's Affairs**
Christian von Bar
March 2006. XXX, 417 pp.
€ 120.- (series price € 93.-)
ISBN 978-3-935808-40-8

**Commercial Agency,
Franchise and
Distribution Contracts**
Martijn Hesselink et al
March 2006. XLI, 371 pp.
€ 120.- (series price € 93.-)
ISBN 978-3-935808-43-9

Service Contracts
Maurits Barendrecht et al
November 2006. LX, 1034 pp.
€ 295.- (series price € 221.-)
ISBN 978-3-935808-41-5

Personal Security
Ulrich Drobnig
June 2007. XXXII, 567 pp.
€ 225.- (series price € 161.-)
ISBN 978-3-935808-42-2

Lease of Goods
Kåre Lilleholt et al
Dec. 2007. XXXVIII, 367 pp.
€ 120.- (series price € 93.-)
ISBN 978-3-935808-64-4

Sales
Ewoud Hondius et al
March 2008. XL, 485 pp.
€ 120.- (series price € 93.-)
ISBN 978-3-935808-61-3

**Non-Contractual Liability
Arising out of Damage
Caused to Another**
Christian von Bar
2009. Approx. 650 pp.
€ 225.- (series price € 161.-)
ISBN 978-3-935808-63-7

Mandate Contracts
Marco Loos/Odavia Bueno Díaz
2009. Approx. 300 pp.
€ 120.- (series price € 93.-)
ISBN 978-3-86653-052-2

Loan Contracts
Edgar du Perron
2009. Approx. 400 pp.
€ 120.- (series price € 93.-)
ISBN 978-3-935808-67-5

Donation
Martin Schmidt-Kessel
2009. Approx. 350 pp.
€ 120.- (series price € 93.-)
ISBN 978-3-86653-051-5

Unjustified Enrichment
S. Swann/C. von Bar
2009. Approx. 450 pp.
€ 120.- (series price € 93.-)
ISBN 978-3-935808-62-0

**Acquisition and Loss of
Ownership of Goods**
Brigitta Lurger/Wolfgang Faber
2009. Approx. 300 pp.
€ 120.- (series price € 93.-)
ISBN 978-3-935808-66-8

**Proprietary Security
Rights in Movable Assets**
Ulrich Drobnig
2009. Approx. 300 pp.
€ 120.- (series price € 93.-)
ISBN 978-3-935808-65-1

Trusts
Stephen Swann
2009. Approx. 600 pp.
€ 225.- (series price € 161.-)
ISBN 978-3-935808-68-2

My Address

....

....

....

....

Date, Signature

....

Prices are subject to change. Free shipping. This order
can be cancelled within 2 weeks after reception of goods.

097

sellier.elp · Geibelstraße 8 · D – 81679 München · Tel + 49 · 89 · 451 084 58-0 · Fax + 49 · 89 · 451 084 58-9 · www.sellier.de

Other Publications

Yes, I would like to order:

Economic Analysis of the DCFR
The work of the Economic Impact Group
within the CoPECL network of excellence
Filomena Chirico/Pierre Larouche (eds.)
Aug 2009. Approx. 416 pp.
Hardcover. € 98.-
ISBN 978-3-86653-113-0

**The Common Frame of Reference:
A View from Law & Economics**
Gerhard Wagner (ed.)
Jun 2009. Approx. 288 pp.
Paperback. € 59.-
ISBN 978-3-86653-110-9

Der Gemeinsame Referenzrahmen
Entstehung, Inhalte, Anwendung
Martin Schmidt-Kessel (ed.)
Feb 2009. XIV, 500 pp.
Paperback. € 69.-
ISBN 978-3-86653-099-7

**Common Frame of Reference
and Existing EC Contract Law**
Reiner Schulze (ed.)
Dec 2008. XII, 356 pp.
eBook (PDF). € 69.-
ISBN 978-3-86653-800-9

European Contract Law
Materials for a Common Frame of Reference:
Terminology, Guiding Principles, Model Rules
Association Henri Capitant des Amis de la
Culture Juridique Française/Société de Légis-
lation Comparée
Jul 2008. XXXIV, 614 pp.
Paperback. € 35.-
ISBN 978-3-86653-067-6

CFR & Social Justice
Martijn W. Hesselink
Nov 2008. VIII, 87 pp.
Paperback. € 69.-
ISBN 978-3-86653-081-2

Franchising in European Contract Law
A comparison between the main obligations of
the contracting parties in the Principles of
European Law on Commercial Agency, Franchi
and Distribution Contracts (PEL CAFDC), Fren
and Spanish law. Odavia Bueno Díaz
Sep 2008. XXVIII, 292 pp.
Paperback. € 35.-
ISBN 978-3-86653-075-1

**Grundregeln des Europäischen
Vertragsrechts**
Teile I und II
German translation of the "Principles of
European Contract Law"
Christian von Bar/Reinhard Zimmermann
Jun 2002. XXXVI, 571 pp.

Hardcover. € 119.-
ISBN 978-3-935808-00-2

Paperback. € 39.-
ISBN 978-3-935808-01-9

**Grundregeln des Europäischen
Vertragsrechts**
Teil III
German translation of the "Principles of
European Contract Law"
Christian von Bar/Reinhard Zimmermann
May 2005. XXVIII, 289 pp.

Hardcover. € 89.-
ISBN 978-3-935808-38-5

Paperback. € 39.-
ISBN 978-3-935808-39-2

sellier.elp · Geibelstraße 8 · D–81679 München · Tel + 49 · 89 · 451 084 58-0 · Fax + 49 · 89 · 451 084 58-9 · www.sellier.de

sellier.
european law
publishers

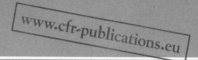

Die Grundregeln des Europäischen Vertragsrechts als Recht grenzüberschreitender Verträge
Friedrich Blase
Jun 2001. XXIII, 409 pp.
Hardcover. € 64.-
ISBN 978-3-935808-55-2

Contract II
General Provisions, Delivery of Goods, Package Travel and Payment Services (Acquis Principles)
Research Group on the Existing EC Private Law (Acquis Group)
May 2009. Approx. 600 pp.
Hardcover. € 150.-
ISBN 978-3-86653-024-9

EC Consumer Law Compendium
The Consumer Acquis and its transposition in the Member States
Hans Schulte-Nölke/Christian Twigg-Flesner/Martin Ebers (eds.)
May 2008. XXVI, 529 pp.
Paperback. € 59.-
ISBN 978-3-86653-063-8

Rules for the Transfer of Movables
A Candidate for European Harmonisation or National Reforms?
Wolfgang Faber/Brigitta Lurger (eds.)
Feb 2008. XI, 268 pp.
Paperback. € 39.-
ISBN 978-3-86653-060-7

National Reports on the Transfer of Movables in Europe
Vol. 1: Austria, Estonia, Italy, Slovenia
Wolfgang Faber/Brigitta Lurger (eds.)
Oct 2008. X, 638 pp.
Paperback. € 59.-
ISBN 978-3-86653-073-7

National Reports on the Transfer of Movables in Europe
Vol. 2: England and Wales, Ireland, Scotland, Cyprus. Wolfgang Faber/Brigitta Lurger (eds.)
Jan 2009. X, 628 pp.
Paperback. € 59.-
ISBN 978-3-86653-096-6

My Address

....

....

....

....

Date, Signature

....

Free shipping for order value higher than 30 EUR. This order can be cancelled within 2 weeks after reception of goods.

097